# CRIMES AND
# THE RICH
# AND FAMOUS

# CRIMES AND THE RICH AND FAMOUS

## Carl Sifakis

☑®
Checkmark Books®
*An imprint of Facts On File, Inc.*

**Crimes and the Rich and Famous**

Checkmark Books
An imprint of Facts On File, Inc.
11 Penn Plaza
New York  NY 10001

**Library of Congress Cataloging-in-Publication Data**

Sifakis, Carl.
Crimes and the rich and famous / Carl Sifakis
p.   cm.
Includes bibliographical references and index.
ISBN 0-8160-4421-X (alk. paper)
1. Celebrities—Crimes against—United States. 2. Criminals—United States. I. Title.
HV6250.4.C34 S53 2002
364.973—dc21          2001017310

Checkmark Books are available at special discounts when purchased in bulk quantities for businesses, associations, institutions or sales promotions. Please call our Special Sales Department in New York at (212) 967-8800 or (800) 322-8755.

You can find Facts On File on the World Wide Web at http://www.factsonfile.com

Text design by Cathy Rincon
Cover design by Nora Wertz

Printed in the United States of America

MP FOF 10 9 8 7 6 5 4 3 2 1

This book is printed on acid-free paper.

# Contents

INTRODUCTION        vii

ENTRIES A - Z        1

PHOTO CREDITS        245

BIBLIOGRAPHY        247

INDEX        251

# Introduction

Probably no type of crime excites the public more than that involving the rich and famous. These selections from the *Encyclopedia of American Crime* represent a cross section of such crimes, but one aspect is apparent in each: the rich and famous are basically more sinned against than sinning, that is, that they tend more often to be the victims rather than the perpetrators of acts of violence or chicanery.

Of course, there are many exceptions. A case in point would be O. J. Simpson, concerning the murders of his wife, Nicole, and her friend Ron Goldman. In many respects the criminal case was well justified being called the "Trial of the Century." Simpson was found not guilty (leaving aside the later civil trial that judged him culpable).

Most analyses of the trial miss a basic truth about crimes, actual or alleged, by the rich and famous. Today, the general opinion is that Simpson, a rich African-American celebrity, was clearly guilty. But his acquittal was not simply the result of his having been tried by a largely African-American jury.

There was a far more pertinent aspect, which may reflect a long-held observation of crime reporters surveying the annals of American murder, that "rich men never burn." One cannot find a case in which a genuinely wealthy person was ever convicted of a capital murder let alone subjected to the death penalty. There is, for instance the case of Texas oilman T. Cullen Davis, the richest man in America ever tried for murder. Davis was charged with staging a shooting spree in his $6 million family mansion during which his 12-year-old stepdaughter and his wife's lover were killed, his estranged wife was severely wounded and a family friend was crippled. Despite the fact that three eyewitnesses named Davis as the killer, the famous and very, very expensive defense lawyer, Racehorse Haynes, won an acquittal for Davis. Similarly, Haynes won a mistrial for the late John Hill, the defendant in the Houston case made famous in the bestseller *Blood and Money*. Hill, too, had the resources to afford the services of the fabled Haynes, of whom one prosecutor said: "He's good, he's very good. But on account of him, there are [a] couple dozen people walking free in Texas who wouldn't blink before blowing somebody's head off. He's a menace to society."

More to the point perhaps is the fact that few will deny that Haynes is "the best lawyer money can buy." The same can be said of

O. J. Simpson who had the wealth that permitted him to assemble a "dream team" defense that rather obviously dissembled a less adequate prosecution. It may be said that Simpson's acquittal outraged more people than Davis's, although Texans might have been cynical enough to understand the disconnect between money and justice. Some cynics, at least with tongue in cheek, find the anger over Simpson's acquittal a form of racial discrimination. Wealthy whites are not found guilty; therefore, they ask, why the tremendous anger about a black man with the same sort of wherewithal being able to enjoy the same benefits in the real world?

Again, though, far more common are cases involving the rich and famous as victims. The murder of famed designer Gianni Versace captured public attention probably as much as the Simpson case. In the process, the murderer, Andrew Cunanan, was elevated by law enforcement and a less-than-discriminating media into a master criminal, which he was not.

Many homicides involving the wealthy have another element that enlivens the case in the public mind. Typical of this was the murder of famous "Scarsdale Diet" doctor Herman Tarnower by Jean Harris, a cultured woman and headmistress of an exclusive Virginia school for girls, who as Tarnower's mistress had to compete with other women for his attentions. The overriding attitude about the murder was "he done her wrong," which to many justified a retribution of murder.

Straight scandal often is enough to whet the appetite of the public, as in the affair involving the multimillionaire and scion of the Bloomingdale's department store family Alfred Bloomingdale and his mistress, Vicki Morgan. So many names could have been dropped in the affair that involved Bloomingdale in sexual perversions and sado-masochistic orgies while he was a close friend of Ronald Reagan and a member of the president's "kitchen cabinet" of political advisers. The affair ended in the tragic murder of Morgan.

No madam in recent years thrilled tabloid readers more than Sydney Biddle Barrows, following her arrest for promoting prostitution in a "call girl" operation that took the guise of an employment agency. Barrows added a new dimension of class, *Social Register* charm and grace, being a descendent of two Mayflower Pilgrims, hence her being dubbed the "Mayflower Madam."

The hunt for scandal sometimes exceeds reality, as the famous are tarred with misbehavior that does not exist. Former teen idol Sal Mineo, his career in deep decline, ended up murdered on a darkened street and as such invited speculation in the press as having been involved in drug dealings, a charge that proved baseless. He had simply been the victim of a random act of violence, the type that could make a victim of anyone.

The cases of crimes involving the rich and famous are varied and their true facts often as startling as the crimes themselves. There is no need to enumerate such additional cases here. They are best told in the complete entries that follow.

# Entries A – Z

**Adams, Albert J.** (1844–1907)   numbers king

A famous and colorful New York City gambler, known as the Policy King, Al Adams was the boss of the most extensive numbers game operation in the city.

Dishonesty has been the keynote of policy games from the time they started in England during the 1700s to the present, but Adams gave them a new wrinkle, not only bilking the public but also swindling other numbers operators in order to take over their businesses.

Adams came to New York from his native Rhode Island in the early 1870s and first worked as a railroad brakeman, a job he found much too taxing. He soon became a runner in a policy game operated by Zachariah Simmons. Duly impressed by Adams' penchant for deviousness, the older man took him in as a partner. Adams developed many ways to rig the game to reduce the winners' payoff. After Simmons died, Adams took over his operation and eventually became the boss of the New York policy racket. At the time, there were scores of independent operators. It was common practice for independent policy men to "lay off" numbers that had been bet too heavily for comfort. They would simply shift part of the action to another operator who had light play on the number, thus spreading the risk. When these operators tried to lay off a heavily played number with Adams, he would note the number and claim he already had too much action on it. He would then lay off the same number around the city, even if he actually had little or no action on it. Thus, a number of operators would become vulnerable to that number. Adams' next move was to fix the results so the heavily played number came out, hitting the owners of many policy shops with devastating losses. To make their payoffs, the operators had to seek loans from Adams, who exacted a partnership as the price of a loan, ultimately kicking the operators out entirely. Some policy operators he simply refused to help, forcing them to make their payoffs (many to Adams' undercover bettors) by dipping into the cash reserved for bribes to politicians and the police. Losing their protection, they were immediately shut down, and Adams simply moved in.

In time, it was estimated that Adams ran between 1,000 and 1,100 policy shops in the city. Over the years his payments to the Tweed Ring totaled in the millions. Even after Tweed fell and reformers came in, Adams was able to operate with the connivance of the police. It was not until 1901 that law enforcement authorities were forced to take action against his nefarious operations, raiding his headquarters. Adams was sent to Sing Sing, where he served more than a year.

When he came out, Adams found that he no longer controlled the New York policy game. The battle for control of the business was turning exceedingly violent, and Adams, who had always operated with bribes and trickery, neither needed nor wanted to be involved in wars to the death. He lived out the next few years in luxury in the Ansonia Hotel and amassed a great fortune through land speculation. However, he was estranged from his family, who was ashamed of his past criminality and blamed him for their inability to lead normal, respectable lives. On October 1, 1907 Adams committed suicide in his apartment.

### Adler, Polly (1900–1962) New York madam

Often called the last of the great madams, Polly Adler achieved such a measure of esteem that in the 1930s and 1940s she was regarded as one of New York City's most illustrious "official greeters." As she said in her memoirs, "I could boast a clientele culled not only from *Who's Who* and the *Social Register,* but from *Burke's Peerage* and the *Almanach de Gotha.*" Her clients, of course, were not limited to high society; they included politicians, police, writers and gangsters. Among the latter were Dutch Schultz, Frank Costello and Lucky Luciano.

The first two were regarded by Polly and her girls as lavish spenders. Luciano was not. If a girl sent by Polly to Luciano's suite in the Waldorf Towers thought she would do much better than the standard $20 fee, she was disillusioned. Luciano might stuff an extra $5 in her bra at the conclusion of a session, but that was all. As he later recalled: "I didn't want to do nothin' different. What do you think I was gonna do—spoil it for everybody?"

Polly almost always used the real names of her clients when introducing them to her girls; the clients did not object, knowing that their secret was safe with Polly. When Dutch Schultz was on the run from the law in 1933 because of an income tax evasion charge drawn by a young federal prosecutor named Thomas E. Dewey, there were 50,000 wanted posters on him. The gang chief nevertheless continued his regular two or three visits a week to Polly's place and was never betrayed.

Despite some memorable police raids, Polly generally operated with little interference out of lavish apartments in Manhattan's fashionable East 50s and 60s. Long laudatory descriptions of the decor in her opulent "homes" appeared in various publications. One establishment at Madison Avenue and East 55th Street was described as having a living room done up in "Louis XVI," a taproom in a military motif colored in red, white and blue, and a dining room that suggested the interior of a seashell. All the baths and "workrooms" were finished in peach and apple green. Free food was always offered and the bar did a thriving business. Many men dropped in just for refreshments and a stimulating chat with the loquacious madam.

Polly became a celebrity in her own right. Interviewed by the press, she commented on

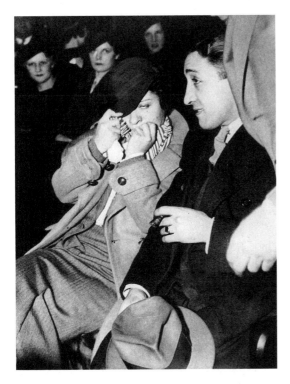

The flamboyant Polly Adler managed to appear dowdyish whenever hauled into court on vice charges, a far cry from the way she paraded with her girls through the Broadway nightclubs.

various past and present events. Her opinion on Prohibition: "They might as well have been trying to dry up the Atlantic with a post-office blotter." Offer the people what they want, she said, and they will buy it. It was a philosophy that served her as well in her field as it did the bootleggers in their area. Madam Adler routinely made the gossip columns and was a regular at nightclub openings, where she would create a sensation marching in with a bevy of her most beautiful girls. She later recalled: "The clubs were a display window for the girls. I'd make a newspaper column or two, the latest Polly

Adler gag would start the rounds and, no matter where we happened to go, some of the club patrons would follow after us and end the evening at the house."

Polly Adler retired from the business in 1944. Encouraged by a number of writer friends, including Robert Benchley, she pursued a writing career after taking a number of college courses, and by the time of her death in 1962, she had become something of a literary light. In her later years Adler, an acknowledged expert on matters sexual, was a dinner companion of Dr. Alfred Kinsey.

### Ah Hoon (?–1909) murder victim

The tong wars of New York's Chinatown were fought with more than guns, hatchets and snickersnee. They were also fought with insult, loss of face and wit. In the 1909–10 war between the Hip Sings and the On Leongs, some of the most telling blows were struck by the celebrated comic Ah Hoon, who was a member of the On Leongs. Ah Hoon used his performances at the venerable old Chinese Theater on Doyers Street to savage the Hip Sings. Finally, the Hip Sings could take no more insults to their honor and passed the death sentence on the comic. They announced publicly that Ah Hoon would be assassinated on December 30. The On Leongs vowed he would not be. And even the white man got into the act. A police sergeant and two patrolmen appeared on stage with Ah Hoon on December 30. The performance went off without a hitch, and immediately after, Ah Hoon was escorted back to his boarding house on Chatham Square. He was locked in his room and several On Leongs took up guard duty outside the door. Ah Hoon was safe. The only window in his room faced a blank wall across a court.

The On Leongs started celebrating this new loss of face by the Hip Sings, who sulked as the On Leongs paraded through Chinatown. When Ah Hoon's door was unlocked the next morning, his shocked guards found him dead, shot through the head. Subsequent investigation revealed a member of the Hip Sings had been lowered on a chair by a rope from the roof and had shot the comic using a gun equipped with a silencer. Now, the Hip Sings paraded through Chinatown. Ah Hoon's killer was never found.

## Alcatraz prison

In 1868 the U.S. War Department established a prison for hostiles and deserters on a stark little island in San Francisco harbor. The Indians called it "Alka-taz"—the lonely "Island of the Pelicans."

By the 1930s Alcatraz had outlived its usefulness to the War Department, but it filled a new need for the Department of Justice, which wanted a "superprison to hold supercriminals," because there just seemed no way to contain them securely in the rest of the nation's federal penitentiaries. The new federal prison on Alcatraz opened on January 1, 1934 under the wardenship of James A. Johnston. Although the warden had previously earned a reputation as a "penal reformer," he would rule "the Rock" with an iron hand.

Hardened criminals were shipped in large batches from other prisons, the schedules of the trains carrying them kept top secret. The first batch, the so-called Atlanta Boys Convoy, excited the public's imagination, conjuring up wild stories of huge gangster armies plotting to attack the convoy with guns, bombs, flamethrowers and even airplanes in order to free scores of deadly criminals. But the first mass prisoner transfer and those following it went off without a single hitch; by the end of the year, the prison, now called America's Devil's Island, housed more than 250 of the most dangerous federal prisoners in the country. The city of San Francisco, which had fought the establishment of a superprison on Alcatraz, now found it had a prime tourist attraction; picture postcards of Alcatraz by the millions—invariably inscribed, "Having wonderful time—wish you were here"—were mailed from the city.

The prisoners, however, wished they were almost anywhere else. Johnston followed the principle of "maximum security and minimum privileges." There were rules, rules, rules, which made Alcatraz into a living but silent hell. A rule of silence, which had to be abandoned after a few years as unworkable, meant the prisoners were not allowed to speak to one another either in the cell house or the mess hall. A single whispered word could bring a guard's gas stick down on a prisoner. But the punishment could be worse; he might instead be marched off to "the hole" to be kept on a diet of bread and water for however long it pleased the warden and the guards.

A convict was locked up in his Alcatraz cell 14 hours a day, every day without exception. Lockup was at 5:30, lights out was at 9:30 and morning inspection at 6:30. There was no trustee system, and thus no way a convict could win special privileges. While good behavior won no favors, bad behavior was punished with water hosing, gas stick beatings, special handcuffs that tightened with every movement, a strait jacket that left a man numb with cramps for hours, the hole, a bread-and-water diet and, worst of all, the loss of "good time," by which all federal prisoners could have 10 days deducted from

U.S. Coast Guard aerial photo of Alcatraz furthers its "superprison" image. In truth, it proved to be a crumbling, inefficient institution.

their sentence for every 30 days with no infractions. But this harsh treatment proved too much for the prisoners and too difficult for the guards to enforce, even with an incredible ratio of one guard for every three prisoners. Within four years the rule of silence started to be modified, and some other regulations were eased.

Incredibly, despite the prison's security and physical isolation, there were numerous attempts to escape from Alcatraz, but none was successful. In 1937 two convicts, Ralph Roe and Teddy Cole, got out of the work-shop area during a heavy fog, climbed a Cyclone fence 10 feet high and then jumped from a bluff 30 feet into the water. They were never seen again, but there is little doubt they were washed to sea. The tide ran very fast that day, and the nearest land was a mile and a quarter away through 40° water. The fact that the two men, habitual criminals, were never arrested again makes it almost certain that they died. Probably the closest anyone came to a successful escape occurred during a 1946 rebellion plotted by a bank robber named Bernie Coy. During the 48 hours of the rebellion, five men died and 15 more were wounded, many seriously, before battle-trained marines stormed ashore and put an end to the affair. Escape attempts proved par-ticularly vicious on Alcatraz because convicts with so little hope of release or quarter were much more likely to kill guards during a break.

Many more prisoners sought to escape the prison by suicide, and several succeeded. Those who failed faced long stays in the hole after being released from the prison hospital. Others escaped the reality of Alcatraz by going insane. According to some estimates, at least 60 percent of the inmates were insane. It remains a moot point whether Al Capone, who arrived there in 1934 from the Atlanta Penitentiary, where he had been serving an 11-year sentence for tax evasion, won parole in 1939 because of the advanced state of his syphilitic condition or because he too had gone stir crazy like so many others.

Alcatraz in the 1930s housed not only the truly notorious and dangerous prisoners but also many put there for vindictive reasons, such as Robert Stroud, the Birdman of Alcatraz, who, along with Rufus "Whitey" Franklin, was one of the most ill-treated prisoners in the federal penal system. The inmate roster included the tough gangsters who truly belonged, like Doc Barker, and those who did not, like Machine Gun Kelly, who had never even fired his weapon at anyone. There were also such nontroublesome convicts as former public enemy Alvin "Creepy" Karpis.

Over the years there were many calls for the closing of Alcatraz. Some did so in the name of economy, since it cost twice as much to house a prisoner on Alcatraz than in any other federal prison. Sen. William Langer even charged the government could board inmates "in the Waldorf Astoria cheaper."

By the 1950s Alcatraz had lost its reputation as an escape-proof prison and had become known simply as a place to confine prisoners deemed to be deserving of harsher treatment.

By the time "the Rock" was finally phased out as a federal prison in 1963, it was a crumbling mess and prisoners could easily dig away at its walls with a dull spoon.

### Allen, John (c. 1830–?)  "Wickedest Man in New York"

One of the most notorious dives in New York City during the 1850s and 1860s—on a par with such later infamous resorts as the Haymarket, Paresis Hall and McGuirk's Suicide Hall—was John Allen's Dance House at 304 Water Street. Allen himself became widely known as "the Wickedest Man in New York," a sobriquet pinned on him first by Oliver Dyer in *Packard's Monthly*. What brought down the wrath of Dyer and other crusading journalists was not simply the vulgarity and depravity of Allen's establishment but his personal background. Allen came from a pious upper New York State family; three of his brothers were ministers, two Presbyterian preachers and the other a Baptist. He himself had initially pursued a similar ministerial career but soon deserted the Union Theological Seminary for the pleasures and profits of the flesh.

With his new wife, John Allen opened a dance hall–brothel on Water Street, stocking it with 20 prostitutes famed for wearing bells on their ankles and little else. In 10 years of operation, the Allens banked more than $100,000, placing them among the richest vice operators in the city.

Despite his desertion of the cloth, Allen never entirely shed his religious training. While he was a drunk, procurer and thief and was suspected of having committed more than one murder, Allen insisted on providing his lurid establishment with an aura of holiness. All the cubicles in which his ladies entertained customers were furnished with a Bible and other religious tracts. Regular clients were often rewarded with gifts of the New Testament. Before the dance hall opened for business at 1 P.M., Allen would gather his flock of musicians, harlots, bouncers and barkeeps and read passages out of the Scriptures. Hymn singing was a ritual; the favorite of Allen's hookers was "There Is Rest for the Weary," apparently because it held out a more serene existence for the ladies in the life hereafter.

> *There is rest for the weary,*
> *There is rest for you.*
> *On the other side of Jordan,*
> *In the sweet fields of Eden,*
> *Where the Tree of Life is blooming,*
> *There is rest for you.*

Eventually, when a group of uptown clergymen took over Allen's resort for prayer meetings, it looked as if the religious aspect of the dance hall had gotten out of hand. Allen had apparently embraced religion entirely, and a lot of uptown devout began attending these meetings to bear witness to the reformation of sinners—especially John Allen. Alas, exposés in several newspapers turned up the sad intelligence that Allen, rather than undergoing a religious rebirth, had actually leased out his establishment to the ministers for $350 a month and seemingly provided some newly reformed sinners for 25¢ or 50¢ a head.

In time, the revivalist movement faded and Allen attempted to return his resort to its former infamy, only to find the criminal element no longer had faith in him, figuring anyone so religiously inclined might be untrustworthy. The last public record of Allen was his arrest, along with his wife and some of his prostitutes, for robbing a seaman. Shortly thereafter, the dance hall closed.

John Allen rented out his dance hall-bordello for prayer meetings and obligingly provided sinners at 25¢ or 50¢ a head.

Allen's fate is obscured by contradictory legends. One had him finally undergoing a complete reformation and even taking up the cloth, but another placed "the Wickedest Man in New York" practicing his tawdry business in a different city under an assumed name. None of these stories has ever been confirmed.

### Allen, Lizzie (1840–1896)  Chicago madam

Next to the fabulous Carrie Watson, Lizzie Allen was Chicago's most successful madam during the 19th century. A native of Milwaukee, she came to Chicago in 1858, at the age of 18, with the clear intention of becoming a madam. She went to work at Mother Herrick's Prairie Queen and, unlike most of the other girls, did not squander her earnings on men. After a stint at another leading brothel, the Senate, Allen opened a house on Wells Street staffed by three prostitutes. Despite the modest nature of the enterprise, she prospered there. Like most other brothel owners, Lizzie was burned out in the Great Chicago Fire of 1871, but she is credited with being the first back in business. She recruited a large staff of unemployed harlots and put them to work in a new house on Congress Street while the carpenters were still working to complete it. With that jump on the competition, Allen accumulated a large fortune and soon became one of the most important madams in the city. In 1878 she formed a relationship with a "solid man," the colorful Christopher Columbus Crabb, and with him as her lover and financial adviser, she flourished still more. In fact, Lizzie Allen was regarded by one local tabloid as "the finest looking woman in Chicago."

In 1888 Allen and Crabb built a 24-room mansion on Lake View Avenue to use as a plush brothel, but police interference doomed the enterprise. They then built an imposing double house at 2131 South Dearborn, which they named the House of Mirrors. Costing $125,000, it was one of the most impressive brothels of its day. (The house was destined to even greater fame under the Everleigh sisters, who took it over in 1900 and made it the most celebrated bawdy house in America.) Lizzie Allen operated the mansion until 1896, when, in poor health, she retired, leasing the property to Effie Hankins. She signed over all her real estate to Crabb and named him the sole beneficiary in her will. The estate was estimated to be worth between $300,000 and $1 million. When Lizzie Allen died on September 2, 1896, she was buried in Rosehill Cemetery. Her tombstone was inscribed, "Perpetual Ease."

See also: EVERLEIGH SISTERS.

## Allison, Dorothy (1925–1999) crime-solving psychic

Among the various psychics who have made the popular press in recent years, one American psychic, a housewife from Nutley, N.J.,

ranked above all others as having some apparent crime-solving ability. Dorothy Allison's visions of peaceful landscapes containing unfound bodies have turned out to be, as *Newsweek* labeled them, "close approximations of grisly reality." In the past dozen years or so, Mrs. Allison had been consulted by police in well over 100 cases and, by her own count, had helped solve 13 killings and find more than 50 missing persons. Many police departments expressed wholehearted, if befuddled, gratitude. "Seeing is believing," said Anthony Tortora, head of the missing persons division of the Bergen County, N.J. sheriff's office. "Dorothy Allison took us to within 50 yards of where the body was found. She's quite a gal."

Some of Mrs. Allison's "finds" have been accident victims and others have been the victims of foul play. In September 1977 two of her finds turned up in different states just one day apart. She pinpointed a swamp area in New Jersey where 17-year-old Ronald Stica would be found and was able to tell police prior to the discovery of the body that he had been stabbed to death. The day before, the body of 14-year-old Susan Jacobson, missing two years, had turned up inside an oil drum in an abandoned boat yard in Staten Island, N.Y. Mrs. Allison had described the corpse site—although she had never been to Staten Island—as a swampy area, with "twin church steeples and two bridges—but one not for cars" nearby. She said she also saw the letters M A R standing alone. All the elements were there, including the letters M A R painted in red on a nearby large rock.

Perhaps Mrs. Allison's most amazing case was one that began at about 6:30 P.M. on Thursday, July 22, 1976, when Deborah Sue Kline left her job as a hospital aide, got in her car and started for her home in Waynesboro, Pa. She never got there. Months of police investigations proved fruitless. Jane Kline, the girl's mother, finally contacted Mrs. Allison, who agreed to come to Pennsylvania. Quite naturally, the first thing the mother asked was if her daughter was still alive. By the end of the day, Mrs. Allison told her the answer: Debbie was dead. Mrs. Allison put on Debbie's graduation ring "to help me feel her presence." She toured the area with police, reporters and a friend of the Klines.

After a while, she was able to reconstruct the crime. She saw Debbie driving home from the hospital and two cars, a yellow one and a black one, forcing her off the road. According to a local newspaper account: "She was taken from her car in one of the other cars to a place where she was molested. She was taken to another place where she was killed with a knife wound. I saw [at the death site] yellow signs, a dump, burnt houses and a swimming pool. I could see her skeleton. It was not underground. The word 'line' or 'lion' came to me."

On January 26, 1977, three days after Dorothy Allison had returned home, police located the body of Debbie Kline. It was not buried and was in an area where junk was dumped. There were no "burnt houses" but the spot was just off the Fannettsburg–Burnt Cabins Road. In the area were yellow traffic signs warning motorists of steep grades on the road. Near the body was a discarded plastic swimming pool. There was no "lion" but there was a "line"—150 feet away was the line between Huntington and Franklin Counties. And Debbie had been stabbed to death.

Then the police confronted a suspect, in jail at the time on another rape charge. His name was Richard Lee Dodson. Dodson broke down and led them to where the body had been found. He and another man, Ronald Henninger, were charged with the crime. Ken Peiffer, a reporter for the *Record Herald,* said: "She told me, among other clues later proven accurate, the first names of the two men involved, Richard and Ronald. She even told me that one of the men had a middle name of Lee or Leroy."

The police of Washington Township, who were in charge of the case, made Dorothy Allison an honorary member of the police department. The citation given to her reads in part, "Dorothy Allison, through psychic powers, provided clues which contributed to the solving of the crime."

Of course, not all of Dorothy Allison's efforts had been triumphs. She was the first psychic called in by Randolph Hearst after daughter Patty disappeared in Berkeley, Calif. Mrs. Allison turned up little of value while on the West Coast. Still, Hearst did not scoff. "Dorothy couldn't locate Patty," he said, "but she is honest and reputable. I wouldn't laugh at it." Allison died December 1, 1999.

**Altgeld, John P.** (1847–1902) Illinois governor
John P. Altgeld, elected governor of Illinois in 1892, was the main player in the final act of the 1886 Haymarket affair, in which a dynamite bomb killed seven policemen and two civilians and wounded 130 others. Altgeld, a wealthy owner of business property, announced he would hear arguments for pardoning three anarchists who had been sentenced to long prison terms for their alleged part in the affair; but no one expected him to free them because it would be an act of political suicide. Four other anarchists had already been hung as a result of Haymarket,

and another had committed suicide in his cell.

In June 1893 Altgeld issued a long analysis of the Haymarket trial, attacking the trial judge, Joseph E. Gary, for ruling the prosecution did not have to identify the bomb-thrower or even prove that the actual murderer had been influenced by the anarchist beliefs of the defendants. "In all the centuries during which government has been maintained among men and crime has been punished, no judge in a civilized country has ever laid down such a rule before." Altgeld also referred to the judge's obvious bias in constantly attacking the defendants before the jury. He then issued full pardons for Samuel Fielden, Michael Schwab and Oscar Neebe, declaring them and the five dead men innocent.

While Altgeld was hailed by labor spokesmen, most newspapers condemned him bitterly. The *New York World* caricatured him as an acolyte worshiping the bomb-wielding, black-robed figure of an anarchist. The *Chicago Tribune* denounced Altgeld, who was German, as "not merely an alien by birth, but an alien by temperament and sympathies. He has apparently not a drop of pure American blood in his veins. He does not reason like an American, nor feel like one." The governor was also hanged in effigy.

Altgeld ignored such criticisms, being content he was "merely doing right," but his act turned out to be political suicide. In 1896 he ran for the U.S. Senate but was defeated. Clarence Darrow later tried to set him up in practice as an associate, but Altgeld, no longer rich, was a tired man, and he died in obscurity six years later. His memory was neglected until Vachel Lindsay placed a poem, "The Eagle That Is Forgotten," on his grave; it read in part:

> *Where is that boy, that Heaven-born Bryan,*
> *That Homer Bryan, who sang*
> *from the West?*
> *Gone to join the shadows with*
> *Altgeld the eagle,*
> *Where the kings and the slaves*
> *and the troubadours rest. . . .*

See also: CLARENCE DARROW.

**Andrews, Shang** (c. late 19th century) publisher
During the 1870s and 1880s a sporting character named Shang Andrews launched a series of publications that chronicled the doings of Chicago's prostitutes.

The Walter Winchell–style tidbits were read as avidly by ladies of the evening as the *Chicago Tribune's* social pages were by matrons of prominence. Portraying the ravages of the profession, they are, no doubt, of sociological value today. The following quotations are taken from the *Chicago Street Gazette*, which like *Sporting Life*, *Chicago Life* and *Chicago Sporting Gazette* among others, made up the Andrews publication list.

> *Lottie Maynard should not be so fresh with other girls' lovers, or she will hear something to her disadvantage.*

> *Ada Huntley is now happy—she has a new lover—Miss Fresh from Pittsburgh.*

> *Lizzie Allen has put on her fall coat of veneer and varnish, and she is now the finest looking woman in Chicago.*

> *Eva Hawkins is on one of her drunks again.*

> *Miss Kit Thompson of 483 South Clark had better let up on taking other girls' men in her room and buying booze for them.*

*Lulu Lee, the little streetwalker, has gone into a house to endeavor and reform herself, but we think it will prove a failure.*

*Lizzie Moss has got sober.*

*What has become of Bad Millie?*

*May Willard, why don't you take a rumble to yourself and not be trying to put on so much style around the St. Marks Hotel, for very near all of the boys are on to you; and when you register, please leave the word "New York" out, for we know it's from the Bridewell you are.*

*We are happy to inform the public that the old-timer, Frankie Warner, has left the city.*

*Mary McCarthy has gone to the insane asylum.*

The true identity of gutter journalist Shang Andrews was never definitely established.

## Annenberg, Moses L. (1878–1942) gambling information czar

Moe Annenberg rose from Chicago's South Side slums to become, for a time, the possessor of the largest individual income of any person in the nation. Using methods not everyone considered legal, he was able to capitalize on two American traits, the desire to read newspapers and the eagerness to bet. However, like Al Capone, he ended up in prison for income tax evasion. For the year 1932 the government said Annenberg owed $313,000; he had paid $308. For 1936 Annenberg owed an estimated $1,692,000; he had paid $475,000. Together with interest and penalties his unpaid taxes totaled $9.5 million. And just as was true with Capone, Annenberg's income tax problems were

merely a logical consequence of his other activities.

Annenberg, who had cut his teeth in the early Chicago circulation wars, was, in the words of Wil-liam Randolph Hearst, a "circulation genius." That "genius" meant selling newspapers with an army of sluggers, overturning the competition's delivery trucks, burning their newspapers and roughing up dealers who sold papers under the impression that it was a free country. Moe first worked in the circulation department of the *Chicago Tribune* and later switched his allegiance to Hearst's new papers in town, the *American* and the *Examiner,* serving as circulation manager of the latter from 1904 to 1906. The roster of Moe's sluggers read like a future public enemies list. A typical Annenberg hireling was Frank McErlane. Former Chicago newspaperman George Murray later wrote of the Annenberg-McErlane alliance: "McErlane went on to become the most vicious killer of his time. Moe Annenberg went on to become father of the ambassador to the Court of St. James."

Moving up in the Hearst organization, Annenberg became one of the highest-paid circulation men in the country. His arrangement with Hearst gave him the right to engage in private business dealings on the side, which included his incursion into the racing information field, on both a legal and an illegal basis. In 1922 he bought the *Daily Racing Form,* and by 1926 his various enterprises had become so vast that he quit Hearst and struck out on his own. In a matter of a few years, he had gathered in his domain the *New York Morning Telegraph, Radio Guide, Screen Guide* and the Nation-Wide News Service. He also took over the century-old *Philadelphia Inquirer* and through it became a power in Republican Party politics.

According to Annenberg, because these activities occurred during a Democratic era, they got him in trouble with the law. Others said that Nation-Wide News Service gave him his great legal problems, as well as huge profits. The service received its information from telegraph and telephone wires hooked into 29 race tracks and from those tracks into 223 cities in 39 states, where thousands of poolrooms and bookie joints operated in violation of local laws. Annenberg became the fifth largest customer of American Telephone and Telegraph, exceeded only by the three press associations and RCA.

The flow of money simply gushed in, becoming so large that, as the *New York Times* reported, "it apparently did not seem worth while to give the government its share." In 1939 Moe and his only son, Walter, were indicted. Walter pleaded not guilty and Moe attacked the charges against him as politically motivated. But finally, in what some observers called great paternal devotion, Moe declared: "It's the best gamble. I'll take the rap." Moe was in his sixties, and his lawyers were hopeful that his guilty plea would lead to the dropping of charges against his son. The gamble paid off. Moe Annenberg drew a three-year prison term and made a $9.5 million settlement with the government.

Nation-Wide News folded up and Moe Annenberg was succeeded as the country's racing information czar by James M. Ragen, who founded Continental Press Service. Walter Annenberg remained a great publishing power and society figure and went on to become ambassador to England under President Richard Nixon.

Further reading: *My Last Million Readers* by Emile Gauvreau.

## Arbuckle, Roscoe "Fatty" (1887–1933)
### accused murderer

Roscoe "Fatty" Arbuckle was at the peak of his career as a comedian, regarded second only to Chaplin, when he was arrested in 1921 for the rape-killing of a delicate young actress named Virginia Rappe, which came to be regarded as Hollywood's worst scandal. The three trials that followed laid bare facts about Arbuckle's private life. What had been amusing on screen for an almost 300-pound buffoon assumed sinister aspects off screen. Somehow the knowledge that Arbuckle had the back seat of his $25,000 Rolls Royce equipped with a built-in toilet came across as more animalistic than humorous when associated with an alleged rapist-murderer.

The facts in the death of 25-year-old Virginia Rappe have never been entirely clear, the picture having been muddled by Hollywood movie studios anxious to protect their investment in a hot comic property. Bribes were paid and witnesses disappeared or changed their stories. But what is clear is that Arbuckle, straight from working on three films without a day off, headed for a session of relaxation in San Francisco with a party of friends, among them Virginia Rappe, who had recently moved up to starring roles on the basis of her delicate beauty rather than any acting ability. Her pretty face at the moment graced the sheet music of "Let Me Call You Sweetheart."

According to some accounts, Virginia thoroughly disliked Arbuckle but kept his company because she felt the fat comedian could aid her career, a common enough belief among aspiring starlets. The young actress was present at a wild party—some later described it as an orgy—that took place in Fatty's St. Francis Hotel suite on September

5, 1921. During the revelry Fatty seized Virginia and hustled her into the bedroom, with the actress showing some or no resistance, according to the conflicting testimony of the witnesses. But what happened next was not disputed.

For 20 minutes no sound was heard from the bedroom and the others in the party simply passed knowing glances. Suddenly, there were hysterical screams and Virginia cried, "I'm dying, he's killing me, I'm dying!"

Arbuckle then walked out of the room wearing Virginia's hat and giggling. "Go in and get her dressed and take her back to her hotel. She makes too much noise."

When the others looked into the bedroom, they saw Virginia's nude, bloody body lying among her ripped clothes. "He hurt me. Roscoe hurt me," she cried. "I'm dying, I'm dying. Roscoe did it."

Arbuckle was unimpressed by Virginia's ravings. "She's acting it up," he said. "She's always been a lousy actress." He warned those present he would throw her out the 12th-story window unless she stopped moaning. Several other women carried Virginia down the hall to another room. Three days later she died.

The three trials of Fatty Arbuckle for felony rape and murder were legal curiosities. At first, courtroom descriptions of what Arbuckle had done were considered so shocking that they were passed back and forth in writing. The official version that Virginia's bladder had been ruptured when the fat man had forced intercourse on her was hardly the complete story. Finally, a witness testified that after the incident Arbuckle had laughingly told others at the party that he had jammed a large jagged piece of ice into her vagina. Later, there was talk about a champagne bottle as well.

The first two trials ended in hung juries, voting 10 to two for acquittal and then 10 to two for conviction. The third trial resulted in a not-guilty verdict, after the jury had deliberated only six minutes. In addition to setting the comedian free, the panel added: "Acquittal is not enough for Roscoe Arbuckle. We feel a great injustice has been done him and there was not the slightest proof to connect him in any way with the commission of any crime." The jurors then stuck around to have their pictures taken with the grateful comic.

While the air was filled with charges that witnesses and jury members had been bribed, the studios set up plans to relaunch Arbuckle's film career. However, it soon became apparent that although a California court had cleared him, the rest of the country did not feel the same way. Theater owners reported that the comedian's unreleased movies would play to empty houses, and his films were junked. Arbuckle spent the next 10 years knocking around in vaudeville and playing second-rate cabarets. He was allowed to direct some minor films under the name of William Goodrich, while he implored the studios to give him another chance. Finally, in 1933 Warner Brothers signed him to do some two-reelers. He finished the first one in New York on June 29. "This is the happiest day of my life," he said. The next morning he was found dead in his hotel room bed of a heart attack.

### Arlington, Josie (1864–1919)   madam

Mary Deubler, better known professionally as Josie Arlington, was perhaps New Orleans' most famous madam. She was certainly regarded as the classiest and her house, the Arlington, gained a reputation as the

## JOSIE ARLINGTON

**225 Basin Street**   **Phone 1888**

*The Arlington*

Nowhere in this country will you find a more complete and thorough sporting establishment than the Arlington. Absolutely and unquestionably the most decorative and costly fitted out sporting palace ever placed before the American public. The wonderful originality of everything that goes to fit out a mansion makes it the most attractive ever seen in this and the old country.

Miss Arlington recently went to an expense of nearly $5,000 in having her mansion renovated and replenished.

Within the great walls of the Arlington will be found the work of great artists from Europe and America. Many articles from the Louisiana Purchase Exposition will also be seen.

One of Madam Arlington's ads in the *Blue Book*, a turn-of-the-century guide to whoring in New Orleans, heralds the ultimate in brothel furnishings and decor.

gaudiest and grandest of bordellos. Her achievement was somewhat remarkable, however, considering her early years in the trade. For nine years, starting at the age of 17, she worked in various brothels on Customhouse Street and Basin Street under the name of Josie Alton. She never stayed long in one place because of her proclivity for brawling with the other girls. In 1886 she engaged in a fierce fight with another prostitute, Beulah Ripley. Josie lost much of her hair, while Beulah staggered from the battle minus her lower lip and half an ear. In 1888 Josie opened her own place at No. 172 Customhouse Street, a house known for having the most quarrelsome residents on the street. The profits enabled Josie to support her lover, Philip Lobrano, who lived in the house, and several members of her family. Lobrano was quite outspoken about relatives living off the income of his women like "a flock of vultures." In 1890, during a fierce brawl in the house involving Josie and all her girls, Lobrano shot and killed Josie's brother, Peter Deubler. New Orleans being New Orleans, Lobrano was acquitted by the courts.

Changing her name to Lobrano d'Arlington, Josie turned over a new leaf. She kicked out her lover, dismissed all her battling prostitutes and announced that henceforth she would fill her establishment with the most gracious of foreign ladies who would entertain only gentlemen of refinement and impeccable taste.

The *Mascot,* a tabloid that reported the doings of the red-light district, trumpeted: "Society is graced by the presence of a bona-fide baroness, direct from the Court at St. Petersburg. The baroness is at present residing incog. at the Chateau Lobrano d'Arlington, and is known as La Belle Stewart." The baroness was soon exposed as being a hoochy-koochy dancer and circus specialist who had graced the Midway at the Chicago World's Fair. Many of Josie Arlington's other imports also proved to be imposters. Despite this, her lavish brothel thrived and when Storyville, a quasi-legal red-light district, was established, Josie opened the Arlington, which was just about the most discrimina-ting in Storyville. Over the next decade Josie Arlington amassed a considerable fortune, which allowed her to buy a mansion in the most fashionable part of New Orleans.

Josie also started to get religion, sending a niece to be educated in a convent. While still in her early forties, she bought a plot in Metarie Cemetery and erected an $8,000 tomb of red marble, with two large flambeaux on top and a crosscut in the back. There was a copper door and carved on it, in bas-relief, was the figure of a kneeling woman, her arms filled with flowers.

Josie leased out the Arlington in 1909 and retired from the business. She died in 1914, at the age of 50, by then Storyville's most-storied madam. Even in death, Josie entertained, in a fashion, the citizenry of New Orleans. The city installed a red traffic light on the street by Metaire Cemetery, and during the night its red glow cast on the two flambeaux gave the illusion of a red light shining over the renowned madam's tomb. Crowds gathered each night to enjoy the spectacle, and nightly sightseeing tours all paused at the cemetery for the show. The city eventually replaced the red light with a white one, making the traffic light one of the most confusing ever installed. In 1924 Josie's niece had the madam's bones transferred to a receiving vault and the gaudy tomb was sold.

## Ashley, John (1895–1924) Everglades gangster

Still regarded as a folk hero in the Florida Everglades, John Ashley headed an unlikely band of criminals who, from 1915 to 1924, robbed a total of 40 banks and stole close to a million dollars. Small-town bankers lived in dread of the sight of the Ashley gang bouncing into town in a Model T and out again with the loot, often waving a gin bottle at the citizens as they went. They were also expert hijackers. Rumrunners, not a spineless sort, blanched when Ashley and his crew mounted one of their transports. A state official called Ashley the worst menace to Florida since the war with the Seminoles. The newspapers likened him to Jesse James, and there was indeed a resemblance save that James never flaunted the law quite as openly as John Ashley.

Once the Ashley gang pulled a job, they would separate and head for the Everglades, where no man alive could track John Ashley, a "cracker" who could move through the swamps with the assurance of an urban pedestrian on well-marked city streets. The story was often told of the time a posse of 12 men went after Ashley when he was alone in the swamp. They failed to catch him but ended up racing out of the swamp panic-stricken, two of them wounded. They suddenly had realized that Ashley was tracking them instead of the other way around.

It was exploits of this sort that made Ashley a hero to a great many crackers who inhabited the pine and palmetto backwoods of Florida. He became a symbol of their resentment toward an encroaching civilization, and a popular belief was that Ashley killed only when he was forced to, lived a life of crime only because he was forced into it. And besides, he sure stuck it to all those the crackers detested—the townies, the revenuers, the police, even them big-city rumrunners importing that foreign stuff and taking away white lightnin' markets. In that last endeavor, the Ashley gang did what the U.S. Coast Guard had failed to do. They virtually halted rumrunning between Bimini, a little spit of sand in the Bahamas, and much of Florida's east coast. The smugglers lost so much liquor to the Ashley gang that they transferred their activities elsewhere.

Perhaps what made the gang so engaging was the fact they did their work so haphazardly; in fact, they were just too lazy to do any advance planning. When Ashley robbed a bank, often the extent of his casing the job was to check the bank's hours to make sure it would be open when he got there. Once when the Ashley mob hit a bank in Stuart, Fla. without bothering to bring along a getaway car, they had an excellent reason: no member of the gang at the time knew how to drive! Ashley figured there'd be someone in the bank who had a car parked outside. Which was exactly how things worked out.

Ashley did get caught a couple of times: following one bank robbery, a member of his own gang accidentally shot him in the eye while firing at pursuers. Ashley was captured as he staggered around on the edge of a swamp, clutching his eye and half-crazed with pain. After that, he wore a glass eye.

Instead of being tried for the bank robbery, Ashley was shipped to Miami to stand trial for the murder of a Seminole Indian sub-chief. There was no hard evidence against Ashley, and he was almost certainly innocent of the murder. The crackers of the swamp knew what was behind it all: the land sellers wanted someone convicted of the killing because they didn't want any Indian trouble scaring away buyers. So why not pin it on John Ashley?

The Ashley gang was incensed and determined to free its leader. Ashley's brother Bob actually made his way into the jailhouse and killed a guard, but he was forced to flee before reaching his brother's cell and was killed shortly thereafter in a fight with police. The frustrated gang then sent an "ultimatum" to the city of Miami that brought the Ashleys nationwide fame. Addressed to the local sheriff, its exact words were

*Dear Sir,*

*We were in your city at the time one of gang Bob Ashley was brutely shot to death by your officers and now your town can expect to feel the results of it any hor, and if John Ashley is not fairly delt with and given a fair trial and turned loose simply for the life of a God-damn Seminole Indian we expect to shoot up the hole God-damn town regardless to what the results might be. we expect to make our appearance at a early date.*

*The Ashley Gang*

It is doubtful the course of Miami justice bent because of this threat, but among the crackers there was a knowing nod of the heads when the murder charge against Ashley was nol-prossed. However, Ashley was convicted of bank robbery and sentenced to 17 years in prison. In a short time, he escaped and returned to take command of his gang.

In 1924 Ashley, tired of bank jobs and the like, pulled one of the most fabulous crimes of the century, though it is little remembered today because the loot turned out to be disappointingly small. During this period of Prohibition most of the rumrunners drew their supplies from the West End Settlement in the Bimini Islands. Ashley decided that instead of going through all the trouble involved in waylaying the rumrunners, it would be a lot less tiring to go to West End and rob whatever money the rumrunners brought there. John and his crew hit the island late one afternoon and within two hours cleaned out all the money the liquor suppliers had on hand. It was the first time in more than 100 years that an American pirate had raided a British crown colony, but Ashley wasn't particularly interested in the distinction. What bothered him was that his master coup had netted a mere $8,000. Just hours before the gang hit the island, an express boat carrying $250,000 in cash had left for Nassau.

Ashley went back to bank robbing, but the end was near. The police now had a stoolpigeon within the gang. His identity has never been established with certainty, but it is widely believed to have been Clarence Middleton, a drug addict member of the gang. The police got a tip in February 1924 that Ashley's father, who'd recently jumped bail on a moonshining charge, was holed up not far from the Ashley home, and that John Ashley was going to visit him.

The hideout was attacked, and Old Man Ashley was killed and a few others wounded. John Ashley, however, escaped. The same source then informed the police that the gang was heading for Jacksonville. A roadblock with a chain and some lanterns was set up at the Sebastian Bridge. It was dark when the Ashley gang's car pulled up. All four men in it—Ashley, Hanford Mobley, Ray Lynn and Clarence Middleton—got out to inspect what they thought was a construction job. A score of gun muzzles were leveled on them. They started to raise their hands.

What happened next is a mystery. The official version is that Ashley made a move for his gun. Twenty law officers fired, and four of the most-wanted men in Florida died. According to another version, told by the crackers, Ashley and the others were handcuffed and then shot to death. This story claims that when their bodies were brought to the funeral parlor, all the dead men's wrists bore the marks of handcuffs.

## assassination

Political assassination came late upon the American scene. The first assassination attempt against a U.S. president occurred in 1835 as Andrew Jackson was strolling out of the Capitol. Richard Lawrence, an out-of-work painter, stepped out from behind a pillar and fired two pistols at Jackson, both of which misfired. Lawrence was judged deranged and committed to an insane asylum, although Jackson remained convinced the would-be assassin's act had been part of a Whig conspiracy to kill him.

The next attack on a U.S. president was the assassination of Abraham Lincoln by John Wilkes Booth in 1865. Besides Booth, who was killed by pursuing troops, four others—Lewis Paine, George Atzerodt, David Herold and Mrs. Mary Surratt—were hanged and several others sent to prison. What followed can best be summarized by a phrase from James McKinley's *Assassination in America,* "After Lincoln, the deluge." While Andrew Johnson was president, 13 political officeholders were shot at and 12 of them killed. During Ulysses S. Grant's two terms, from 1869 to 1877, there were 20 attacks, resulting in 11 deaths.

Assassinations became a part of American political life from the late 19th century on. Some important assassinations and attempts included the following:

*1881:* President James A. Garfield was shot in Washington, D.C. on March 13 by a disappointed office seeker, Charles Julius Gaiteau. Garfield died on September 29 and Gaiteau was hanged in June 1882.

*1901:* President William McKinley was shot in Buffalo, N.Y. on September 6 by Leon Czolgosz. McKinley died on September 14 and Czolgosz was executed the following month.

*1910:* New York mayor William J. Gaynor was shot and badly wounded by

In what many experts regard as the greatest crime photo ever taken, New York mayor William J. Gaynor is shown seconds after he was shot by a disgruntled city employee in 1910 aboard an ocean liner as he prepared to sail for Europe. Gaynor survived. When Charles Chapin, city editor of the *Evening World,* saw the picture he exclaimed, "Look, what a wonderful thing! Blood all over him—and exclusive too!"

James J. Gallagher, a disgruntled city employee, but the mayor recovered.

*1912:* Former President Theodore Roosevelt was shot in Milwaukee by a demented man named John N. Shrank, but Roosevelt was saved when the passage of the bullet was slowed by a folded 50-page speech and the spectacle case in his pocket. The bullet nevertheless, penetrated the former president's chest in too dangerous a position ever to be removed. Shrank was confined in mental institutions until his death in 1943.

*1933:* President-elect Franklin D. Roosevelt was shot at in Miami, Fla. on February 15 by Joseph Zangara. The shot missed Roosevelt and instead hit and fatally wounded Chicago mayor Anton J. Cermak. Some historians insist Zangara never intended to shoot Roosevelt (despite his own claims to that effect) but had been hired by elements of the Capone mob to get rid of Cermak. The mayor himself clung to that belief on his deathbed. Zangara died in the electric chair in March 1933.

*1935:* Sen. Huey P. Long of Louisiana was shot and killed by Dr. Carl Austin Weiss, who in turn was cut down by Long's bodyguards.

*1950:* On November 1 two Puerto Rican nationalists, Oscar Collazo and Griselio Torresola, attempted to storm Blair House to assassinate President Harry S Truman. They never reached Truman but killed a guard, Leslie Coffelt. Torresola was also killed and Collazo wounded. Collazo was sentenced to life imprisonment. In 1979 President Carter granted him clemency and he returned to Puerto Rico.

*1963:* President John F. Kennedy was shot to death in Dallas, Tex. by Lee Harvey Oswald. Oswald was later assassinated by Jack Ruby while in police custody.

*1965:* Malcolm X was shotgunned to death in New York City on February 21 by three assassins as he addressed his Organization of Afro-American Unity. Thomas "15X" Johnson and Norman "3X" Butler, both reputed Black Muslim enforcers, and Talmadge Hayer were all convicted of murder and given life imprisonment.

*1968:* Dr. Martin Luther King, Jr., was gunned down in Memphis, Tenn. on April 4 by James Earl Ray, who was convicted of the shooting and sentenced to 99 years in prison.

*1968:* Sen. Robert F. Kennedy was fatally shot in Los Angeles on June 5 by Sirhan Sirhan, who was subsequently convicted of the murder and sentenced to life imprisonment.

*1972:* Gov. George Wallace of Alabama was shot and permanently paralyzed in Laurel, Md. on May 15 by Arthur H. Bremer. Bremer was sentenced to 53 years in prison.

*1975:* An adherent of Charles Manson, Lynette Alice "Squeaky" Fromme, pointed a gun at President Gerald Ford in Sacramento, Calif. on September 5, but she was immediately seized by a Secret Service agent. Fromme received a sentence of life imprisonment.

*1975:* In the second attempt on President Ford's life in 17 days, Sara Jane Moore fired a revolver at him in San Francisco, Calif. on September 22, but an on-looker shoved the gun off target. Moore was sentenced to life in prison.

*1981:* President Ronald Reagan was shot in the left lung on March 30 by 25-year-old John W. Hinckley, Jr., who fired a total of six shots at the president as he left a Washington, D.C. hotel. Reagan's press secretary, a Secret Service guard and a city policeman were also severely wounded. Reagan recovered.

## Astor Place Riots

One of the worst riots in New York City's history started on May 10, 1849, ostensibly as an outgrowth of a rather silly theatrical feud between the English tragedian William Charles Macready and the American actor Edwin Forrest. Actually, the riots were fomented by a notorious political rogue, Capt. Isaiah Rynders, who capitalized on the poor's general class hatred and anti-British

feeling to regain a measure of public power following the unexpected defeat of his Democratic Party in 1848.

Macready had been chosen instead of Forrest to perform in *Macbeth* at the Astor Place Opera House. When the English actor appeared on stage, he was met by a mob who had gathered in response to a fiery tirade by Capt. Rynders and one of his chief lieutenants, Edward Z. C. Judson, better known as Ned Buntline. Rynders' thugs broke up the performance by hurling rotten eggs, pennies and even chairs onto the stage. Others threw pieces of paper filled with gunpowder in the chandeliers. Macready was driven from the stage but no one was injured. The noted actor was induced by the righteous element, led by Washington Irving and other prominent citizens to try once more on May 10, but Rynders was again prepared.

Offering free drinks, passes and rabble-rousing handbills, Rynders produced a crowd of 10,000 to 15,000. Twenty of Rynders' thugs entered the theater with orders to kidnap the hated foreigner right off the stage. However, the police foiled the plot and locked them all up in the basement, where they unsuccessfully tried to burn down the building. Meanwhile, the mob outside was running wild. They bombarded the barricaded windows of the theater with cobblestones gathered from a nearby sewer excavation and ripped down street lamps to use as clubs, plunging the area into darkness.

The police managed to evacuate the building and got Macready out wearing a disguise, but they couldn't contain the rioting. When Edward Judson was arrested, the mob turned even more violent. Officers were stoned to their knees, and the Seventh Regiment was called into action. Even the cavalrymen were knocked off their horses, and the infantry fell back on the sidewalk on the east side of the opera house. When the crowd tried to seize their muskets, the soldiers were ordered to fire, and several volleys tore into the rioters, who fell by the dozens. Twenty-three persons were killed, and the injury list on both sides totaled more than 120.

The mobs returned the following night determined to wreck and burn the opera house, but they were driven off by reinforced troops and artillery, which had been set up to sweep Broadway and the Bowery. For several days thereafter, crowds gathered in front of the New York Hotel, where Macready had been staying, calling on him to come out and be hanged. However, the actor had rushed to New Rochelle on May 10 and gone on by train to Boston, where he sailed for England, never to return to America.

For his part in fomenting the trouble, Edward Judson was fined $250 and sentenced to a year in the penitentiary. Rynders also was tried for inciting to riot. At the farcical trial, prosecution witnesses retraced the genesis of the plot back to Rynder's Empire Club, where the original plotting had been done, but they could not recall anything involving him directly. The jury acquitted Rynders in two hours and 10 minutes.

**Bailey, F. Lee** (1933– ) defense attorney

Not quite as flamboyant as some other present-day criminal defense lawyers, such as Richard "Racehorse" Haynes and Percy Foreman, F. Lee Bailey is nonetheless recognized as one of the best in the business. Virtually a specialist on homicide, he has, at least until recent years, flown from case to case, around the country in his own private jet, causing courtroom foes and some of the more staid members of the bar to nickname him "the Flying Mouth."

Bailey has proven to be a miracle worker in court: he freed Dr. Sam Sheppard after he had been convicted of murdering his wife when represented by other well-regarded attorneys; he won acquittal for army captain Ernest L. Medina on charges of killing South Vietnamese civilians at My Lai; and perhaps most remarkably of all, he prevailed upon the state of Massachusetts to try Albert DeSalvo, the notorious Boston Strangler, on noncapital charges.

Of course, Bailey has had some notable failures—because, his supporters say, he refuses to run away from the really tough cases. Thus, he lost the Patricia Hearst case and one out of two murder cases against Dr. Carl Coppolino. In his courtroom oratory Bailey lacks the bombast typical of some of today's leading defense lawyers. He is not given to cheap moralizing and has been described by *Newsweek* magazine "as unsentimental as a cat, and equally predatory." Bailey is also cunning. In pre-1972 murder cases—before the Supreme Court temporarily halted the death penalty—he went out of his way to get prosecutors to smile amiably during the trial. "To ask for the death penalty successfully," he explained, "a prosecutor must be like an Old Testament figure—deeply serious, righteously angry. No smiling man can properly ask for another man's death."

Bailey is accomplished at what has been long recognized as a defense lawyer's most important function: picking the right jurors. In the first Coppolino trial, one of his notable successes, he asked prospective jurors if they would be prejudiced because the defendant "may have stepped out of line" during his marriage. One man replied, "I step out of line myself occasionally." When the courtroom laughter subsided, the man added, "You look like you might have played around a little yourself."

"Right there and then," Bailey later said, "I knew he was my man, and I grabbed him. For some reason, the prosecution didn't challenge. And when the jury went out, my man dragged his chair to the window and said, 'I vote not guilty. Call me when the rest of you are ready to agree with me.'"

However, Bailey does not rely on such lucky happenstance. At many of his trials he posts beside him a hypnotist aide who advises him on juror selection and who allegedly is able to tell Bailey how a potential female juror will react to a lawyer based on the way she crosses her legs when answering questions.

Some observers say that in recent years the glow has rubbed off Bailey. He reputedly was chosen to defend Patty Hearst only because the family's first choice, Racehorse Haynes, had asked for double the fee Bailey wanted. But Bailey's detractors are no doubt motivated, in large part, by jealousy. His reputation with the public is probably best typified by one prospective juror's comment under questioning: "I think the man's guilty already. He wouldn't have the most important lawyer in the U.S. otherwise."

See also: PATRICIA HEARST.

## Baker, Rosetta (1866–1930) murder victim

Few murder trial verdicts were ever based so much on racial stereotypes as that in the Rosetta Baker case, although this was one of the few times the decision went in favor of a member of a minority.

A wealthy San Francisco widow in her sixties, the woman was found dead by her Chinese houseboy, Liu Fook. In the course of their investigation, detectives zeroed in on Liu Fook, who was about the same age as the victim, as the only logical suspect. Witnesses revealed that Liu Fook and his "boss missy" had quarreled often, and on the day of the murder, he had scratches on his face and an injured finger—as though it had been bitten. In addition to that, a broken heel and a shirt button found on the floor beside the body belonged to the houseboy.

In spite of this and still more incriminating evidence, the jury at Liu Fook's trial in 1931 acquitted him. Some of the jurors said they had simply been swayed by the defense lawyer's repeated insistence that Liu Fook could not have been guilty because no Chinese employed in this country had ever murdered his employer. Immediately after the trial, Liu Fook took a fast boat for Hong Kong.

## Bakker, Rev. Jim (1940– ) "Praise the Lord for Suckers"

On a par with the bank and Wall Street scoundrels of the 1980s, some in televangelist circles were also grabbing headlines as scamsters. At the top of the list was the Reverend Jim Bakker and his hectic sexual and Ponzi-like shenanigans. Bakker had built up a television network, the PTL (for "Praise the Lord," or "People That Love"), that reached more than 13 million American households.

It was a sexual dalliance that precipitated Bakker's downfall. In December 1980, the youthful-looking Bakker had met a 21-year-old comely brunet named Jessica Hahn, a secretary at a Pentecostal church in Massapequa, N.Y., during a visit to Clearwater, Fla. At the time, Bakker's 19-year marriage to his wife, Tammy Faye, who cohosted his religious television show, was rough going. Bakker and Hahn had sex, and to hear Hahn tell it, she suffered great emotional distress as a result of the encounter. In any event, her pain and suffering were so great that $265,000 was to be paid her as compensation for her silence.

Bakker's secret remained safe for a time; the story was eventually broken in the *Charlotte* (N.C.) *Observer*, a newspaper near the headquarters of the PTL ministry. In addition to the television show featuring Jim and Tammy Faye, the PTL empire included Heritage USA, a Christian resort complex and amusement park in Fort Mill, S.C. In the PTL's peak year, the ministry took in $129 million, and in the recent few years, it had garnered $158 million by offering promises of lifetime vocations—which Bakker could not provide. Instead, huge sums were diverted to the couple, which allowed the Bakkers to live in opulence. In March 1987, Bakker was forced to resign his ministry and later was charged with fraud and conspiracy. At his trial (with Tammy Faye—by now regarded as something of an American original—vowing to stand by her man), a former reservation supervisor at Heritage USA said that in the last year of Bakker's regime at PTL, between 1,300 and 3,700 lifetime contributors had been turned away every month from lodgings that had been promised but did not exist.

Bakker was convicted on all 24 counts against him and sentenced to 45 years in prison and fined $500,000. He would not be eligible for parole for 10 years. In passing sentence, U.S. district judge Robert Porter said, "Those of us who do have religion are sick of being saps for money-grubbing preachers and priests. I just feel like there was massive fraud here, and it's going to have to be punished."

Once again, Tammy Faye promised to stand by her man, but she later filed for divorce and planned to marry a businessman who likewise divorced his wife. In the meantime, Hahn had appeared on the cover of *Playboy* magazine and was paid an estimated $750,000 for a photo display and an interview in which she informed readers that "I'm not a bimbo." She later devoted her talents to hosting a late-night show advising viewers via special 800 numbers how to find "love."

After Jim Bakker was freed, he remarried and devoted himself to activities helping the unfortunate, an undertaking that won him considerable accolades from the media.

### Barrows, Sydney Biddle (1952– ) the "Mayflower Madam"

The 1980s infatuation with the sins of the rich and famous extended even to the world of prostitution, a field that was withering not so much due to a rise in morals but because, as one practitioner put it, "the sexual revolution is killing us. There are just too many women willing to just give it away." Thus, the nation's tabloids were thrilled by the appearance of Sydney Biddle Barrows—the "Mayflower Madam."

For the scandal-minded press, the story harkened back to the glorious old days of high-paid sex, "little black books" and erudite madams. Intellectually, the swooning press declared, Barrows could have held her own with Polly Adler, the "Madam Elite" of the 1930s and 1940s. Sydney Barrows, a descendant of two *Mayflower* Pilgrims, also added a new dimension in class: *Social Register* charm and grace.

Sydney Biddle Barrows, the "Mayflower Madam" who ran a plush Manhattan bordello, celebrates after getting off with just a $5,000 fine.

Thirty-two-year-old Barrows was indicted in December 1984 in New York City for promoting prostitution in the guise of a temporary-employment agency, through which she ran three escort services that actually were expensive call-girl operations. The press was much impressed that the call girls she trained garnered as much as $2,000 a night, in her 20-woman, $1 million-a-year business.

When the tabloids uncovered her connection with the *Mayflower* (which linked her with Elder William Brewster, the minister who had played a leading role in the 1620 Plymouth Rock landing), they quickly dubbed her the "Mayflower Madam."

Barrows pleaded guilty in July 1985 to a lesser charge of fourth-degree promotion of prostitution and paid a $5,000 fine. The press saw this as a plea-bargain deal to sup-

press those eternal little black books. In fact, under the agreement, the prosecution returned seized documents that bore information about her clients, said to include "scores of prominent businessmen."

Now famous, Barrows appeared on the *Donahue* television show unrepentant and complaining that nobody had gone to jail in the state in the last 100 years for what she had done. She earned the attention of the press by writing about her call-girl business: "As I saw it, this was a sector of the economy that was crying out for the application of good management skills—not to mention a little common sense and decency." She expressed the opinion that all women are prostitutes since they withhold favors from their husband when they are angry. But she assured the eager public that, in her own life, "I am monogamous and rather old-fashioned."

Barrows did qualify as a trailblazer in the world's oldest profession by employing only well-informed, articulate women and letting her ladies choose the nights they wished to work. She even allowed clients to pay for services *after* they were rendered, truly a revolutionary practice in the field.

Barrows was a graduate of New York's Fashion Institute of Technology and had studied business management and merchandising. After a stint as a fashion buyer, she got a job through a friend answering the phone for an escort service. She decided she could do it better with her own service, one with very special wrinkles.

Barrows would not even concede that her *Mayflower* ancestors necessarily would have censured her activities. "Had they lived in a more enlightened era," she opined, "they would have understood that the private behavior of consenting adults is not the business of the state."

When TV host Phil Donahue wondered what Barrows' grandmother—who died after her granddaughter's arrest and conviction—had thought about it all, Barrows answered, "She was not amused."

Her post-business activities proved most rewarding for Barrows. Her book soared to the best-seller lists and was condensed in a top women's magazine, and she remained much sought after for lucrative television appearances.

## Beckwourth, Jim (1800–1866 or 1867)
### mountaineer and thief

Trader, scout and all-around frontiersman, Jim Beckwourth was easily the most famous of the black adventurers of the West.

Beckwourth was born in Virginia, the son of Sir Jennings Beckwith (who was descended from minor Irish aristocrats) and a mulatto slave woman. In 1822 Beckwourth (the spelling he adopted) appeared in Missouri as a free black man. Two years later, he joined Gen. William Ashley's expedition to the Rocky Mountains. It is difficult to measure Beckwourth's accomplishments because his own accounts make him easily the greatest Indian fighter and lover of Indian women of all time; yet his reputation grew quickly, and migrants coming West in wagon trains bid high for his services as a guide through the Sierras. Beckwourth also did a thriving business supplying these migrants with horses. To that end, he formed the biggest gang of horse thieves in California's history, together with famed mountain men Old Bill Williams and Pegleg Smith. The gang's greatest raid occurred in 1840, when, with a large band of Indians, they slipped undetected over Cajon Pass. On May 14 Juan Perez, the administrator at San Gabriel Mission, reported to the authorities that every ranch in the valley from San Gabriel to San Bernardino had been stripped of its horse stock. Although posses occasionally caught up to the horse thieves, they were beaten off. Finally, a posse of 75 men under Gov. Jose Antonio Carillo cornered the gang at Resting Springs. In the ensuing gun battle, Beckwourth justified the tales of his prowess with a gun, killing or wounding several members of the posse. Scores of horses were killed and others so badly wounded they had to be destroyed, but Beckwourth and company still got away with more than 1,200 head.

Eventually, Beckwourth turned to ranching, managing to build up his stock with stolen horses until 1855, when he barely got out of the state ahead of vigilantes out to hang him. He moved to the Colorado Territory, scouted again for the army and later took up city life in Denver as a storekeeper. This activity bored him, and in 1864 he went back to the wilderness, acting as a guide for John M. Chivington in the infamous Sand Creek Massacre. Perhaps unwisely, Beckwourth then started trading with the Indians again, and in 1866 he was allegedly poisoned by the Crows while visiting their village. Other reports have him dying in 1867 near Denver.

## Benson family murders   a not-so-ideal son

During the 1980s—the decade of greed—it was inevitable that scandals and homicides among the rich and famous received a great deal of attention. The Benson family murders in Florida were a case in point.

Mrs. Margaret Benson, a 58-year-old widow and heiress to a $10 million tobacco fortune after the death of her wealthy husband in 1980, moved herself and her grown children to a life of self-indulgent ease in Naples, Fla. She supported her children: a married daughter, Carol Lynn Benson Kendall; her older son, Steven; and her young adopted son, Scott. Of the boys, Steven—seemingly the ideal son—was by far the more responsible and dependable and had taken charge of managing the family's affairs. Twenty-one-year-old Scott, by contrast, was always a problem, prone to violence and the use of drugs, snorting cocaine and inhaling nitrous oxide (laughing gas). Given to expensive clothes and flashy sports cars, Scott had difficulty living within a $7,000-a-month allowance. On occasion, he beat his mother and sister, and once the police had to haul him away to a drug-treatment center. Still, the members of the Benson family remained loyal and loving toward him.

In 1985, Steven bought a $215,000 home complete with tennis court and swimming pool, which aroused his mother's suspicions about how he could afford to do so. She began to realize he had been skimming money from a company the family owned. She made plans to have an audit conducted and hinted at disinheriting Steven. One summer day in 1985, the family climbed into their Chrevolet Suburban van for a drive when Steven said he had forgotten something and reentered the Benson mansion. While he was gone, two pipe bombs sent off in the van. Mrs. Benson, now 63, and young Scott died instantly, and Carol was badly injured.

After recovering, Carol told investigators that Steven had made no effort to aid her after the explosion and had shown little emotion at the scene. He was eventually charged with murder. At Steven's trial in 1986, Carol shocked the court by revealing that Scott Benson was actually her son and that her mother—actually Scott's grandmother—had adopted him.

Steven Benson's defense was that the pipe bombs had probably been made by the drug-crazed Scott, who was seeking to destroy the family. The pipe bombs, the defense argued, must have gone off sooner than Scott had anticipated. However, prosecution witnesses contradicted that line of reasoning; one of them testified that Steven had once declared he had learned how to make pipe bombs years before. A purchase order for materials used for such devices was found to bear Steven's finger- and palm prints.

While no one had actually seen Steven plant the bombs, the circumstantial evidence was strong enough for the jury to quickly bring in a guilty verdict. Steven, then 35, was sentenced to two consecutive terms of life imprisonment with no parole for at least 50 years.

## Bergdoll, Grover Cleveland (1893–1966)
### World War I draft dodger

No draft dodger in American history was as infamous as Grover Cleveland Bergdoll, a handsome Philadelphia millionaire playboy who refused to report to his local draft board in 1917. Bergdoll was not captured until January 1920; eventually, he was sentenced to five years imprisonment. In a bizarre escape, Bergdoll talked his military escort into allowing him to retrieve a gold cache of $105,000 he said was hidden in his home, took them there and then eluded them. Over the next two decades the federal government spent millions of dollars trying to recapture him. Private "vigilantes" tried to kidnap, lynch or murder him. During this time Bergdoll flitted between America and various hideouts in Europe, but remarkably, he spent a large portion of the time hidden in the family mansion in Philadelphia with his wife and children.

An overview of newspaper headlines perhaps best illustrates the comic quality of the desperate hunt. Some read:

*SEAS SEARCHED IN BERGDOLL HUNT . . . BERGDOLL DISGUISED AS WOMAN POSSIBLY. . . SEARCH FRUITLESS. . . . BANKER COUNSELS PATIENCE IN BERGDOLL CASE: HAS NO CLUE TO THE FUGITIVE . . . INDIANA MARSHAL SAYS DRAFT DODGER WENT INTO KENTUCKY . . . MAN IN FEMALE GARB TAKEN FOR BERGDOLL. . . BERGDOLL NEARING MEXICO . . . SEEK BERGDOLL IN MOHAWK TOWNS. . . BERGDOLL SUSPECT FREED . . . BERGDOLL CAPTURE HOAX OF SUMMER . . . ONEONTA PRISONER NOT BERGDOLL . . . BERGDOLL REPORTED NEAR CITY . . . BERGDOLL 'ARRESTED' AGAIN.*

Perhaps the most frantic headline of all appeared in the *New York Times:* BERGDOLL'S INITIALS AND ARROW ON TREE.

Finally tiring of the chase, Bergdoll—who had slipped in and out of the country at least a half-dozen times—surrendered on May 27, 1939, sailing into New York aboard the German liner *Bremen*. Reports said he had fled Hitler's Germany to avoid being drafted into the army there; however, as an American citizen, Bergdoll was not subject to German military service. Bergdoll's case was debated in Congress and pressure was put on President Franklin D. Roosevelt to deny amnesty that had been granted to all other draft evaders and deserters. Bergdoll was sentenced to a total of seven years at hard labor. He was released early in 1944. Nineteen years later, suffering mental deterioration, he was confined to a psychiatric hospital in Richmond, Va. He died there on January 27, 1966.

### Berger, Meyer (1898–1959) reporter

Although totally lacking the flamboyance of such other great crime reporters as Ike White, Charles MacArthur and Ben Hecht, Meyer "Mike" Berger was probably the greatest of his or any other day. He brought a sense of quiet, self-effacing dignity and a devotion to accuracy for which the field was hardly renowned. All doors were open to Berger, whether they belonged to distinguished citizens or secretive mobsters. Whenever a rampaging horde of crime reporters from the more than 10 New York City newspapers then in existence would descend on the home of a well-known citizen drawn into a criminal investigation, they would shove Berger to the front and announce: "This is Mr. Meyer Berger of the *New York Times.* He would like to ask some questions." This same respect for the *Times* man was shown in a most unusual way by Arthur (Dutch Schultz) Flegenheimer after the reporter had covered one of his many trials. An incensed Schultz sought out Berger, demanded to know if he had written the story in which someone was quoted as saying Dutch was a "pushover for a blonde." Quaking, Berger admitted he was. "Pushover for a blonde!" the gangster raged. "What kind of language is that to use in the *New York Times*?"

Berger was nominated for a Pulitzer Prize in 1932 for his stories on Al Capone's

Chicago trial that had captured the character of America's most famous gangster far better than the more so-called definitive efforts. When Abe Reles, the Murder Inc. informer, "went out the window" of a Coney Island hotel in which he was being held under police "safekeeping," Berger climbed out on the ledge where Reles would have stood—if indeed he had gone willingly—and told his readers what Reles saw and heard and what he must have felt. Berger won a Pulitzer Prize for his brilliant coverage of the 1949 shooting of 13 persons in Camden, N.J. by an insane veteran named Howard Unruh. The reporter followed the mad killer's trail, talking to 50 persons who had watched segments of Unruh's movements. The account, written in two and a half hours and running 4,000 words, was printed in the *Times* without any editorial changes.

When Berger died nine years later, very few of his colleagues knew that he had given his prize money to Unruh's aged mother.

## Berkman, Alexander (1870–1936) anarchist and would-be assassin

In one of the most tortured assassination attempts ever, anarchist Alexander Berkman tried but failed to kill a leading industrialist of the late 19th century.

Few men were more hated by labor and radical forces in this country than Henry Clay Frick, chairman and strongman of the Carnegie Steel Co., who was blamed as much or more for the company's abysmal working conditions as his partner, Andrew Carnegie.

During the terrible Homestead Steel Strike of 1892, Carnegie left for a vacation in Scotland to avoid being around when the great labor crisis erupted over the workers' refusal to accept a reduction in wages. Carnegie wanted the strike crushed by any means, and no one was more capable and indeed eager to do so than Frick. He recruited a private army of 300 Pinkertons and fortified the company's mills at Homestead, Pa. Then, under cover of night, he sent the Pinkertons by barge up the Monongahela River. They opened fire on the strikers without warning, killing several, including a small boy, and wounding scores of others. The strikers countered with burning oil, dynamite and homemade cannon. With his army stymied, Frick turned to the governor for aid and 8,000 militiamen were dispatched to the scene.

During the stalemate Frick continued his opposition to unionization despite a rising anger in the country. On July 23, 1892 Frick was in his private office with his chief aide, John Leishman, planning company strategy when a young man posing as an agent for a New York "employment firm" received permission to enter.

Actually, the man was 21-year-old Alexander Berkman, a fiery anarchist and lover of another famous anarchist, Emma Goldman. Berkman was outraged at Frick's behavior during the strike and resolved to assassinate him as an act of liberation on behalf of his working comrades. He first tried to do so by making a bomb but failed to produce a workable model. Emma then went into the streets as a prostitute to raise money in order to buy a gun. She was picked up by a kindly older man who guessed her amateur status and sent her home with $10. With that, Berkman bought the assassination weapon.

The actual attempt was best described by a contemporary account in *Harper's Weekly*:

*Mr. Frick had been sitting with his face half turned from the door, his right leg thrown over the arm of his chair . . . and almost before he had realized the presence of a third party in the room, the man fired at him. The aim had been for the brain, but the sudden turning of the chairman spoiled it, and the bullet ploughed its way into the left side of his neck. The shock staggered Mr. Frick. Mr. Leishman jumped up and faced the assailant. As he did so another shot was fired and a second bullet entered Mr. Frick's neck, but on the left side. Again the aim had been bad. Mr. Leishman, who is a small man, sprang around the desk, and just as the assailant was firing the third time, he seized his hand and threw it upward and back. The bullet embedded itself in the ceiling back of where the man was standing . . . Mr. Frick recovered almost instantly from the two shots and ran to the assistance of Leishman, who was grappling with the would-be assassin . . . The exertion made the blood spurt from his wounds and it dyed the clothing of the assailant.*

*The struggle lasted fully two minutes. Not a word was spoken by any one, and no cry had been uttered. The fast-increasing crowd in the street looked up at it open-mouthed and apparently paralyzed (Frick's upper-floor office could be readily seen into from across the street). There were no calls for the police and no apparent sign of excitement, only spellbound interest. The three men swayed to and fro in struggle, getting all the time nearer to the windows. Once the assailant managed to shake himself loose, but before he could bring his revolver again into play, Mr. Leishman knocked his knees from under him, and the combined weight of himself and Mr. Frick bore the man to the floor. In the fall, he succeeded in loosening one hand and with it he drew an old-fashioned dirk-knife from his pocket and began slashing with it. He held it in his left hand. Mr. Frick was trying to hold him on that side. Again and again, the knife plunged into Mr. Frick until seven distinct wounds had been made, and then Mr. Frick succeeded in catching and holding the arm.*

*At the first sign of the knife the crowd in the street seemed to recover itself and there*

Anarchist Alexander Berkman is shown after his assassination attempt on steel magnate Henry Clay Frick during the Homestead Steel Strike of 1892.

*were loud calls of "Police!" "Fire!" The clerks in the main office recovered from their stupefaction, and rushed pell-mell into the office of their chief. Deputy Sheriff May, who happened to be in the office, was in the lead. He drew a revolver, and was about to use it, when Mr. Frick cried: "Don't shoot! Don't kill him! The law will punish him." The deputy's hand was seized and held by one of the clerks, while half a dozen others fell on the prostrate assailant. The police were in the office in a few minutes and took the man away. Fully two thousand people had gathered in the street, and there were cries of "Shoot him! Lynch him!"*

Despite a total of nine wounds, Frick was back at his desk within a week, but Berkman spent 14 years in prison before being pardoned in 1906. Like most acts of terrorism, his attack on Frick had not helped the intended beneficiaries. In fact, the strikers generally denounced the act, though many with seemingly little conviction. From 1906 until 1919, when they were deported in the Red Scare roundups, Berkman and Goldman became the primary spokespersons for American anarchism. They were sent back to their native Russia, where they were welcomed by the new Soviet government, but the incompatibility of anarchism and communism soon forced them both to leave. Berkman settled first in Sweden, then Germany and finally in France. He continued his anarchist writing and organized and edited many of Goldman's work. He did some translating and ghostwriting for European and American publishers but needed contributions from friends and comrades to survive. Both despondent and ill, he committed suicide in 1936. H. L. Mencken wrote of Berkman that he was a "transparently honest man . . . a shrewder and a braver spirit than has been seen in public among us since the Civil War."

### Bickford, Maria (1823–1845) murder victim

The murder of Maria Bickford by Albert Tirrell in Boston on October 27, 1845 was noteworthy because the young man was of the Weymouth Tirrells, one of New England's wealthiest and most socially prominent families. However, the case was to become even more noteworthy since it represented the first effective use of sleepwalking as a defense.

The 25-year-old Tirrell was the bane of his family. Although married, he was notorious for picking up a whore and going off with her for a week or longer at a time. In one of the family's constant efforts to get Albert to reform, they sent him on the road as a representative for one of the Tirrell businesses, Tirrell's Triumphant Footwear. Exactly how providing Albert with such an ideal opportunity for whoring would lead to his reformation was, at least in retrospect, a mystery. In New Bedford, Mass., he met 23-year-old Maria Bickford and was soon pursuing his usual desires. But in the case of this woman, it was a matter of true love; Tirrell brought Bickford back to Boston, ensconcing her in a waterfront flat where he could visit her regularly, while continuing to pretend to his family that he had indeed become a solid citizen.

However, the Tirrell-Bickford love affair was not a quiet one. They screamed, fought, got drunk frequently and eventually were evicted for boisterous behavior. Tirrell's conduct became the talk of Boston. The family could no longer ignore this, and finally, Tirrell's wife and brother-in-law brought criminal charges of adultery against him. In the year 1845 in Boston, adultery was a word spoken only in whispers. Indeed, the act was punishable by a fine and six months imprisonment. Even worse, a convicted man would almost certainly be treated as a pariah, shunned by society. Painfully aware of this, Tirrell was most contrite when visited in his cell by the family. "He implored his young wife for forgiveness," says an account of the day. The fact that he was in the process of "drying out" added to the heart-rending scene. Finally, on October 20 the family, including Tirrell's wife and brother-in-law, capitulated. They withdrew the charges and the prodigal son was turned loose upon signing a bond promising to "keep the peace and observe propriety in his behavior."

Back home for an hour, Tirrell kissed his wife and said he had to go out "on business." Like a homing pigeon, he headed for the house of Joel Lawrence on Cedar Lane in the Beacon Hill district, where Maria Bickford had taken up residence. Tirrell brought with him a demijohn of rum. During the reunion of the lovers that followed, landlord Lawrence later said that he thought the house was falling down. Eventually, the lovers quieted a bit until the following evening. Then the revelry started again but soon turned into a nasty quarrel when Tirrell found some letters written to Maria by a new admirer. Over the next several evenings the pair's frolicking was increasingly interrupted by harsh arguments, a matter compounded when a Miss Priscilla Moody from down the hall, unaware that Tirrell was around one afternoon, dropped by to ask Maria to help her out since she had two gentlemen calling on her shortly. When Tirrell erupted in anger, Maria just laughed and said if she did anything like that, it would just be "funning."

The Tirrell-Bickford funning came to an end at 4:30 the morning of October 27. Smoke was seen pouring out of Maria's window, and the landlord, who had been awakened about an hour earlier by another of the incessant screaming matches between the lovers, broke in. Someone had deliberately set fire to the room. It was not Maria. She was lying on the floor, totally nude, her throat slit almost from ear to ear. When Lawrence viewed the scene, he shouted out, "Where's Albert?"

Albert had headed for the Boston docks, he joined a ship's crew and sailed away as a common seaman. It was not until February 27, 1846 that he was apprehended aboard the schooner *Cathay* in New York and returned to Boston to face murder charges. There was little reason to doubt that Tirrell would be convicted. There were witnesses who saw him leave the Lawrence house moments before the fire. Those who had seen him testified that he wore no shirt under his coat—his bloody shirt had been found in the murder room. An acquaintance of Tirrell's, Sam Head, told of how young Albert had turned up at his home and asked, "Sam—how came I here?" He stank of rum.

With such a strong case against him, Tirrell was considered as good as convicted. Nevertheless, the Tirrell family decided to strive mightily to save the errant son, recoiling in horror from the stigma that would attach to all if Albert were hanged for murder. The Honorable Rufus B. Choate was retained to defend Albert. Choate, then at the height of his oratorical powers, was rightly considered a courtroom wizard, but everyone was convinced that in this case he was espousing a hopeless cause. It would take a miracle to save Tirrell. Which was exactly what Choate came up with.

Choate stunned the court when he conceded that his client had indeed killed "this unfortunate woman." However, the lawyer said, "I will prove that he cannot be held responsible under the law because he was asleep at the time." While the courtroom buzzed with an argument never heard before in an American court of law, Choate continued:

*I do not mean, of course, that he was asleep in the usual physical sense. He was mentally asleep. Although he was capable of physical movement and action, he had no knowledge or judgment of what he was doing. His mental and moral faculties were in deepest slumber. He was a man in somnambulism, acting in a dream. Gentlemen, I will show that the defendant Tirrell has been a sleepwalker since early youth, and that while in a condition of somnambulism that often lasted for many hours, he performed feats of almost incredible complexity and dexterity.*

Witness after witness took the stand to tell of Tirrell's past sleepwalking escapades and accomplishments. His mother said her son had first shown sleepwalking tendencies at the age of three. He had been found in the kitchen sound asleep smearing jam on the walls. He started sleepwalking regularly. Mrs. Tirrell took to tying his son to his bed, but the boy showed a slumbrous ability to untie knots he could not undo when awake. After the lad had been discovered to have climbed out of his bedroom window and perched precariously on the porch roof, Mrs. Tirrell, according to the testimony of a workman, ordered an iron grill over the window "to keep the tyke from killing himself."

The family physician reported that at the age of 10, the sleepwalking boy, barefoot and in only his nightgown, had been found in the late hours of a winter night just as he completed building a snowman. "The boy came near dying of pneumonia as a result of that," the doctor testified.

According to the evidence presented, Tirrell's sleepwalking escapades became less frequent in adulthood but tended to be more dangerous and violent. His wife Cynthia awoke one night to find him trying to strangle her. Her desperate screams awakened him, and he expressed surprise and contrition, begged her forgiveness and then lapsed into a peaceful sleep. A sailor from the *Cathay* told of watching the sleeping and stark-naked Tirrell cross the ice-covered deck of the vessel, climb high in the mast and then come down safely, all the while acting "like a man in his sleep."

Lawyer Choate then recalled the words of Samuel Head, who had seen Tirrell shortly after Maria Bickford's murder. "He seemed like a man coming out of a stupor. He said, 'Sam, how came I here?'"

Despite the prosecution's attempts to knock down Choate's unique defense of his client, the jury was duly impressed. It took less than two hours to bring in a verdict that established a legal milestone. Albert Tirrell was found not guilty and freed. As time passed, the Tirrell verdict did not sit well with the public, which clearly felt the family money had gotten him off. A man who could slit a pretty girl's throat and—allegedly—not remember it was, general opinion held, more likely rum soaked than in a somnambulistic trance. Finally, bowing to public opinion, the family had Albert confined where he would no longer be a danger, sleeping or awake.

## Black Sox Scandal   baseball betting coup

Before 1919 the fixing of baseball games for betting purposes was by no means unheard of. But in that year it went too far; the "unthinkable" happened: a World Series was fixed by eight star players for the Chicago White Sox who managed to lose the series to the underdog Cincinnati Redlegs five games to three (the series that year was being played in an experimental nine-game set).

All the details of what was to be called the Black Sox Scandal were never fully exposed, primarily because there was an attempted cover-up by the baseball establishment, in general, and White Sox owner Charles A. Comiskey, in particular. The offending players were not even suspended until there were only three games left to play in the following season, when confessions by three players to the grand jury forced Comiskey to act.

The throwing of the series appears to have been thought of initially by Chicago first baseman Charles Arnold "Chick" Gandil, who passed the word to Boston gamblers that he could line up several teammates for a lucrative killing. The other players involved were Eddie Cicotte and Claude Williams, star pitchers who between them had won 52 games during the season; left fielder Shoeless Joe Jackson; center fielder Oscar Felsch; third baseman George "Buck" Weaver; shortstop Charles "Swede" Risbergand; and utility infielder Fred McMullin. The gamblers first approached were Joseph "Sport" Sullivan of Boston and William "Sleepy Bill" Burns of New York. Because they felt they needed more capital to finance a gigantic killing, they approached the country's leading gambler, Arnold "the Brain" Rothstein. It is debatable whether or not Rothstein entered the plot or turned them down and then simply went ahead and bet at least $60,000 on Cincinnati (and collected $270,000) because he knew the fix was in and saw no need to pay out any bribe money himself. In any event, the main operator behind the fix became Abe Attell, the ex-featherweight boxing champion. A caller to Attell's hotel suite in Cincinnati later told of seeing money stacked on every horizontal surface in the room, on tables, dresser tops and chair seats, after the Reds won the first game.

In the first two games Cicotte's invincible "shine ball" failed him, and he was knocked out in the fourth inning; Williams was uncharacteristically wild and lost 4–2. By the end of the second game, rumors of the fix were rampant, and the Reds were big favorites to take the series. It was impossible to find a professional bookmaker who would bet on Chicago, that action being played strictly by amateur bettors. It took a

yearlong grand jury investigation to crack the case, with confessions coming from Jackson, Cicotte and Williams. Comiskey was forced to fire all the players except Gandil, who had already "retired."

Testimony showed that most of the players had gotten $5,000 for their parts in the fix, while Gandil had kept $35,000 for himself. How many hundreds of thousands the gamblers made was never really determined. When several of the players left the grand jury room, a group of small boys awaited them. One said to Shoeless Joe Jackson: "It ain't true, is it, Joe?"

"Yes, boys," the outfielder replied, "I'm afraid it is."

The conversation has come down in folklore as the boy wailing plaintively, "Say it ain't so, Joe."

Another bit of folklore is that the baseball establishment excised this cancer as quickly as possible. In fact, the baseball magnates provided legal aid to the players, and indeed, the jury acquitted them and carried some of the defendants out of the courtroom on their shoulders. However, Judge Kenesaw Mountain Landis, appointed commissioner to oversee the integrity of "the Game," was not satisfied. He never let any of the players don a Comiskey uniform again.

**Bloomingdale-Morgan affair** perversion in high places

This sex scandal caused considerable dismay in the Reagan White House and concluded later in a savage murder that was judged to be unconnected to it. The scandal erupted when a beautiful playgirl-model filed a $10 million palimony suit in 1982. Thirty-year-old Vicki Morgan filed the claim against multimillionaire Alfred Bloomingdale and

Vicki Morgan's long-running love affair with multimillionaire Alfred Bloomingdale bared perversions in high political and social circles.

later against his estate, charging she had long been "kept" by him for sexual perversions and sadomasochistic orgies. Bloomingdale was the scion of the Bloomingdale's department store family and a longtime friend of Ronald Reagan. His wife, Betsy, was a particularly close friend of the president's wife, Nancy.

The affair had started in 1970 when Morgan was 17 and Bloomingdale was 53. Bloomingdale had spotted Morgan on Sunset Boulevard and followed her into a restaurant and struck up a conversation with her. He insisted on having her phone number before he would leave. Morgan later said,

"He was so persistent, I had lunch with him."

Lunch was not what the encounter was all about, and within a week of "wooing," Morgan was mired into Bloomingdale's bizarre world of leather and chains, with Bloomingdale as a demanding dungeon master. Vicki stripped naked along with as many as three other women so that Bloomingdale could whip them and have them engage in an endless number of sexual "games."

The end result: Vicki "found herself falling in love" with Bloomingdale. If love was not enough, there was the matter of compensation. Bloomingdale paid Morgan's rent, provided her with spending money to the tune of a trifling—for him—$18,000 a month and got her launched on a movie career that never amounted to much. This went on for 12 years.

For all his weird activities Bloomingdale still had time to do his thing on the social circuit. He extended his fame and fortune by developing the Diners Club credit card. For a time he was also a Hollywood agent and producer and was a big booster of actor Ronald Reagan's career in state and, later, national politics. After Reagan became president, Bloomingdale, as a member of Reagan's "kitchen cabinet" of political advisers, harbored hopes of becoming ambassador to France. However, he got no such appointment, and it was said later by some observers, this was because the public image–conscious president was obviously aware of his pal's swinging lifestyle. A year later, Bloomingdale became a member of Reagan's Foreign Intelligence Advisory Board, composed of "trustworthy and distinguished citizens outside the government" who reviewed the operations of U.S. intelligence and counterintelligence agencies.

Early in 1982, the 66-year-old Bloomingdale was diagnosed with throat cancer and hospitalized. It was during this period that his wife discovered he had been providing Morgan an $18,000 monthly allowance. Furious, Mrs. Betsy Bloomingdale had the payments stopped. Morgan countered by filing a $5 million palimony suit, claiming she was Bloomingdale's confidante, business partner and traveling companion. Shortly after, she raised the ante another $5 million for Betsy having cut off her $18,000 stipend.

Before the case came to court, Bloomingdale died, on August 20, 1982. The following month, a court threw out most of the $10 million claim, declaring the relationship had been no more than a "wealthy, older paramour and a young, well-paid mistress." The judge permitted to stand Morgan's claim that she had a written contract guaranteeing her a $10,000 payment each month as a partner in Bloomingdale's business interests.

While litigation against the Bloomingdale estate continued, the depressed and angry Morgan moved into a North Hollywood condominium, which she eventually shared with an old friend, Marvin Pancoast, a homosexual with major psychological problems of his own. The condominium became the site of frequent drug and drinking bouts. Arguments between the two over money, mainly that Pancoast could not come up with his share of the expenses, became tense.

On July 7, 1983 Pancoast used a baseball bat to beat Morgan to death. He notified the police and confessed to the crime, but later recanted.

Meanwhile, the embarrassing political fallout continued when an attorney practicing criminal law announced he had been asked to represent Pancoast at this trial and said he had videotapes showing Bloomingdale and Morgan in group and sadomasochistic sex with a number of top government officials. The lawyer said one person so involved "would definitely embarrass the president, just like Mr. Bloomingdale did."

Shortly thereafter, he insisted the tapes had been stolen, and the following day porno publisher Larry Flynt said he had a deal with the lawyer to pay $1 million for the tapes, but that the lawyer never showed up to complete the deal. The lawyer later denied having talked to Flynt. The tape story was considered to be a hoax and the lawyer was charged with having filed a false report.

Pancoast pleaded innocent to the murder of Vicki Morgan by reason of insanity. Records indicated that over the previous 13 years, he had been diagnosed as masochistic, manic-depressive and psychotic-depressive. It turned out he had once even confessed to the Sharon Tate and related murders, which actually were committed by the Charles Manson family. Besides trying to discredit Pancoast's previous confession, the defense also stressed that others had had reasons to murder Morgan because of her claims of depraved sex with government officials. The jury rejected such theories and convicted Pancoast. He was sentenced to 26 years to life in prison.

In December 1984, a jury finally ordered the Bloomingdale estate to pay $200,000 to Morgan's estate, on the grounds that Bloomingdale had promised in a letter in February 1982 to pay $240,000 for Morgan to spend time with him in the hospital during his terminal illness. Morgan had received $40,000 before these funds also had been cut off. Under the law, the money went to her 15-year-old son, who had been fathered during an affair Morgan conducted during a brief breakup with Bloomingdale early on in their relationship.

## Boesky, Ivan (1937– ) "Ivan the Terrible" of stock deals

Until the mid-1980s Ivan Boesky was regarded as the most controversial high-rolling stock speculator on Wall Street. Few such operators were more feared than "Ivan the Terrible," as he was called. Boesky gambled tens of millions on risky securities deals. Later, when the secrets of his methods were uncovered, he was regarded as one of the biggest crooks in the financial world.

The son of a Russian immigrant in Detroit, Boesky was graduated from law school in 1962 and moved to New York four years later. He did stints in an investment firm and then a brokerage house, and then was attracted to the wild world of risk arbitrage—risking huge sums buying and selling stocks of companies that appeared to be likely to merge or be taken over by other firms.

Boesky launched his own arbitrage firm with $700,000 in capital, and 11 years later had a financial empire worth some $2 billion. He lived with his wife and four children in a 10-bedroom mansion on a 200-acre estate in suburban Westchester County and maintained a lavish river-view apartment in Manhattan. Corporations competed to get him on their boards, and he gave huge sums to charities while making increasing profits on his stock dealings.

Unfortunately, Boesky didn't do this on the up-and-up. He sought out insider tips and paid generously for such illegal information. In May 1986, Dennis Levine, one of Boesky's key illegal sources and a wheeler-dealer in his own right, was trapped by government investigators and started to "sing." The man he gave to the government was Boesky, and Boesky in November of that year made an agreement to pay $100 million in penalties for violating securities laws. To cut his potential prison time, Boesky started to outwarble Levine and turned in his fellow lawbreakers. He even agreed to let investigators tape his phone conversations as he carried out his stock deals. Numerous heads rolled as a result, and Drexel Burnham Lambert, one of the giant financial institutions on Wall Street, plunged to near collapse, turning into a shell of its former self.

In a plea bargain Boesky got off with a three-year sentence, saying he was "deeply ashamed" of his past actions. Many observers thought he had paid a very tiny price for the ruined financial fortunes of so many shareholders. Even his $100 million penalty—the largest of its type in history—left him a most wealthy man. When he left prison, Boesky did, however, face a host of legal actions undertaken by ex-partners and victimized shareholders.

See also: DENNIS LEVINE.

## Bonnie and Clyde    public enemies

As professional thieves, Bonnie and Clyde—Bonnie Parker and Clyde Barrow—never qualified as public enemies. Most of their thefts were of the minor-league variety: grocery stores, filling stations, luncheonettes and a few small-town banks. Their greatest haul was no more than $3,500. But they were brutal, killing at least 13 persons and escaping police ambushes with incredible pluck.

In a sense, Clyde Barrow was cut from a heroic mold, unlike many other gangsters of the 1930s, such as Baby Face Nelson, Pretty Boy Floyd and even John Dillinger. When trapped, he never abandoned his woman, often fighting his way back to her and leading her to safety. It was an odd relationship: a homosexual and a near nymphomaniac.

Born in extreme poverty in Texas in 1909, Clyde followed his older brother into crime, first stealing turkeys and then graduating to cars. The pair committed several robberies in the Dallas area. Finally, after holding up a gas station in Denton, Tex., they were forced to make a 90-mile-an-hour run from the police with Clyde behind the wheel. Buck was shot during the chase, and when Clyde wrecked the car in a ditch, he left Buck for the law, fearing his brother would bleed to death otherwise. Buck got five years.

In January 1930 Clyde met 90-pound, golden-haired 19-year-old Bonnie Parker, who was "sort of married" to a convict, Roy Thornton, serving 99 years for murder. Bonnie described herself in that period as "bored crapless." They started living together, and Clyde tried to support them by playing the saxophone. It was a futile effort and he quickly reverted to robbery. It wasn't long before Dallas lawmen arrested Clyde for a burglary in Waco: he had left his fingerprints behind. The judge sentenced him to two years.

Buck Barrow escaped from prison, and he and his wife, Blanche, joined up with Bonnie. On a visit soon afterwards, Bonnie passed a narrow-handle .38 Colt through the jail bars to Clyde. After he made his break, Bonnie stayed put for a while to keep the law occupied. The law caught up with Clyde in Ohio.

This time Barrow was sent to the prison farm at Eastham, Tex., one of the most brutal institutions in the state. Clyde endured many tortures there and became a far more hardened criminal and a confirmed homosexual. He served 20 months, gaining a pardon after his mother tearfully pleaded his cause with Gov. Ross Sterling. Clyde Barrow said he would never see the inside of a prison again. "I'll die first," he said, and he was right.

Following Clyde's release, Bonnie teamed up with him on various robberies, but after a confrontation with the police, they became separated and Bonnie was caught. She served three months for the robbery of a car the couple had seized trying to escape. Clyde went on committing robberies and killed his first two lawmen in Atoka, Okla.

When Bonnie rejoined him, they fell in with a gunman named Ray Hamilton, an incorrigible young thief and killer who in many ways was a more spectacular criminal than Clyde. His relationship with Bonnie and Clyde, however, was more meaningful than just the addition of greater firepower on their holdups. Hamilton regularly slept with Bonnie and at times with Clyde as well. It was, by all accounts, a well-adjusted triangle, at least for brief periods. Eventually, the sexual pressures probably became too much for the three, and Hamilton broke away. Both Bonnie and Clyde apparently needed a more submissive love partner; Hamilton was just too tough to give them their way. After leaving them the last time, he pulled off a long string of crimes and several jailbreaks before finally dying in the electric chair in 1935.

While Bonnie and Clyde's robberies continued to be on the minor side, their escapades were often extremely violent. They stuck up a butcher, and when the man came at Clyde with a cleaver, Clyde avoided the blow and emptied his gun into him. In November 1932 the pair held up a filling station and kidnapped the attendant, William

Bonnie and Clyde are snapped in a playful mood. Gag photos such as these did much to capture the public's attention.

had been identified, and their exploits made front-page news from coast to coast, which pleased Bonnie no end. She deluged newspapers with samples of her "poetry." Editors eagerly printed her poem "The Story of Suicide Sal." They also printed pictures of her smoking a cigar and brandishing a machine gun. Bonnie said these were "horsing around" pictures and resented the light in which the newspapers had put them. During their getaways the gang often kidnapped lawmen, one of whom was chief of police Percy Boyd. When they let him go, Bonnie told Boyd: "Tell the public I don't smoke cigars. It's the bunk."

They fought their way out of a trap in Joplin, Mo., killing two officers, but it was apparent that the gang could not continue to escape capture or death. In July 1933 the gang was hiding out in the deserted fair grounds in Dexter, Iowa when a posse closed in. Buck Barrow was fatally wounded and Blanche captured. Bonnie and Jones were also wounded, but Clyde got both of them away.

In the next few months, Bonnie and Clyde killed four more lawmen. During this period Jones took the first opportunity to desert them. When picked up in late 1933, he told of his incredible career of crime and suffering with the pair and begged to be sent to prison, where he would be safe from Bonnie and Clyde. The law obliged.

Bonnie knew the end was near. She mailed newspapers "The Ballad of Bonnie and Clyde," which concluded:

> *The road gets dimmer and dimmer,*
> *Sometimes you can hardly see,*
> *Still it's fight man to man,*
> *And do all you can,*
> *For they know they can never be free.*
>
> *If they try to act like citizens,*
> *And rent them a nice little flat,*

Daniel Jones. After learning who his captors were, Jones joined up with them and replaced Ray Hamilton in their affections. He later described his experience as "18 months of hell."

Meanwhile, Buck Barrow had been in and out of jail again, this time pardoned by the new governor, Mrs. Miriam "Ma" Ferguson, who had granted pardons to some 2,000 felons during an earlier term. With Buck and Blanche in tow, the gang now numbered five and was ready for the big time. Brandishing newly obtained machine guns, they held up a loan company office in Kansas City. They

*About the third night they are
invited to fight,
By a submachine-gun rat-tat-tat.*

*They don't think they are too
tough or desperate,
They know the law always wins,
They have been shot at before
But they do not ignore
That death is the wages of sin.*

*From heartbreaks some people have suffered,
From weariness some people have died,
But take it all and all,
Our troubles are small,
Till we get like Bonnie and Clyde.*

*Some day they will go down together,
And they will bury them side by side.
To a few it means grief,
To the law it's relief
But it's death to Bonnie and Clyde.*

The pair stayed on the run until May 23, 1934, when they attempted to hook up with Henry Methvin, a convict they had freed once while busting out Ray Hamilton in a daring prison raid. With the law closing in on all sides, they felt Methvin was the only one left outside of family whom they could trust. But Methvin sold them out, informing the law about a roadside rendezvous he was to have with them. In exchange, he was not prosecuted for charges pending against him in Louisiana and Texas.

A trap was set up at Gibland, La., near the Texas border, under the command of Capt. Frank Hamer of the Texas Highway Patrol, an ex–Texas Ranger who for the past three and a half months had been assigned exclusively to tracking down Bonnie and Clyde. Hamer and five other lawmen waited at an embankment armed with a Browning automatic rifle, three automatic shotguns and two rifles.

Bonnie and Clyde drove up to the rendezvous site. Clyde was driving in his socks; Bonnie was munching on a sandwich. They had in their car a shotgun, a revolver, 11 pistols, three Browning automatic rifles and 2,000 rounds of ammunition.

There is some argument about whether they were given a chance to surrender or even knew they had run into a trap. The lawmen opened fire and the pair died instantly. They dug 25 bullets out of Clyde and 23 out of Bonnie.

### Borden, Lizzie (1860–1927) accused murderess

A well-respected, religious spinster of 32, Lizzie Borden of Fall River, Mass., became without doubt America's most celebrated accused female murderer, charged with the 1892 killing of her father, Andrew, and her stepmother, Abby.

On August 3 of that year, Mr. and Mrs. Borden were both taken ill with severe stomach pains. Lizzie had bought some prussic acid just a short time before, but no connection was ever developed.

Between 9 and 9:30 on August 4, a hot, sweltering morning, someone entered a second-story bedroom of the Borden house and axed Abby Borden to death, bashing her skull 19 times. At the time, Lizzie's sister Emma was away from home, and the only ones known to be in the house besides the victim were Lizzie and Bridget Sullivan, the Irish maid. If either of them was the murderer, they certainly concealed it from the other for the next hour to 90 minutes, each going about their business without indicating any knowledge of the body in the bedroom. At about 10:30 Andrew Borden returned home from his business activities. He lay down on a sofa in the downstairs sitting room to take a nap, and the murderer crept up on him and hit him 10 times with an ax, killing him.

The police charged Lizzie Borden with committing the crimes, strictly on circumstantial evidence, not all of it very strong. For one thing, although the walls of both murder rooms were splashed with blood, no blood was found on Lizzie or her clothes. There was a theory that Lizzie had stripped naked to do the deeds and then had put her clothes back on, but that certainly would have involved a great risk of her being seen by the maid. The authorities claimed but never really proved that Lizzie had burned a dress in the kitchen stove a few days after the murders.

After being held in jail for nearly a year, Lizzie was subjected to a 13-day trial, with the entire nation hanging on every word. Rather than play down the gruesome nature of the murders, her defense attorney stressed this aspect. He then pointed to the prim, very feminine, charity-minded Lizzie and said: "To find her guilty, you must believe she is a fiend. Gentlemen, does she look it?"

The verdict in the case of Lizzie Borden, perhaps this country's most enduring cause célèbre, was not guilty. The jury had needed only an hour to arrive at it.

Lizzie made one statement to the press expressing her elation but then refused to say any more, even though reporters parked in front of the Borden home for weeks and weeks, searching for more morsels to feed their hungry readers. Lizzie enjoyed a considerable public sympathy during her ordeal and through her acquittal, but over the years public opinion seemed to turn, with more and more people regarding her as guilty. After a time she was considered guilty, as the popular rhyme went, of the charge that she "gave her mother forty whacks."

Lizzie and Emma inherited their parents' $500,000 estate, but they soon sold the house and moved into a lavish mansion in Fall River. Lizzie returned to her charitable works. Although she demanded anonymity, it is believed she financed several college educations.

In 1905 Emma moved out of the mansion after an argument. She too had lived under a cloud, and there was even speculation that she was the killer. At the time of the murder, Emma had been staying overnight with friends, but some authorities on the Borden case insisted she could have returned home, committed the crimes and returned to her friends' unseen.

The sisters never spoke again. When Lizzie died in 1927, she left nothing to Emma. Aside from some bequests to servants, she willed the bulk of her estate, $30,000 in cash and large holdings in stocks, to the Animal Rescue Leagues of Fall River and Washington, D.C. She was buried in the family plot beside her mother, father and stepmother.

### impact of Lizzie Borden case

No murder case in American history caused more public repercussions than that involving Lizzie Borden, the 32-year-old spinster who was tried and acquitted of killing her father and stepmother with an ax in their home in Fall River, Mass. in 1892. The case was the subject of an endless number of books, magazine articles and newspaper accounts. Edmund Pearson explained the public's fascination with the case may have resulted from its very "purity." The murders, and Lizzie's guilt or innocence, were uncomplicated by such sins as ambition, robbery, greed, lust or other usual homicidal motives. Innocent or guilty, Lizzie became an American hero.

The verse and doggerel on the case varied from the anonymous children's jump rope rhyme:

*Lizzie Borden took an ax*
*And gave her mother forty whacks;*
*When she saw what she had done,*
*She gave her father forty-one.*

to A. L. Bixby's almost endearing:

*There's no evidence of guilt,*
*Lizzie Borden,*
*That should make your spirit wilt,*
*Lizzie Borden;*
*Many do not think that you,*
*Chopped your father's head in two,*
*It's so hard a thing to do,*
*Lizzie Borden.*

The *New York Times* informed its readers that controversy over Lizzie Borden's innocence or guilt was directly responsible for 1,900 divorces. Such was the grip of "Bordenmania" on the entire nation.

## Bowers, J. Milton (1843–1904) accused murderer

The Bowers case, involving a handsome young San Francisco doctor who lost three wives to early deaths, was one of the 19th century's most sensational, controversial and protracted. The doctor, J. Milton Bowers, was convicted of murder and later cleared, although not to the satisfaction of the police or a substantial portion of the public.

Bowers' third wife, 29-year-old Cecelia, had been ill for two months before dying from what appeared to be an abscess of the liver. Dr. Bowers appeared appropriately grief stricken over the death of his wife of three years. But an anonymous letter triggered an investigation, and an autopsy was ordered. When the body was found to contain phosphorus, Bowers was charged with murder. He was pilloried in the press, and the public seemed obsessed with the fact that Cecelia was the third of Bowers' wives to die after a short-lived marriage. In addition, all three had been duly insured. There were also charges that Bowers was a criminal abortionist. At Bowers' trial much damning evidence was presented by his brother-in-law, Henry Benhayon, who testified that the doctor had prevented his wife from receiving outside care during much of her illness. Bowers was convicted of first-degree murder and incarcerated pending a decision on his appeal for a new trial.

In October 1887 Henry Benhayon was found dead in a rooming house. Police discovered a bottle of potassium cyanide and three suicide notes. One of the notes, addressed to the coroner, confessed that Benhayon had poisoned Mrs. Bowers. While this sensational development appeared to clear Dr. Bowers, the police were not convinced that the suicide note was genuine or that Benhayon's death was a suicide. Tracing purchases of potassium cyanide, the police located a druggist who identified one John Dimmig as a purchaser. They then discovered that Dimmig had visited Bowers in his jail cell.

Although he denied having bought the poison or being involved in Benhayon's death, Dimmig was charged with murder. The first trial ended in a hung jury. In the meantime, Dr. Bowers' motions for a new trial were rejected. Dimmig was tried again in late 1888 and acquitted. In August 1889 Dr. Bowers was released from jail, where he had been confined for four years. He eventually married a fourth time, and when he died in 1904 at the age of 61, the murder of

Cecelia Bowers was still being carried in police files as "unsolved."

## Bremer, Arthur Herman (1950– ) would-be assassin

On the afternoon of May 15, 1972, George Wallace was campaigning at a Laurel, Md. shopping center in his quest for the Democratic presidential nomination. He left the bulletproof podium and was shaking hands with people when a young blond man called several times, "Hey, George, over here!" Wallace moved toward that area, and the youth pulled a gun and fired several shots at Wallace, hitting him four times. In the ensuing struggle with Wallace's guards, the assassin emptied his weapon, wounding three others, all of whom recovered. Wallace himself remained paralyzed afterwards because of a bullet that lodged near the spinal column.

The would-be assassin was identified—how soon was to be a matter of some concern later—as Arthur H. Bremer, a young man in his twenties who had been a janitor's assistant and a busboy in Milwaukee, Wis. In November 1971 Bremer had been charged by Milwaukee police with carrying a concealed weapon, but this was reduced to a disorderly conduct charge and the gun confiscated. Shortly thereafter, he went out and bought two other guns.

On March 1, 1972 Bremer started following the Wallace campaign trail. During that period he spent about $5,000, although his total earnings for 1971–72 came to only $1,611. At times, he left the Wallace trail. On April 7 and 8 he stayed at the Waldorf-Astoria Hotel in New York, where Hubert Humphrey was staying. Bremer then traveled to Ottawa, Canada, where he stayed at the expensive Lord Elgin. He also checked into a number of motor inns along the Wallace campaign route. Where he got the money for the bills has remained a mystery, especially since it was established that he had not received any money from his parents.

As is customary in such cases, Bremer was initially reported to be a "loner," but that does not appear to have been very accurate. He had quite a few friends in Milwaukee, including Dennis Cassini, an individual officials never got to question. He was found dead of a heroin overdose, his body locked in the trunk of his own automobile. Although this was reported to the FBI, there is no indication that its director, L. Patrick Gray, ordered any inquiry into the matter. Other odd facts or circumstances developed. Bremer had been seen in Ludington, Mich. in the company of a man described as having a "New Joisey brogue." Roger Gordon, who was a former member of the Secret Army Organization (SAO), a right-wing intelligence organization, said the man was Anthony Ulasewicz, a White House operative later to win fame in the Watergate scandal. Gordon later left the country.

There were prominent reports that White House aide Charles W. Colson ordered E. Howard Hunt (two more Watergate personalities) to break into Bremer's apartment and plant Black Panther Party and Angela Davis literature. More explosive than that charge was the allegation that the order was given within one hour of the attempt to kill Wallace.

Commenting on these details in an interview with Barbara Walters, Wallace said: "So I just wondered, if that were the case, how did anyone know where he lived within an hour after I was shot?"

A practical political result of the attempted assassination of Wallace was to force him out of the 1972 race, in which he was expected to run as a third-party candidate. A week before the election, voters were polled on how they would have voted had Wallace run. The results were Nixon, 44 percent; McGovern, 41 percent; Wallace, 15 percent. Such a result, because of how the vote broke down, would likely have thrown the election into the House of Representatives, where Wallace would have had considerable influence. With Wallace out of the race, virtually all his supporters went to President Nixon.

Arthur Bremer has steadfastly refused to state why he shot Wallace. He was sentenced to 63 years, over objections by his attorneys that he was unbalanced. He has been described as a loner in the Maryland State Penitentiary, working in the print shop.

"Bremer does not give interviews," Warden George Collins said in 1979. "In fact, he won't even see his mother. She came in all the way from Milwaukee at Christmas, and he talked to her for about five minutes and went on back down inside. He just doesn't want to be bothered. He just doesn't want any hassle." The warden did add Bremer was "a very good inmate, so far as obeying institution rules is concerned."

**Buchanan, Dr. Robert** (?1855–1895) murderer
Dr. Robert Buchanan, one of New York's most famous 19th-century killers, was a vain murderer who modeled his crime on a similar one committed by a young medical student, Carlyle Harris, for which the latter went to the chair. Dr. Buchanan, possessing higher scientific knowledge than that of a mere medical student, improved on Harris' method but also went to the chair.

Buchanan's background is a bit murky. He had lied about his age and education so that he could practice medicine in Canada without a license. When he got caught, he went to Chicago for a couple of years and then returned to Halifax, Nova Scotia, where he married the daughter of a wealthy manufacturer. Buchanan talked his in-laws into sending him to Edinburgh, Scotland to complete his medical education. When he returned, he and his wife moved to New York, where he set up a modest practice in Greenwich Village.

By 1890 when he divorced his wife and sent her back to Nova Scotia, Buchanan had developed a taste for the seamier side of life and had formed an attachment with big, fat, ugly Annie Sutherland, who lived in the Village but ran a call house in Newark. Annie had one very redeeming quality: she had $50,000 in the bank. When he proposed marriage, Annie Sutherland jumped at the chance. For her, marrying a doctor meant respectability. For Dr. Buchanan, the marriage meant $50,000.

About that time the Carlyle Harris case was coming to trial. Harris, a medical student had secretly married a young girl named Helen Potts. After tiring of her, he disposed of Helen by poisoning her with morphine. He had been caught because a doctor noticed her pupils were pin points, the universal sign of morphine poisoning.

One evening Buchanan was drinking in Macomber's, a Village watering hole. He slammed a fist on the bar and said: "And I tell you Carlyle Harris was a fool! If Harris had known anything about medicine, he could have gotten away with it easily."

"How, Doc?" a drinking companion asked.

"Never mind," said Buchanan. "We of the profession cannot have laymen mindful of such information."

Buchanan would say no more, but he was in fact to put his opinion to the test. In 1892 he announced he was going to Edinburgh by himself, but four days before he was scheduled to leave, he canceled the trip because his wife had taken sick. Buchanan promptly called in not one but two other physicians to treat her. Both of them were with her when she died. Clearly, the doctors had no reason to view the woman's death as anything other than apoplexy, the result of a cerebral hemorrhage; their patient did not appear to have been poisoned since her pupils were not contracted. Apoplexy and morphine poisoning produced similar symptoms except for that one basic difference: in apoplexy there is no change in the pupils of the eyes, but in morphine poisoning the pupils greatly contract.

Some of Mrs. Buchanan's friends, from her brothel in Newark, were sure the doctor had not only married her for her money but had also killed her for it. Although the police wouldn't listen to such shady characters maligning an apparently respectable medical man, Ike White, a star reporter for the *New York World* who had a reputation for breaking cases, did listen. He had worked on the Carlyle Harris case and was intrigued by the story of a doctor who had married a madam.

White asked the physicians who had attended Mrs. Buchanan about her symptoms and raised the possi-bility of morphine poisoning; he was told that the woman's pupils had definitely not contracted. An average investigator or reporter might have given up right there, but White kept checking. He discovered that a mere three months after Mrs. Buchanan's death, the doctor had announced he was going to Edinburgh. Instead, he went back to Nova Scotia and remarried his first wife. The major difference

in the doctor's present marital condition was that he was $50,000 better off. There was a story here, and White knew it.

He also knew that in the 1890s, before the psychiatric couch came into vogue, the average man imparted his deepest secrets to either his priest or his bartender. He also knew that Dr. Buchanan was not a churchgoer. This theory is what finally led the reporter to Macomber's. He talked with Old Man Macomber about a number of things, including sports, current events, murders—especially the Carlyle Harris case—and people in the neighborhood who had died, such as Mrs. Buchanan. Finally, the matter of Dr. Buchanan's statement about Harris' stupidity was raised.

"Now how could Harris not have been found out?" White said derisively.

The bartender leaned forward. "The doc told me," he said. "One night he said he wouldn't tell anybody how it could be done, but by closing time he was so plastered he whispered to me that if I'd set up one for him, he'd tell just me. I did and he said, 'If you've ever been to the eye doctor, and he's put drops in your eyes, chances are the eye drops were atropine, which makes the pupils dilate or enlarge. If Harris had used some atropine when he gave his wife the morphine, his wife's eyes would have ended up looking normal, and no one would have suspected.'"

White ran his story, and Dr. Buchanan was indicted. An autopsy showed that his wife had in fact been killed by morphine poisoning. At his trial the prosecution went so far as to kill a cat in the courtroom with morphine and then administer atropine to show how the pin pointing could be prevented.

On July 1, 1895 Dr. Buchanan went to the electric chair as a result of drunken remarks he never remembered making.

## Bulette, Julia (1832–1867) madam and murder victim

Julia Bulette was the reigning madam of Virginia City, Nev. during the town's wide-open mining days, and her murder in 1867 became a cause célèbre of the time. In a larger sense, it marked the beginning of the taming of the West.

It is hard to separate fact from legend when talking about Julia. In later years it was believed that she was buried in a solid silver coffin, that a parlor car on the Virginia and Truckee Railroad was named in her honor, that she was enormously rich and that she charged as much as $1,000 a night for her company. Probably only the last two items were really true.

This beauty of Creole origin turned up in Virginia City in 1859, when it was no more than a town of clapboard houses and tents inhabited by 6,000 miners and a handful of women. Julia immediately set up business as a prostitute, starting to entertain men as soon as a floor was laid for her cabin, while other grateful miners went about putting up the walls and roof. Julia's enterprise flourished and within a year she employed six other girls to handle business. She opened a parlor house that became the town's center of elegance, one that offered French cuisine and wines and had fresh flowers brought in daily from the West Coast by Wells Fargo. Julia was made an honorary member of the Virginia City Fire Co., the only woman so honored, and on the Fourth of July, she led the parade through town, riding a fire truck adorned with roses.

Much beloved by miners, mine owners and railroad tycoons, Julia was frequently pictured as the prostitute with the Golden Heart. Her praises were often sung by a young reporter for the *Territorial Enterprise* who had just adopted the pen name of Mark Twain. During the Civil War she was one of the biggest contributors to fund-raisers for the Sanitation Fund, the Red Cross of its day. When a fever epidemic hit the area, Julia turned her pleasure palace into a hospital and pawned much of her jewelry and furs to raise money to care for and feed the sick. After the sickness passed, the establishment returned to its fabled bagnio status.

During her early years in town, Julia always sat in the orchestra of the local theater surrounded by a swarm of admirers, but with the arrival of more virtuous ladies and gentlemen in Virginia City, she was forced to sit in a box on the side, curtained off from their cold stares. Civilization was coming to the West, and Julia's days as queen of Virginia City society were clearly coming to an end.

On January 20, 1867 Julia was found strangled in her bed, most of her valuables gone. She had been murdered by either a thief or a client.

The miners of Virginia City were outraged. Quickly, suspect after suspect, 12 in all, were arrested, questioned and finally released after proving their innocence. Had one been judged guilty in those angry days just following murder, a lynching would have resulted, despite the attitudes of the more righteous elements.

Unable to bring the culprit to justice, the men of Virginia City gave Julia Bulette the biggest funeral the town had ever seen. All mines, mills and stores were shut down and draped in black bunting. Led by the fire company and the Metropolitan Brass Band, the cortege paraded through town with hundreds of weeping men in the line of march. We are told that the respectable women of the town shuttered their windows for fear of seeing their own husbands in the procession. After Julia's body was laid in the ground, the band marched back to town, playing the rollicking "The Girl I Left Behind Me."

Several months after the murder, the culprit, John Millain, described in the local press as a "trail louse," was captured following an attempt to rob and kill another madam. Many of Julia's jewels and other prize possessions were found on him. Despite his claims that others were responsible for the murder, Millain was convicted after a quick trial.

The community attitude toward Millain was probably best reflected in the district attorney's summation to the jury:

*Although this community has, in times past, seen blood run like water, yet in most cases there was some cause brought forward in justification of the deed, some pretext. But on the morning of the 20th of January last, this community, so hardened by previous deeds of blood, was struck dumb with horror by a deed which carried dread to the heart of everyone—a deed more fiendish, more horrible than ever before perpetrated on this side of the snowy Sierra. Julia Bulette was found lying dead in her bed, foully murdered, and stiff and cold in her clotted gore. True, she was a woman of easy virtue. Yet hundreds in this city have had cause to bless her name for her many acts of kindness and charity. So much worse the crime. That woman probably had more real, warm friends in this community than any other; yet there was found at last a human being so fiendish and base as to crawl to her bedside in the dead hour of the night, and with violent hands, beat and strangle her to death—not for revenge, but in order to plunder her of*

*these very articles of clothing and jewelry we see before us. What inhuman, unparalled barbarity!*

That philosophy reflected the thinking of virtually the entire male population of Virginia City, but not that of some of the women. During his confinement in jail, many of the good ladies of the area virtually lionized Millain, bringing him delicacies to fortify his spirits. A woman's committee went so far as to circulate a petition for commutation of his sentence. The *Territorial Enterprise* was incensed by the effort, commenting: "We believe that the man will be hung. If he is not, we do not know where a fit subject for hanging is to be found."

After Millain was sentenced to be hanged on April 24, 1868, so many people wished to attend the event that it had to be shifted to a great natural ampitheater one mile to the north of the city. On that day all the mines on the Comstock shut down once again; it was the second major holiday Julia Bulette had provided.

## Burdell, Dr. Harvey (1811–1857) murder victim

The murder of Dr. Harvey Burdell was New York's most sensational case during the 1850s, marked by too many suspects and too many motives, and ending with the public paying P. T. Barnum a fortune to view a baby whose claim to fame was not having been fathered by the late dentist Burdell.

In 1857 Dr. Burdell, at the age of 46, was no pillar of righteousness in the community. When the police relayed news of Burdell's murder to his own brother, Theo, the man declared, "I am not surprised, for he was a dirty"—here even the more sensational of the city's press concealed the words— "... .. . ..... !"

As the police pressed their investigation, they found that no one seemed to have a good word to say about the departed wealthy dentist. He was described as a sly scoundrel, an accomplished thief, a slick cheat, a welsher, a cheap swindler, a liar "whose word was not worth a cough," a man who quarreled with everyone including his patients. One redoubtable Irishman even insisted Burdell had been a secret agent in the pay of the British government. And why not? Anything was possible when speaking of a man who could woo a girl, go to the church to marry her, pull her father aside and say the wedding was off unless he was paid $20,000, and indeed call the wedding off if no agreement in principle was reached.

Dr. Burdell was paid back in full by his murderer; he died in painful and lingering fashion. He had been stabbed 12 times, and sometime during that ritual, in between or afterward, the murderer or murderess paused to strangle him for good measure. He was found in the master bedroom of his Bond Street home by a young boy who came each morning to make a fire in the fireplace. The boy had trouble pushing open the door to the bedroom, and the obstruction turned out to be Burdell's body. The place was spattered with blood.

There were three other people living in the Burdell mansion. One was a comely widow, Mrs. Emma Cunningham, who, on a sublet deal with the dentist, rented out rooms to boarders. She was about the most distressed person the police found. When informed of the crime, she shrugged and said, "Well those things happen."

A bachelor businessman, John J. Eckel, who rented a room in the house, was not quite as heartbroken. In fact, a contemporary historian insisted he danced a jig when he learned of Burdell's passing. The other tenant was George Snodgrass, who was the son of a Presbyterian minister, a shy and effeminate-looking youth, broke into a big smile when told about the murder and supposedly went out to celebrate, got drunk and tried to attack a hulking longshoreman. Snodgrass was to become a prime suspect after the police found various female undergarments, which he evidently liked to wear, secreted in his rooms. This struck the lawmen as somehow highly significant in a murder investigation.

But there were other major suspects. Dr. Burdell was known to owe a bundle to Honest John Burke, the crookedest gambler in town. Honest John took the loss of his money quite well when informed of his patsy's death. As a matter of fact, he ordered drinks set up for everyone in his favorite tavern, including the officers who brought him the tidings. A rich old Connecticut Yankee, Spawl, now living in New York, had much the same reaction as Honest John, although he didn't spend any money to exhibit his joy. Dr. Burdell had also pursued his daughter, Miss Lucy Spawl, until Spawl sent him away. Burdell had become so incensed that he beat up the old man.

Unfortunately for the police, Honest John, Spawl and several other suspects all had alibis for the time of the murder. This left authorities with the three persons living in the Burdell mansion, Cunningham, Eckel and Snodgrass. And in fact, since the house was shut tight from the inside and the fireplace boy had his own key to get in, the murder certainly appeared to be an inside job. If it hadn't been, then how had the killer entered and left?

Mrs. Cunningham became a prime suspect when she suddenly laid claim to a widow's portion of Burdell's estate, stating she had married him secretly a short time before his murder. She even produced a rather senile minister to attest to the marriage. Yes, the minister said, he had married the woman to a Harvey Burdell. But he wasn't at all sure if this Burdell fellow resembled the deceased. In fact, the minister allowed that the groom looked a little like roomer Eckel.

The coroner decided there wasn't all that strong a case against any of the three alone, so he ruled all three were involved in the murder and should be charged. The prosecutor in the case was A. Oakley Hall, a district attorney who was later to become the most rapacious and, according to some, the most dishonest district attorney in the history of New York City, known as O. K. Haul. But at this stage of the game, Hall was merely out to make a name for himself so he could pave the way for his future misdeeds.

Mrs. Cunningham was to be tried first, under Hall's plan, and her supposed confederates later. One reason for this was that doctors had found Burdell had been stabbed by a left-handed person—and Mrs. Cunningham, or Mrs. Burdell, was left-handed. But aside from that detail and motive and opportunity, there was little direct evidence linking the woman with the crime.

All the while the district attorney was presenting his case, the defendant sat in a chair demurely knitting little blue and pink things. Finally, Hall had had enough and he protested this bizarre behavior. Emma's lawyer, Henry L. Clinton, a descendant of a former vice-president of the United States, defended his client's action. Mrs. Burdell—as he insisted on calling her—was pregnant and would soon be giving birth to the deceased's child.

In the end, that as much as anything caused the jury to bring in a not-guilty verdict. With the woman free, the prosecution gave up efforts to convict the two men. The men quickly disappeared, but Mrs. Cunningham-Burdell stayed much in evidence, pressing her claim to the Burdell fortune. Now that she was with child, she stood to inherit virtually the entire estate. Her pregnancy, however, had an odd quality to it. She seemed to grow bigger, but she would not permit her doctor to examine her. She was, she said, of the old, old school, and no male hands would ever touch her body.

Finally, the doctor decided he was being used and went to the district attorney to say he suspected the woman was stuffing her dress with cushions. The authorities put a watch on her and soon found she was dickering to buy a new-born baby. She offered a young unmarried girl about to give birth $1,000 if she would slip her baby right over to the Burdell home. The girl took the money, and as soon as her baby was born, it was sent over to the alleged Mrs. Burdell, who planned to inform her doctor that a little event had happened during the night. But the police were watching and stormed into the bedroom of the bogus mother-to-be and arrested her.

Many people thought that since Mrs. Cunningham wasn't pregnant, it somehow meant she had indeed murdered Burdell. But the fact was she had been acquitted of that charge. Fraud charges were brought against her but they were later dropped. The Burdell case was to remain unsolved, although for many years the press continued to present various theories. The *Police Gazette* came out with an exclusive that the murderer was a man named Lewis, who had just been executed in New Jersey for another murder.

Lewis had told the Gazette that he had done the job by mistake, meaning to kill another Burdell.

Whoever did kill Dr. Burdell, now firmly established as New York's favorite murder victim, never paid for his sins, but at least the guilty party did not gain financially from his or her crime. The only one to make out well moneywise was the bogus Burdell baby. Her mother, already $1,000 ahead on the deal, rented her out for $25 a week to P. T. Barnum, who displayed the tot at his museum for all the eager New Yorkers wishing to see what a baby impostor looked like.

## Burr-Hamilton duel

The most famous duel in this country's history was between Alexander Hamilton and Vice President Aaron Burr on the banks of the Hudson River at Weehawken, N.J. on July 11, 1804.

There had been a festering hatred between the two men since 1801, when Hamilton refused to join in the conspiracy to keep Thomas Jefferson from the presidency and persuaded a number of key Federalist congressmen to choose Jefferson in the runoff against Burr, whom Hamilton called "a cold-blooded Cata-line." At the signal, Burr fired, and Hamilton rumbled forward mortally wounded. Hamilton's gun had discharged into the air, and many of his supporters claimed he had deliberately fired high. A coroner's jury called for Burr's arrest, but he fled to the South. After the duel, Hamilton's reputation was enhanced, while Burr became an outcast. A typical poem attacking him read:

*Oh Burr, oh Burr, what hast thou done,*
*Thou hast shooted dead great Hamilton!*

*You hid among a bunch of thistle*
*And shooted him dead with*
*a great hoss pistol!*

## Butcher, Jake (1937– ) the $700-million bank man

Of all the high finance scam operators whose depredations came to the fore in what came to be known in financial circles as the "Greedy 1980s," Jake Butcher had the distinction of being the most punished by the law, ending up with much more prison time than such offenders as Ivan Boesky, Michael Milken, and Charles Keating, Jr., among others.

Jacob "Jake" Franklin Butcher was a former Democratic candidate for governor of Tennessee and organizer of the 1982 World's Fair in Knoxville. Considered a respected figure in Tennessee banking circles, Butcher defrauded his own banks (he controlled 26 in Tennessee and Kentucky) of millions of dollars so that many of them failed and went bankrupt. Butcher's depredations, which financed his flamboyant lifestyle—such as the purchase of such "toys" as a 60-foot yacht for a mere $400,000—ended up costing the Federal Deposit Insurance Corporation (FDIC) well over $700 million, with Butcher and his wife having personal debts of more than $200 million.

It was said at the time that by his actions alone, Butcher had destroyed the deep-held faith that people had put in their banks since the reforms of the 1930s. The public grasped clearly the threats to their banks and savings and that they would have to pay for FDIC losses through their taxes. As a result, there was universal praise for the sentence imposed on Butcher—two 20-year concurrent terms, the maximum allowed.

## Capone, Alphonse "Scarface Al"
### (1899–1947) gang leader

Al Capone was a mindless, brutal and obscure Brooklyn hood in his teens, but by the age of 26 he had become the most powerful crime boss of his day and could boast that he "owned" Chicago, that city of gangsters, during the Prohibition years.

At its zenith the Capone mob had probably upward of 1,000 members, most of them experienced gunmen, but this represented only a portion of Capone's overall empire. Capone often proclaimed, "I own the police," and it was true. Few estimates would place less than half the police on the mob's payroll in one way or another. Capone's hold on the politicians was probably greater. He had "in his pocket" aldermen, state's attorneys, mayors, legislators, governors and even congressmen. The Capone organization's domination of Chicago and such suburban areas as Cicero, Ill. was absolute. When Capone wanted a big vote in elections, he got out the vote; when he wanted to control the election returns, his gangsters intimidated and terrorized thousands of voters. The

politicians he put in power were expected to act the way the Big Fellow desired. The mayor of Cicero once took an independent action. Capone caught him on the steps of City Hall and beat him to a pulp; a police officer standing nearby had to look elsewhere to avoid seeing the violence.

Capone was born in Brooklyn in 1899 and attended school through the sixth grade, when he beat up his teacher, got beaten by the principal and quit. After that, he learned his lessons in the streets, especially with the tough teenage James Street gang, run by an older criminal, Johnny Torrio, as a subsidiary of the notorious Five Points Gang, to which Capone eventually graduated. Among his closest friends, both in school and in the gang, was a kid who grew up to become a major crime boss, Lucky Luciano, and the two remained lifelong friends.

When he was in his late teens, Capone was hired by Torrio as a bouncer in a saloon-brothel he ran in Brooklyn. Capone picked up a huge scar on his left cheek in an altercation with a tough hood named Frank Galluccio, who slashed him with a knife in a

This mug shot of Al Capone was taken in 1929 in Philadelphia, where he allowed the police to arrest him in order to "take off some heat" brought on by the St. Valentine's Day Massacre.

dispute about a girl. Later, Capone would claim he got the wound serving with the "Lost Battalion" in France during World War I, but he was never in the army.

In 1920 Torrio, who had relocated in Chicago to help his uncle, Big Jim Colosimo, the city's leading whoremaster, ply his trade, summoned Capone to come and help him. What Torrio wanted to do was take advantage of Prohibition and gain control of the booze racket, an endeavor that promised profits in the millions. But he was being thwarted by Colosimo, who was so rich and content he saw no need to expand. Torrio soon decided Colosimo would have to be eliminated so that he could use Big Jim's organization for his criminal plans. He and Capone plotted Colosimo's murder and imported New York talent to do the job.

The Torrio-Capone combine was then on the move, taking over some mobs that bowed to their threats and going to war with those that failed to cooperate. Their biggest coup was the assassination in 1924 of Dion O'Banion, the head of the largely Irish North Side Gang, utilizing the talents of Frankie Yale of Brooklyn, the same man who had rubbed out Colosimo. However, the O'Banion killing resulted in all-out war with the rest of the North Siders. Torrio was badly shot in an ambush and hovered near death in a hospital for days. When he got out in February 1925, he told Capone, "Al, it's all yours," and retired back to Brooklyn with an estimated $30 million.

It was a sobering experience for the 26-year-old Capone, who found he now needed to use brains instead of muscle to run things. He had to become a top executive, bossing a firm employing more than 1,000 persons with a weekly payroll of over $300,000. He demonstrated he could do this as well as work with other ethnic groups, such as the Jews, the Irish, the Poles and the blacks. Capone appreciated any man provided he was a hustler, crook or killer, and he never discriminated against any of them because of their religion, race or national origin, being perhaps the underworld's first equal opportunity employer.

Capone's secret of success was to limit his mob's activities mainly to rackets that enjoyed strong demand from the public: liquor, gambling and prostitution. Give the people what they want and you have to gain a measure of popularity. Al Capone was cheered when he went to the ball park. Herbert Hoover was not.

Capone surrounded himself with men in whom he could place his trust, a quality he in turn inspired in many of his underlings. He was even smart enough to hire Galluccio, the thug who had scarred him, as a bodyguard, an act that demonstrated to the underworld the Big Fellow's magnanimity. Still, he faced many assassination attempts, including an effort to poison his soup. In September 1926 the O'Banions sent an entire convoy of cars loaded with machine-gunners past Capone's Cicero hotel headquarters. They poured in 1,000 rounds, but Capone escaped injury.

One by one, Capone had his North Side enemies eliminated, and he did the same to others who resisted bending to his will. His most famous killing involved treachery within his own organization. Hop Toad Giunta and Capone's two most competent killers, John Scalise and Albert Anselmi, were showing signs of planning to go independent. Capone invited them to a banquet in their honor and, at the climax of the evening, produced an Indian club with which he bashed their brains in.

By this time, Capone started to look invincible, but he erred terribly when he ordered the St. Valentine's Day Massacre in an effort to kill Bugs Moran, the last major force among the old O'Banions. Seven men were machine-gunned to death by Capone hit men masquerading as police officers. Suddenly, the public had had enough of the savage bootleg wars. Washington began applying intense pressure, and while he could not be convicted of murder, Capone was nailed for income tax evasion and sentenced to the federal prison at Atlanta for 11 years.

He was transferred to Alcatraz in 1934 and within a few years his health began to deteriorate. When released in 1939, he was a helpless paretic, a condition generally attributed to the ravages of syphilis contracted in his early whorehouse days. Chances are he had also gone "stir crazy," a common fate among Alcatraz inmates.

Capone retired to his mansion in Miami Beach, no longer capable of running the Chicago mob. For several years he wavered between lucidity and mental inertia. He died on January 25, 1947.

Al Capone had left an imprint on America and the rest of the world. Even in the minds of foreigners, he was the "Chicago gangster" personified. His impact on Chicago was significant and long lasting. During his reign Capone ordered the extermination of more than 500 men, and an estimated 1,000 died in his bootleg wars. The pattern of violence he set and the organization he built did not disappear with either his imprisonment or death. It is still not dead.

See also: ALCATRAZ PRISON.

## Carroll's orgy  Prohibition offense

What may have been the silliest arrest in the entire era of Prohibition, but one with tragic personal consequences, was that of Broadway producer Earl Carroll for an "orgy" held on February 22, 1926 at the Earl Carroll Theatre after a performance of his *Vanities*.

With typical Broadway irreverence, Carroll was honoring the Countess Vera Cathcart, who had just beaten an Immigration Service effort to prevent her from remaining in this country on the grounds of "moral turpitude" because of her sensational divorce from the earl of Cathcart. Climaxing the party onstage, a bathtub was filled with champagne and a nude model climbed in while men eagerly waited to fill their glasses or at least ogle at the naked beauty. When reports of the big bash got out, producer Carroll was hauled before a federal grand jury to explain his unique violation of the Volstead Act. Carroll tried to avoid prosecution by declaring there was no champagne in the bathtub, merely ginger ale. For this heinous distortion, he was convicted of perjury, fined $2,000 and sentenced to the federal prison at Atlanta for a year and a day. Carroll suffered a nervous breakdown on the way to the penitentiary. Because of his mental state, his fellow prisoners were ordered never to mention bathtubs in his presence. He was released after serving four months.

## Carson, Ann (1790–1838) counterfeiter

A strange set of circumstances turned Ann Carson into one of early America's most notorious female criminals. The daughter of a naval officer, she was the lovely and vivacious wife of Capt. John Carson of the U.S. Army, who disappeared in 1810 on a mission in the West against the Indians. Carson was listed as presumed dead. In 1812 Ann Carson met Lt. Richard Smith, who was stationed near her home in Philadelphia. After a short courtship they were married and lived happily until January 20, 1816, when her first husband arrived at his home and banged loudly on the door. He told Smith who he was. Smith, who later insisted he had been confused, drew a revolver and shot Carson dead. Within days Smith was brought to trial, and it was soon evident that everyone assumed he had killed Carson rather than give up his wife.

While the trial was going on, Ann Carson made a desperate attempt to kidnap the governor of Pennsylvania, Simon Snyder, and hold him as a hostage to gain her second husband's release. She failed, and Smith was convicted and, on February 4, 1816, hanged. Ann Carson lost all respect for law and order and became the head of a band of hardened criminals. Drawing on her military background, she organized the gang under strict regulations that made them most effective. While they engaged in some violent crimes, Ann Carson's gang were most competent at counterfeiting, passing notes for six years with brilliant efficiency. After they were finally rounded up, all were given long prison terms in 1823. Ann Carson died in Philadelphia Prison in 1838 while working on her memoirs.

## Caruso, Enrico (1873–1921) Black Hand extortion victim

Few Italians coming to America around the turn of the 20th century expected to escape the terrors and tribulations they had experienced at the hands of criminals in their native country. Rich or poor they could expect threats on their lives—so-called Black Hand threats that promised death unless they paid money. These were not the work of any "Black Hand Society" but extortions performed by the Mafia or other criminals, and not even the most famous were immune. During a triumphal engagement at the Metropolitan Opera shortly before World War I, the great Italian tenor Enrico Caruso received a Black Hand letter, with the imprint of a black hand and a dagger, demanding $2,000. The singer quietly paid, considering an appeal to the police both useless and foolhardy.

However, when this payment was followed by a new demand for $15,000, Caruso knew he had no choice but to go to the police. If he did not, he realized the criminals would continue to increase their demands and drain him dry. Caruso had been instructed to leave the money under the steps of a factory, and after the police set a trap, he did so. Two prominent Italian businessmen were seized when they tried to retrieve the loot. The two were convicted of extortion and sent to prison—one of the few successful prosecutions of Black Hand criminals. Even so, Caruso was considered to be in such great danger in case the criminals sought their usual vengeance on an informer that he was kept under police and private detective protection, both in this country and in Europe, for several years.

## Casey, James P. (?–1856) murderer

One of the most famous and infamous victims of the San Francisco Committee of Vigilance, James Casey was the editor of the *Sunday Times* and a member of the city's Board of Supervisors during what many regard as the most politically corrupt decade in San Francisco's history. Ruffians, outlaws, thieves and murderers controlled the city in the 1850s and were protected by equally crooked politicians, one of whom was Casey.

An arch rival of Casey was James King, editor of the *Evening Bulletin,* who publicized Casey's involvement with corrupt elements and his previous history, which included serving 18 months in Sing Sing prison for larceny. In 1855 King's voice was the most virulent in calling for the reestablishment of the 1851 vigilance committee to clean up the city. On May 14, 1856 King launched a vigorous attack against Casey and said he deserved "having his neck stretched." As King left his newspaper's offices later that day, Casey accosted him, shoved a revolver against his chest and ordered him to "draw and defend yourself." Casey then shot and mortally wounded his foe without even giving him a chance to draw a weapon, which in any case he did not have. After the shooting Casey was taken into custody. However, fearing the political powers would permit him to escape justice,

Drawing shows James Casey being conveyed through heckling San Franciscans to be hanged by the vigilance committee.

the vigilance committee swung into action. A thousand men enrolled in a special armed force, and militiamen guarding Casey in jail wired their resignation to the governor, stacked their arms and joined the vigilantes. King clung to life for six days before dying on May 20. He was buried two days later, with an estimated 15,000 to 20,000 men and women following his body to the grave. By the time the last of the throng returned to the city, Casey and another murderer, Charles Cora, were hanged from the windows of the vigilante headquarters on makeshift gallows.

Casey's political friends buried him and had inscribed on his tombstone, "May God

Forgive My Persecutors." It should also be noted that in the two months following Casey's execution, not a single murder occurred in San Francisco, a period of tranquility never again experienced in that city.

### Cermak, Anton J. (1873–1933) Chicago mayor and murder victim

Mayor Anton J. Cermak of Chicago was with Franklin D. Roosevelt in Miami on February 15, 1933 when Joseph Zangara attempted to assassinate the president-elect and fatally shot Cermak instead. Cermak became a martyr.

At the time he was shot, Cermak cried, "The President, get him away!" He told Roosevelt, "I'm glad it was me instead of you." Roosevelt, who cradled the wounded mayor, said: "I held him all the way to the hospital and his pulse constantly improved. . . . I remember I said, 'Tony, keep quiet—don't move—it won't hurt you if you keep quiet and remain perfectly still.'"

Cermak lingered for three weeks. From his deathbed the mayor expounded a theory, long held by some historians after his death, that he, not Roosevelt, was the intended victim all the time. Judge John H. Lyle, probably as knowledgeable as any non-Mafia man on the subject of Chicago crime, stated categorically, "Zangara was a Mafia killer, sent from Sicily to do a job and sworn to silence." It was not an outlandish theory, the concept of the sacrificial hit man having a long history in the annals of the Mafia.

In theory, Cermak was a great reformer, but that must be measured in light of what constituted reform in Chicago. Born in Prague and brought to America when he was one year old, Cermak went into politics at an early age and soon won the nickname Ten

Percent Tony, since that figure was said to be his standard skim in kickbacks and other deals. By the time Cermak had served three terms in the state legislature, he was worth $1 million. Before he took office as mayor, his net worth was $7 million. In the words of a contemporary writer, Cermak was guilty of using "surreptitious means such as wire taps, mail drops, surveillance and stool pigeons to ferret out information concerning the weaknesses and foibles of administrative and political friends, taking great pains to learn the identities of his enemies."

Cermak did not attempt to purge Chicago of gansterism but only of the Capone element, which he sought to replace with others who had supported his campaign, headed by Gentleman Teddy Newberry. Some writers have claimed that Cermak moved to take over all crime in Chicago after the imprisonment of Al Capone. Later court testimony indicated that the mayor had dispatched some "tough cops" to eradicate Frank Nitti, Capone's regent during his absence. Nitti was searched, found to be unarmed and was about to be handcuffed when an officer leveled his gun at the gangster and shot him three times in the neck and back. The officer then shot himself in the finger. Nitti was taken to the hospital to die, and the police announced he had been wounded while resisting arrest, as the officer's injured finger proved. Unfortunately for the mayor, Nitti recovered and a full-scale war ensued, one of the early victims being Cermak's favorite gangster, Newberry. At the time, Cermak was taking the sun in Florida on a rather extended vacation, said to have been so arranged to keep him away from the Capone gangsters. Cermak had left Chicago for Florida on December 21, 1932, and he was still there February 15, 1933.

Some cynics suggested that the mayor was seeking the protective wing of the president-elect to stay alive. Others contended that Cermak was merely cementing relations with the incoming administration and just possibly talking to Roosevelt's campaign manager, James J. Farley, about an indictment said to be pending against him for income tax evasion.

Zangara, who had been overwhelmed by guards and the crowd after firing the shots, died in the electric chair on March 21, 1933. He insisted Roosevelt was the man he had meant to kill.

See also: JOSEPH ZANGARA.

## Chadwick, Cassie (1857–1907) swindler

One of the most audacious swindles ever worked in this country was accomplished in the 1890s by a Canadian woman and incorrigible thief, Mrs. Cassie Chadwick, who married into Cleveland society. She was, she hinted, the illegitimate daughter of Andrew Carnegie, the steel magnate. In fact, she did more than hint—she flashed all sorts of promissory notes supposedly signed by Carnegie and then deposited some $7 million worth of allegedly valid securities in a Cleveland bank. She told the banker to keep her secret, which meant, of course, that the news spread like wildfire throughout the banking community and soon among the city's social set. Clearly, Mrs. Chadwick was somebody, and she was invited to the best functions. Bankers too volunteered their services without asking. Yes, Mrs. Chadwick acknowledged, she might be able to use a little loan or two against future payments from her tycoon father. She took a few small loans, all under $100,000, and repaid them promptly by taking out other loans from different banks and private lenders. She then went whole hog, borrowing millions. Mrs. Chadwick paid high interest, but with all that Carnegie money behind her, she seemed good for it.

The hoax was simplicity itself, being so outrageous that it was never questioned. Certainly, no one was going to approach Carnegie for confirmation. The Chadwicks now traveled frequently to Europe and, when they were in Cleveland, entertained lavishly. Mrs. Chadwick was also a leading public benefactor. In less than a decade, it was later estimated, she took banks and private lenders for upwards of $20 million.

The bubble burst in 1904, when the *Cleveland Press* heard of a Boston creditor who had become dubious about getting his money back. The newspaper checked on Mrs. Chadwick's background and found out her real name was Elizabeth Bigley, a convicted forger who had been pardoned in 1893 by Gov. William McKinley of Ohio. When the news came out, Charles T. Beckwith, president of the Citizens National Bank of Oberlin, to whose institution Mrs. Chadwick owed $1.25 million, promptly keeled over from heart failure. There was a run on the bank and on scores of others that were found to have made loans to the woman.

Mrs. Chadwick, who was in New York on a spending spree when the unpleasantness surfaced, was arrested and extradited back to Cleveland, where she was tried and sentenced to 10 years in prison. She died there in 1907. It was believed at the time of her death that many of her victims had still not come forth, some individuals hoping to avoid ridicule and the banks to avoid runs. Remarkably, there were still those who firmly believed that Mrs. Chadwick was indeed Carnegie's daughter and that he would in due course make good on her debts. All of which made Cassie Chadwick's swindle among the most enduring ever concocted.

### Champion, Nathan D. (1857–1892) victim of Johnson County War

Even today in some quarters of Wyoming, the name of Nate Champion is a hallowed one, that of a man killed solely because he defied the great cattle barons. Others regard him as a cunning rustler, the head of the notorious Red Sash Gang that allegedly stole thousands of head of cattle. Whatever the truth may be, it is certain that he was on a "death list" composed by the executive committee of the Wyoming Stock Growers' Association on the basis of "nominations" received from members.

Champion, a powerfully built man, had been a trailherder for several years until the early 1880s when he collected his pay after a drive and settled in Johnson County. Similar to many others, Champion became a homesteader and built up a little herd of cattle, thus earning the enmity of the cattle barons, who wanted an open range for their huge herds. These absentee cattlemen sent Pinkerton agents onto the range and were assured by them that there was organized rustling of their stock in Johnson County, mainly the work of the Red Sash Gang bossed by Nate Champion. Other observers believed that the charge was a self-serving lie and the only connection Champion had with any mythical Red Sashers was the fact that he, like a great many other homesteaders who came up from Texas, wore a *vaquero*-type red sash.

In the early morning hours of April 11, 1892, a small army of about 50 gunmen, most hired for the occasion, attacked Champion's cabin, which he shared with a cowboy named Nick Ray. Ray went outside in the snow to chop some wood and was cut down by a hail of bullets. Champion rushed out and hauled the severely wounded Ray to safety. He then kept up a barrage of fire that held off his attackers. By afternoon Ray had died, but so had two of the invaders and several others were wounded.

During lulls in the battle Champion kept a diary of his ordeal. One entry read: "Boys, there is bullets coming like hail. They are shooting from the table and river and back of the house." Another went: "Boys, I feel pretty lonesome just now. I wish there was someone here with me so we could watch all sides at once." The final entry was made that evening, about 12 hours after the first attack. "Well, they have just got through shelling the house like hail. I heard them splitting wood. I guess they are going to fire the house tonight. I think I will make a break when night comes, if alive. Shooting again. It's not night yet. The house is all fired. Goodbye, boys, if I never see you again."

Champion signed his pathetic diary and then charged out the back door, firing two guns. How many bullets cut him down could not be determined because his dead body was strung up and used for target practice. Later, 28 bullets were removed from the body. Champion's slayers also pinned a card on the body—"Rustlers beware."

The killings of Champion and Ray were the opening shots in the Johnson County War, one in which the cattle barons' mercenary army would go down to ignoble defeat. Because a reporter accompanying the stockmen's hired army found their victim's diary, Nate Champion was to emerge as the folk hero of the struggle.

## Chapman, Mark David (1955– ) murderer of John Lennon

The murder of 40-year-old rock star John Lennon, a former member of the Beatles, on December 8, 1980 by Mark David Chapman was a long time in the making. Chapman had waited all that wintry day and evening in front of the Dakota, a celebrated New York apartment building, where the singer and his wife, Yoko Ono, lived. He had come prepared for the weather, wearing two pairs of long underwear, a jacket, an overcoat and a hat. He also carried a .38-caliber Charter Arms revolver.

Chapman had been living in Honolulu since 1977, arriving there from Decatur, Ga., his home state, and had apparently been afflicted with John Lennon fantasies for a considerable period. Lennon's wife was Japanese, and although Chapman's wife was not Japanese, she was of Japanese descent. In the fall of 1980 Chapman decided to "retire," at the age of 25. After all, Lennon was retired. Later, a psychiatrist would testify that the more Chapman imitated Lennon, "the more he came to believe he was John Lennon." He eventually began to look upon Lennon as a "phony."

In September 1980 Chapman sold a Norman Rockwell lithograph for $7,500, paid off a number of debts and kept $5,000 for a "a job" he had to do. He contacted the Federal Aviation Administration to inquire about the best way to transport a revolver by plane. He was advised that he should put the gun in his baggage but was warned that the change in air pressure could damage any bullets. When Chapman left his job as a security guard at a Honolulu condominium development for the last time, he scrawled the name John Lennon on the sign-out sheet. On October 29 he flew to New York, taking a gun but no bullets.

Frustrated in New York by an inability to obtain bullets for his weapon or to gain access to Lennon, Chapman left on November 12 or 13 to return to Honolulu. After his arrival there he made an appointment at the Makiki Mental Health Clinic for November 26 but didn't keep it. On December 6 he flew back to New York.

Two days later, Chapman waited outside the Dakota for Lennon to appear. About 4:30 P.M. the singer and his wife left the building. When he saw the couple, Chapman held up his copy of Lennon's recently released *Double Fantasy* album, and Lennon stopped to autograph it. After the Lennons departed, the doorman asked Chapman why he lingered, and he said he wanted to wait to get Yoko Ono's autograph as well.

At 11 P.M. Lennon and his wife returned. Chapman stepped out of the darkness and said, "Mr. Lennon." As Lennon turned, Chapman fired his revolver five times. Four bullets struck Lennon, killing him. When the police arrived, Chapman was reading his copy of *Catcher in the Rye* by J. D. Salinger.

A few weeks later, John W. Hinckley, Jr. recited into a tape recorder: "I just want to say goodbye to the old year, which was nothing, total misery, total death. John Lennon is dead, the world is over, forget it." In March 1981 Hinckley attempted to assassinate President Ronald Reagan.

Chapman pleaded guilty to the Lennon killing. On August 24, 1981, appearing in court with what looked to be a bulletproof vest underneath his T-shirt, evidently to protect him from possible retribution by distraught Lennon fans, he was sentenced to 20 years to life. Under New York State law he would have to stay in prison for 20 years before becoming eligible for parole.

## Clutter family murders  *In Cold Blood* case

The Clutter family murders in 1959 were a brutal, senseless affair that became the subject of Truman Capote's best-selling book *In Cold Blood*.

The Clutters were sought out, robbed and killed by two ex-jailbirds and vagrants named Richard E. Hickock and Perry E. Smith. Hickock had learned of the Clutters while sharing a prison cell with a convict named Floyd Wells, who had once worked for Clutter, a well-to-do wheat farmer in Holcomb, Kan. Hickock pumped Wells about Clutter's wealth and whether he kept a safe in his home and how much money he was likely to have on hand. When Hickock was paroled from the Kansas State Penitentiary, he hooked up with Smith, and the two headed for the Clutter home. They invaded it on November 15, 1959. After terrorizing the family, the pair killed Clutter and his wife, Bonnie, both 45, daughter Nancy, 16, and son Kenyon, 15. Clutter's body was found in the basement of his home with his throat cut and shot in the head. His wife and two children had been killed with shotgun blasts at close range. All the victims were bound by the wrists.

When news of the murders reached the penitentiary, Wells went to the warden and told him of Hickock's interest in the Clutters. This put the police on Hickock's trail, and he and Smith were captured in Las Vegas. Both men made confessions, each trying to shift more of the blame on the other. While they had expected to find $10,000, they had netted less than $50 for the four murders. Smith said of Clutter: "He was a nice gentleman. . . . I thought so right up to the moment I cut his throat."

At the trial the jury was urged by the prosecuting attorney not to be "chicken-hearted" and to find them guilty of first-degree murder. The jury did so, and after a number of appeals, Hickock, 33, and Smoth, 36, were hanged in April 1965.

## Colt, John C. (1819–1842?)  murderer

John C. Colt was the central figure in a classic murder case in 1841 that started with a solution but concluded in a mystery.

Colt was a member of one of New York's millionaire merchant families and the brother of Samuel Colt, inventor of the Colt revolver and the Colt repeating rifle. At 22 John was tall, slim and handsome, with curly blond hair and steel gray eyes. The darling of society, he fancied himself a writer of sorts and numbered among his close friends Edgar Allan Poe, Washington Irving, James Fenimore Cooper, John Howard Payne, George Palmer Putnam and Lewis Clark.

Despite his literary bent, Colt had a quick, uncertain temper, and in a nasty argument he killed Samuel Adams, a printer he had hired to produce a book of his. Colt was tried speedily and sentenced to be hanged. There were those who said Colt would never hang, that his family was too powerful. Press exposés of Colt's treatment in the city's new prison, the Tombs, informed the public that Colt lived an exceedingly happy life for a condemned man. He had flowers on his table and a pet canary. A young Charles Dana reported: "In a patent extension chair he lolls smoking an aromatic Havana. . . . He has on an elegant dress-gown, faced with cherry-colored silk, and his feet are encased in delicately worked slippers." His food was "not cooked in the Tombs, but brought in from a hotel. It consists of a variety of dishes—quail on toast, game pates, reed birds, ortolans, fowl, vegetables, coffee, cognac."

The greatest concession to Colt's grand station was the permission granted by prison authorities that he be allowed to marry his fiancée Caroline Henshaw on the morning of November 18, the day of his execution. Newspaper announcements of the bizarre nuptials-gallows ceremony brought out thousands of thrill seekers who jammed Centre (later Center) Street at dawn. Miss Henshaw was forced to come by carriage to a side street entrance to the Tombs at about 11:30. During the actual wedding ceremony, carpenters assembling the gallows in the courtyard politely suspended their hammering, a fact a guard relayed to the crowd outside. The crowd moaned at that. It moaned again when word was passed, "They're married." Other news was passed as it happened. "The guests have gone. . . . There are silk curtains across the cell door. . . . They've ordered champagne. . . . They're testing the gallows!"

Shortly after 1 P.M. the new Mrs. Colt was advised that she had to leave, and she did so "smiling bravely." Later, there would be much conjecture over whether Caroline slipped her groom a large dagger with which he could stab himself in the heart and thus escape the noose. At 3:30 P.M. the Rev. Henry Anton, who had officiated at the wedding, was ordered to offer his final services to the condemned man. At that moment the tinder-dry wooden cupola atop the adjacent Hall of Justice mysteriously caught fire. Within three minutes smoke was pouring into the interior of the prison. Panic broke out and several guards raced out of the building. Convicts banged on their bars and begged to be let out, and some apparently were by the few remaining keepers. In the smoke-filled confusion, Rev. Anton rushed up to Sheriff Monmouth Hart and cried:

"Mr. Colt is dead! He has a dagger in his heart!"

Instead of proceeding to the cell, the sheriff rushed around in search of the doctor who was there to pronounce Colt dead after his now unnecessary execution. At 7 P.M. a hurriedly convened coroner's jury officially declared Colt had committed suicide. It was a remarkable hearing, with no official identification of Colt being made. Not even Rev. Anton was called to testify. The body was released and buried that same night in the yard of St. Mark's Church. Afterward, the recently widowed Mrs. Colt disappeared.

At first, the newspapers focused on the source of the death dagger, including in the speculation every member of the wedding party. Only when it later was conceded by officials that a number of prisoners had escaped during the fire, did it suddenly occur to anyone that Colt could have escaped in the confusion—if there was a body to substitute for him.

The *New York Herald* commented, "We have no doubt that Governor Seward will order an investigation at once into this most unheard of, most unparalleled tragedy." No investigation was ever held, however, although even George Walling, who was appointed chief of police shortly therafter, gave considerable credence to the idea of a substitute corpse. So too did Colt's friends. In 1849 Edgar Allan Poe received an unsigned manuscript from Texas written in the unmistakable hand of John Colt. He took the manuscript to Lewis Clark, editor of *The Knickerbocker* magazine, and found Clark too had gotten a copy. They concluded it was Colt's way of letting them know he was alive and still trying for a literary career. Then in 1852 Samuel Everett, a close friend of Colt, returned from a visit to California and told others in the Colt circle of friends that he had met John Colt while horseback riding in the Santa Clara Valley. According to Everett, Colt lived in a magnificent hacienda with his wife, the former Caroline Henshaw.

Many students of crime dismiss the substitute corpse theory and regard Everett's story as apocryphal, insisting it was just an exotic fillip to an incredible tale. Others find the chain of events too mired in coincidence. That Colt should commit suicide just at the moment of a mysterious fire during which several prisoners escaped, they say, staggers the imagination. And why did the widowed Mrs. Colt disappear from New York City after her husband's death?

### Cook, Dr. Frederick A. (1865–1940) explorer and land fraud conspirator

Dr. Frederick A. Cook is most famous for his dispute with Commodore Robert E. Peary over who was the first to reach the North Pole. For a brief time, Dr. Cook was hailed throughout the world after announcing he had reached the North Pole. However, shortly thereafter, Peary made the same claim and labeled all of Cook's claims false. In the controversy that followed, Peary clearly gained the upper hand, and Cook was to keep only a few believers. He returned home disheartened and in disgrace, and things were to get worse for him. In the 1920s Cook's name was used to promote a Texas oil-land sale that was branded fraudulent. While there was much reason to believe that Cook was not an active member of the fraud, he had a famous name and thus made an excellent target. He was convicted of using the mails to defraud and sentenced to 14 years. After working as a prison doctor in Leavenworth, he was released in 1931. Con-

sidering that the lands in question were now selling at prices well above the so-called fraud figure, it would indeed have been unseemly to hold him longer. President Franklin D. Roosevelt granted Dr. Cook a presidential pardon shortly before the latter's death in 1940.

### Costello, Frank (1891–1973) Prime Minister of the Underworld

No syndicate criminal in this country ever enjoyed as much political pull as did Frank Costello, who was the advocate within the national crime syndicate of the "big fix." He believed in buying favors and even paying for them in advance. Scores of political leaders and judges were beholden to him. An entire array of New York's Tammany Hall bosses "owed" him. They ranged from Christy Sullivan to Mike Kennedy, from Frank Rosetti to Bert Stand and from Hugo Rogers to Carmine DeSapio. Costello had done them favors, had raised money for them, had delivered votes that really counted. And when it came time to make appointments, Costello practically exercised the equivalent of the Senate's prerogatives to advise and consent. Tammany kingpin Rogers put it best when he said, "If Costello wanted me, he would send for me."

It was the same with judges. In 1943 Manhattan district attorney Frank Hogan obtained a wiretap on Costello's telephone. Investigators were treated to this enlightening conversation on August 23 between Costello and Thomas Aurelio just minutes after the latter had learned he was getting the Democratic nomination to become a state supreme court justice:

"How are you, and thanks for everything," Aurelio said.

At the pinnacle of his power during the Kefauver Committee hearings in the early 1950s, Frank Costello, as Prime Minister of the Underworld, was the mob's representative in dealings with politicians, judges and the police.

"Congratulations," Costello answered. "It went over perfect. When I tell you something is in the bag, you can rest assured."

"It was perfect," Aurelio said. "It was fine."

"Well, we will all have to get together and have dinner some night real soon."

"That would be fine," the judge-to-be said. "But right now I want to assure you of my loyalty for all you have done. It is unwavering."

Despite the disclosure of the wiretap, the grateful Aurelio went on to be elected to the judgeship after beating back disbarment proceedings. Clearly, when Costello said something was in the bag, it was in the bag.

Born Franceso Castiglia in Calabria, Italy in 1891, he came to New York with his family at age four. At 21 he had a police record of two arrests for assault and robbery. At 24 he was sentenced to a year in prison for carrying a gun. He did not return to prison for another 37 years. Beginning in the early days of Prohibition, his best friends were Lucky Luciano, a Sicilian, and Meyer Lansky, a Polish Jew. These three were to become the most important figures in the formation of the national crime syndicate during the 1930s. While

Luciano and Lansky did most of the organizing among criminals, Costello's mission was to develop contacts and influence among the police and politicians. By the mid-1920s the trio's varied criminal enterprises, mostly bootlegging and gambling, were making them rich. To protect these interests, they were paying, through Costello, $10,000 a week in "grease" directly into the police commissioner's office. Within a few years, during the regimes of commissioners Joseph A. Warren and Grover A. Whalen, the amount rose to $20,000 a week. In 1929, just after the stock market crash, Costello told Luciano he had to advance Whalen $30,000 to cover his margin calls in the market. "What could I do?" Costello told Luciano. "I hadda give it to him. We own him."

No one ever questioned whether Costello always dispensed mob money the way it was intended. Costello was a man of honor on such matters. Besides, the results were there for the mob to see, with cases never brought to court, complaints dropped and so on.

Costello became the most vital cog in the national crime syndicate after the forceful purging of the old mafiosi or "Mustache Petes." The gangs cooperated, and Costello supplied the protection. As part of his reward, Costello got the rights to gambling in the lucrative New Orleans area.

He was respected by all the crime family heads and was considered the Prime Minister of the Underworld, the man who dealt with the "foreign dignitaries"—the police, judges and politicos. Much has been made of the fact that Costello was not a murderer, but he sat in on all syndicate decisions concerning major hits, and while he may have often been a moderating force, he was a party to murder plans. His general reluctance to use violence was not due to squeamishness; it was just that he felt hitting a man over the head with a wad of greenbacks could be more persuasive than using a blackjack.

One of the prime accomplishments of the Kefauver investigation during the 1950s was the exposure of Costello's vast influence in government. While he insisted that only his hands be shown on television, that minor subterfuge could hardly cover up his activities. When he left the stand, Costello knew his term as prime minister was at an end. He was too hot for everyone, those who appreciated the mob's favors and the mob itself.

Through the 1950s, with Luciano deported to Italy, Joe Adonis being harassed and facing the same fate, and Costello facing tax raps that would finally send him to prison, Vito Genovese moved to take over the syndicate. In 1957 Genovese engineered an attempt to assassinate Costello; he survived by perhaps an inch or two, his assailant's bullets just grazing his scalp. Later that same year Genovese arranged the rub-out of Albert Anastasia, the Lord High Executioner of Murder, Inc. and a devoted follower of Costello and Luciano.

It looked like Genovese was in. Meanwhile, Costello really wanted out, to retire in peace and concentrate on his battles with the government about his citizenship and tax problems. But Genovese's blueprint for power was soon destroyed. Costello, Lansky, Carlo Gambino and Luciano masterminded a drug operation that involved Genovese. As soon as he was mired deeply in it, evidence was turned over to prosecutors, and in 1959 Genovese went to prison for a term of 15 years. He would die there in 1969. During this period Costello did a short stint in Atlanta Penitentiary, the same one Genovese was in; it was said the two had a sentimental reconciliation there. Genovese may have been sincere, but Costello certainly was not. When he left prison, he felt no pangs of sorrow for Genovese.

Costello went into quiet retirement after that, living the life of a Long Island squire until his death in 1973.

### Craft, Gerald (1965–1973) kidnap victim

Although not very well known in white circles, the kidnap-murders of eight-year-old Gerald Craft and six-year-old Keith Arnold in Detroit on December 1, 1973 stand as the "black Lindbergh case."

Gerald Craft was actually a familiar face to most of the country's whites, being famous, if anonymously, for a television commercial in which he gobbled down big helpings of fried chicken with a devilish grin on his face. On that December 1, a Saturday afternoon, Gerald was playing football with a friend, Keith, in front of his grandmother's house when both suddenly disappeared. The next day a hoarsely whispered telephone call demanded a ransom of $53,000 for the return of the children. This was an amount the families could not pay. With the help of the Detroit police, a bogus package of ransom money was dropped at a designated spot, which the police staked out. Two men came to retrieve it, but officers moved too slowly to capture them before they drove off. Two days later, the bodies of the two boys, both shot twice, were found in a field near Detroit's Metropolitan Airport.

The *Detroit News* offered a $5,000 reward for information leading to the capture of the kidnappers and set up a "secret witness" phone number for informers. Within a week the information received through this source led to the arrest of three 21-year-old men and a teenage girl and the solution of the case. The girl provided evidence that convicted the men, Byron Smith, Geary Gilmore and Jerome Holloway. All three were given mandatory life sentences.

As big a news splash as the kidnapping made in the black press around the country, few whites ever heard much about it.

### Crane, Stephen (1870–1900) writer and police victim

Few writers have suffered as much harassment from the police as did Stephen Crane during the last four years of his life. Crane's troubles began in September 1896, when the author, already famous for his book *The Red Badge of Courage*, visited the vice-ridden tenderloin section of Manhattan to collect material for a series of sketches on the district. A tall, broad-shouldered policeman named Charles Becker walked up to a free-lance prostitute, Dora Clark, and started beating her to a pulp. Becker over the years was to become famous as "the crookedest cop who ever stood behind a shield," and in 1915 he died in the electric chair for the murder of gambler Herman Rosenthal. His prime concern during his days in the tenderloin was not to drive out the prostitutes but to make sure he got his share of their income.

Dora Clark was definitely not soliciting when Becker started roughing her up and arrested her. Crane, having witnessed the entire incident, so testified at her hearing. The Clark woman complained she had been subjected to Becker's constant harassment and demands for money. The judge chose to believe Crane over Becker and released the woman.

Becker was brought up on police departmental charges before Commissioner Frederick Grant, who at the time was considered one of the department's looser administrators and an opponent of reforms advocated by another commissioner, Theodore Roosevelt. Becker's defense tried to shift the case to one against Crane, accusing him of regularly consorting with prostitutes and of being an opium smoker. Despite attacks by the newspapers, Commissioner Grant allowed a long line of questioning on such points, causing the *Brooklyn Daily Eagle* to lament that "the reputation of private citizens is permitted to be assailed without comment or protest, while so much is done to shield one of a body of men that collectively was lately shown to be one of the most corrupt, brutal, incompetent organizations in the world." Other newspapers joined in observing that the rank treatment of Crane showed the police had hardly reformed since the revelations of their crookedness by the Lexow Committee two years previously.

Becker escaped without suffering any major penalties for his conduct, and the police thereafter kept up a steady campaign of intimidation and harassment against Crane. His rooms were raided, and police insisted they had found opium there. (The conventional wisdom was that they had brought the opium with them.) The police vendetta against Crane reached such intensity that the author was forced to flee the city for a time. As soon as he returned, the police resumed their persecution of him. When a policeman saw Crane at the theater with a woman, he loudly accused her of being a "goddam French whore" and only beat a retreat after realizing the other member of the Crane party was a priest.

By 1898 the malicious attacks on Crane again forced him to leave the city. When next he returned, there was no need for the police

to reactivate their campaign a third time. Crane was dying of tuberculosis.

## Crater, Joseph Force (1889–1937?) missing judge

On August 6, 1930 a portly 41-year-old man wearing a high-collared shirt, brown pin-striped double-breasted suit and extremely polished and pointed shoes stepped into a taxi in front of a Manhattan restaurant, waved good-bye to a friend and rode off into history, to become known as America's greatest vanishing act. The man was Justice Joseph Force Crater of the New York Supreme Court. From that day forth, Crater was never seen again—alive or dead. His disappearance provided grist for the mills of jokers, playwrights, graffiti writers, cartoonists and amateur detectives over the next half century.

Crater was born in Easton, Pa., graduated from Lafayette College and earned a law degree at Columbia University. He established a successful New York practice and formed important political connections, later rising to the presidency of the Cayuga Democratic Club, an important part of the Tammany organization. In April 1930 Gov. Franklin D. Roosevelt appointed him to the New York Supreme Court.

Crater cut short a vacation in Maine to return to the city in order to take care of some business. He was seen in his court chambers on August 5 and 6 and had his aide cash two checks for him totaling $5,150. Later that day he met some friends at a restaurant and then stepped into the taxi and oblivion.

The investigation into his disappearance eventually mushroomed into a months-long grand jury probe that quizzed hundreds of witnesses but produced no leads to explain what happened to him. One theory was developed about why he had vanished. The grand jury uncovered considerable evidence of corruption in the Cayuga Democratic Club, which brought on the much publicized Seabury probe.

Meanwhile, the tantalizing mysteries of the case continued. Under New York City law, cabbies were required to keep records of all their trips, starting points and destinations. But despite many appeals from the police, a $5,000 reward offered by the city and a $2,500 reward offered by the *New York World*, the cabbie who picked up Judge Crater never came forward nor offered any information concerning the case. If he had, Crater's movements could have been traced at least one more step.

On countless occasions in the 1930s, the case seemed to be a fraction of an inch from being solved, but each lead fizzled. There was no limit to the type of leads the police ran down over the years. The missing Crater was identified wrongly as a gold prospector in the California desert country; a human torch who died of self-inflicted burns in Leavenworth, Kan.; a skeleton at Walden, Vt.; an unidentified murder victim in Westchester County, N.Y.; a man who hanged himself from a tree less than 15 miles from the Crater summer home at Belgrade Lakes, Maine; an amnesia victim in the Missouri State Insane Asylum; a sufferer of "daytime somnambulism."

Then again he was a Hollywood race tout; a free-spending American tourist in Italy; an ill-shaven door-to-door beggar in Illinois ("I didn't pull his whiskers but I'm pretty sure they were false," one Chicago housewife bubbled to police). Perhaps the best of all was the GI who returned from overseas in

Twenty-five years after Judge Joseph Force Crater's disappearance, his wife, since remarried, calls for a renewal of the hunt for him.

1946 with the emphatic intelligence that Crater was operating a bingo game in North Africa for a strictly Arab clientele.

Jokers, of course, got into the act. Assistant Chief John J. Sullivan was sitting at his desk one day when a call from Montreal was switched to him. A very calm voice said: "I can't tell you my name, because I don't care to get mixed up in it, but Judge Crater is now in room 761 at my hotel. I am in the hotel now, but I don't dare give you my name." In a matter of minutes Sullivan had the Montreal police breaking into the room of a honeymooning couple.

Throughout the country a number of dying bums felt compelled to make deathbed confessions, each admitting that he was the judge. One in the Midwest, who lived long enough for the police to question him, admitted finally that he was just trying to "get myself a decent burial instead of being laid in that pauper's plot all the other boys end up in."

In 1937 Judge Crater was ruled legally dead, and his widow remarried. At the time, it was estimated the hunt for Crater had expended 300,000 Depression dollars. Even by the 1950s the Judge Crater legend had not faded. Former police commissioner Edward P. Mulrooney, under whose supervision the case was first investigated, revealed he still carried a picture of Crater in his pocket at all times. "You never know but that someday you might run into him," he said. "I'd give my right arm to find him." During the following decade the police were still up to the search, digging up a Yonkers, N.Y. backyard in the hope of finding the judge's bones. Nothing came of it.

## Crazy Eddie's insane fraud  their prices and their stock offerings were truly insane

In the 1980s few television pitches bombarded Easterners more than of Crazy Eddie's, an appliance and hi-fi chain that declared ad nauseum "our prices are insane." And they were—and so was their accounting system, their tax payments and their Wall Street deals.

Crazy Eddie's went public at a time when Wall Street was mad about rapidly growing companies. In effect, proprietor Eddie Antar and his cousin Sam were telling the best brains in the financial community: "You want super growth, we got super growth."

The Antars realized that super growth thanks to Sam Antar's creative accounting. As the law was later to determine, the Antars had been skimming money from the business for years. In fact, they were making money not only from actual profits but just as lucratively from avoiding sales taxes. It was as near to a Marx Brothers operation as possible. But then an even more insane inspiration hit the Antars:

"Why don't we go public?" Why not indeed.

Of course, to be a super growth company they had to show explosive profits. Nothing was easier for the boys. All that had to be done was to cut back on the family skimming. With the abrupt reduction in the skim, profits seemingly ballooned from $1.7 million to $4.6 million. That figure for 1984 truly astounded Wall Street brokers, and a public stock offering was a resounding success. The Antars had barely warmed up.

In the quest for more imaginary profits, the family bought up imaginary merchandise so that gross profits by 1986 had soared to the level of 40 percent. For a second time Wall Street put out a stock issue that was even more successful than the first.

Alas for the Antars and their investors, there was no way Sam Antar could produce more bogus profits. Hungry Wall Streeters now were expecting an additional $20–$30 million for 1987.

"My pencil is only so long," Sam informed Eddie. The boys tried to move inventories from store to store so that auditors would count the same goods time after time. Unfortunately, that was the end of the road. Auditors were not that insane.

Jail sentences followed, but this did not end the Antar saga. In later years Sam Antar made speeches to such groups as the National Association of Fraud Examiners, outlining the crookedness of Crazy Eddie's. His theme to the experts and to credulous investors was that fraud is so easy—insanely so.

## Cunanan, Andrew (1969–1997) murderer of Gianni Versace

Andrew Cunanan was, if there is such a thing, just an average multiple killer—until he gained notoriety from shooting and killing famed fashion designer Gianni Versace outside his Florida mansion. Clues left at the scene soon identified Cunanan as the killer, just as telltale evidence of his identity clumsily littered the scenes of crimes he'd committed previously.

To the sensation-hungry media, such behavior was reflective of his stature as one of the most daring and brilliant criminals of the century: he disdained covering things up because he knew he could always elude his hunters, utilizing among other attributes his mastery of the art of disguise. One had to assume he was like that "damned elusive" Scarlet Pimpernel—here, there and everywhere—and the police, like the French, knew not where.

In *Three Month Fever: The Andrew Cunanan Story* Gary Indiana noted that Cunanan's killing of Versace instantly made him a world-famous "diabolic icon." According to Indiana, the tabloid press magnified the stories of his many disguises, among other matters, to fashion "a homosexual golem to absorb every scary fantasy about the gay community."

Cunanan did indeed spin his disguises and deceptions through a lifetime of lies going back to childhood to aggrandize his relatively humdrum existence. Thus at times he could pose as the son of a Filipino plantation owner who had fled from the oppression of the Ferdinand Marcos regime, or as having a multimillionaire Israeli father who doted on him and gave him anything he wanted, or then again that he was himself a major international drug dealer. In point of fact Cunanan's father had fled the States after embezzling $106,000 from his company, after which his mother was reduced to living in public housing in Eureka, Ill. As for his being a major drug dealer, for a time he was actually a drugstore clerk who sold prescription drugs such as Prozac and Xanax on the street. Flashiness and lies were part of his nature, and none of his acquaintances took him seriously for long, forcing him to constantly reinvent himself.

While still in his teens he learned the art of living off very rich men. It would be wrong to say that Cunanan was a simple hustler. He was rather a compensated companion. He was very good looking and lent a touch of class to the men he escorted, being well-versed in current events, fine wines and etiquette. His companions tended to be very friendly and generous to him. With younger men Cunanan was apparently into sado-masochism.

Thus Cunanan reinvented himself to accommodate two different lifestyles. His most successful and fruitful relationship with an older man was with an arts patron in San Diego who moved among the La Jolla elite. There were lavish gifts for Cunanan as well as a grand tour of Europe with his patron. Then Cunanan mixed his two lifestyles. He complained to his millionaire friend that he was worth more. He got a hefty allowance, a lavish apartment and more, but he was not satisfied. Now his patron started viewing him as more of a cheap hustler than a cherished companion. The millionaire kicked him out, giving him severance variously stated to have been $15,000 or $50,000. Cunanan was crushed. He realized it would be harder to reestablish himself in social circles. He was getting older and going to paunch. He tried to maintain his ties to younger friends and companions.

One was David Madsen, a young blond architect from Minnesota. Madsen wanted to end his relationship with Cunanan, suspecting him of being involved in some "shady dealings." Madsen headed back to Minnesota in April 1997. Now low on funds and overdrawn on his credit cards, Cunanan managed to scrape up the money for a one-way ticket to Minneapolis. Madsen took his visitor to dinner but seemed to maintain a certain aloofness. Cunanan found Madsen now had become closer to another friend, Jeffrey Trail, whom he did not like and had that feeling returned from Trail. Trail often objected to Cunanan's use of drugs. Fresh from rejection by his wealthy patron, Cunanan suspected there was no way he could be a part of the Madsen-Trail relationship.

Now the situation became unclear. Cunanan invited Trail to come to Madsen's loft apartment. It is unclear if Madsen was present. What was a fact was that Cunanan beat Trail to death with a claw hammer and rolled the corpse in a carpet and stayed with it for two days. On the second day, Madsen reappeared. The pair were seen walking a dog and later, without the dog, the pair drove to a lake outside Minneapolis. Cunanan shot Madsen with Trail's pistol and dumped the body where it was later found by fishermen.

Authorities readily determined that Cunanan was staying with Madsen but had disappeared. Plenty of evidence was found to link him to the two murders.

But where was Andrew Cunanan?

It turned out Cunanan had moved on to Chicago. Somehow he got to know Lee Miglin, one of Chicago's most successful real estate developers. Apparently Cunanan used a fake gun to force the millionaire into his garage, where he was bound and eventually murdered, his throat cut with a bow saw. Miglin was wrapped in masking tape in bondage mask style. There were also wounds from a garden tool on Miglin's body, indicating Cunanan had tortured him to reveal where his money and some gold coins were. Then Cunanan drove off in Miglin's green Lexus.

Again there were plenty of clues left that linked Cunanan, the murderer of Madsen and Trail, to the Miglin murder as well. Madsen's red jeep was left behind. Again Cunanan was gone.

How he wound up in a Civil War cemetery in Pennsville, N.J., not far from Philadelphia, was never determined except that he may have decided he needed new wheels. He shot caretaker William Reese to death in the cemetery office, deserted the Lexus as too hot and made off with a pickup truck.

Because most, but not all, his victims were gay, homosexuals around the country grew rather tense about meeting young, dark-haired men.

It was known that Cunanan spent a few days in Manhattan and then passed through Florence, S.C. But where was he bound?

In *Homicide: 100 Years of Murder in America*, Gini Graham Scott, Ph.D., surmised: "Knowing what we do now, there seems only one reason Cunanan went all the way to Miami: He was going to kill Versace because—there seems no other explanation—he admired him yet had no way to enter his circle of friends."

It has never been established that Cunanan knew Versace. Cunanan had been present at a lavish party in San Francisco to greet the fashion designer in celebration of the work he'd done on a production of the Richard Strauss opera *Cappricio*. According to Cunanan, Versace had thought he recognized him and introduced himself but that he, Cunanan, brushed him off, saying, "If you're Versace, I'm Coco Chanel." That would have been a typical claim for Cunanan to make, true or not.

In Miami Beach Gianni Versace went about his life. He never suspected his lavish mansion and grounds in South Beach were being watched. On Tuesday morning, Versace left to buy some publications at a newsstand, then turned around and walked back home. He was in the process of inserting a key in the lock to the gate when, innocuous in black shorts, gray T-shirt, black cap and white tennis shoes, Cunanan stepped up behind him. He fired two shots, leaving the designer dying.

Again there were tons of clues identifying the culprit, fingerprints and more. And now knowing what part of the country he was in the law could marshal its forces in vast numbers. Authorities located a garage where Cunanan had stored the cemetery pickup. He had a considerable library of clippings there covering the manhunt for him.

The question was whether Cunanan was still in the Miami area. Was he not, the media noted, a master of disguise? He could be anywhere. The tabloids were very grateful when some authorities speculated that Cunanan might be disguised as a woman.

While the authorities pressed their search, Cunanan had broken into a houseboat moored across from the luxury hotels and condos on Collins Avenue. It had been lavishly furnished by the owner, a Las Vegas club operator. Cunanan was comfortably ensconced in surroundings of wealth. It was where he always wanted to be. But where could he go next? The media had no problem; he was a serial killer who would continue with his killing spree.

But the shadows were closing in on Cunanan. He had all the fame he could ever hope to achieve. He was at a dead end. He knew sooner or later such vessels are checked for intruders. There was no way he dared leave and there was no way he dared stay.

Finally a caretaker did show up and spotted signs of an intrusion. He called police. A SWAT team responded and moved slowly through the boat. They found Cunanan's body propped up on two pillows in the bedroom of the master cabin on the second level. He was dead, his gun in his lap.

The search for the master killer who had dared so often for the authorities to catch him—or was so clumsy he left a parcel of clues wherever he went—was over.

Fittingly, the houseboat Cunanan occupied was demolished in January 1998. But the legend of a mythic killer still remains.

### Czolgosz, Leon (1873–1901) McKinley assassin

The crowd at the Pan-American Exposition in Buffalo, N.Y. at noon on September 6, 1901 was jubilant over the opportunity to meet William McKinley, the president of the United States, face to face. They queued up excitedly after the president had agreed to shake hands with all comers. At the end of the line was a dark little man of 28, his right hand swathed in a white bandage. When he was about sixth in line, the man lowered his head to keep from being spotted. He had lived in nearby West Seneca for some time and was known to police as a dangerous anarchist.

The president was smiling as he stepped toward Czolgosz. Czolgosz waited until he was just a few feet from the president and then flipped a pistol out from under the phony bandage and fired. The first shot hit a button and bounced away, but the second penetrated the president's abdomen. McKinley stiffened a moment but did not lose consciousness as guards and soldiers pounced on his attacker. "I done my duty," Czolgosz cried. A guard took careful aim and smashed his fist into Czolgosz's face. "Be easy with him boys," the president said weakly.

Eight days later, McKinley died of gangrene of the pancreas. Latter-day opinion contended that bungled medical care was as much the cause of death as Czolgosz's bullet. Nine days after the president's death, Czolgosz was put on trial, a matter in which the defendant took no interest. He said nothing to his court-appointed lawyers, refused to take the stand and showed no reaction when a verdict of guilty was announced. All he would do was affirm his anarchist beliefs, even though long before the assassination an anarchist publication, *Free Society,* had urged others to avoid him, denouncing Czolgosz as a dangerous crank and possibly a spy or police agent.

When Czolgosz went to the electric chair at Auburn Prison, he said: "I killed the President because he was the enemy of the good people—the good working people. I am not sorry for my crime." When he was placed in his coffin, sulfuric acid was poured on his body, and experts predicted his corpse would decompose in 12 hours.

After McKinley's death, the third presidential assassination in 36 years, the new president, Theodore Roosevelt, ordered the U.S. Secret Service to take over full responsibility for guarding the chief executive.

## Darrow, Clarence Seward (1857–1938)
### defense lawyer

America's greatest lawyer, Clarence Darrow, had been practicing before the bar for 16 years when in 1894 he took on the case of a convicted murderer who was appealing to a higher court. Darrow lost and the man, Robert Prendergast, was hanged. He was the first—and last—Darrow client to be executed, although the famous lawyer represented more than 50 accused murderers, many of whom were definitely guilty.

Born in the Ohio farmlands in 1857, Darrow's formal education ended after he finished the equivalent of one year of high school. He continued to study law books at night, however, and saved up enough money to go to law school. In 1878 Darrow was admitted to the bar and soon became a political reformer, backing the ill-fated John Peter Altgeld's efforts in Illinois. Later, he was a well-paid corporation lawyer, but his natural sympathies lay with the working man, and in 1894 he rejected the business world to defend labor leader Eugene V. Debs in connection with the Pullman strike. He earned the permanent enmity of business when in 1906 he successfully defended radical labor leader Big Bill Haywood on a murder charge. However, he was forced to plead labor men James McNamara and John J. McNamara guilty in the 1910 bombing of the *Los Angeles Times,* a decision that had a shattering effect on the Western labor movement. The unions refused to pay him his $50,000 fee in the case, and the prosecution, prodded by *Times* publisher and rabid anti-unionist Harrison Gray Otis, tried to convict him of jury tampering. Darrow beat the charges, but he never again took a labor-related case.

He continued to achieve considerable success, however, in leading criminal cases. Darrow's secret, he admitted, was his ability to pick a jury, which he considered the most important part of any case. "Get the right men in the box," he said, "and the rest is window dressing." Darrow would seldom accept a German or a Swede for a jury. A German, he felt, was too bullheaded and too "law and order" oriented and a Swede also too stubborn. His favorite jurors were Irishmen and Jews. Both, he felt, were highly emotional and easily moved to sympathy. He often said the perfect jury was six Irishmen and six Jews. "Give me that combination in the box," he remarked often, "and I could get Judas Iscariot off with a five dollar fine."

Darrow also preferred older men to younger ones. An older man, he said, was more sympathetic to the jams other men got into. In important cases Darrow assigned investigators to look into the lives of prospective jurors and would come into court with a dossier on all the veniremen, aware of their foibles, their likes and dislikes, and their prejudices. Through the years Darrow was never troubled by the testimony of experts against his clients. His handling of a medical witness called to testify that an accident victim would soon be up and around was typical; it ran:

> *"You came here from out of town to testify for the company, Doctor?"*
> *"Yes."*
> *"And you had a nice trip?"*
> *"Yes, Mr. Darrow."*
> *"How much are you getting for testifying, Doctor—over and above the expenses of your trip?"*
> *"Three hundred dollars."*

Darrow then turned to the jury, raised his eyebrows and, still looking at the jurors rather than the witness, growled, "That will be all, Doctor."

Once Darrow implied that an expert was a money grubber, he never deigned to concern himself with what the witness had to say—and usually neither did the jury.

There is no record of how much money Darrow made in a year. There were years when he made over $100,000, but others when, bogged down in cases with penniless clients, he netted very little. Even in what was perhaps his most famous case—that of

thrill-slayers Nathan Leopold and Richard Loeb in 1924, two wealthy Chicago youths whom he saved from execution—his clients, the boys' parents, reneged on paying him the major part of his fee.

The Leopold and Loeb case showed Darrow's courtroom genius at its best, passing up a jury trial in favor of making his case to a judge. From experience, Darrow knew that while a juror might convict and thus doom a defendant if his vote was only $1/12$ of the decision, that same juror would draw back if his vote alone was the deciding factor. He shrewdly viewed the judge, a humane jurist, John Caverly, as no different than the average juror.

Although both sides presented expert psychiatric testimony, Darrow knew in the end that he would have to sway the judge with his summation, in part because he himself probably recognized his two clients were homicidal. Throughout the trial Darrow had had trouble keeping them from smirking in court and hamming it up for photographers outside the court. Public opinion had been against the two rich boys from the beginning and became even more so because of their mannerisms during the trial.

For two days Darrow summarized his case, maintaining his clients were not murderers but two boys who had taken a human life because they were mentally and morally sick, victims of complicated, often misunderstood forces, buried deep in their past. He ended by declaring: "Your Honor, if these two boys hang, *you* must order them to hang. It will be entirely up to *you*, Your Honor. There must be no division of responsibility here, Your Honor. The sentencing of these boys to die must be an act on *your* part alone. Such a sentencing must be your own cold, deliberate, premeditated act, without

The Great Defender, Clarence Darrow, is shown in shirt sleeves, at the Monkey Trial. Standing behind him in light jacket is schoolteacher John Scopes.

the slightest chance to shift any part of the responsibility. Your Honor alone stands between these boys and the trap door of the scaffold."

Darrow's gamble of bypassing a jury trial worked. The judge sentenced the pair to life imprisonment.

The following year Darrow won worldwide acclaim in Tennessee's famous Monkey Trial, in which he dueled with William Jennings Bryan over the theory of evolution. Darrow's client, a young schoolteacher named John Scopes, was convicted of teaching evolution, a decision that was almost inevitable considering the time and the place, and fined $100, but the famous lawyer clearly won the case against Bryan in the world of public opinion.

Darrow published his autobiography in 1932, six years before he died at the age of 81.

See also: JOHN P. ALTGELD

## Dekker, Albert (1905–1968) accidental or deliberate death?

The death of veteran actor Albert Dekker in early May 1968 had the element that the tabloids love best in Hollywood scandals—kinkiness. Dekker, long famed for his career in the theater and later in top Hollywood films, was in a sense best known to a gener-

Albert Dekker won great fame in "mad" and kinky roles. In that sense his death was his kinkiest role ever.

ation of young moviegoers for playing the title role in *Dr. Cyclops,* about a mad scientist who shrinks people to doll size. Perhaps that Cyclops association somehow fit the gruesome death he suffered.

Dekker was found in a scene that was called a "grotesque nightmare." Police had to break into the bathroom of his Hollywood apartment, where they found him dead and naked except for some female underwear. His wrists were handcuffed and he was bound with leather ropes around his neck, chest, waist and ankles. There were punctures on his arms and buttocks caused by a hypodermic needle that lay beside the body. Scrawled on his body with bright red lipstick were a number of words, among which the tamer were *whip* and *slave.* There was a drawing of

a vagina on his lower stomach. He had been choked to death by the leather rope.

If Dekker was into kink, it was something neither his friends nor his longtime fiancée, fashion model Geraldine Saunders, seemed to know. It was Saunders, unable to reach him by phone the previous two days, who had sounded the alarm.

In the entertainment world Dekker was known to be cultured and intellectual. He had served two years in the 1940s in the California legislature as a liberal Democrat. His liberal stance and his attacks on Sen. Joseph McCarthy led to his being blacklisted as an actor for several years. During the last year of his life, although his career was very much on track, Dekker was despondent over the death of his 16-year-old son Jan, who accidentally shot himself.

The official verdict on Albert Dekker's death was first said to be suicide but was later changed to accidental death. This seemed to be rather logical since the bathroom door had been chainlocked from the inside. But many observers found the idea unconvincing, declaring that Harry Houdini, and lesser sorts, would know it is as easy to lock a chainlock from the outside as from the inside. And Houdini certainly could have escaped the restraints on Dekker but might have had a bit more difficulty getting in them without help of some sort. The way Dekker was bound and choked indicated 1) that he had not been alone and 2) that he was unconscious at the time of his death.

Then there was the drug that had certainly been injected in him. Officials could not identify it.

On a more prosaic crime level, it was known that Dekker had $70,000 in cash in his apartment. The money was missing, as was an expensive camera.

But to officials an autoerotic asphyxiation thesis was more fitting to write *fini* to the life of an actor who had played so many spooky roles.

## DeLorean, John (1925– ) accused multimillionaire drug smuggler

He was one of the most flamboyant automotive entrepreneurs to come out of Detroit. He was also perhaps the only American multimillionaire ever busted for alleged drug trafficking. Federal authorities were reportedly ecstatic over netting such a big fish in a huge sting operation. However, the results did not turn out the way the government wanted.

John DeLorean was reputed to be both a wunderkind and incorrigible playboy. From the very beginning of his career in the automotive industry at Chrysler he showed the signs of developing into a swashbuckler—"hustler" not seeming to suitably reflect his style. From Chrysler DeLorean shifted to Packard and was by then generally known as a real "comer." In 1956 DeLorean hopped to General Motors and at age 44 was general manager of the Chevrolet division. In 1972 he was a vice president with much more expanded duties. Observers of the automotive scene cast him as a logical candidate to eventually become president of GM if he could keep his personal ardor under control. But DeLorean took his own measure of his status; he regarded most of GM's leadership as dinosaurs. He felt he could do wonders for company policies without their interference, and he ignored objections to his "fast lane" lifestyle, which included marrying a 20-year-old fashion model. In 1973 after a divorce he married 22-year-old fashion model Cristina Ferrare.

About this time GM and DeLorean came to a parting of the ways. DeLorean resigned from his post, which paid him $650,000 a year in salary and bonuses. The way DeLorean told it, he "fired" GM.

DeLorean was by then totally involved in developing his "dream car"—a state-of-the-art sports car. He made an offer to the British government that it could not refuse. Britain was to invest $110 million for his dream car, and he would build a "showcase" auto factory in Belfast where thousands of jobs would go to that strife-torn and unemployment-ridden area. The British government coughed up loads of grants and low-interest loans, and, attracted by DeLorean's reputation for genius, a number of rich American investors put up additional backing.

The first of DeLorean's gleaming products came off the assembly line in 1981, most of the cars targeted for the American market at a then eye-popping $25,000. Unfortunately for DeLorean and his governmental and private backers, the roll-out coincided with a worldwide recession. Sales were, to say the least, disappointing.

The following year the British government could no longer keep a stiff upper lip and was obliged to put DeLorean's company in receivership. Later the Belfast factory was to be shut down permanently.

However, when the shoe dropped it was not then DeLorean's major worry. The very day of the announcement of the shutdown, DeLorean was arrested in Los Angeles by federal authorities, who charged him as being involved in a $50-million cocaine deal. It was a shocking story for the American and British public.

Federal prosecutors were sure they had an iron-clad case. They had videotapes involving DeLorean and federal agents posing as drug dealers going over details of the negoti-

Flamboyant automotive hot shot John DeLorean produced his "dream car," which turned out to be a bust. Then he was accused of being the only American multimillionaire ever busted for alleged drug trafficking.

ations. When authorities broke in on the scene and arrested DeLorean, he was defiant, declaring, "I am absolutely an innocent man" and that the case was "a pure frame-up and FBI cheap shot."

Usually sting operations of this type easily go the prosecution's way, since, to use a law enforcement phrase, a "dog was caught with the meat in his mouth." But after a 22-week trial in which DeLorean was charged with conspiracy to sell $24 million worth of cocaine, as well as other charges involving possession and distribution of drugs, proved no easy sell to the jury. The defense made much of what it called improper entrapment

and that federal agents had set up DeLorean because he was known to be desperate for funds to bail out his ailing dream car enterprise. At the time a congressional inquiry had subjected such stings to severe criticism. The jury felt the same way about the DeLorean case and voted not guilty on all charges.

Clearly enraged by the verdict, prosecutors brought new charges accusing their elusive quarry with wire and mail fraud, interstate transportation of stolen money and income-tax evasion. DeLorean was accused of funneling millions into a Dutch bank. However, once again a federal jury was not buying the charges and cleared DeLorean on all counts.

All told, DeLorean's company owed more than $100 million to creditors, and finally a federal bankruptcy court okayed an agreement under which a shade more than $9 million settled the company's debt.

In later years John DeLorean lived in reclusion in his New Jersey mansion.

## Dewey, Thomas E. (1902–1971) prosecutor and near assassination victim

Thomas E. Dewey was only one of several prosecutors, especially in New York State, to use his crime-fighting prowess to advance himself politically, moving on to the governorship and twice running for president, in 1944 and 1948. Dewey had started off as a Wall Street lawyer, and observers would note that as a prosecutor of industrialists, businessmen and financiers, he showed limited brilliance and effectiveness. In prosecuting gangsters, however, the Dewey zeal was limitless and telling. In various roles—U.S. attorney, special prosecutor and district attorney—he clapped in prison the likes of Waxey Gordon, Louis Lepke, Gurrah Shapiro and Lucky Luciano.

Before he got Luciano, Dewey set his sights on Dutch Schultz, the king of Harlem policy rackets and numerous other criminal enterprises. Although the Dutchman was a brilliant criminal leader, he was also a bit of a flake, fond of solving pressing problems with a gun. When Dewey's investigators closed in on his operations, Schultz went before the national board of the crime syndicate to demand that the prosecutor be assassinated as a solution to both Schultz's present problems and the future ones of others. When the crime syndicate was formed, a firm rule was agreed upon, as

Luciano stated it, that "we wouldn't hit newspaper guys or cops or DAs. We don't want the kind of trouble everybody'd get."

Led by the forces of Luciano and Lansky, the crime board voted down Schultz. "I still say he ought to be hit," the mad dog underworld leader is reported to have snarled in defiance. "And if nobody else is gonna do it, I'm gonna hit him myself."

At first, the syndicate decided that Schultz was simply blowing off steam, but then it was discovered in October 1935 that Schultz was setting an assassination plot in place. He had Dewey's Fifth Avenue apartment staked out by a man who posed each morning as the father of a child pedaling a velocipede. What could be less suspicious than a devoted parent strolling with his offspring? Dewey and the two body guards always at his side passed them without suspicion on their way to a nearby drug store, where Dewey made his first phone call of the morning to his office from one of several booths. He did not use his home phone for fear it might be tapped.

Once the "caser" with the child learned this, a murder plot was worked out; a killer carrying a gun with a silencer would be inside the drug store first and shoot Dewey when he entered one of the booths. Dewey's bodyguards waiting outside would not be aware of a thing as the killer walked out past them.

Schultz's mistake was involving Albert Anastasia in the plot. Anastasia was close to Luciano, and although he also favored killing Dewey, he would never betray Luciano. He passed the word about the plot to Luciano and others in the syndicate. Luciano was horrified. So were most of the others. An immediate trial was held and the death sentence passed on the absent Schultz. According to

Martin A. Gosch and Richard Hammer in *The Last Testament of Lucky Luciano,* Meyer Lansky, while not casting a dissenting vote, told Luciano: "Charlie, as your Jewish *consigliere,* I want to remind you of something. Right now, Schultz is your cover. If Dutch is eliminated, you're gonna stand out like a naked guy who just lost his clothes. The way La Guardia and the rest of them guys've been screamin' about you, it's ten to one they'll be after you next."

Luciano allowed that Lansky could be right, but the syndicate had no other choice than to eliminate Schultz. The vote taken was unanimous On October 23, 1935 Schultz was shot to death in a chop house in Newark, N.J.

Dewey did not learn of his "almost assassination" until 1940, when it was revealed to him by Murder, Inc. prosecutor Burton Turkus. Dewey listened impassively to the step-by-step details, but his eyes widened perceptibly when mention was made of the proud papa with the tot on the velocipede. After five years he apparently still remembered them.

By that time, as a result of Dewey's efforts, Lucky Luciano had been sent to prison for 30 to 50 years on a charge of compulsory prostitution, the longest sentence ever handed out for such an offense. After the end of World War II, Dewey backed a parole board's recommendation that Luciano be released, an action for which Dewey was roundly criticized by political opponents. The move was made because of Luciano's aid to the war effort, Dewey said, but it may also have been based to some degree on what had to remain an unspoken gratitude for Luciano's having saved his life. Perhaps somewhat ingraciously, Luciano to his dying day insisted there was yet another reason; the mob had contributed $90,000 in small bills to Dewey's campaign fund.

### Dillinger, John Herbert (1903–1934) public enemy

John Dillinger was the consummate public enemy, certainly the "superstar" gangster of the 1930s. But what is really amazing is that he achieved this status in a criminal career that spanned a mere 11 months, from September 1933 to July 1934. Dillinger and his mob—he actually was not the leader but merely a member among equals of the first so-called Dillinger mob—robbed between 10 and 20 banks. They also plundered three police arsenals, engaged in three spectacular jail breaks and fought their way out of police traps, murdering 10 men and wounding seven others in the process. This last fact was never considered very important by the public, just as Missourians did not hold such indiscretions against Jesse James a half-century earlier.

Dillinger captured the public's imagination with his style and verve; he displayed dash and derring-do in a spectacular but apocryphal "wooden gun" jail escape, had a casual impudence toward authority and often displayed a form of chivalry during robberies, especially flirting with older women bystanders, that turned him into a Depression-day Robin Hood. After all, he just robbed banks, not people, and on occasion told depositors to hang on to their money, that all the gang wanted was the bank's money. Undoubtedly, Dillinger was smart enough to understand such behavior stood him well with the public and could conceivably help him out of a tight spot someday.

John Dillinger (second from left) is photographed at arraignment in Arizona, the last time he would be taken alive.

Dillinger was a master bank robber. His gang's jobs were all well planned and timed to precision. During his nine-year stretch in prison for attempting to rob a grocer, he had learned the meticulous "Baron Lamm method" of bank robbery, named after a former Prussian army officer turned American criminal, which called for careful casing of a bank beforehand, pretested and timed getaway routes, and the like. Dillinger followed the technique to the utmost detail but added his own daring touches. The day before one robbery, two of his men cased a bank posing as journalists and were taken on a grand tour of the institution by its chief officer. During

another caper the townsfolk thought they were witnessing a rehearsal for the filming of a movie; a "movie director"—reputedly Homer Van Meter, the daring clown of the gang—had visited the scene the day before to publicize the event.

The product of an unhappy home life—John's mother died when he was three and his father subsequently remarried—young Dillinger became a juvenile delinquent. As a member of a youth gang called the Dirty Dozen, he was charged with stealing coal from the Pennsylvania Railroad's gondolas to sell to residents of his Indianapolis neighborhood; he was in the sixth grade at the time.

So far as the record shows, Dillinger did not get involved in serious crime until 1924, following a stint in the navy from which he just "walked away." That year he and an older, more seasoned criminal, Ed Singleton, attempted to rob a grocer whom they knew carried the day's receipts on him. The two men accosted their victim, B. F. Morgan, on a darkened street, and Dillinger, armed with a .32, struck him on the head with a bolt wrapped in a handkerchief. The grocer stayed erect and struggled, and Dillinger's gun went off. The hapless robbers then fled. Apprehended quickly, Dillinger drew a sentence of 10 to 20 years, although he had been assured by the local prosecutor that as a first offender, he would be treated lightly if he pleaded guilty. Dillinger's accomplice, 10 years older, was brought before a different judge and drew a far shorter sentence; he was released after doing two years. Dillinger ended up serving nine and the experience embittered him.

In 1934 Indiana governor Paul V. McNutt's secretary, Wayne Coy, would observe: "There does not seem to me to be any escape from the fact that the State of Indiana made John Dillinger the Public Enemy that he is today. The Indiana constitution provides that our penal code shall be reformative and not vindictive. . . . Instead of reforming the prisoner, the penal institutions provided him with an education in crime."

Doing time first in the Indiana State Reformatory at Pendleton and then in the state prison at Michigan City, Dillinger came in contact with criminals who became his mentors and later his accomplices, among them accomplished bank robbers like Harry Pierpont, John Hamilton, Homer Van Meter, Far Charley Makley, Russell Clark and Wal-

ter Dietrich. Despite his youth and relative inexperience, Dillinger was accepted as a member of this clique of hardened criminals because of his personal trustworthiness and willingness to help other prisoners. These were qualities much respected by men behind bars, even causing Pierpont, the group's nominal leader, to overlook a failing in Dillinger that he tolerated in no other associate—having an "old lady" prison lover.

Several members of the Pierpont clique had unsuccessfully attempted to break out of the prison, leading most of them to conclude their only chance for escape was a scheme based on having aid from outside and making the proper payoffs inside. Dillinger, soon to be paroled, was designated the "outside man." As such, he would have to raise a lot of money and fast, and the group, which included a number of "jugmarkers" (men who had knowledge of good banks to be robbed), told him how to go about it. Pierpont and others also supplied him with names of trustworthy accomplices to use on various capers. Dillinger's duties were to get enough money to make the proper payoffs, buy guns, obtain getaway cars and clothes, and find a hideout for the escapees. With only limited experience but a vast amount of criminal knowledge, Dillinger emerged from prison to become the greatest public enemy in the history of American crime.

He was released in May 1933, after a petition bearing the signatures of almost 200 residents of his adopted hometown of Mooresville, Ind., including that of his grocer victim, was presented to the governor. Dillinger immediately set about committing robberies to raise the funds needed for the mass escape. Many of his capers were pulled with criminals little more experienced than he was and were badly bungled, often clearing less than $100. But Dillinger kept trying for bigger scores and finally pulled off a bank robbery that netted $10,600, no small sum for a bank in a Depression-racked area, and then a payroll heist that yielded more than $24,000. He now had enough funds to spring the Pierpont group, being totally unmindful at the time that Capt. Matt Leach of the Indiana State Police had identified him as the busy holdup artist. Leach had an alarm out for Dillinger and had just missed catching him on a number of occasions.

Meanwhile, Dillinger gave a large part of the escape money to Mary Kinder, a 22-year-old woman whose brother was one of the convicts slated to be in on the escape and who would become Pierpont's mistress. The complete story about the Michigan City breakout of 10 convicts was never fully revealed. Payoffs were made, that much is certain. In addition, Dillinger traveled to Chicago, where through an intermediary he bribed the foreman of a thread-making firm to conceal several guns in a barrel of thread destined for the prison's shirt shop. The barrel was marked with a red X so that the escapees would recognize it.

On September 26, 1933 Pierpont and nine others took several hostages and made their way out of the prison, a feat that resulted in all sorts of political recriminations in Indiana. The new McNutt administration contended that holdover Republican guards or some who had been dismissed must have been involved, but the former Republican governor, Harry Leslie, blamed the breakout on the 69 new guards appointed by the Democrats. It mattered little to the Pierpont bunch. They were free. It mattered less to Dillinger. He had in the meantime been captured in Dayton, Ohio while visiting one of several new girlfriends.

The Pierpont bunch were stunned when they learned from Mary Kinder that Dillinger had been arrested. There was no question of what they were going to do about it. Dillinger had kept his word and freed them, and now they were going to free him. They planned a raid on the jail in Lima, Ohio where Dillinger was being held. Dillinger had been informed of the escape plot in advance and asked that another of his girlfriends, Evelyn "Billie" Frechette, a half Indian in her mid-twenties, be waiting for him when he got out.

The grateful Pierpont would deny Dillinger nothing. Billie, the wife of a bank robber then in Leavenworth, was brought to an apartment in Cincinnati to await Dillinger's release. On October 12, Columbus Day, Pierpont, Makley and Clark broke into the Lima Jail, mortally wounded Sheriff Jess Sarber and freed Dillinger. On the way out of the jail, Dillinger paused to look at the dying sheriff, who had treated him kindly and whom Dillinger had developed an affection for, and said sharply to Pierpont, "Did you have to do that?"

Pierpont shrugged. He might not have taken such a rebuke from another man, but he genuinely liked and respected Dillinger.

The "Dillinger mob" was now ready for action, although at the time, it should have been called the "Pierpont mob." Dubbing it the Dillinger mob was the idea of lawman Matt Leach, who thought he might produce friction between the pair by making Dillinger into a greater criminal than he was. However, Leach's ploy failed. Nothing would come between Dillinger and Pierpont, and in fact, the latter wanted Dillinger to assume a more active leadership. He quickly grasped that Dillinger inspired confidence, trust and loyalty, vital qualities in a criminal organization, and could bring peace between feuding gangsters.

The mob pulled off a string of somewhere between 10 to 20 bank robberies; the number could not be determined because the gangsters never confessed which ones they had perpetrated and which were falsely attributed to them. This first so-called Dillinger mob functioned until January 1934, by which time the gang, after going to Florida for a rest, had moved to Tucson, Ariz. Several members were captured there by police work that was partly brilliant, partly pure luck and partly a result of tips from persons who recognized some of the gang from detective magazine pictures.

Dillinger was caught with Billie Frechette. Pierpont, Makley and Clark were taken with Mary Kinder and another woman. The three men were shipped to Ohio to be charged with the murder of Sheriff Sarber. Dillinger was flown to Chicago, where that city's entire "Dillinger Squad," 40 officers permanently assigned to the job of capturing him, and 85 other policemen met the plane. A 13-car convoy then took America's most famous prisoner to an "escape-proof" jail in Crown Point, Ind.

It was here that Dillinger was to electrify the nation with his famous "wooden gun" escape. According to the first version of the story, he used a knife to whittle a wooden gun out of the top of a washboard, colored it with shoe polish and used it to escape. But how did America's number one criminal get hold of a knife in jail? All right, change that to a razor blade. Both versions were sheer nonsense. Dillinger's wooden gun was a real one. The true story behind his escape from the Crown Point Jail was that his lawyer, an incredible rogue named Louis Piquett, had met with a prominent Indiana judge on the grounds of the Century of Progress in Chicago and handed over an envelope containing several thousand of dollars. In return, the judge agreed to smuggle a gun into the jail. Dillinger used the gun to capture and lock up several guards and then made his way to the warden's office, where he grabbed two machine guns.

He gave one of the machine guns to a black prisoner, 35-year-old Herbert Youngblood, and together they locked up several more officers; snatched the car of a lady sheriff, Mrs. Lillian Holley, from the jail parking lot; and made good their escape, taking two hostages with them. Dillinger later released the two hostages, giving one, an auto mechanic, $4 for his troubles.

Naturally, the supposed wooden gun escape made headlines. Sometime later, however, a secret investigation conducted by the Hargrave Secret Service of Chicago on orders of Gov. McNutt turned up the true story about the gun. McNutt and Attorney General Philip Lutz, Jr. decided not to reveal the information because they quite properly didn't want Dillinger to know that certain informants whom he might trust again in the future had talked to private detectives. By the time Dillinger was killed, the judge too had died, and the findings about the gun never were made public.

Meanwhile, Dillinger basked in the glory of the wooden gun story and sought to perpetuate it. In a letter to his sister, he told her not to worry about him and that he was "having a lot of fun." Concerning the gun, he added:

> . . . [the reports] I had a real forty five Thats just a lot of hooey to cover up because they don't like to admit that I locked eight Deputys and a dozen trustys up

*with my wooden gun before I got my hands on the two machine guns. I showed everyone the wooden gun after I got a hold of the machine guns and you should have seen thire faces. Ha! Ha! Ha! Pulling that off was worth ten years of my life. Ha! Ha!*

Dillinger's intention obviously was to cover up the fact that a real gun had been smuggled to him and to satisfy his ego. It was not the only time he had done that. Dillinger had often tormented his chief pursuer, Matt Leach, with phone calls and letters. And on one occasion he supposedly sent a book entitled *How to Be a Detective* to the excitable Leach. When he was captured in Arizona, Dillinger had been asked if he had in fact sent the book. He replied, "I was there when it was sent." That too was sheer nonsense. The book had been sent to Leach as a practical joke by Jack Cejnar, the bureau chief of the International News Service in Indianapolis.

After their escape Dillinger and Youngblood immediately separated. Thirteen days later, on March 16, 1934, Youngblood was mortally wounded in a gun battle with lawmen in Port Huron, Mich. As evidence of the loyalty Dillinger inspired in men, the dying Youngblood falsely told police that Dillinger had been with him the day before.

Immediately, Dillinger put together the real Dillinger mob, including among others Van Meter, jugmarker Eddie Green, Hamilton, Tommy Carroll and a newcomer, a short, violent-tempered punk named Lester Gillis, better known as Baby Face Nelson. It took considerable skill on Dillinger's part to keep Nelson and Van Meter, and occasionally some of the others, from shooting at one another. Dillinger undoubtedly disliked Nelson but he needed him. Nelson was the sort who would never desert his post in a robbery, and Dillinger had to commit several rob-

beries fast. He had to get money to provide a legal defense for Pierpont, Makley and Clark, who were to be tried for murdering Sheriff Sarber.

Dillinger sent the money, but it did little good. All three were convicted: Clark got life and the other two were sentenced to the electric chair.

Time was running out for Dillinger as well. The same month as his breakout from the Crown Point Jail, he barely escaped in a barrage of machine-gun fire during a confrontation with FBI agents in St. Paul. Dillinger was wounded in the leg, but Billie Frechette drove him to safety. The next month, April 1934, Dillinger and the rest of the mob were hiding out at Little Bohemia Lodge, a closed summer resort about 50 miles north of Rhinelander, Wis., when the FBI closed in. Warned by barking dogs, Dillinger and his men escaped. Baby Face Nelson killed Special Agent W. Carter Baum and wounded another agent and a local police officer. The FBI wound up capturing only three of the mob's women, who were found hiding in the basement. They also managed to shoot two innocent bystanders, a salesman and a Civilian Conservation Corps (CCC) cook, and kill another young CCC worker, all of whom they thought were escaping gangsters.

It was a debacle for the FBI and, in a sense, another laurel for Dillinger. Will Rogers got into the act, writing, "Well, they had Dillinger surrounded and was all ready to shoot him when he come out, but another bunch of folks come out ahead, so they just shot them instead. Dillinger is going to accidentally get with some innocent bystanders some time, then he will get shot."

Dillinger and Van Meter both submitted to plastic surgery to alter their faces and fingerprints. Neither job was overly effective. Ironically, Dillinger "died" on the operating cot. Given a general anesthetic, he swallowed his tongue and stopped breathing. One of the panicky outlaw doctors managed to pull out his tongue with a forceps and applied artificial respirations, and Dillinger started breathing again.

By this time Hamilton had died of wounds received in a shoot-out with pursuing officers, and while Dillinger was recovering from the plastic surgery, Tommy Carroll was killed near Waterloo, Iowa. The mob was falling apart, and Dillinger could only think of making a few big scores and then fleeing to Mexico.

Still, Dillinger's facial surgery gave him enough confidence to venture openly in the streets. Using the identity of Jimmy Lawrence, he took up with a 26-year-old Chicago waitress named Polly Hamilton. Polly shared rooms with a friend, Anna Sage, whose real name was Ana Cumpanis. Sage had come to America from Romania just after the war and had operated whorehouses in Gary, Ind., and East Chicago, Ill. She had twice been convicted of operating a disorderly house but had won pardons from Indiana governor Leslie. Recently, however, Sage had been convicted a third time and Gov. McNutt had refused her request for a pardon. The Immigration Bureau was seeking to deport her as an undesirable alien.

Dillinger felt safe with Polly Hamilton and Anna Sage; he had never had trouble with women betraying him. It is doubtful that Hamilton knew his true identity, but Anna Sage soon discovered it. Dillinger felt comfortable talking to her. She was 42, an older woman and perhaps even a mother figure for him. Sage listened to his stories and ramblings and perhaps would not have informed

on him merely because there was a $10,000 reward for his capture. But through a police contact in East Chicago, she made a deal with the FBI to betray Dillinger in exchange for a promise that the deportation proceedings against her would be dropped and the reward money would be given to her. Melvin Purvis, agent in charge of the Chicago office of the FBI, agreed to help with those matters as far as possible.

On July 22, 1934 Dillinger took the two women to a Chicago movie. Earlier in the day Sage had called the FBI to tell them about Dillinger's plans, but at that time she did not know which of two movies they would attend. The FBI staked out both and waited. As planned, Sage dressed in red so that the FBI men would recognize her. The agents at the Biograph Theater saw Dillinger and the two women enter. FBI inspector Sam Cowley, in charge of the nationwide hunt for Dillinger, telephoned J. Edgar Hoover and the decision was not to try to take Dillinger inside the movie house but to wait until he came out. When Dillinger and the women walked out of the theater, Purvis lit a cigar, the signal that identified Dillinger. Then he called on Dillinger to halt. The gangster looked about suddenly, and he saw that his female companions had vanished. In that brief instant he must have realized he had been betrayed by a woman. He pulled a Colt automatic from his right pants pocket and sprinted for the alley at the side of the movie house. Three FBI agents fired. They wounded two women passing, but they also shot Dillinger. One bullet went through his left side, another tore through his stooped back and came out his right eye. Dillinger fell dead.

Within a few months the second Dillinger mob was completely wiped out. Eddie Green was shot by the FBI. A month after Dillinger died, Homer Van Meter was also killed in an alley, this one in St. Paul, after being betrayed by friends. In November, Baby Face Nelson killed two FBI agents but died himself of wounds received in the gun battle. Meanwhile, Pierpont and Makley attempted to escape from the death house at the Ohio State Prison in Columbus by imitating Dillinger's mythical wooden gun ruse. With guns carved out of soap, they succeeded in overpowering one guard and were trying to batter their way out through the door leading from the death house when a riot squad opened fire. Makley was killed and Pierpont wounded. A month later, Pierpont died in the electric chair.

### Dillinger double

The death of John Dillinger in July 1934 marked the end of crime's greatest folk hero of the 20th century, and it was therefore hardly surprising that his death was not accepted by many. This has been a common behavioral reaction. For decades there were people who believed Jesse James had not been shot by Bob Ford, that a substitute corpse had been used. And for decades one "real Jesse James" after another turned up. In the cases of the Apache Kid and Butch Cassidy, the weight of opinion seems to favor the theory that they survived their alleged demises, but the identification of their corpses was far more controversial.

The disbelief about John Dillinger started instantly after his death and continued for years. In a book entitled *Dillinger: Dead or Alive?* (1970), Jay Robert Nash and Ron Offen made perhaps the most complete case that the great public enemy had not been killed by FBI agents. Their basic premise was that the FBI had been duped into thinking the dead man was Dillinger, and when the

agency discovered otherwise, it could do nothing but develop a massive cover-up.

What makes this case less than totally acceptable is the number of people such a plot would have required. Certainly Anna Sage, "the woman in red," and her East Chicago police contact or contacts. And someone would have had to have planted a phony Dillinger fingerprint card days before the killing. According to this theory, "Jimmy Lawrence" was not a Dillinger alias but the name of a real minor hoodlum whose career was rather hazy.

Proponents of the fake Dillinger theory make much of glaring discrepancies found in Dillinger's autopsy report, which was allegedly lost for more than 30 years. For instance, in the report the dead man's eyes were listed as brown, Dillinger's were blue. But this was an autopsy performed in Cook County during the 1930s, a time when coroners' findings nationwide were notorious for being replete with errors. The autopsy was performed in a "looney bin" atmosphere. A reporter for the *Chicago Tribune* appeared in news photos propping up Dillinger's head and was identified as the "coroner." Even after the autopsy was performed, Dillinger's brain was actually "mislaid" for a time. If all errors made in autopsies of that period were taken seriously, probably just half the victims of violent deaths could really have been considered dead.

Another question that must be raised is how John Dillinger lived happily ever after and on what. By all accounts, he had less than $10,000 available to him for a final, permanent escape. Could he stay away from crime forever? And if he could not, would he not have been identified sooner or later? And what of Anna Sage? Despite promises made to her by the FBI, she was deported back to her native Romania. She could undoubtedly have bought a reprieve from that fate had she come forward with the true facts about a Dillinger hoax.

In sum, the "Dillinger lives" theory appears to be a case of wishful thinking, one fostered by the fact that John Dillinger was too good—or too bad—to be allowed to die.

## DNA evidence    convicting the guilty, freeing the innocent

The crime was probably as worthy of the death penalty as any. Robert Lee Miller, Jr., was convicted by an Oklahoma jury in 1988 for the rape and asphyxiation of two women, 92-year-old Zelma Cutler and 83-year-old Anne Laura Fowler. Miller was sentenced to death in 1988 and remained under that sentence for 10 years until a judge dismissed the case because of insufficient evidence. "Insufficient" was not quite the word for it. DNA in a semen sample turned out not to match Miller's DNA but did match that of an already convicted rapist.

DNA has revolutionized the field of crime. It has frequently convicted the guilty and in many cases kept innocent people from being prosecuted; in fact, it has often freed the innocent. However DNA testing involves utilizing human beings in the process and therein can lie the rub. There remains a crying need for competence and thoroughness during an investigation. Robert Hayes was convicted in 1991 in Florida for the rape and murder of a coworker. The conviction was based largely on DNA evidence taken from hair found in the victim's hands. Hayes was released in 1997 by the Florida Supreme Court when it was learned the hair was from a white man. Hayes was black.

DNA could be said to have had its birth in 1953 when English physicist M. H. F. Wilkins, together with Francis Crick and an American.

John Watson, worked on the acids comprising the cell nucleus. They discovered DNA.

The great breakthrough in crime detection occurred in 1984 when Dr. Alec Jeffreys in England came up with chemical typing of "genetic fingerprints." Through Dr. Jeffreys' research it was established that the only persons in the world with identical "bar codes" were identical twins.

Dr. Jeffreys first applied the technique in paternity cases and in 1987 he made the great breakthrough in a murder case. Colin Pitchfork raped and strangled two teenagers three years apart. In a sweep that would never get compliance in the United States but did in Britain, authorities gained the cooperation of 4,600 men for blood samples. Pitchfork realized something was up although he did not understand what was involved and got a stand-in to give blood for him. Unfortunately, the police discovered the trickery and Jeffreys got his man.

Within a short time DNA testing started being used extensively in the United States. The FBI started doing DNA testing in rape and rape-homicide cases in 1989. The agency only gets the cases when there has been an arrest or an indictment and then does DNA testing to confirm or exclude the suspect. In one out of four cases where they get a result, the primary suspect is excluded.

The noted DNA expert Barry Scheck, has asked, "How many of those people would have been convicted had there been no DNA testing?"

Scheck is codirector, with Peter Neufeld, of the Innocence Project at the Benjamin N. Cardozo School of Law in Manhattan. As of 1999 well over 60 persons, more than half of them with the aid of project, had their convictions overturned because of DNA testing. In eight of those cases, the convicts were on death row. More important, thousands of others, said Scheck, "have been exonerated after an arrest, in the middle of a trial, things like that." Still, in 70 percent of the Innocence Project cases, the evidence the investigators wished to test could not be located.

On August 23, 1999 the *New York Times* stated that since capital punishment was reinstated by the United States Supreme Court there had been 566 executions, and at the same time 82 awaiting executions were exonerated—one in seven. There was no estimate of how many of those executed had been afforded the opportunity to use DNA evidence. This was not to be unexpected. Back in 1957, in *Not Guilty,* a trailblazing book examining the extent of wrongful convictions, Judge Jerome Frank, noted, "No one knows how many innocent men, erroneously convicted of murder, have been put to death by American governments. For . . . once a convicted man is dead, all interest in vindicating him usually evaporates." A "scorecard" of sorts could be offered by the death penalty experiences in Illinois to show 12 persons executed and in that same period 12 other inmates exonerated.

It is not always easy to free a defendant even after it has been proved that he is not guilty. There have been cases of prosecutors simply refusing to drop the charges even after the defendant has been released. In other cases it is a matter of gamesmanship to even introduce DNA evidence. This is especially the case when there is what some critics call "quickie deadlines" on new evidence. In Virginia the statute of limitations is 21 days, which left Earl Washington, Jr., in hard luck. In 1994 his DNA testing arrived too late. An optimist might say he still had some good luck. Subsequently his sentence was com-

muted to life imprisonment. David Botkins, a spokesman for Mark Earley, Virginia's attorney general, announced, "The inmates who have been granted clemency and had their death sentences commuted show the system works."

Some reformers do not see this as making the system work, and they have called for federal legislation to guarantee inmates an opportunity to require DNA testing. At the time only New York and Illinois offered such requirements.

Above all, this would require that DNA testing be done correctly. In the celebrated murder trial of ex-football star O. J. Simpson, Barry Scheck persuaded the jury in the criminal proceeding to disregard DNA evidence offered by the prosecution by demonstrating how such evidence could be misused.

Also required would be the fair use of the DNA evidence. In 1992 Randall Padgett was convicted of the stabbing death of his estranged wife. Virtually the entire case against Padgett was based on blood samples left at the scene, which were tested for DNA. It turned out the FBI crime laboratory had concluded the blood was not Padgett's. The Alabama prosecutors simply suppressed that fact. Padgett was acquitted at a retrial and was released after spending five years on death row.

There were indications by late 1999 that a bit of a sea change was taking place concerning the death penalty, especially in light of the DNA record. In some cases reforms were even supported by vocal death-penalty supporters. In Illinois, the house passed a resolution calling for a moratorium on executions and for the formation of an independent group to study how the death penalty was being applied in the state. In Nebraska, death penalty foes and proponents joined forces to pass a law that would stop executions for two years.

But in other jurisdictions the push remained strong for speedier executions. In fact, in August 1999 a conference organized by the United States Court of Appeals for the 11th Circuit, known to attorneys as hardline, was held to find ways to expedite capital punishment. Some states have cut financing, in some cases to zero, for lawyers representing death row inmates for their appeals.

Calling for the rights to every death row inmate to have access to DNA testing, a decent attorney and the opportunity to introduce evidence of innocence no matter when it is uncovered, the *New York Times* editorialized: "It is the rare death-row inmate who does not claim to be innocent. But many states are finding, to their horror, that it is not a rarity that this claim is true . . . A wrongful conviction, of course, means that the real killer has gone free."

And of course the *Times* reiterated the long-standing view of reformers: "There is no way to know how many innocent people have been executed because the dead do not search for champions to prove their case."

Against this, many death penalty supporters tend to demand a date certain on all executions. A fairly standard call is for a definite cut-off after five years of conviction. Proponents argue that the absence of a date-certain provision makes a mockery of capital punishment. One who might have fallen victim to such a schedule for death would be Gregory Wilhoit, who was convicted in 1987 for killing his estranged wife in her sleep in Oklahoma. The prosecution relied on an expert who testified that Wilhoit's teeth matched bite marks on the victim's body. Later the state appeals court

ruled that Wilhoit's counsel had failed to challenge the expert's claim. The court said at the time he—the defense attorney was "suffering from alcohol dependence and abuse and brain damage during his representation of appellant." At a new trial, 11 experts were brought in to testify that the bite marks did not match, and Wilhoit was freed.

However, this was six years later—beyond the so-called five-year limit.

## Draft Riots

Beginning early on the morning of July 13, 1863 and continuing for three more bloody days, great riots broke out in New York City, leaving, according to the best estimates, 2,000 dead and another 8,000 wounded. The cause of the rioting was indignation over President Lincoln's draft, fanned by racial hatred, Irish resentment at occupying the lowest level of the social and economic order, and the greed of the great criminal gangs of the Bowery and the Five Points, which saw a chance to loot the city much as had been done during the earlier anti-abolitionist and anti-English Astor Place riots of the 1830s and 1840s.

There were minor disturbances of the peace in opposition to the draft in Boston, Mass., Portsmouth, N.H., Rutland, Vt. and Wooster, Ohio, but none approached the size or ferocity of the New York riots. There the city's poor, largely Irish, allied with the Democrats in opposition to the war, rioted to protest the draft, which they saw as trading rich men's money for poor men's blood through a provision in the law that allowed a potential draftee to buy out of the service for $300. Since this was a monumental sum to the Irish, it meant they had to do the fighting and dying in the conflict between the North and the South.

What had started out as violent protest against the draft turned by the second day into savage lynching of blacks—the cause of the war in the Irish poor's eyes—and wholesale looting, as rioters and criminals sought to seize armory supplies, overpowering and then torturing, mutilating and murdering defending soldiers. Some saw in the great riots a Roman Catholic insurrection, which they were not, although along with the "No Draft" signs were some that sang the praises of the pope and proclaimed, "Down with the Protestants." Considerable church properties of various Protestant faiths were among the 100 buildings burned to the ground by the rioters, but none belonging to the Catholic faith were touched. Lone Catholic priests turned back rioters bent on looting and killing, but Catholic archbishop Hughes refused to counsel the rioters to disband until the fourth day, when the violence had run its course. On that day he addressed a pastoral letter entitled "Archbishop Hughes to the Men of New York, who are called in many of the papers rioters." Later, the archbishop was to acknowledge that he had "spak too late."

The rioters were bent on mayhem, and some of their crimes were heinous indeed. Policemen and soldiers were murdered, and the children of the rioters picked the bodies clean of every stitch of clothing, proudly wearing the bloodstained garments as badges of honor. Great throngs—estimated to be between 50,000 and 70,000 persons in all—stormed across Manhattan from the Hudson to the East Rivers, looting stores, burning buildings and beating every black they saw. At least three black men were hanged before sundown of the first day, and thereafter, the

Burning of the Second Avenue Armory caused many deaths.

sight of bodies hanging from lampposts and trees were common throughout the city. The blacks' bodies were all viciously mutilated, slashed with knives and beaten with clubs. Often, they were mere charred skeletons, the handiwork of the most ferocious element in all early American riots—women. Trailing behind the men, they poured oil into the knife wounds of victims and set the corpses ablaze, dancing beneath the awesome human torches, singing obscene songs and telling antiblack jokes.

The black settlements were the scene of much of the violence, the target of those of the rioters more concerned with bloodletting than looting. A house of prostitution on Water Street was burned and its occupants

Drawing shows the corpse of a policeman killed in the riot being abused by children and women following in the wake of the mob.

tortured because they refused to reveal the hiding place of a black servant. In New Bowery three black men were cornered on a rooftop and the building set afire. For a time the men clung by their fingers to the gutters while the mob below chanted for them to fall. When they did, they were stomped to death.

Meanwhile, as other groups of rioters attacked armories in search of weapons and police stations in anger at the police resistance to them, a mob sought to destroy the offices of Horace Greeley's prodraft *New York Tribune*. They started several blazes that forced the staff to flee by the back stairway. Greeley was compelled to take refuge under a table in a Park Row restaurant. A police garrison of 100 men retook the newspaper's premises and extinguished the fires, and the following day 100 marines and sailors took up guard in and around the building, which bristled with Gatling guns and a howitzer posted at the main entrance.

By late evening the mobs moved further uptown, leaving the scene behind them filled with numerous fires. At 11 o'clock a great thunder and lightning storm extinguished the blazes. Had it not, many historians believe the city would have been subjected to a conflagration far worse than the Great Chicago Fire a few years hence. Complicating the firefighting was the fact that several fire units had joined the rioters and others were driven away from many of the blazes by the rampaging mobs.

Probably the greatest hero of the first day of the riots was Patrolman George Rallings, who learned of a mob's plan to attack the Negro Orphanage at 43rd Street and Fifth Avenue where 260 children of freed slaves were sheltered. He spirited the children away before the building was torched. Only one tiny black girl was killed by the ax-wielding rioters. Overlooked in the exodus, she was found hiding under a bed and axed to death.

The fighting over the ensuing three days reflected the tides of military battle, as first the rioters and then the police and various militia units took control of an area. A pitched battle that left an estimated 50 dead was fought at barricades on Ninth Avenue until the police finally gained control of the thoroughfare. Rioters captured Col. H. J. O'Brien of the Eleventh New York Volunteers, tied a rope around his ankles and dragged him back and forth over the cobblestones. A Catholic priest intervened long enough to administer the last rites and then departed. For three hours the rioters tortured O'Brien, slashing him with knives and dropping stones on his body. He was then allowed to lie suffering in the afternoon sun until sundown, when another mob descended on him and inflicted new tortures. Finally, he was dragged to his own backyard, where a group of vicious Five Points Gang women squatted around him and mutilated him with knives until at last he was dead.

On July 15 militia regiments sent toward Gettysburg were ordered back to the city, and by the end of the 16th, the rioters had been quelled. The losses by various military units were never disclosed, but the toll of dead and wounded was believed to have been at least 350. The overall casualties in the riots, 2,000 dead and 8,000 wounded, were greater than those suffered at such famous Civil War battles as Bull Run and Shiloh; virtually every member of the police force had suffered some sort of injury. The number of blacks lynched, including bodies found and others missing, was believed to total 88. Property losses probably exceeded $5 million. Among the 100 buildings totally burned were a Protestant mission, the Negro Orphanage, an armory, three police stations, three provost marshals' offices as well as factories, stores and dwellings. Another 200 buildings were looted and partially damaged.

Even while the riots were going on and in the days following them, Democratic politicians seeking to embarrass a Republican president and a Republican mayor, demanded the police and troops be withdrawn from their districts because they were "killing the people." As a result of political influence

By the second day most of the rioters' fury was taken out on blacks, many of whom were lynched.

almost all of the hundreds of prisoners taken in the last two days of the riots were released. This was especially true of the gang leaders of the Five Points and the waterfront who were caught leading looting expeditions during the fighting. In the end, only 20 men out of the thousands of rioters were brought to trial. Nineteen of them were convicted and sentenced to an average of five years in prison. No one was convicted of murder.

On August 19, the city now filled with troops, the draft drawings resumed, and those who could not pay $300 were sent off to war.

## Elwell, Joseph Bowne (1875-1920) murder victim

Joseph Bowne Elwell was *the* bridge expert of the day and a notorious ladies' man. He was the author of *Elwell on Bridge* and *Elwell's Advanced Bridge,* or so it seemed. In fact, the books were written by his wife, later ex-wife, Helen Darby, whose high social position gave Elwell entrée into the world of society. This was vital for Elwell because the bridge books did not really bring in the kind of money needed to afford him the really good life. Elwell was basically a card hustler who milked the rich. With his ill-won wealth he established himself as one of them, becoming the owner of a racing stable, a yacht, an art collection and several cars.

Elwell was also the owner of what the tabloids referred to after his death as a "love index," a roster of 53 women, married and single, who boasted both high social affiliations and considerable allure. He maintained another list for male acquaintances and more run-of-the-mill females. Clearly, Elwell was a womanizer, a fact that proved to be something of a minor mystery in itself

since after death he was revealed to have been toothless and bald, owning a collection of no less than 40 toupees.

Early one morning in 1920, just as dawn crept over Manhattan's West 70th Street, someone put a .45-caliber bullet into Elwell's head as he was reading a letter in his study. His housekeeper found him near death when she came to work; he was not wearing his toupee or his false teeth. The housekeeper, Marie Larsen, was a devoted servant who, while doctors labored over Elwell, hid a pink kimono she found in the house. Later, it was discovered, but the young lady who owned it had an alibi for the time of the shooting. Almost all of the ladies on the love index and those in Elwell's larger file had been sound asleep at the time of the murder.

The newspapers had a field day with this first sex-and-murder scandal of the decade. All sorts of filmy underclothes were found secreted in Elwell's bedroom. It undoubtedly took a keen mind to remember which belonged to whom and perhaps a slip of this kind is what did Elwell in. All sorts of theories developed, featuring jealous women, their husbands or other lovers, gambling rings, gambling victims, mysterious spies (according to this postulation, Elwell, who had been a secret government agent in the war, was killed by spies he had uncovered) and even rival horse owners. One could have a pick of suspects and motives, but the public clearly preferred the idea that some fashionable matron (or her daughter) committed the murder for reasons of passion. Yet a .45 was hardly a woman's weapon and Elwell, a notoriously vain man, would never have admitted a female to his presence without putting in his teeth and donning his toupee. The answer to that argument was, of course, that a woman murderer might use a .45 and then remove his plates and wig precisely to make it look like the work of a man. Russel Crouse, the playwright and a former crime reporter, who had a keen eye for such things, once observed, "'*Cherchez la femme!*' will echo every time the murder of Joseph Bowne Elwell is mentioned. And the fact that she will never be found will not still the whispers."

## Everleigh sisters   madams

Some experts on the subject insist there has not been a genuine bordello in America since 1910, when Chicago's Everleigh Club, run by sisters Ada and Minna Everleigh, shut its doors. And when it did, the sisters, still in their early thirties, retired with, among other things, $1 million in cash; perhaps $250,000 in jewelry, much of which had come from grateful clients; paintings, statues, rare books, rugs and other valuables for which they had paid $150,000; about 50 brass beds inlaid with marble and fitted with specially designed matresses and springs; and 25 gold-

plated spittoons worth $650 apiece. For the Everleighs the wages of sin had been enormous.

Coming from a small Kentucky town, the Everleighs inherited about $35,000 between them. Everleigh was not their real name—it may have been Lester—but one they adopted in honor of their grandmother, who signed her letters, "Everly Yours." For a time the sisters joined a theatrical troupe while they looked for a nice town in which to invest their money. Early in 1898 they decided on Omaha, Neb., then readying for the Trans-Mississippi Exposition, which was expected to bring big crowds. At the time, Ada was 23 and Minna not quite 21, but they were hard-headed businesswomen and coolly analyzed what type of business would please a fun-seeking exposition crowd. So they went out and bought a whorehouse, a field in which they had no experience. They brought in all new girls and charged the highest prices in Omaha. It worked during the exposition, but when the crowds left, the sisters found out there was no way the sports of Omaha were going to pay $10 for a girl and $12 for a bottle of wine. So they packed up and moved to Chicago. The sisters bought the lease to and girls at the brothel of Madam Effie Hankins at 2131-3 South Dearborn Street for $55,000. On February 1, 1900 they opened the incredible Everleigh Club. Describing it, the *Chicago Tribune* said, "No house of courtesans in the world was so richly furnished, so well advertised, and so continuously patronized by men of wealth and slight morals."

On opening night the club took in $1,000. Never again were revenues so small, as word got around about the fabulous services offered. Separate soundproof parlors were called the Gold, Silver, Copper, Moorish, Red, Green, Rose, Blue, Oriental, Chinese,

Egyptian and Japanese rooms and were appropriately furnished. The *Tribune* described the Japanese Room as "a harlot's dream of what a Japanese palace might look like." Every room had a fountain that squirted a jet of perfume into the air.

Quite naturally, the charges were hardly cheap for the era, ranging from $10 to $25 to $50, depending on how long a client wished to avail himself of a prostitute's company. The $10 price was really little more than the cost of admission; if a man failed to spend at least $50, he was told not to return. The costs of running such a magnificent house—which included a library, an art gallery, a dining room, rooms where three orchestras played and a Turkish ballroom with a huge indoor fountain—were enormous. Overhead ran to $75,000 a year, including $30,000 for servants, music and entertainment and probably protection, since the sisters were never bothered and the name of the club did not appear on the police lists of bawdy houses. Also on the payroll were 15 to 25 cooks. This was an excellent investment because, while a good sport might spend $50 or $100, and gentleman throwing a dinner party for a small group of friends (with wine at $12 a bottle) could easily run up a tab of $1,500 for an evening's fun.

Madame Minna met each visitor in the grand hallway, clad in a silk gown and bedecked with jewels, including a diamond dog collar. The sisters permitted no lineup of their girls but had them drift from parlor to parlor, talking to a man only after a formal introduction. Everleigh Club prostitutes were much sought after by other bordellos and a girl who made it in the club had her future assured in the business—if she did not go directly from the business to marriage of a wealthy patron.

"I talk with each applicant myself," Ada once explained. "She must have worked somewhere else before coming here. We do not like amateurs. . . . To get in a girl must have a good face and figure, must be in perfect health, must understand what it is to act like a lady. If she is addicted to drugs, or to drink, we do not want her." For the girls the work was lighter and the pay higher than elsewhere, so the sisters always had a waiting list of applicants. Those accepted got regular classes in dress, manners and makeup and had to read books from the establishment's library.

A man who partied at the Everleigh Club even once could boast of it for years. The real secret of the sister's success was their understanding of male chauvinism and fantasies. One much appreciated gimmick used at times was to have butterflies to flit about the house. As a rival madam, Cleo Maitland, observed, "No man is going to forget he got his behind fanned by a butterfly at the Everleigh Club."

The list of celebrities who patronized the club was almost endless. Prince Henry of Prussia enjoyed a mighty orgy there in 1902, and repeat callers included John Barrymore, Ring Lardner, heavyweight boxing champion James J. "Gentleman Jim" Corbett, George Ade, Percy Hammond and Bet-A-Million Gates. One of the rave reviews of the establishment was offered by newsman Jack Lait, who said, "Minna and Ada Everleigh are to pleasure what Christ was to Christianity."

Other madams and whoremasters were jealous of the sisters' success and tried to fabricate charges of clients being robbed or drugged there, but the Everleighs paid the highest graft in the city and the authorities would not listen to such nonsense. One resourceful bordello operator, Ed Weiss, opened up next door to the Everleigh Club and put taxi drivers on his payrolls so that when a particularly drunken sport asked to be taken there, he would be deposited at the Weiss place instead without knowing the difference.

The great reform drive against vice in Chicago in 1910 forced the Everleigh Club to close. The sisters had no intention of doing battle with the authorities, who were under attack from do-gooders. Most Everleigh clients could not believe such a palace of pleasure would ever go out of business. The trauma was much worse for them than for the sisters, who took a year's grand tour of Europe and on their return settled in New York City in a fashionable home off Central Park. They lived out their lives in genteel fashion, Minna dying in 1948 and Ada in 1960.

See also: NATHANIEL FORD MOORE.

**Fall, Albert Bacon** (1861–1944)  political grafter
The central figure in the Teapot Dome scandal, Secretary of the Interior Albert B. Fall was the most tragic figure in the Harding administration. Unlike many of the other grafters, his motive was not so much avarice as a genuine need for money. There is evidence that he resisted temptation until he saw clear cases of corruption by Attorney General Harry M. Daugherty and the rest of the Ohio Gang.

Born in Frankfort, Ky. in 1861, Fall was forced by ill health to move to a Western climate. He taught school for a short time in Indian Territory in the Oklahoma area and then became a cattle drive rider, later trying his hand at mining and oil prospecting. In New Mexico he became a close friend of Edward L. Doheny, was admitted to the bar and started to develop a huge ranch at Three Rivers, N.M.

Fall also turned to politics, holding several positions in the territorial government, and in 1912, after New Mexico had achieved statehood, he became one of the state's first two senators. In 1921 his friend Warren

Harding named him to the cabinet as secretary of the interior. It was a welcomed opportunity for Fall, whose personal fortunes had sagged badly. His ranch needed many repairs and improvements, and all his properties were heavily mortgaged. In 1922 Fall secretly leased the Elk Hills, Calif. and the Teapot Dome, Wyo. oil lands, which were held by the government as a reserve in case of war, to Doheny's Pan-American Co. and Harry F. Sinclair's Mammoth Oil Co. It is doubtful if Fall would have done this had it not been for his long friendship with Doheny. Furthermore, Congress had authorized the leasing of the oil lands, although not the secret way Fall had gone about it or, of course, as a quid pro quo for bribes. Doheny gave Fall $100,000, and Sinclair arranged to have Fall receive a "loan" of $260,000 in Liberty Bonds.

The affair became public when a Wyoming oil man wrote his congressman demanding to know how Sinclair had leased Teapot Dome without competitive bidding. In the resulting senatorial inquiry the story of the payoffs to Fall was unraveled. Fall at first insisted that he had gotten the $100,000 as a

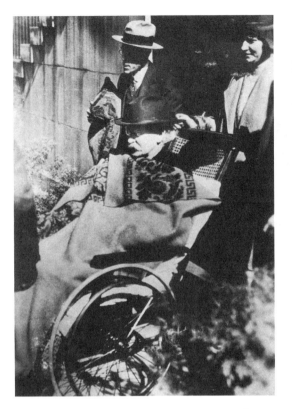

Albert Fall, secretary of the interior during the Harding administration, was broken physically by the time of his conviction and imprisonment and remained an invalid the rest of his years.

loan from the eccentric millionaire Edward B. McLean. When McLean then surprised him by denying such a loan, Fall admitted getting the money "in a black bag" from Doheny.

Over the next several years Fall went on trial eight times, sometimes with Doheny or Sinclair and sometimes alone. On the witness stand, Doheny told a tale of how the two young friends started out together, with one eventually striking it rich in oil while the other had nothing but bad luck. "Why shouldn't I lend him $100,000 and tear his name off the note?" he asked. "He was an old friend." Then Doheny called the $100,000 "a mere bagatelle," and the newspapers and public were outraged. It was said that remark did more to doom Fall than any evidence against him. While the two oil men were finally acquitted of the charges against them (Sinclair did get nine months for contempt for having a Burns detective follow the jurors during one trial), Fall was convicted, drawing a year in prison and a fine of $100,000. The money penalty was dropped when Fall signed a pauper's oath, and because he was suffering from tuberculosis, he was allowed to serve his sentence in the New Mexico State Penitentiary, into which Fall, his face ashen, was carried on a stretcher. He came out of the prison an invalid, needing the constant attention of his family until he died poverty-stricken in El Paso in 1944.

See also: OHIO GANG, TEAPOT DOME SCANDAL.

**Fallon, William J.** (1886–1927) defense attorney
William Joseph Fallon was New York's greatest criminal lawyer during the Roaring Twenties. Fallon was the Great Mouthpiece, as his biography by Gene Fowler was entitled, for pimps, madams, prostitutes, thieves, stock swindlers, second-story men, gangsters and murderers. Few Fallon clients ever spent a day in jail pending trial. Even if a Fallon client were not acquitted, he almost certainly benefitted from long delays due to hung juries. The novelist Donald Henderson Clarke called Fallon "the Jail Robber."

A large number of Fallon's cases never made it to a courtroom. Fallon paid off cops and bought people working in district attorneys' offices who could see to it that the evidence against his clients disappeared. On one occasion, during a court recess, the prosecutor was called to the telephone; he took along his briefcase, which contained the prosecution's case against the defendant. On the telephone, he was startled to hear an anonymous female voice inform him his wife was guilty of infidelity. The prosecutor walked out of the telephone booth in a daze and down the corridor. When he remembered his briefcase and went back for it, it had "disappeared." In court, Fallon demanded the trial continue; without the state's key evidence, his client was cleared.

Unlike those defense lawyers who never take on murder cases when the evidence is overwhelming, in order to protect their claim of never losing a client to the electric chair, Fallon took on any number of individuals who seemed doomed. Still, not one of his clients ever went to the chair. In 12 years before the New York bar, he defended about 100 murderers. About 60 percent of them were acquitted, and the rest got off with comparatively light sentences. Fallon's technique was to badger prosecutors and judges, confuse prosecution witnesses, and fool jurors. Above all, his specialty was producing a hung jury. He would address his entire summation to a single juror, picking out the one he judged to be most susceptible to such flattery. After some years a Hearst newspaper would point to Fallon's almost endless record of cases with juries hung by 1-to-11 votes. When he judged his skills were not winning the battle, Fallon was not above bribing a juror. He often paid them off in the courthouse elevator, giving them half in advance and half afterwards. He reputedly never made a second payment.

His courtroom performances were replete with trickery. In one case he defended a Russian who stood accused of arson and against whom the case looked strong indeed. The man twice previously had been convicted of setting fire to stores he had owned in attempts to bilk insurance companies. Fallon realized his only hope was to discredit the prosecution's witnesses. A fireman testified to entering the burning structure and smelling kerosene on a number of wet rags. Fallon insisted the rags were soaked with water and demanded the fireman submit to a test to see if he could tell the difference. The lawyer produced five bottles number 1, 2, 3, 4 and 5 and asked the fireman to sniff the contents of each and say if it was kerosene or water. The fireman sniffed bottle number 1 and announced it was kerosene. So too were bottles 2, 3, 4 and 5, he declared.

Fallon then took a sip of bottle number 5 and told the jury: "The contents of this bottle does not taste like kerosene to me. This bottle—this bottle that the gentleman on the witness stand would have you believe contains kerosene—doesn't contain kerosene at all. It contains water. When you get into the jury room, I wish you would all help yourself to a taste of its contents. If what you taste in the slightest resembles kerosene, I think it is your duty to convict my client. If what you taste is water, then it is your duty to acquit my client."

Fallon's client was of course acquitted because the liquid was pure water. What he had done was to have the fireman inhale deeply of the first four bottles all of which contained kerosene. Then when he sniffed the water, the fumes from the first four bottles were still in his nostrils.

In 1924 Fallon himself was brought to trial for allegedly bribing a juror in one of his 1-to-11 specialties. Reporters for Hearst's *New York American* had followed a number of jurors who had voted the Fallon way until they found one who was spending an unseemly amount of money after being the lone holdout in a jury hearing the case against two stock swindlers. It appeared Fallon had extracted $25,000 from his clients for the bribing of the juror, offered the man $5,000, given him $2,500 and kept the balance.

The juror confessed, and Fallon was brought up on charges. The famous lawyer ran his own defense, even putting himself on the stand, and proceeded to make William Randolph Hearst, rather than William Joseph Fallon, the defendant. The lawyer insisted Hearst had trumped up the charges because he, Fallon, had gone to Mexico and uncovered the birth certificates of twins fathered by Hearst with a well-known Hollywood actress. While the jurors sat agog at the testimony, the prosecution tried to knock out all references to Hearst. But the point had been scored. It took the jury only five hours, with time out for dinner, to bring in a not-guilty verdict.

Fallon bounded out of his chair and thanked each juror, and then as the crowds of well-wishers thinned out, he approached the press table, where Nat Ferber, the *American* reporter who had dug up the case against him, was sitting. "Nat," he whispered, "I promise you I'll never bribe another juror!"

Actually, Fallon went on operating the way he always had for another couple of years, but by then drink was taking its toll. He died in 1927 of heart disease complicated by alcoholism. He was only 41.

## Finch, Mrs. Barbara (1923–1959)
### murder victim

The murder of Mrs. Barbara Finch by her California doctor husband and his mistress was one of the most sensational in recent decades. The case required three jury trials before a verdict was given.

Dr. Raymond Bernard Finch and his wife were prominent in social circles in Los Angeles and popular members of the Los Angeles Tennis Club. By 1957 the couple had drifted apart and Dr. Finch, using another name, rented an apartment where he regularly met with a 20-year-old married ex-model, Carole Tregoff. In 1958 Tregoff got a divorce, but Finch's wife refused to give him one.

Finally, she decided to seek a divorce. Under California divorce laws, when the grounds for divorce are desertion, cruelty or adultery, the courts can award all the property to the innocent party instead of dividing it equally. Suing on grounds of desertion, Mrs. Finch claimed all the property, including her husband's interest in a medical center, and demanded heavy alimony. If she won, Dr. Finch would have been left in virtual poverty.

Thereafter, according to later court testimony, Dr. Finch and Tregoff sought to obtain compromising evidence against the doctor's wife and, for that purpose, involved a petty crook named John Patrick Cody to make love to her. Later, according to Cody, he was offered money to kill Mrs. Finch. Cody said Carole Tregoff offered him $1,400 to shoot her. He claimed she stated, "If you don't kill her, Dr. Finch will . . . and if he won't, I'll do it."

On July 18, 1959 Dr. Finch and Carole Tregoff drove to the Finch home for a conference with Mrs. Finch. There was a shot, and Mrs. Finch lay dead on the driveway with a .38 bullet in her back. Dr. Finch's version was that during an argument his wife had pointed a gun at him and he had seized it and tossed it over his shoulder. The gun went off, he said, and fatally wounded his wife.

The prosecution's version was somewhat different. It claimed the pair had come to the Finch home with a so-called murder kit for the purpose of killing Mrs. Finch. The first plan, according to the prosecution, called for injecting an air bubble in her bloodstream; and if that failed, injecting a lethal dose of sodium seconal. An alternate plan, the prosecution contended, involved driving the unconscious woman over a cliff in back of the house. The prosecution contended the shooting was deliberate and presented scientific testimony that "the woman was in flight" when shot.

Dr. Finch took the stand and, with tears coursing down his face, gave a heartrending version of his wife's last words to him after the "accident." They were: "I'm sorry . . . I should have listened to you . . . I love you . . . take care of the kids. . . ." It was a rather novel defense, almost as though the victim was apologizing for being killed.

Nevertheless, the doctor's testimony was effective, resulting in a hung jury after eight days of deliberations. Finch and Tregoff, who had not spoken a word to each other throughout the trial, were retried a second time and again the jury failed to agree. On the third try, Dr. Finch was convicted of first-degree murder and Carole Tregoff of second-degree. Both were sentenced to life imprisonment. As they left the courtroom, Finch tried to kiss Tregoff but she turned away. Carole Tregoff was paroled in 1969; she never answered any of the many letters Finch wrote to her. Dr. Finch was freed in 1971.

## "Four Hundred" assassination list
### Secret Service suspects

In the social world, the Four Hundred is a reference to status, but the "400" listing put together by the Secret Service's Protective Research Section refers to the most active potential political assassins in this country. Obviously, the 400 is not a complete or definitive grouping, but it does represent an effort to glean the most likely candidates for political violence out of a computer listing of 30,000 suspects maintained by the Secret Service.

Most of the persons on the larger list have made verbal or written threats against the president or are suspect for some other reason. They are routinely checked on whenever the president visits their locality. Members of the 400 are subjected to closer scrutiny. Since they are often mentally disturbed or have a history of violence, every effort is made to keep them far away from a presidential appearance. If legal or family restraints prove ineffective, the 400 suspect is put under close surveillance, an operation which may require the work of as many as 15 agents on a 24-hour basis.

Watching the 400 to make sure they don't harm the president can be dangerous for the agents. Many of them are well known to the agents, and this familiarity is a danger in itself. A case in point occurred in 1979. That year the Secret Service had Joseph Hugh Ryan committed to a mental hospital outside Washington, D.C. after he tried to break through a gate at the White House. Following his release, Ryan turned up in the Denver, Colo. office of the Secret Service to complain that he was being harassed by agents. Stewart Watkins tried to calm him down, but when the agent moved close to him, Ryan draw a .45-caliber pistol from under his coat and shot Watkins twice, killing him. Another agent then shot Ryan dead as the killer tried to turn his weapon on him.

Of course, neither the 400 grouping nor the larger computer listing is foolproof. Sara Jane Moore did not qualify for either of them despite the fact that she had threatened to kill President Gerald Ford and had one of her guns confiscated by San Francisco police the day before she took a potshot at the president in 1975. Moore was interviewed by two Secret Service agents but found to be "not of sufficient protective interest to warrant surveillance." Although she had a long history of erratic behavior, her name was not put on the computer listing because of the fact that she was simultaneously an informer for the FBI, the San Francisco police and the Treasury Department's Bureau of Alcohol, Tobacco and Firearms. It is possible that the Secret Service considered Moore's "kookie behavior" merely a cover for her other activities.

## Gentlemen's Riot

Easily the "classiest" riot in American history was staged in 1835 in Boston by the "broadcloth mob," a crowd of 3,000 wealthy and socially prominent men, most of whom were dressed in broadcloth. On October 21 they gathered to protest a lecture being given by the famous English abolitionist George Thompson on behalf of the Boston Female Anti-Slavery Society. The mob planned to tar and feather the speaker, but Thompson had been forewarned and fled the city. The mob, angered at losing the victim, vented its frustration on William Lloyd Garrison, who published the antislavery newspaper *Liberator*. Garrison was bound with ropes and hauled away some distance, and by this time it was probably uncertain if the intent was a tar and feathering or a hanging. Garrison, however, was rescued by a number of friends and the police who carried him through the crowd to the city jail and kept him there overnight for protection. The disturbance became known as the Gentlemen's Riot. No convictions ever resulted.

## Gillette, Chester (1884–1908) murderer

Chester Gillette was the real-life Clyde Griffiths of Theodore Dreiser's classic novel *An American Tragedy*.

An ambitious factory worker who wanted to make it into high society, Gillette worked at his uncle's skirt factory in Cortland, N.Y. As the relative of a well-to-do businessman in town—Gillette had been deserted at the age of 14 by his own parents, who had gone off around the country to spread the Salvation Army gospel—he was accepted into local society and could look ahead to the time when he would marry a wealthy girl. Those future plans, however, did not prevent Gillette from partaking in the pleasures of the present, especially an affair with Billie Brown, an 18-year-old secretary at the factory.

Things went along well for the 22-year-old youth up to the time he received a letter from Billie saying she was pregnant. She did not ask Gillette to marry her but kept sending him heart-rending letters, which were intended sooner or later to persuade him to "do the right thing." Gillette ignored Billie's plight until she wrote warning him that she would tell his uncle. Seeing his world threatened, Gillette informed Billie he not only would do right by her but also intended to take her on a glorious holiday.

On July 8 the couple spent the night in Utica, registering in a hotel as man and wife, and from there moved on to the North Woods section of the southern Adirondacks. After some time at Tupper Lake, they moved on to Big Moose Lake, where Gillette asked for "any old hotel where they have boats to rent." They were sent to the Glenmore Hotel, where Billie registered under her right name while Gillette used a phony. They got separate rooms.

On the morning of July 11, the couple took along a picnic lunch and a tennis racket and rowed out on the large lake. Chester Gillette was not seen again until almost 8 o'clock that evening; Billie Brown was never seen alive again. Her body washed ashore at Big Moose Lake on July 14. The medical report revealed that she had died from blows to her face, which had been badly battered, not from drowning. The same day, Gillette was arrested for murder at the Arrowhead Hotel on Eagle Bay, where he had since registered. Under some newturned moss on the shore, the police found a buried tennis racket and asserted it was what Gillette had used to kill Billie. He denied it and told many conflicting stories. One was that Billie had committed suicide by jumping overboard; another was that the boat had capsized accidentally and that she had drowned after hitting her face on the side of the boat.

During Gillette's trial, which lasted 22 days, 109 witnesses appeared. So many of them came from the Cortland skirt factory that it had to shut down. Numerous women said they could not believe this charming, calm and handsome young man was capable of murder. From his cell Gillette sold photos of himself for $5 apiece and thus could afford to have his meals sent in from the local inn. Despite what his female supporters thought, the jury found differently, convicting him of premeditated murder. After more than a year of appeals, Chester Gillette went to the electric chair at Auburn Prison on March 30, 1908, refusing to admit his guilt.

### Gonzales, Thomas A. (1878–1956) medical examiner

Dr. Thomas A. Gonzales, chief medical examiner of New York City from 1937 to 1954, was recognized as one of the country's foremost forensic pathologists. His evidence convicted hundreds of murderers and saved a number of other innocent men, some of whom were accused of crimes that never happened. Often Dr. Gonzales needed only a moment's view of the corpse to tell immediately, for instance, that a husband who strangled his wife had tried to make it appear a case of suicide by gas inhalation.

Clearing an innocent suspect gave Dr. Gonzales the most satisfaction. Such was the case when an elderly tenant was found dead 15 minutes after he had had a heated argument with a muscular real estate agent over the rent and repairs. The old man's body was discovered just inside the door of his apartment, his face bruised and marked and his scalp deeply gashed. Several pieces of furniture in the foyer were overturned or moved out of position. Police learned of the angry dispute from neighbors and arrested the agent. He denied striking the old tenant, but the case against him was strong indeed. There was the confrontation, the obvious signs of a fight, a witness in the hallway who said no one entered the apartment after the agent left and the fact that the victim was dead just a quarter of an hour later.

Dr. Gonzales inspected the scene, diagrammed the position of the furniture and then performed an autopsy. As a result, charges against the real estate man were dropped. The old man had not been beaten to death. He had suffered a heart attack and stumbled around the foyer, displacing the furniture in his death throes. The diagrams of the furniture placement demonstrated how the old man had suffered each of the injuries he received.

Dr. Gonzales, a tall, spare man, was one of the top assistants to Dr. Charles Norris, who founded the Medical Examiner's Office in 1918. He took over following Dr. Norris' death in 1935, first as acting head and later as the chief medical examiner, after outscoring all other competitors in the tests given for the position. During his career he testified in many famous cases in New York and elsewhere in the country and coauthored *Legal Medicine and Toxicology,* still regarded as a classic in the field. He often said only medicine could solve many cases.

One common puzzle in many violent deaths was whether the cause had been homicide or suicide. He once proved that a man who had allegedly stabbed himself through his shirt had actually been murdered. (Suicides, he found, almost invariably preferred to strip away their clothing before stabbing themselves.) In another case Gonzales solved a stabbing that had police baffled. A man was found stabbed through the heart in a third-floor bathroom that was locked from the inside. The only window had been painted shut. It was clearly a case of suicide except there was no knife. The case was a stumper for the detectives but not for the medical examiner. "Never mind what happened here," he told the police. "See if you can find out about a knife fight anywhere in the area." The police checked and found that the victim had been stabbed in an altercation. As Dr. Gonzales later explained, it was quite possible for a man stabbed in the heart to walk a block, climb a couple of flights of stairs, lock himself in a bathroom and then finally collapse. Such victims often head for the bathroom to clean themselves up, not realizing they have been fatally wounded.

Dr. Gonzales retired in 1954 and died two years later.

## Graham, Barbara (1923–1955) murderess

Barbara Graham was a call girl and murderess who worked with a California gang of notoriously savage robbers and killers who often tortured their victims to extract loot from them. She was subsequently immortalized in *I Want to Live!,* perhaps the phoniest movie ever made about a female criminal.

Admittedly, Barbara was the product of an unhappy childhood. When she was two years old, her mother was sent to a reformatory for wayward girls, and Barbara was raised in a rather indifferent manner by neighbors. Later, mother and daughter were reunited, but Barbara ran away at the age of nine. Ironically, she ended up doing time in the same institution where her mother had been confined.

Barbara was drawn into organized crime circles in the 1940s. In 1947 she was a star call girl in San Francisco for Sally Stanford, the city's most infamous madam. Following her fourth marriage, to a man named Henry Graham, she gave birth to her third child and took up drugs. She also joined a murderous

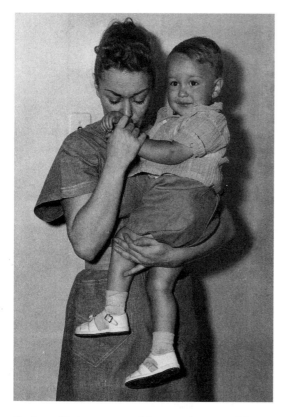

Barbara Graham, on trial for murder, posed for photographers with her 19-month-old son.

robbery ring headed by Jack Santos. Santos' gang included Emmett Perkins, second-in-command, a brute as vicious as Santos himself; John L. True, a deep-sea diver who later turned state's evidence; and Baxter Shorter, who eventually tried to turn state's evidence, was kidnapped and was never seen again.

Among the crimes the gang committed were the December 1951 torture and robbery of a gold buyer, Andrew Colner, and his wife; the December 1951 murder of Edmund Hansen, a gold miner; the October 1952 murder of a grocer, Guard Young, his two little daughters and a neighbor's child; and the March 1953 brutal beating murder of Mrs. Mabel Monahan, a 63-year-old crippled Bur-

bank widow believed to have had a large amount of jewels.

Of these crimes the only one that Barbara Graham was definitely tied to, primarily by True's confession, was the Monahan killing. She was to get the gang into the house by asking to use the telephone. According to True, the original plan called for the four men to crowd in as soon as the door was opened, tie up, gag and blindfold Mrs. Monahan and then ransack the house, grab the treasure and leave. The plan went awry when Barbara ran amok.

She struck the widow to the ground, seized her by the hair and began beating her over the head with the butt of the gun she was carrying. The old woman, bewildered and in agony, started moaning, "Oh, no, no, no!" One of the men egged Barbara on, "Give her more!" She did, cracking her skull and killing her. Later, a veteran prosecutor was to tell a jury the victim looked "as if she had been hit with a heavy truck traveling at high speed. The savage brutality of the attack is like nothing I have seen in 20 years of experience. I can scarcely believe that human beings could do that to an elderly woman against whom they had nothing, merely because they wanted money."

The gang, however, got no money. There was no large sum in the house and no valuable jewelry. They had simply been misinformed.

At her trial Barbara tried to prove her innocence by producing two alibis, both of which were probably false. Meanwhile, a police officer posing as an underworld agent offered to furnish her another alibi if she paid $25,000. Barbara agreed, and the plot was then exposed in court complete with taped recordings. Barbara lost her composure and cried out chokingly: "Oh, have you ever been desperate? Do you know what it means not to know what to do?"

On June 3, 1955 Barbara Graham, Santos and Perkins died in the San Quentin gas chamber. Barbara asked for a blindfold. "I don't want to have to look at people," she said bitterly.

In 1958 actress Susan Hayward won an Academy Award for her film portrayal of Barbara Graham.

**Grant, Ulysses S.** (1822–1885) traffic offender
Both before and after he entered the White House, Ulysses S. Grant was a notorious speedster with horse and rig. On at least two occasions, Grant, while in command of the Union armies, was fined $5 in precinct court. Such an offense was not so readily handled during Grant's first presidential term. President Grant was apprehended in the nation's capital for racing his horse and buggy at breakneck speed on M Street between 11th and 12th. The arresting constable, a man named William H. West, was dragged some 50 feet after seizing the horse's bridle. When Constable West recognized Grant, he started to apologize, but the president said, "Officer, do your duty." The horse and rig were impounded for a time but finally returned to Grant when no charges were pressed. A constitutional dilemma developed, much as it would a century later in the Watergate scandal, about whether it was possible to indict a president without first impeaching him.

**Graves, Thomas T.** (1843–1893) murderer
The murder of a rich elderly lady named Josephine Barnaby by Dr. Thomas Graves in 1891 ranked as New England's second most celebrated mystery during the 1890s, sur-

passed only by the case of Lizzie Borden. What especially offended the Victorian mores of the day was that a physician had done in his patient for profit. It was something "doctors don't do," a contemporary account noted.

The estranged wife of a Providence, R.I. businessman, Mrs. Barnaby inherited a paltry $2,500 upon her husband's death. Dr. Graves, who had treated the woman for a number of years, masterminded Mrs. Barnaby's campaign to reverse the will and eventually succeeded. The grateful widow gave her doctor power of attorney over her finances, whereupon the good doctor proceeded to loot her assets.

To make the task easier, Dr. Graves prescribed long trips for his patient's health. The old woman eventually grew suspicious, and when she insisted upon returning home and taking charge of her own affairs, the doctor warned her that he might have her declared incompetent and put in a home for the aged. Initially, Mrs. Barnaby was too petrified to protest any further, but then she let the doctor know she was returning from California and planned to take care of her estate personally.

On her trip back home, Mrs. Barnaby stopped off in Denver, Colo. to visit with a friend, a Mrs. Worrell. When she arrived there, she was greeted with a package from the East. It contained a bottle of whiskey on which was pasted a note reading: "Wish you a Happy New Year's. Please accept this fine old whiskey from your friend in the woods."

The two women used the whiskey in mixed drinks, found it rather "vile" but downed it all. Both of them died six days later. When the gift of whiskey was discovered, one of Mrs. Barnaby's daughters financed an autopsy on her body that turned up evidence of poison. Suspicion soon centered on Dr. Graves, who was much reviled in the press despite his denials of the crime. But suspicion was one thing and proof another, and although Dr. Graves was arrested, he was soon released on $30,000 bail. The lack of proof of any connection between the doctor and the poisoned whiskey made it appear that he would eventually be cleared, and numerous patients continued to visit him, declaring their belief in his innocence.

However, at Dr. Graves' trial the prosecution brought forth a newly discovered witness, a young man named Joseph Breslyn who told of Dr. Graves approaching him in November 1890 in the Boston train station and asking him to write a note, claiming he himself could not write. This was the note pasted on the poisoned whiskey bottle. Convicted, Graves was awaiting a retrial after a successful appeal when he committed suicide in April 1893 with poison smuggled into his jail cell.

## Greenlease, Robert C., Jr. (1947–1953)
kidnap-murder victim

The first major kidnapping of the post–World War II period was the abduction of six-year-old Bobby Greenlease, Jr., the son of a wealthy Kansas City, Mo. automobile dealer, on September 28, 1953. Using the ruse that the child's mother had suffered a heart attack and was calling for her son, one of the kidnappers, 41-year-old Bonnie Brown Heady, posed as the boy's aunt to get him out of the French Institute of Notre Dame de Scion, one of the city's most exclusive schools for small children.

She and her accomplice, Carl Austin Hall, the 34-year-old ne'er-do-well son of a respected lawyer and an alcoholic who had turned to crime, then drove the Greenlease boy across the state line to Kansas, where Hall attempted to strangle him in a field. The feisty youngster fought back fiercely, several times breaking from Hall's grasp and striking back. Finally, Hall drew a revolver from his pocket and shot the child twice.

The kidnappers put the corpse back in their car and later buried it in the garden of Mrs. Heady's home in St. Joseph, Mo. Then, by letter and telephone, they demanded and received $600,000 in ransom from their victim's frantic parents. It took several fouled-up efforts to get the money to the kidnappers, but the child was not returned. On October 6, 1953 the two were arrested by police in St. Louis after they had gone on a drunken spree and attracted the suspicions of a cab driver.

Justice came swiftly. They were found guilty the following month, and on December 18, 1953 they died together in the gas chamber. As they were strapped into their chairs, Bonnie Heady's main concern was that her lover not be bound too tightly. "You got plenty of room, honey?" she asked. Hall replied, "Yes, Mama." The gas was turned on and they died.

An unanswered question was what happened to that part of the ransom money that Hall had placed in two metal suitcases. After the pair's arrest the suitcases were brought to the Eleventh Precinct Station in St. Louis. When the money was counted, it totaled only $295,140. Since the couple had spent just a few thousand dollars, the FBI determined, the missing amount was $301,960. It was an open secret that the FBI suspected a member or members of the St. Louis police force, but no charges were ever lodged.

## Guiteau, Charles Julius (1844–1882) assassin of James A. Garfield

It is generally agreed that no assassin today could kill a president of the United States with the ease that Charles J. Guiteau, a disgruntled office seeker, shot President James A. Garfield in a Washington railroad station on July 2, 1881. First of all, it is doubtful an assassin could get as close as he got. Moreover, Guiteau fired and missed on his first shot: now, he would almost certainly be dropped before he had a chance to squeeze the trigger a second time.

Only after Guiteau's second shot did the president's guards pin his arms behind him and hustle him off to jail. It may have been the quietest assassination on record. But the president did not die immediately, lingering the whole hot summer with a bullet lodged so deep behind his pancreas that an operation to remove it was impossible. He finally died, after much suffering, on September 19, 1881.

"How could anybody be so cold-hearted as to want to kill my baby?" Garfield's mother asked.

Guiteau was eager to answer the question. He was busy in his jail cell writing his memoirs. He had had an erratic background as a sort of self-styled lawyer. Abandoning his wife, a 16-year-old waif he found in the streets, he had moved to Washington, D.C., where he did volunteer work for the Republican Party and picked up syphilis. When Garfield won the nomination, Guiteau mailed the candidate a disjointed speech he had written for Garfield to use and passed printed copies of it at meetings. Garfield never utilized the unsolicited speech, but Guiteau became convinced that his words provided Garfield with his margin of victory and thereby petitioned the newly elected president for the post of ambassador to France. He did not get it and resolved to gain vengeance by shooting Garfield. He bought a .44-caliber pistol and practiced shooting at trees along the Potomac. When he considered

Charles J. Guiteau shoots President Garfield in a Washington railroad station.

himself a credible marksman, he started dogging Garfield. When he was unsure of the president's schedule on a certain day, he simply asked the White House doorman, who told him. He once got near to Garfield in church but decided not to shoot because he feared others would be hit. On another occasion he passed up a golden opportunity to shoot the president because Mrs. Garfield was present, and Guiteau considered her "a dear soul."

Shortly before he finally shot Garfield Guiteau visited the District of Columbia jail to see what his future accommodations would be like and concluded it was "an excellent jail."

Brought to trial two months after the president's death, Guiteau subjected the courtroom to venomous outbursts during the 10½-week trial. He leaped up and launched into long diatribes against the witnesses and called them "dirty liars." The prosecutor was alternately "a low-livered whelp" and an "old hog." At other times, he was most civil; after the Christmas and New Year's recesses, Guiteau assured the judge that he "had a very happy holiday."

When in his cell, Guiteau made a point of strutting back and forth behind the bars so that visitors and crowds outside could gawk at him. In his own defense, he told the jurors that God had told him to kill. "Let your verdict be, it was the Deity's act, not mine," he demanded. When he was found guilty, he shook his finger at the jury box and snarled, "You are all low, consummate jackasses!"

In the days before his scheduled execution, Guiteau was relaxed and unrepentant during his waking hours, but his jailers insisted he moaned all night and slept in terror with his blankets over his head. At dawn on June 30, 1882, the date of his execution, Guiteau insisted on shining his shoes. He ate a hearty meal and memorized a poem he had written to recite on the scaffold. Guiteau went silently to the gallows, but after mounting the scaffold, he wept for a moment and, as the hangman came forward, recited his verse. "I am going to the Lordy," it started.

Then Guiteau was gone.

**Hargraves, Dick** (1824–1882) gambler and killer
Probably the epitome of the Mississippi gambler, Dick Hargraves cut a dapper and deadly figure on the river in the 1840s and 1850s.

A fashion plate who ordered boots from Paris and clothing from his native England, Hargraves came to New Orleans at the age of 16 and went to work as a bartender. He turned to professional gambling after winning $30,000 in a legendary poker game. Thereafter, he was a fixture on the river, where he became famous as an honest but pitiless gambler. Since at least 90 percent of all Mississippi gamblers were dishonest operators, Hargraves prided himself on being "square" and always felt that characteristic made it totally unnecessary for him to feel any sympathy for those he won money from. He supposedly shot at least eight or 10 men who sought vengeance after losing their money and often all their possessions to him. At the peak of his prosperity, Hargraves was worth an estimated $2 million.

As the best-known gambler in New Orleans, it was inevitable that women would be attracted to Hargraves. One of his numerous affairs resulted in scandal and death rivaling a Greek tragedy. Hargraves became involved with a banker's wife and was challenged to a duel by the enraged husband. He killed the banker with dispatch, and when the dead man's brother warned he would shoot the gambler on sight, Hargraves met him at a Natchez-under-the-Hill gambling den and killed him in a desperate battle. When Hargraves returned to New Orleans, the banker's widow stabbed him and then committed suicide. He recovered from his wounds and married a girl whose life he had saved in a fire. Tired of river gambling, he joined a filibustering campaign to Cuba and during the Civil War served as an officer in the Union Army. After the war Hargraves, a wealthy but ill man, moved to Denver, where he died of tuberculosis in 1882.


**Harris, Jean** (1923– ) "he done her wrong"
Certain cases rise little above the level of the tawdry in their facts but take on special import because of the role they play in influencing social attitudes affecting the American

Jean Harris' murder of the famous "Scarsdale Diet" doctor, Herman Tarnower, energized many women in their demands for social equality in court.

scene. Many crime aficionados would eschew Jean Harris' murder of famous "Scarsdale Diet" doctor Herman Tarnower as a minor event in the annals of homicide. She shot him, made no real effort to escape, was easily apprehended and insisted it was an accident resulting from a lover's quarrel. However, the Harris-Tarnower case had an important impact on the nation's views, occurring as it did on the tide of rising female expectations and demands for social equality with men. For decades, verdicts delivered in "heat of the moment" legal cases were seldom harsh. Jean Harris represented fair

turnaround, or, as one female put it in a reversal of a popular refrain, "He done her wrong."

On March 10, 1980, Dr. Tarnower, the 69-year-old cardiologist and author of the best-selling book *The Complete Scarsdale Medical Diet,* which brought him millions, was shot and killed in the bedroom of his luxurious home in Purchase, N. Y. The police were summoned by the Tarnower maid and picked up 56-year-old Jean S. Harris before she drove away.

Harris, a cultured woman and headmistress of the exclusive Madeira School for Girls in McLean, Va., had had a love affair with Tarnower for 14 years. Known to her students as "Integrity Harris," she had spent many weekends and vacations with the doctor and had helped him in the writing of his book. Over the years, Tarnower had spoken often of marriage to Harris but had called off an impending wedding on one occasion. During the years, Harris had shut her eyes to the more than 30 relationships Tarnower had maintained with other women, and she had tolerated other women's nightclothes, underwear, cosmetics, and the like, which littered the Tarnower bedroom.

But it was Mrs. Lynne Tryforos, 18 years younger than Harris, whom the headmistress came to regard as her main threat. The two women carried on a fierce struggle for the doctor's affections, cutting up each other's clothes, and Harris accusing Tryforos of making obscene phone calls. Harris contemplated plastic surgery as a means to regain the doctor's affections.

Just a few days before Tarnower's death, Harris mailed him a letter from Virginia, calling Tryforos a "dishonest adultress . . . a slut and a psychotic whore."

Hoping to spend the weekend with Tarnower, Harris drove up from Virginia and arrived in advance of her letter. She and the doctor got into a violent argument in the bedroom after Harris came across a nightgown and hair curlers belonging to some other woman. In the ensuing struggle, Harris pulled a .32-caliber handgun from her purse, and the doctor began pushing her and was heard to cry out, "Get out of here. You're crazy."

Four shots were fired, and Tarnower keeled over, bleeding profusely. He died about an hour later in the hospital. Meanwhile, Harris gave a rambling statement to the police who apprehended her. "He wanted to live," she said. "I wanted to die." She claimed she had carried the revolver and a number of amphetamines to give her courage, saying she had planned to persuade Tarnower to shoot her and that her shooting of him (with three hits) had been accidental.

Harris' three-month-long trial started in November 1980 and was a field day for the tabloid press, as much testimony centered on Tarnower's lifestyle and love affairs. A great deal was made of the intimate clothing so many women had left behind. At one point, even Harris' own underwear was introduced as evidence, much to her discomfort.

Although many women sympathized with Harris and felt she had been demeaned by Tarnower, the jury of eight women and four men found that she had deliberately set out to kill the lover who had spurned her. On March 20, 1981, she was sentenced to a mandatory term of 15 years to life imprisonment. An attempt to gain clemency, which was supported by many women, failed, and she was confined at Bedford Hills Correctional Facility, not eligible for parole until 1996. Harris became active in prison reform and, in 1988, wrote a book entitled *They Always Call Us Ladies* about her prison experience.

Harris began experiencing heart problems and in January 1993, Harris, then 69, had her sentence commuted by Gov. Mario Cuomo, after serving not quite 12 years of her minimum 15-year term.

## Harris, William and Emily kidnappers of Patricia Hearst

The bizarre hunt for kidnapped heiress Patricia Hearst ended on September 18, 1975, when Hearst and 32-year-old Wendy Yoshimura were captured by the FBI in an apartment in the Mission District of San Francisco. About an hour earlier, William and Emily Harris, 30 and 26, respectively, were picked up on a street corner by FBI agents. The Harrises were considered to be the last of the Symbionese Liberation Army, a radical terrorist group that had taken Hearst from her Berkeley, Calif. apartment in February 1974. Some three months after her abduction, Hearst renounced her parents and said she was joining her SLA captors.

It appeared the Harrises had been with Hearst during virtually the entire period of her kidnapping and witnessed her startling behavioral conversion from prisoner to willing partner. In the San Francisco apartment agents found a portion of William Harris' autobiography describing the Hearst abduction and her later transformation to a willing member of the SLA, a development that startled the Harrises. The manuscript quoted Hearst as labeling her parents racists.

In August 1978 the Harrises pleaded guilty to "simple kidnapping" rather than to the more serious charge of "kidnapping for ransom and with great bodily harm." Before they were sentenced in October, William Harris accused Patricia Hearst and her family of "lies, distortions and exaggerations" about her life with the SLA. He said: "She was not brainwashed, beaten, tortured or raped. She was not coerced into rejecting her family and remaining with the people of the SLA." This had been Hearst's defense at her own trial on charges of taking part in a bank robbery with other SLA members.

With credit for time served and good behavior, the Harrises were released in 1983 and went their separate ways.

See also: PATRICIA HEARST.

## Harsh, George S. (1907–1980) murderer and war hero

Once sentenced to death for a senseless "thrill killing," George S. Harsh went on to become a much storied World War II hero and an author and spokesman against capital punishment.

In 1929 Harsh and Richard G. Gallory confessed to the shooting of a drugstore clerk during an Atlanta holdup that the newspapers called a thrill killing. The two were also charged in six other robberies and the killing of another clerk. Both defendants came from wealthy and socially prominent families. Harsh's family put up an elaborate and expensive defense, including testimony from 12 psychiatrists that he suffered from "psychological irresponsibility and hereditary taints." Harsh was nonetheless found guilty and sentenced to die in the electric chair, but this was later commuted to life imprisonment on a Georgia work gang. In 1940 he was granted a parole after helping to save a fellow inmate's life by performing an appendectomy on him.

Harsh joined the Royal Canadian Air Force. Shot down by the Germans, he was captured and sent to a Nazi prison camp. He played a key role in the tunnel breakout of 126 Allied soldiers from the camp, 50 of whom were later apprehended and executed. The movie entitled *The Great Escape* was based on this incident. Harsh was eventually freed from captivity, and after the war he turned to writing about his life and his moral redemption, relating his experiences in a book entitled *A Lonesome Road*. He also crusaded against capital punishment, writing in 1972: "Capital punishment is a law zeroed in on the poor, the underprivileged, the friendless, the uneducated and the ignorant. I was convicted of a senseless crime and sentenced to die in the electric chair. This sentence would have been carried out had I not come from a white, wealthy and influential family. This Mosaic law of death is drawn from the worst of all human motives, revenge."

Harsh died on January 25, 1980 in Toronto, Canada.

## Hart, Brooke (1911–1933) kidnapping and murder victim

The kidnap-murder of a 22-year-old hotel and department store heir in California in 1933 probably triggered more official approval of vigilantism than any other crime in this century.

Brooke Hart was seized by two 24-year-old youths of comfortable middle-class backgrounds, John Maurice Holmes and Thomas H. Thurmond, the latter having no criminal record at all. The pair abducted Hart as he left the family's department store in San Jose on November 9 and, using the victim's car, drove to the San Mateo–Hay-

Thomas Thurmond's body dangled from a tree after he was dragged from his cell by angry Californians and hanged. Gov. Sunny Jim Rolfe called the lynching "the best lesson ever given the country."

ward Bridge. Hart was knocked unconscious and his body, weighted down with cement blocks, heaved into the bay. Hart regained consciousness on hitting the water and, screaming, tried to stay afloat whereupon Thurmond shot him several times until his body disappeared. An hour later, the kidnappers were on the telephone to the victim's father, Alex Hart, demanding a ransom of $40,000 for the safe return of his son. Several more calls were necessary to arrange a pickup spot for the money, and on November 15 police traced a call to a San Jose garage and arrested Thurmond while he was still on the phone with the elder

Hart. Thurmond confessed and named Holmes as his accomplice, each man accusing the other of devising the plot and committing the murder.

On November 24, young Hart's body washed ashore and the San Jose community, especially the college students who knew Hart as a recent graduate, were enraged. By that evening, a crowd of 15,000 had gathered outside the jail where the two quarreling killers were being held in separate cells. The college students took up a cry of "We want a touchdown," a chant that chilled not only the prisoners but Sheriff William Emig as well. He called Gov. James "Sunny

Jim" Rolfe requesting troops, but his plea was rejected. Gov. Rolfe insisted there was no need. For the next several hours local and state police held off the crowd, which was growing bigger and more ugly by the minute. They held them back with high-powered hoses and tear gas but the mob continued to surge toward the jail. Alex Hart appeared on the scene and begged the would-be vigilantes to leave, but he was ignored. Not long before midnight, the mob moved in, battered down the jail door and poured past the handful of police guards. Holmes was attacked in his cell, stripped of his clothes and beaten so badly an eyeball dangled from its socket. When the mob located Thurmond's cell, they found it empty. Then while everyone grew silent, they could hear labored breathing and spotted him hiding in the pipes over the cell's toilet. Thurmond was beaten badly, dragged outside to a park and hanged from a tree. A pleading Holmes was hanged next, while the crowd chanted, "Get that ball!"

Authorities never charged anyone in the lynchings, although many identifications could have been made. Newspapers in California and the rest of the nation condemned the lynchings, but it was clear the popular and official California reaction approved of the acts. Gov. Rolfe described the lynchings as "the best lesson ever given the country. I would pardon those fellows if they were charged. I would like to parole all kidnappers in San Quentin and Folsom to the fine patriotic citizens of San Jose."

## Hearst, Patricia (1955– ) kidnap victim

Few crimes in recent history were as sensational and involved as many bizarre twists as the kidnapping of Patricia Hearst, who was taken from her Berkeley, Calif. apartment on February 5, 1974 by members of the Symbionese Liberation Army (SLA), a radical terrorist organization.

At first, the kidnappers offered to return the 19-year-old heiress if her father, newspaper publisher Randolph Hearst, would start a food program for the poor in the San Francisco Bay area. Later, however, a tape-recorded message from Patty said she had "chosen to stay and fight" with the SLA for the "freedom of the oppressed people." She adopted the SLA name of "Tania" and was subsequently linked to the armed robbery of a San Francisco bank on April 15. Hearst refused to believe his daughter was acting of her own free will, but photographs of the bank robbery and reports by eyewitnesses indicated she "absolutely was a participant." In later tapes sent by the SLA, Patty ridiculed the idea that she had been brainwashed.

Meanwhile, law enforcement authorities pressed their hunt for the handful of SLA members and cornered six of them in a Los Angeles hideout on May 17. All six including Donald DeFreeze, alias "Field Marshal Cinque," the alleged leader of the group died in an ensuing gun battle and fire. Actually, subsequent evidence indicated the real leaders were a dynamic female trio Patricia Soltysik, Nancy Ling Perry and Camilla Hall, all of whom perished with guns in their hands during the desperate shoot-out. Fears that Patty was among the dead proved unfounded, and although she was still missing, she was indicted on a charge of bank robbery.

Finally, 19 months after her original kidnapping, Patty Hearst was captured in a hideout in San Francisco. With her was 32-year-old Wendy Yoshimura, who had joined her after she had gone into hiding. The hunt ended with Patty telling FBI agents, "Don't shoot. I'll go with you." Just an hour earlier agents had arrested William and Emily Harris, the last remaining members of the SLA group that originally seized Patty.

At Patty's trial, defense attorney F. Lee Bailey stressed the brutality of the kidnapping by the SLA and claimed she had endured hardships and constant terrorization during her captivity. He argued the bank robbery had been staged by the SLA just to make Patty believe she could not return to society. The lawyer also said that DeFreeze had familiarity with brainwashing techniques and "knew just enough about this process to start it moving" on "a particularly vulnerable, frightened 19-year-old girl."

In her testimony Patty said her early treatment by her abductors had included a number of death threats. She insisted she had been forced to have sex with DeFreeze and another SLA member, William Wolfe. The prosecution presented psychiatric testimony to refute any contention that Patty had been anything but a "voluntary member of the SLA." Dr. Joel Fort cast doubt on her tale of sexual abuse while with the SLA, noting that she had been "sexually active at age 15," and Dr. Harry Kozol described her at the time of her kidnapping as a "rebel in search of a cause."

Patty Hearst was found guilty of the bank robbery charge and sentenced to seven years imprisonment. She served a total of 28 months, including time in prison before and after her trial. William and Emily Harris were given 10 years to life for the kidnapping.

When Hearst was released, she married and settled into what was described as a very establishment lifestyle. She was pardoned by President Clinton in January 2001.

See also: DOROTHY ALLISON, F. LEE BAILEY, WILLIAM AND EMILY HARRIS.

## Hecht, Ben (1894–1964) crime reporter

Many of the fascinating facts that typified novelist and playwright Ben Hecht's writing were drawn from his earlier experiences as a Chicago crime reporter. He started out as what was called a "picture chaser" for the *Chicago Journal,* assigned to acquire, by any means possible, photographs of ax murderers and the like and their victims, sometimes pilfering them from the family mantelpiece. Before long he advanced to reporter, which in the Chicago journalism of the day did not require an undue concern for accuracy.

Hecht became expert at writing stories that began, e.g., "If Fred Ludwig is hanged for the murder of his wife, Irma, it will be because of the little gold band he slipped on her finger on his wedding day, inscribed with the tender words, 'Irma—Love Forever—Fred.'"

If Hecht and his favorite crony, Charles MacArthur of the rival *Examiner* and later the *Daily News,* sometimes purpled their facts, they also solved many a case that had the police stumped. It was basically Hecht who cracked Chicago's famed Case of the Ragged Stranger, in which a pregnant woman named Mrs. Ruth Wanderer was shot by a ragged stranger as she and her husband were returning from a movie the night of June 21, 1920. At the time, her husband, Carl, according to his statement, was carrying the Colt .45 service automatic that he had kept upon discharge from the army after World War I, and he blazed back at the attacker. A total of 14 shots were fired, and when the smoke cleared, Mrs. Wanderer was dead and so was the ragged stranger. Only Carl Wanderer was unscathed.

Wanderer was celebrated in the press and by a public fearful about the rise in violent crime. But Hecht and MacArthur both were skeptical. MacArthur traced the gun found on the ragged stranger back to a relative of Carl Wanderer's. That man, a cousin, had given it to Wanderer. Hecht in the meantime befriended Wanderer and learned much of his private life, including that he was a homosexual who was appalled at the thought of being father to a woman's baby. When Hecht found letters Wanderer had written to a male lover, the husband confessed he had tricked an unidentified stranger, whom he had met in a skid row bar, into waiting in the vestibule for him. When he and his wife arrived, Wanderer pulled two guns and opened up on both his wife and the stranger.

Ironically, the two reporters spent much time with Wanderer in the death house at the Cook County Jail, playing cards with him (and winning his money), and prevailed upon him to read attacks on their city editors as his last words on the gallows. The reporters forgot that a condemned man is bound hand and foot when hanged. At his execution Wanderer could only glance unavailing at the speeches strapped to his side. Shrugging at the reporters, he did the next best thing he could think of, bursting forth in a rollicking version of "Dear Old Pal O' Mine."

After the trap was sprung, MacArthur turned to Hecht and said, "You know, Ben, that son of a bitch should have been a song plugger."

Even after Hecht went on to bigger and better things as an author, playwright and screenwriter, his Chicago crime-writing days came back to haunt him. In Hollywood during the early 1930s Hecht wrote the screenplay for *Scarface*, starring Paul Muni, for Howard Hughes' studio. One night there was a knock at his hotel room in Los Angeles, and two sinister-looking gentlemen confronted him with a copy of the screenplay.

"You the guy who wrote this?" one said, brandishing the script.

Hecht couldn't deny it.

"Is this stuff about Al Capone?"

"God, no!" Hecht assured them. "I don't even know Al." He rattled off the names of Chicago underworld characters he had known—Big Jim Colosimo, Dion O'Banion, Hymie Weiss.

His visitors seemed satisfied, one saying: "O.K. then. We'll tell Al this stuff you wrote is about them other guys." As they started to leave, however, the other one had a thought. "If this stuff isn't about Al Capone, why are you calling it *Scarface*? Everybody'll think it's him."

"That's the reason. Al is one of the most famous and fascinating men of our time. If you call the movie *Scarface*, everybody will want to see it, figuring it's about Al. That's part of the racket we call showmanship."

"I'll tell Al. Who's this fella Howard Hughes?"

"He got nothing to do with it. He's the sucker with the money."

"O.K. The hell with him." And Capone's men left placated.

## Helter Skelter   Manson murder code

Originally the title of a rock song by the Beatles, "Helter Skelter" took on a grim meaning within the notorious Charles Manson "family." In August 1969 the words were found printed in blood outside the home of two of the Manson family's murder victims, Leno and Rosemary La Bianca. The words meant, according to Manson, that blacks were destined to rise up and wipe out the entire white race, with only Manson and his family permitted to survive.

See also: CHARLES MANSON.

## Hill, Joan Robinson (1930–1969) alleged murder victim

One of the most notorious, headline-provoking murder cases in modern American history was the alleged "murder by omission" of beautiful and wealthy Joan Robinson Hill by her husband, a leading plastic surgeon in Houston, Tex. After he walked out free as a result of a mistrial, he was assassinated by a paid gunman, which kept the case boiling for years.

Joan Robinson was the daughter of oil multimillionaire Ash Robinson, a man who epitomized Texas-style money and power. Robinson was highly influential in state politics and had the ability to get what he wanted. But few things meant as much to him as Joan. She had been through a couple of marriages when she met Dr. John Hill in 1957. The two were married in a mammoth, Texas-sized wedding paid for by Ash Robinson. Hill's career kept him away from his wife a good deal, but Joan, an accomplished horsewoman, didn't seem to mind and old Ash was perfectly happy because he still had his daughter around so much of the time.

By 1968, however, the marriage was breaking up. Joan became aware that Hill was seeing other women. They argued often. In March 1969 Joan grew ill, and after considerable delay her husband put her in a small hospital, which didn't have the facilities to handle what developed into a very serious condition. During the course of her treatment, she had a sudden heart failure and died. The following morning a most peculiar event occurred. When doctors arrived to perform an autopsy, they found the body had been sent to a funeral home "by accident." Upon reaching the funeral home, they discovered the body had already been drained of fluids and was partly embalmed, making a

really thorough autopsy most difficult. Back at the hospital a brain said to be Joan Hill's showed signs of meningitis, but there was some reason to suspect it was not Joan's brain since the brain stem in the body failed to produce the same symptoms.

From the time of Joan's funeral, old Ash Robinson pressured the district attorney to get a murder charge brought against Hill. In addition, Robinson had a parade of his important friends approach the DA with the same demand. Then, three months after the death of his first wife, John Hill married a woman with whom he had been linked while his marriage to Joan was disintegrating. That galvanized Robinson to further action. He hired detectives to follow Hill and lined up medical testimony, even bringing in the New York City medical examiner to reexamine the body. Two grand juries were convened but both refused to indict Hill. A third grand jury, however, received some additional material. By that time, Hill's second wife, Ann, had divorced him and testified Hill had confessed to her that he had killed Joan. Moreover, she claimed Hill had tried to kill her on more than one occasion. Hill was indicted for murder by neglect, technically "murder by omission," in that he willfully denied his wife adequate medical attention.

Hill's murder trial ended in a mistrial when his second wife blurted out that Hill had told her he had killed Joan. Such a statement could not be permitted in court, since under the law she could only testify about the period before she married Hill.

Before a new trial could be held, Dr. Hill married a third time. Just after returning from his honeymoon in September 1972, he was shot and killed by an assassin wearing a Halloween mask. The murderer was identified as a young Houston hood, Bobby Vandiver, who had brought along a prostitute to keep him company while he waited to ambush Hill in the latter's home. Vandiver confessed he had gotten $5,000 for the job, and his story implicated a number of people, among them Ash Robinson. The killer said that Ash had let it be known he would pay for the execution of his ex-son-in-law and that his intermediary in the hit contract was a Houston woman named Lilla Paulus, a former prostitute and madam. The Paulus woman was indicted, but before her trial began, Bobby Vandiver was killed while attempting to escape jail. Despite this development, Paulus was convicted on the testimony of the young prostitute who had accompanied Vandiver. The prostitute, however, could produce no admissible evidence linking anyone else to the crime. Lilla Paulus was sentenced to life imprisonment but refused to implicate anyone else in the murder.

Following the verdict, Ash Robinson continued to deny to the press any involvement in Hill's murder. He successfully fended off a civil suit against him by the Hill family, and it appeared that with Joan Robinson dead, John Hill dead and Ash Robinson growing old, the Hill-Robinson murders were destined to remain one of the most bizarre mysteries of modern times. In 1981 a four-hour miniseries dramatization of the case was shown on television; it had already been the subject of a best-selling book, *Blood and Money* by Thomas Thompson. Joan Robinson was played by Farrah Fawcett, and the actress, or her publicity agent, took special pains to let it be known that Ash Robinson, the surviving principal in the case and then 84 years old, had voiced his "casting approval" of Farrah as the "ideal choice" to play his deceased daughter. Rumor also had

it that Robinson had suggested he portray himself in the film.

## Hinckley, John W., Jr. (1955– ) accused assailant of Ronald Reagan

On March 30, 1981 Ronald Reagan became the eighth sitting president of the United States to be subjected to an assassination attempt and the fourth—after Andrew Jackson, Harry Truman and Gerald Ford—to survive. Reagan was shot by a 25-year-old drifter, John W. Hinckley of Evergreen, Colo., as he left the Washington Hilton Hotel, where he had addressed a labor audience. The assailant was seized immediately after having fired four to six shots from a .22-caliber revolver, a type known popularly as a Saturday Night Special. The president was hit by a bullet that entered under the left armpit, pierced the chest, bounced off the seventh rib and plowed into the left lower lobe of the lung. Reagan froze for a moment at the door of his limousine and then was brusquely pushed inside the car by a Secret Service agent. Remarkably, the president did not realize he had been shot but thought he had simply been injured when shoved into the car. Only upon arrival at the hospital was it determined that he had been shot.

Also wounded were three others: the president's press secretary, James S. Brady; a Secret Service agent, Timothy J. McCarthy; and a District of Columbia police officer, Thomas K. Delahanty. All three survived, although Brady remained hospitalized for many months after the assassination attempt.

Hinckley turned out to be the son of an oil executive who had grown up in affluence in Dallas and moved with his family to Colorado in 1974. He had attended Texas Tech University on and off through 1980 but never graduated. At times he had traveled across the country, and in 1978 he had enrolled himself in the National Socialist Party of America, generally known as the Nazi Party of America. A spokesman for that organization said the group had not renewed Hinckley's membership the following year because of his "violent nature."

Hinckley had evidently flown from Denver to Los Angeles on March 25 and then boarded a Greyhound bus for Washington the following day, arriving March 29, the day before the attack. Following Hinckley's arrest for the attack on President Reagan, it was discovered that he had been in Nashville, Tenn. on October 9, 1980, when then-President Jimmy Carter was there. Hinckley was arrested at the airport in Nashville when X-ray equipment disclosed he had three handguns and some ammunition in his carry-on bag. The weapons were confiscated, and he paid a fine of $62.50. Despite his arrest, federal authorities did not place Hinckley under security surveillance thereafter. Four days after his release, Hinckley turned up in Dallas, where he purchased two .22-caliber handguns in a pawnshop. One of these weapons was alleged to have been used in the attack on Reagan.

A bizarre sidelight to the case was the discovery that Hinckley had been infatuated with movie star Jodie Foster, then a student at Yale University. He had written her several letters, and an unmailed letter dated March 30, 1981, 12:45 P.M.—one and three-quarter hours before the attack—was found in his Washington hotel room. It read:

> Dear Jody,
>     There is a definite possibility that I will be killed in my attempt to get Reagan. It is for this very reason that I am writing to you now.

Hinckley went on to say he loved her and that

> although we talked on the phone a couple of times, I never had the nerve to simply approach you and introduce myself . . . Jody, I would abandon this idea of getting Reagan in a second if I could only win your heart and live out the rest of my life with you, whether it be in total obscurity or whatever. I will admit to you that the reason I'm going ahead with this attempt now is because I just cannot wait any longer to impress you. I've got to do something now to make you understand in no uncertain terms that I am doing all this for your sake. By sacrificing my freedom and possibly my life, I hope to change your mind about me.

It appeared that Hinckley had been influenced in his alleged actions by the film *Taxi Driver,* in which Foster had played a child prostitute. At one point in the film, the protagonist, a taxi driver, is planning to assassinate a presidential candidate.

In August 1981 Hinckley was indicted by a federal grand jury in Washington, D.C. on charges of attempting to kill President Reagan as well as the other three men. The FBI reportedly concluded that Hinckley had acted alone. In a verdict that shocked the nation, he was acquitted by a jury on grounds of insanity. He was then committed to a mental institution.

### Hoffman, Harold Giles (1896–1954) governor and embezzler

One of the most flamboyant politicians in recent American history, Harold G. Hoffman lived a double life, that of an elected public official and an embezzler, whose total depredations remain undetermined. At the high point of his career, in 1936, he was groomed by New Jersey Republicans for president of the United States. At the low point in his life, in 1954, investigators closed in on him and he became an almost certain candidate for prison.

Hoffman was an army captain in World War I, a small-town banker, mayor of South Amboy, assemblyman, congressman, state commissioner of motor vehicles and, lastly, governor of New Jersey. At the age of 33, he began looting money. By the time he left the governorship in 1937, he had stolen at least $300,000, a considerable sum in Depression dollars. He spent the last 18 years of his life juggling monies in order to cover his embezzlements.

As near as could be determined, Hoffman started stealing from his South Amboy bank, dipping into dormant accounts to keep up his free-spending ways. Whenever an inactive account became active, Hoffman was able to shift money from another quiet account to cover his looting. Some of Hoffman's stolen funds went to promote his political career. Eventually, he reached Congress. Happily, Washington was not too far away from South Amboy, so he could keep a lid on things at the bank. When Hoffman suddenly left Congress to take the post of state commissioner of motor vehicles, which to many seemed a political step-down, some observers theorized that the move was part of Hoffman's plan to eventually run for governor, but the real reason was that he needed access to public funds. Sooner or later, an examiner might discover the shortages at the bank, so it was extremely advantageous for Hoffman to be able to juggle the funds of the motor vehicle department. When money had to be at the bank, it was there; when it had to be in the state coffers, it was there. In the

process, more and more stuck to Hoffman's fingers.

When Hoffman won the governorship at the age of 39, he enjoyed wide popularity in his state and grew to be a national political power. However, he became a center of controversy in the sensational Lindbergh kidnapping case. His interference and attempts to reopen the investigation after Bruno Richard Hauptmann was convicted brought him widespread criticism. When he granted Hauptmann a few months' reprieve, he provoked a storm of criticism. He would never again be elected to any public office. Upon completing his term, Hoffman was named director of the unemployment compensation commission, an agency with a budget of $600 million, and he was able to continue his money-juggling operations.

While still governor, Hoffman had become president of the Circus Saints and Sinners, a group devoted to the twin duties of providing help to old circus folk and providing themselves with a good time. Hoffman became known as a boisterous buffoon, but inside he must have been a frightened, lonely man trying to keep his crimes hidden.

In 1954 newly elected Gov. Robert B. Meyner suspended Hoffman pending investigation of alleged financial irregularities in his department. Exorbitant rentals were apparently being paid for some department offices, and the state's attorney general subsequently found that favored groups stood to make nearly $2 million from a modest investment of $86,854. Other irregularities appeared in the purchase of supplies.

Hoffman put up a joyous front. The day following his suspension he appeared before the Circus Saints and Sinners. Harry Hershfield, the famous wit, cracked, "I knew you'd get into trouble in Jersey, fooling with a

Meyner." Hoffman answered, "I can't even laugh." And he broke into raucous laughter.

The next two months, however, were lonely ones for Hoffman as he waited for the ax to fall. One morning in June he got up in the two-room Manhattan hotel suite provided by the Saints and keeled over with a fatal heart attack.

Later, more and more facts came out. The state became concerned when they discovered Hoffman had deposited $300,000 of public money in his own bank in a non-interest-bearing account. Officials then learned that not only was the interest missing but so was the principal.

Hoffman had written a confession to one of his daughters to be opened only upon his death. It said, ". . . until rather recently I have always lived in hope that I would somehow be able to make good, to get everything straight."

See also: LINDBERGH KIDNAPPING.

**Insull, Samuel** (1860–1938) **stock manipulator**

Among the most grandiose swindlers of the 20th century, Samuel Insull built up a multi-billion-dollar Midwest utility empire, one of the great financial marvels of the 1920s, by merging troubled small electric companies into an apparently smooth-running combine. He was hailed by the nation's press as the financial genius of the age, and lucky was the banker from whom Mr. Insull deigned to borrow money.

Clearly outdoing even Horatio Alger, Insull began his career as a 14-year-old dropout in his native London and rose to the pinnacle of high finance. He first worked as an office boy for $1.25 a week and later became a clerk for Thomas A. Edison's London agent. He was so impressive that he was recommended to Edison as a youth worth bringing to America, and the great inventor made him his secretary in 1881; Insull was 21 at the time.

Soon, Insull was handling the organization of several Edison companies, and by 1902 he was president of Chicago Edison. In 1907 he merged all the electric companies there into Commonwealth Edison. He then struck out on his own, joining small, often poorly run utilities into one operation. By the 1920s he was among the nation's richest men, worth $100 million, and people felt they were making the smartest investment in America when they purchased his stock.

The secret of Insull's success was to have one of his electric companies sell properties to another of his companies at a handsome profit over the original cost. The second company would not be hurt because it would later sell other properties to yet another Insull company. Thus, even in 1931, at the depths of the Depression, Insull's Middle West Utilities group reported the second most profitable year in its history. Of course, by this time Insull had to do more than sell properties to himself. He started cutting depreciation allowances in his various utilities or eliminating them entirely.

Then Insull had to spend huge sums—which he took in from gullible investors—to fight off takeover bids from other Wall Street operators eager to latch onto a strong financial organization. The problem was that if a takeover occurred the buyers would soon discover that Insull had done it all with mirrors. The swindler spent $60 million in the battle and won, but his financial empire was now so weak the bubble had to burst. The collapse came in June 1932, with investor losses estimated at $750 million.

Broke at the age of 72, Insull fled to Paris, where he lived on a yearly pension of $21,000 from a few companies of his that hadn't gone under. Facing extradition back to the United States on embezzlement and mail fraud charges, the old man left France and went to Greece. The Greek government let him stay a year but then bowed to U.S. pressure and ordered him out. For a time Insull drifted about the Mediterranean in a leased tramp steamer, but he finally had to put in at Instanbul for supplies. The Turks arrested him and shipped him back home for trial.

Because Insull's financial capers were so involved and often fell into areas where the law was not really clear, the government failed to prove its charges and he was able to go back to Paris. He dropped dead on a street there at the age of 78. At the time, he had assets of $1,000 cash and debts of $14 million.

### Irving, Clifford (1930– ) Howard Hughes book forger

In 1971 writer Clifford Irving pulled off what was undoubtedly the most celebrated literary hoax of the 20th century when he swindled the McGraw-Hill Book Co. out of $765,000 for a fake autobiography of billionaire recluse Howard R. Hughes. Irving also conned *Life* magazine, which planned to print excerpts of the book with 20 pages of handwritten letters by Hughes. After examining the letters, a

Clifford Irving's phony biography of Howard Hughes earned him a dubious distinction from *Time* magazine.

number of handwriting experts had declared all of them to be genuine.

Together with a friend who was a children's book author, Richard Suskind, Irving wrote an engrossing 1,200 page book, which veteran newsmen who had long covered the enigmatic Hughes found to be most "authentic." The scheme was so daring and so outrageous it was widely accepted even after Hughes said in a telephone call from his hideaway in the Bahamas that he had never met with Irving and that the work was "totally fantastic fiction." Irving's hoax was finally wrecked when a Swiss bank broke its vow of secrecy to reveal that a

$650,000 check from the book publisher to Hughes had been cashed in one Swiss bank by "H. R. Hughes" and deposited in another under the name "Helga R. Hughes"—actually Irving's wife.

On March 13, 1972 Irving pleaded guilty to federal conspiracy charges. He was forced to return what was left of the publisher's money and was sentenced to two and a half years in prison. He served 17 months.

In 1977 Irving was asked by the editors of the *Book of Lists* to compile a list of the 10 best forgers of all time. He listed Clifford Irving as number nine.

## Jackson, Andrew (1767–1845) victim of assassination attempt

On January 3, 1835 the first attempt on the life of a United States president took place when Andrew Jackson was attacked in the rotunda of the Capitol while attending the funeral of a South Carolina congressman, Warren Ransom Davis. A house painter named Richard Lawrence stepped up to President Jackson and, at a distance of 6 feet, fired two pistols at him. Both misfired and Jackson's would-be slayer was seized. Lawrence, who believed he was the rightful heir to the English throne, was committed to an insane asylum.

## Jackson-Dickinson duel

In the famous, or infamous, duel between Andrew Jackson and Charles Dickinson in 1806, there was no quarter given. Although Dickinson was considered to be the best shot in Tennessee, Jackson had challenged him after he had made disparaging remarks about Jackson's wife, Rachel. The duel was fought at a range of 24 feet. Dickinson got off the first shot, which crashed into Jackson's chest, missing his heart by only an inch. Blood gushed through his clothes, but Jackson managed to keep his feet, though unsteadily. He took dead aim at Dickinson, who broke and ran from the line of fire. The seconds ordered Dickinson back to his previous position, as the dueling code required, and he stood awaiting Jackson's shot with his arms crossed to protect his heart. Jackson aimed a bit lower at his target and fired, hitting Dickinson in the groin. Death came slowly and excruciatingly to Dickinson. Jackson carried the lead ball he had received until the end of his days, it being too close to the heart to be removed.

## Kahane, Rabbi Meir (1932–1990) murder victim

It was a November 5, 1990, meeting for the supporters of Rabbi Meir Kahane in the conference room of a Midtown New York hotel. The turnout was approximately 70 persons who generally agreed with the extremist founder of the Jewish Defense League in the United States and the anti-Arab Kach Party in Israel. Kahane outlined his proposal for the "transfer" or expulsion of Arabs from Israel and the occupied territories.

Just as Kahane finished his speech, a shot rang out and a bullet hit him in the neck that then exited through his cheek. It was a fatal shot.

A member of the audience ran from the room, gun in hand. According to police, the gun-toting man shot and wounded an elderly bystander as he fled the room. Out on the street he commandeered a taxi at gunpoint. A block later he jumped out of the cab and came face-to-face with an on-duty Postal Service policeman, Carlos Acosta. The police said the gunman fired a shot that bounced off the officer's bulletproof vest and wounded the policeman in the arm. Acosta returned fire and his bullet hit the gunman in the neck and lodged in his chin.

The alleged assailant was identified by police as Sayyid A. Nosair, an Egyptian immigrant who had become a U.S. citizen the previous year and at present worked for a city agency. Nosair was hospitalized in serious condition, but recovered. On November 20 Nosair was charged with multiple crimes: second-degree murder, second-degree attempted murder, aggravated assault of a police officer, second-degree assault, three counts of criminal possession of a weapon, reckless endangerment and coercion. Investigators also warned six prominent New York City Jews that their names appeared on a list held by Nosair, but at the time nothing developed to prove he had ties to Palestinian groups or international terrorists.

As a matter of fact, officials were going to have great difficulty tying Nosair to the murder, even though they felt their case was overwhelming and the press openly described Nosair as Kahane's murderer. On December 21, 1991, Nosair was acquitted of the main

Rabbi Meir Kahane, extremist founder of the Jewish Defense League in the United States, was shot dead before 70 persons at a conference in a New York hotel after he outlined his proposal for the "transfer," or expulsion, of Arabs from Israel and the occupied territories.

charges against him, those of killing Kahane and shooting the post office policeman Acosta.

Later it was determined the jury felt the prosecution had not presented sufficient evidence to prove that Nosair had shot Kahane, and in interviews some noted no one testified to seeing Nosair firing a shot. All one witness testified to was to seeing Nosair pointing a gun at Kahane moments after the shooting. Jurors also said the state did not prove that the gun found in the street near Nosair was the one that had been used in the murder.

The noted defense attorney William M. Kunstler insisted Kahane had been killed by a dissident member of the JDL in a finan-

cial dispute. After the verdict several newspaper accounts noted that Kunstler seemed quite stunned that he had basically won his case.

Nosair did not go free, however, and in 1995 he was tried with a number of defendants in the World Trade Center bombing and was also convicted on federal charges for the Kahane murder.

## Keating, Charles H., Jr. (1923– ) savings and loan scandal figure

Throughout the entire savings and loan (S&L) scandal, which rocked American finance in the late 1980s, Charles H. Keating Jr. remained the most blatant participant. Keating's case—estimated to have cost U.S. taxpayers some $2.6 billion—even jeopardized the reputation of the U.S. Senate because of the actions of the so-called Keating Five. It was a prime example of unfettered S&L officials living high on the hog and playing fast and loose with depositors' and investors' money.

The Keating story can be told in the form of a chronology:

*February 1984*—American Continental Corp., formed by Keating, buys the Lincoln Savings and Loan of California for $51 million.

*March 1986*—The Federal Home Loan Bank in San Francisco starts an examination of Lincoln's rapid growth and hectic investment activities.

*Mid-1986*—San Francisco bank examiners urge Washington officials to come down hard on Lincoln for questionable accounting and loan procedures.

*November 1986*—Five U.S. Senators—Alan Cranston of California, John Glenn of Ohio,

Donald W. Riegle of Michigan and Dennis DeConcini (all Democrats) and Republican John McCain of Arizona—meet with examiners on behalf of Keating, who has made large political contributions to them.

*May 1987*—Examiners recommend that Lincoln be seized for operating in an unsound manner and dissipating its assets. Nothing happens.

*April 12, 1989*—American Continental files for bankruptcy protection, making its junk bonds worthless.

*April 14, 1989*—The government now takes control of Lincoln and puts the bailout at an eventual cost of $2.6 million, the most expensive in history.

*September 1990*—A California grand jury charges Keating and three others with securities fraud, saying they had deceived investors into buying junk bonds without telling them the risk. Many Lincoln investors thought they were buying government-insured bonds.

*February 1991*—After a three-and-a-half month investigation, the Senate Ethics Committee renders a verdict in the case of the Keating Five. It declares there was "substantial credible evidence" of misconduct by Senator Cranston (leading to a severe rebuke from the Senate in November). Riegle and DeConcini are described as giving the appearance of impropriety, but no further action is taken against them. Glenn and McCain are criticized less severely.

*December 4, 1991*—After a four-month court case, Keating is convicted of securities fraud and sentenced to a 10-year state jail term in California. He still faces federal charges.

*July 3, 1993*—Keating, convicted of federal charges of fraud, is sentenced to 12 years and seven months, the sentence to run concurrently with the state sentence.

The S&L scandal provoked a tightening of regulations against such institutions, which took their investments far afield. The impact on politics was immense so that by 1999 only John McCain of the Keating Five still was in the Senate.

## kidnapping

Kidnapping for ransom was hardly an American invention, the practice dating back to ancient times. However, probably nowhere else was the crime committed as frequently as it was in the United States during the early 1930s, typified best by the Lindbergh baby kidnapping in 1932.

Although there were many early kidnappings in America, especially of children—girls for the purposes of prostitution—and free blacks, the first major kidnapping for ransom case in this country is generally regarded to have been that of four-year-old Charley Ross, who was abducted on July 1, 1874. Technically, the case was never solved and "little Charley Ross," which became a household phrase, was never found. It is almost certain that he was murdered by his kidnappers, two notorious criminals named William Mosher and Joey Douglass and an ex-policeman named William Westervelt.

The question kidnappers always face is whether or not to kill the victim. When the victim is murdered the crime usually occurs immediately after the abduction. Conversely, the victim's family must decide whether or not to pay the ransom, since paying may only lead to the killing of the victim. A general rule of thumb is that a so-called amateur kidnapper will tend to kill the victim, but a true professional will let him or her live, realizing that murdering the victim lessens the chance of collecting a ransom for the next kidnapping. This perspective evolved in the 1920s, when organized criminals were kidnapped by other organized criminals and held for ransom. Killing the victims under such circumstances would have eliminated the "goose that lays the golden eggs." Underworld ransom kidnappings were very profitable because the racketeer-victims seldom were able to appeal to the law for assistance. Equally important, such victims hardly wished to let it be known that they had been unable to defend themselves. As a result, their kidnappers received scant public attention. Around 1930 organized kidnap rings started to victimize private citizens, and the public not only grew aware of kidnappings but demanded the authorities put a halt to them. The FBI's success in smashing several kidnapping gangs did much to alter that agency's tarnished image.

### Major Kidnappings in American History

*1900:* Edward A. Cudahy, Jr., 16, in Omaha, Neb. Released after $25,000 ransom paid. Pat Crowe confessed but was acquitted.

*1927:* Marion Parker, 12, in Los Angeles, Calif. $7,500 ransom paid but victim had already been murdered and dismembered. Edward Hickman convicted and executed.

*1932:* Charles A. Lindbergh, Jr., 20 months, in Hopewell, N.J. $50,000 ransom paid but victim had already been murdered. Bruno Richard Hauptmann convicted and executed.

*1933:* William A. Hamm, Jr., 39, in St. Paul, Minn. Released after $100,000 paid. Alvin "Creepy" Karpis convicted and sentenced to life.

*1933:* Charles F. Urschel, in his forties, in Oklahoma City, Okla. Released after $200,000 paid. Kathryn and George "Machine Gun" Kelly and four accomplices convicted and sentenced to life.

*1936:* Charles Mattson, 10, in Tacoma, Wash. $28,000 ransom demanded but never collected. Victim found dead. Case remains unsolved.

*1937:* Charles S. Ross, 72, in Franklin Park, Ill. $50,000 ransom paid but victim then murdered. John Henry Seadlund convicted and executed.

*1953:* Robert C. Greenlease, six, in Kansas City, Mo. $600,000 ransom paid but victim had already been murdered. Carl A. Hall and Bonnie Brown Heady convicted and executed.

*1956:* Peter Weinberger, 32 days old, in Westbury, N.Y. $2,000 ransom demanded but not paid. Victim found dead. Angelo John LaMarca convicted and executed.

*1963:* Frank Sinatra, Jr., 19, in Lake Tahoe, Calif. Released after $240,000 ransom paid by father. John W. Irwin, Joseph C. Amsler and Barry W. Keenan convicted and sentenced to prison.

*1968:* Barbara Jane Mackle, 20, in Atlanta, Ga. Released after $500,000 paid. Gary Steven Krist and Ruth Eisemann-Schier convicted and sentenced to prison.

*1974:* Patricia Hearst, 19, in Berkeley, Calif. $2 million ransom paid but victim not released and later charged with joining her captors. Except for William and Emily Harris, all of victim's kidnappers killed in gun battle with police. Harrises convicted and sentenced to 10 years to life.

*1974:* E. B. Reville of Hepzikbah, Ga. and wife, Jean, kidnapped; $30,000 ransom paid. E. B. found alive; Jean Reville found dead.

*1974:* J. Reginald Murphy, 40, an editor of *Atlanta Constitution,* freed two days later after $700,000 ransom paid. William A. H. Williams arrested and most of the money recovered.

*1976:* 26 children and bus driver in Chowchilla, Calif. Ransom demanded but victims escaped. Frederick Newhall Woods, IV, James Schoenfeld and Richard Allen Schoenfeld convicted and sentenced to life.

*1992:* Sidney J. Reso, oil company executive, seized April 29; dies May 3. Arthur Seale and his wife, Irene, arrested June 19. Seale pleads guilty and is sentenced to life; Irene Seale gets 20-year prison term.

1996: Marshall J. Wais, 79, owner of two San Francisco steel companies, kidnapped from his home and released unharmed the same day after half-million dollar ransom paid. Thomas Taylor and Michael Robinson arrested the same day.

## King, Dot (1894–1923) murder victim

The murder of playgirl Dot King in New York in 1923 was the classic Broadway drama which, as Russel Crouse wrote, "might easily be credited to a hack and his typewriter. Its characters are creations at a penny a word—the Broadway butterfly, the 'heavy sugar daddy,' the dark, sinister lover, the broken-hearted mother, and even the Negro maid, for comedy." Countless books on the "sins of New York" have described the Dot King case with varying degrees of accuracy.

Born into an Irish family living in an uptown slum, Anna Marie Keenan married a chauffeur when she was 18 but dumped him shortly afterwards as she began making it big as a model. To fit her new image, she changed her name to Dot King and, with her stunning looks, natural blonde hair and sparkling blue eyes, became a hostess in a plush speakeasy. It was here that she met "Mr. Marshall," the sugar daddy who made her the envy of her nightclub coworkers. Within a year after she met Mr. Marshall, he had showered some $30,000 in cash and jewelry on her.

On March 15, 1923 Dot King was found dead on her bed, at first glance an apparent suicide. An empty bottle of chloroform lay nearby, and the telephone had been shifted away from the bed as far as the cord would stretch. On closer inspection, the police noticed Dot's arm was twisted behind her back as if it had been put in a hammer lock, and the suicide theory was discarded for one of murder. But who had done it? There were many suspects, but the most logical one was the missing Mr. Marshall, whom the victim's maid described and who had written scores of "spicy" letters. One, which the newspapers delighted in publishing, read: "Darling Dottie: Only two days before I will be in your arms. I want to see you, O, so much, and to kiss your pretty pink toes."

And there was Dot's "kept" man, a Latin named Alberto Santos Guimares, upon whom the Broadway butterfly seemed to bestow gifts with almost the same frequency as she received them from Mr. Marshall. Police soon had evidence that Guimares, who apparently survived by petty swindling and exploitation of women, repaid Dot for her generosity by beating her up regularly. As a suspect, however, Guimares had drawbacks. He claimed that at the time of the murder he was in the arms of another woman, a leading socialite who backed up his story. If the tabloid readers suffered any disappointment over that development, they were overwhelmingly compensated by the identification of Mr. Marshall, who had already revealed his identity to the police. They had tried to shield him because they accepted his word that he had nothing to do with the murder—and because he was someone worth protecting. However, an enterprising newspaper reporter learned who he was.

His name was J. Kearsley Mitchell, the wealthy son-in-law of E. T. Stotesbury, the most prominent millionaire on Philadelphia's Main Line. Gossip writers ran amok with tales of twisted passions and plots of blackmail. Had Kearsley wanted to leave Dot and was she blackmailing him? The police said no, but their theories weren't respected since they had admitted attempting to hide Kearsley's identity to protect the millionaire's socially prominent wife and their three children from scandal.

Eventually, the police fell back to a theory that was safest of all, although devoid of social scandal, lurid romance and the like. It was that Dot had been the victim of robbers who had chloroformed her a bit too thoroughly. About a year later, another Broadway butterfly, Louise Lawson, suffered the same kind of death. Police learned that Louise, whose apartment, like Dot's, was stuffed with cash and baubles from an admirer, had opened the door to two men who said they had a package for her.

Undoubtedly, a woman—like Dot King—who had a sugar daddy would almost certainly open her door for someone saying he was bearing gifts. Of course, the public did not like the robbery theory. They much preferred a story of Main Line society, twisted and violent jealousy, and since the Dot King case remained unsolved, they never had to abandon that version.

## Koehler, Arthur (1885–1967) wood detective

Shortly after Bruno Richard Hauptmann was convicted in the 1932 kidnap murder of the Lindbergh baby, Edward J. Reilly, the chief defense counsel, told an interviewer: "We would have won an acquittal if it hadn't been for that guy Koehler. What a witness to ring in on us—somebody they plucked out of a forest. Do you know what he is? He's a—a xylotomist." While the dictionary defines a xylotomist as one who studies wood anatomy and is proficient in the art of preparing wood for microscopic examination, the lawyer said the word as if he were mouthing an obscenity.

Arthur Koehler was not an obscenity but the nation's foremost wood detective. Until his retirement in 1948 Koehler spent 36 years with the U.S. Forest Service including 34 years at the famous Forest Products Laboratory in Madison, Wisc., where he was the chief wood identification expert for the government. While Hauptmann's counsel had not heard of him, law officials in the Midwest had long relied on Koehler to crack perplexing criminal cases. His evidence was vital in convicting a Wisconsin farmer named John Magnuson for the 1922 dynamite-by-mail murder of Mrs. James A. Chapman and the crippling of her wealthy farmer husband. Fragments of the wood portions of the bomb were given to Koehler, who identified the pieces as elm. Although the suspect denied he had elm lumber on his farm, the police swept up wood shavings from the floor of his workshop. Koehler identified the sweepings as particles of elm and matched up their cellular structure with the wood used in the construction of the bomb. Magnuson was convicted.

Koehler's reputation in the Midwest became so great that on one occasion the mere mention that he was being brought into an investigation caused an arsonist to confess. In another case his testimony trapped a tree rustler who had made off with a huge amount of choice logs. Koehler traced the logs back to a certain valuable timberland and even identified which log was cut from which tree by matching saw cuts and the structure of the annual rings to the tree stumps. He also was instrumental in convicting Michael Fugmann, a triple murderer whose bomb packages had terrorized a Pennsylvania coal mining town during a union dispute in 1936.

In the Lindbergh case Koehler presented the damning evidence that one of Hauptmann's tools had been used to construct the kidnap ladder and that one of the ladder's rails came from Hauptmann's home. Despite many subsequent attempts by certain writers to prove Hauptmann's innocence, Koehler's expert evidence has never been successfully challenged.

Koehler had spent 18 months tracing the wood used in the kidnap ladder. At one point, about six months before Hauptmann's capture, he was so close on the trail of the culprit that the two men were in the same lumberyard at the same time. Hauptmann, apparently warned by instinct, had fled the yard, leaving behind a 40¢ plywood panel he had paid for. If one of the yard employees had mentioned the matter to Koehler, it is conceivable that the Lindbergh case would have closed six months earlier in a most dramatic fashion.

See also: LINDBERGH KIDNAPPING.

## LeBlanc, Antoine (?–1833) murderer

Although the claim may be dubious, Antoine LeBlanc is generally known as the fastest murderer in America.

LeBlanc arrived from France on April 26, 1833, and by May 2, 1833 he had committed three murders. Upon his arrival he had gone to work on the estate of the Sayre family in rural New Jersey and apparently could not cope with his lowly position which required him to sleep in the woodshed. On May 2 LeBlanc crept up on Mr. and Mrs. Sayre, battered them to death with a shovel and buried their bodies under a pile of manure. LeBlanc thought the Sayre's black maid was away, but when he discovered her presence in the attic of the house, he murdered her as well. He did not immediately flee the area, believing he could remain a while and say that his employers had gone away for a short time. The more scandalous purveyors of the news in that era later reported that LeBlanc, a tall, handsome rogue, entertained a number of young ladies in the Sayre home. In any event, friends of the missing couple found the bodies and captured the Frenchman. He was quickly tried and convicted and hanged on September 6, 1833 on the Morristown green before a crowd of 12,000. It is unclear how many were attracted by his savage crimes and how many by his romantic reputation since, as one historian of the day related, of those in attendance "the majority were females."

## Leibowitz, Samuel S. (1893–1978) defense attorney and judge

A flamboyant lawyer who built his reputation with highly remunerative defenses of gangsters, Samuel S. Leibowitz ran up an amazing record: he represented 140 persons charged with murder and lost only one to the electric chair. However, he won international fame for his defense of the Scottsboro Boys, nine young blacks charged with the rape of two "Southern ladies"—actually hobo-style prostitutes—aboard a freight train in Alabama in 1931. In a total of 10 trials and retrials, the stirring defenses by the "New York Jew nigger lover," as he was called by many citizens and much of the press in the

Attorney Samuel Leibowitz (left), shown with one of the Scottsboro Boys, was famous for losing only one client to the electric chair out of 140.

South, resulted in the dropping of charges against four of the nine and played a huge part in winning paroles for four others; the last, Haywood Patterson, the alleged ring-leader, escaped but eventually was captured and sent to prison for another crime. One of Leibowitz' most important accomplishments was winning a Supreme Court decision that the exclusion of blacks from jury service was unconstitutional, a finding that over the years was to have a profound effect on the administration of justice in the South.

Leibowitz was born in Romania and came to the United States at the age of four. He worked his way through law school and became a lawyer in 1916. Within a few years he established himself among criminal defendants as a miracle lawyer, with a knack for assembling "friendly juries" and an ability to demolish eyewitness testimony.

Leibowitz firmly believed in prescreening jurors, an entirely legal procedure few defense lawyers bother with because of the expense and tediousness of the research involved. Leibowitz wanted to know how many times each prospective member of the panel had served on a criminal case jury, how they had voted and much about their personal life and beliefs, and he was usually blessed with high-paying clients who had no trouble financing such research. The prosecution, aided by the vast investigative machinery at its disposal has always engaged in the screening of potential jurors, often to a far greater extent. Once Leibowitz had the background information, he picked jurors whom he felt would be sympathetic to the defense and disposed of those more likely to vote for conviction. Even district attorneys admitted no lawyer could pick a more "friendly" panel than Leibowitz.

Leibowitz generally had contempt for eyewitness testimony, knowing how faulty it could be. He firmly believed circumstantial evidence was, on the whole, more dependable. Out of court, Leibowitz delighted in exposing the unreliability of eyewitness evidence, staging events to show the contradictory stories told by witnesses. In one classic demonstration he performed at legal seminars and at law school lectures, Leibowitz would ask regular smokers of Camel cigarettes, "Is the man leading the camel or sitting on its back?" In one typical result, two out of five said the man was leading the camel, two out of five that he was sitting on the camel and only one in five correctly stated there was no man in the picture.

In his famous defense of Vincent "Mad Dog" Coll, a gangster who had gunned down five children on a Manhattan street, one of them fatally, Leibowitz got his client off by shifting the focus of the trial to eyewitnesses of the tragedy until it almost seemed as if they were the defendants.

Leibowitz successfully represented many of the top mobsters of the day, once rather easily getting Al Capone acquitted of a murder charge. He secured acquittals for Pittsburgh Phil Strauss, Abe Reles, Buggsy Goldstein and Bugsy Siegel, admittedly before the existence of Murder, Inc. and he turned down a $250,000 fee to defend Louis Lepke when that investigation was breaking in 1939. By that time Leibowitz had tired of the role of defense attorney and was seeking appointment to a judgeship.

When in 1940 the Democratic Party of Brooklyn proposed him for judge of the King's County Court, his nomination brought forth vigorous opposition. "Elect Leibowitz and he'll open the doors of the jails," his political opponents cried. "He'll turn loose every crook who comes before him."

It was a fear never realized. He turned out to be what is known as a "hanging judge," meting out extremely harsh sentences to professional criminals. On his retirement from the bench in 1970, eight years before his death, he observed, "I was tough with hardened criminals, toughness is all they understand."

Still, Leibowitz remained true to his belief in the right of every defendant to proper counsel.

In a typical scene in his court, a defendant would be brought up on robbery and assault charges.

"Let's see now," the judge would say. "You first appeared in juvenile court when you were fifteen. Since then you've been charged with crime, twelve times; everything from petty larceny to manslaughter. You've been convicted four times, and you've spent ten years behind bars. Bail is fixed at fifty thousand dollars. Have you got a lawyer?"

"I got no money to pay a lawyer," the defendant would reply.

"You need a good lawyer," Leibowitz would declare. "I'm going to appoint the best defense lawyer I know to represent you, without pay."

That was the law, according to Sam Leibowitz.

## Leopold and Loeb  thrill murderers

One day in May 1924 two youths, the sons of two of Chicago's wealthiest and most illustrious families, drove to the Harvard School for Boys in the suburb of Kenwood, Ill. to carry out what they regarded as the "perfect murder." Eighteen-year-old Richard "Dickie" Loeb, the youngest graduate of the University of Michigan, was a postgraduate student at the University of Chicago, and 19-year-old Nathan "Babe" Leopold, a Phi Beta Kappa from Chicago, was taking a law course there. The pair had perpetrated several minor crimes before they decided to commit the perfect murder. The killing, they felt, would be fun and an intellectual challenge, one worthy of their superior mental abilities.

Working out their plot for seven months, they picked as their victim 14-year-old Bobby Franks, the son of millionaire businessman Jacob Franks and a distant cousin of Loeb. The Franks boy, who was always flattered when the pair took note of him, happily hopped into their car when they pulled up in front of his school. They drove the boy to within a few blocks of the Franks residence in fashionable Hyde Park and then grabbed him, stuffed a gag in his mouth and smashed his skull four times with a heavy chisel. Following the murderous assault Leopold and Loeb casually motored to some marshy wasteland and carried the body to a culvert along tracks of the Pennsylvania Railroad. After dunking the boy's head under swamp water to make sure he was dead, they poured hydrochloric acid on his face to complicate identification and then stuffed the body in a drain pipe.

Satisfied with their work, the pair repaired to Leopold's home, where they played cards and drank liquor. At midnight they called the elder Franks and informed him he would receive instructions on how to ransom his missing son. By the time their typewritten note demanding $10,000 was received, workmen had found the boy's body. Despite their self-proclaimed mental abilities, the two young killers weren't very good criminals. They were easily caught. Leopold had dropped his eyeglasses near the spot where the body was hidden and police checked the prescription until it led back to him. Furthermore, the ransom note was traced to Leopold's typewriter.

Dickie Loeb broke first, and then Leopold confessed as well. A shocked city and nation fully demanded and expected that the pair would be executed.

The parents of the two called in famous lawyer Clarence Darrow to defend them. For a fee of $100,000 Darrow agreed to seek to win the best possible verdict, one that would find them guilty but save them from execution. The trial began in August. Both sides produced psychiatrists to prove or disprove their mental competence. Darrow had less trouble with the opposing psychiatrists than he did with his clients, who turned the court proceedings into a circus. They clowned and hammed through the sessions, and the newspapers caught their frequent smirks in page-one pictures. The public, always against the two "poor little rich boys," became even more hostile.

Still Darrow prevailed. He put the human brain on trial and presented evidence that Leopold was a paranoiac with a severe manic drive; Loeb was pictured as a dangerous schizophrenic. He derided their supernormal intelligences and portrayed them as having the emotional capacities of seven-year-olds. For two days Darrow talked. "Do you think you can cure the hatreds and the maladjustments of the world by hanging them?" he asked the prosecution before Judge John R. Caverly, chief justice of the Criminal Court of Cook County, who was hearing the case without a jury. "You simply show your ignorance and your hate when you say it. You may heal and cure hatred with love and understanding, but you can only add fuel to the flames with cruelty and hating."

Then Darrow wept. In macabre detail he described how the state planned to hang the defendants. He invited the prosecution to perform the execution. Even the defendants were gripped by Darrow's presentation. Loeb shuddered, and Leopold got hysterical and had to be taken from the courtroom for a time. The lawyer refused to let up. He wept for the victims and he wept for the defendants and he wept for all other victims and defendants. In the end, Darrow won. Sentenced on September 10, the defendants got life for the murder of Bobby Franks plus 99 years for kidnapping him. Ironically, Darrow was paid only $40,000 of the much larger fee due him, and most of that only after he had dunned the two families a number of times.

Thrill killers (at left) Richard Loeb (left), who would later be killed in prison, and Nathan Leopold were saved from execution by the efforts of defense attorney Clarence Darrow. Leopold (at right) in 1957 shortly before he won parole.

The public was not through with Leopold and Loeb, however. There were subsequent exposés of the favored treatment they received in prison. Unlike many other prisoners at Joliet, each was put in a separate cell. They were provided with books, desks and filing cabinets. Loeb kept two canaries. They ate in the officers' lounge, away from the other prisoners, and had their meals cooked to order. They freely visited one another and they were allowed to keep their own garden.

Over the years Loeb became an aggressive homosexual, noted for pursuit of other convicts. In January 1936 he was slashed to death in a brawl.

Leopold, on the other hand, made tremendous adjustments in his behavior. Nevertheless, his appeals for parole were rejected three times. During his fourth appeal poet Carl Sandburg pleaded his case, saying he would be willing to allow Leopold to live in his home. Finally, in March 1958 Leopold was paroled. He said: "I am a broken old man. I want a chance to find redemption for myself and to help others." He published a book, *Life Plus 99 Years,* and went to Puerto Rico to work among the poor as a $10-a-month hospital technician. Three years later, he married a widow. Leopold died of a heart ailment in 1971.

See also: CLARENCE DARROW.

### Levine, Dennis (1953– ) Wall Street inside trader

It was the "singing" of Dennis Levine that broke open the 1986 Ivan Boesky scandal that exposed the boundless avarice existing on Wall Street. The Securities and Exchange Commission discovered that Boesky, a millionaire hard-ball stock trader and arbitrager, had agreed to pay Levine a total of $2.4 million for his illegal tips. But Levine was also an illegal stock trader in his own right.

Over a period of five years Levine illegally traded in at least 54 stocks and stashed away $12.6 million in profits. At the time he was unmasked, Levine was a hotshot managing director of the investment banking firm of Drexel Burnham Lambert. He conducted his personal trading through a secret bank account in the Bahamas.

Using his Wall Street position, Levine profited from information about various companies' dealings before that information reached the public. The extent of Levine's ease in making illegal profits was typified by his 1985 activities in Nabisco stock. With inside information he had obtained, Levine made two phone calls on the stock and walked away with almost $3 million in illicit profits. Later Levine would tell the CBS news show *60 Minutes*: "It was this incredible feeling of invulnerability. . . . That was the insanity of it all. It wasn't that hard. . . . You get bolder and bolder and bolder, and it gets easier, and you make more money and more money, and it feeds upon itself. And looking back, looking back I realize that I was sick, that it became an addiction, that I lived for the high of making those trades, of doing the next deal, making the bigger deal."

After he was caught, Levine pleaded guilty to securities fraud, perjury and tax evasion, and cut a deal for himself by exposing Boesky and his own circle of wheeler-dealers. Levine gave up $11.6 million in illegal profits and served 15 months in the federal penitentiary in Lewisburg, Pennsylvania. He was released in 1988 and thereafter claimed to have turned his life around, lecturing college students around the country about what he'd learned from his past mistakes and operating his own financial consulting firm.

Some questioned how much Levine had changed. Since that time Levine was involved in a number of dubious "up-front" deals, bringing together struggling businesspeople needing financing and supposed financial institutions willing to make money available in exchange for an up-front commission. For his part Levine also received thousands of dollars in fees. The only trouble was no monies were ever advanced and some Levine clients said they were out almost $200,000. One Levine client said he had been told by Levine that a person named Jim Massaro could help out on the deal. The client said Levine described Massaro as a friend he'd done business with during his days at Drexel. Levine actually met him at Lewisburg where they had been jailmates.

Levine insisted he had exercised the required "due diligence" in all cases and that it was not accurate for him to be described as the consummate con man. He insisted, "I have never conned anybody in my life. . . . People are entitled to their own opinions, but it's not true. I have to live with myself. I don't think I've done anything wrong."

### Lincoln, Abraham (1809–1865) assassination victim

By present-day standards, the protection of Abraham Lincoln at the time of his assassination in 1865 bordered on the criminally

Four of those charged with the crime, Mrs. Mary Surratt, Lewis Paine, David Herold and George Atzerodt, were hanged, although to the end most people expected Mrs. Surratt's death sentence to be commuted.

negligent. On the night of April 14 President and Mrs. Abraham Lincoln attended the performance of *Our American Cousin* at Ford's Theatre in Washington, D.C. Attending with them as substitutes for Gen. and Mrs. Ulysses S. Grant, who had canceled (because Mrs. Grant could not abide Mrs. Lincoln), were the daughter of Sen. Ira Harris and his stepson, Maj. Henry Rathbone. Earlier that day the president had asked the War Department to provide a special guard. Oddly, the request was refused, a matter of considerable puzzlement to historians. The only presidential

bodyguard that night was a shiftless member of the Washington police force, who after the start of the performance, incredibly left his post outside the flag-draped presidential box to adjourn to nearby Taltavul's tavern for a drink.

While there, he may well have rubbed elbows with another imbiber, John Wilkes Booth, who had been drinking heavily for several hours, determined that tonight he would kill Lincoln. At 26 Booth, a noted Shakespearean actor, had long made no secret of his Southern sympathies. The War

Department undoubtedly knew of his drunken boasting about a plot to kidnap Lincoln and drag him in chains to Richmond, where he would be held until the Union armies laid down their arms. As a matter of fact, Booth and a small group of conspirators had waited in ambush about three weeks earlier to attack the Lincoln carriage outside the city limits but were thwarted by the president's change of plans.

After that failure Booth shifted to the assassination attempt. The plan called for him to kill Lincoln while other members of the group simultaneously attacked Vice President Andrew Johnson and various Cabinet members.

At 10 o'clock Booth left the bar and went to the theater, pausing long enough to bum a chew of tobacco from a ticket taker he knew. In the foyer of the theater Booth caught the eye of actress Jennie Gourlay, who later recalled he had appeared pale and ill and distraught with "a wild look in his eyes."

Booth entered Lincoln's unguarded box, leveled his one-shot Derringer behind the president's left ear and pulled the trigger. As Lincoln slumped, Booth cried out, *"Sic semper tyrannis"* ("Ever thus to tyrants"), dropped his gun and pulled a dagger. He slashed Maj. Rathbone as the officer lunged for him. Booth hurdled the rail of the box in what he undoubtedly visualized as a dramatic appearance on the stage, shouting, "The South is avenged." However, his spur caught in the flag outside the box and he almost fell on his face. Somehow he kept his footing and limped on a fractured left leg across the stage and out into the street. There he mounted his horse and rode off.

Were it not for his leg injury, Booth might have made good his escape, crossing the Potomac and losing himself among the sol-

diers being demobilized following Lee's surrender. But the pain slowed his flight. He met up in Maryland with David Herold, another of the conspirators, who had failed in a simultaneous attempt on the life of Secretary of State William Seward, and the pair located Dr. Samuel Mudd. After Mudd set Booth's leg the two left the doctor's home and made it to the Potomac River awaiting an opportunity to cross into Virginia.

Meanwhile, the hunt for the assassin was pressed, some observers said later with considerable incompetence. Certainly, greed for the reward money being offered and hysteria hindered the search, and it was not until April 26 that the fugitives were cornered in a tobacco shed on a farm near Port Royal, Va.

The commander of the Union troops, a Lt. Baker, ordered the pair to surrender or the building would be set on fire. Booth called out, "Let us have a little time to consider it."

Five minutes later Booth declared: "Captain, I know you to be a brave man, and I believe you to be honorable; I am a cripple. I have got but one leg; if you withdraw your men in one line one hundred yards from the door, I will come out and fight you."

Baker rejected the offer and Booth then shouted, "Well, my brave boys, prepare a stretcher for me."

Then the soldiers heard loud voices from the shed and Booth's voice could be heard saying: "You damned coward, will you leave me now? Go, go; I would not have you stay with me." Then Booth yelled, "There's a man in here who wants to come out."

A trembling Herold surrendered himself.

The structure was set afire, and the troopers could see a dark figure hobbling about. Suddenly, there was a shot—possibly by Booth himself and possibly by a Union zealot, a soldier named Boston Corbett—and Booth fell. Soldiers rushed into the barn and pulled Booth outside.

"Tell mother I die for my country," Booth whispered before breathing his last.

Even before Booth's death, the government had implicated several other persons in the assassination—Herold, George A. Atzerodt, Lewis Paine, Mary E. Surratt, her son John H. Surratt, Edward Spangler, Dr. Mudd, Samuel Arnold, and Michael O'Laughlin. All except John H. Surratt, who eluded capture, were tried before a military commission, on the ground that Lincoln was the commander in chief and had fallen "in actual service in time of war." The trial, which ran from May 9 to June 30, was a bizarre spectacle conducted under decidedly unfair conditions and amidst postwar hysteria. Somehow the defendants were linked to the deeds of the Confederate government and Jefferson Davis. Many of the charges dealt with such irrelevancies as starvation of Union prisoners in notorious Andersonville Prison and the plot to burn New York City.

At the same time, important witnesses were never called to testify. John F. Parker, who negligently left Lincoln unguarded, was not summoned (nor was he dismissed from the police force or even reprimanded). Even men who had harbored Booth for a week after the assassination were not forced to appear. Most observers felt that the case against Mrs. Mary Surratt was singularly weak, depending largely on the word of a known liar and an infamous drunkard. Her sole offense seems to have been owning the rooming house where much of the plotting had taken place.

Nonetheless, Mrs. Surratt was sentenced to hang along with Paine, Herold and Atzerodt. Mudd, Arnold and O'Laughlin received life sentences and Spangler got six years. The executions were carried out on July 7, 1865, ironically with umbrellas held over the prisoners' heads on the gallows to protect them from the sweltering sun. To the very end, it was thought that Mrs. Surratt would be pardoned. Paine told the executioner: "If I had two lives to give, I'd give one gladly to save Mrs. Surratt. I know that she is innocent, and would never die in this way if I hadn't been found at her house. She knew nothing about the conspiracy at all. . . ." However, there was no last-minute reprieve and the four were executed at the same moment.

The hunt for John Surratt became a world chase and he was finally located in Italy serving in the Swiss Guards. Brought back to trial in 1867, when the hysteria had died down, Surratt went free when the jury could not agree on his guilt.

The weakness of the case against the imprisoned men also became apparent in time, and by March 4, 1869 President Andrew Johnson had pardoned all of them except O'Laughlin, who had died in prison in 1867.

### Defense attorney

Attorney Abraham Lincoln of Illinois "rode the circuit" around Springfield in the practice of his profession. While most of his cases were civil, involving land disputes, livestock claims and financial matters, he also defended a number of clients on criminal charges. Most of these cases involved prosaic allegations, such as theft, drunkenness and the like, but he conducted a murder defense that brought him statewide fame.

William "Duff" Armstrong was accused along with James Norris of killing James "Pres" Metzker in a drunken brawl near Havana, on August 29, 1857. It was estab-

"Riding the circuit" made young Abraham Lincoln one of the best-known lawyers in downstate Illinois.

lished beyond doubt that Norris had hit Metzker with an ox-yoke. Tried separately, he was convicted and given eight years in the penitentiary. However, young Armstrong denied he had struck the victim another deadly blow with a slung shot, insisting he had done all his fighting with his fists.

Lincoln took the case without fee because, as he would tell the jury, the defendant was the son of Jack and Hannah Armstrong, who had provided the now-famous lawyer with a home when he was "penniless, homeless, and alone." The inference Lincoln would make was that such a fine couple could not possibly have raised a killer.

The trial opened in Beardstown, Ill. on May 7, 1858. The prosecution's case was based primarily on the testimony of a house-painter named Charles Allen, who said he had seen every detail of the murder, which had occurred at 9:30 in the brilliant light of a full moon. Lincoln took Allen over the details of the crime several times, drawing from the witness again and again a description of the brilliant moonlight that had enabled him to see the events so clearly. Then Lincoln produced a farmer's almanac and turned to the page for August 29, the day of the murder. It showed that the moon had been just past its first quarter, providing little help for the witness. In addition to discrediting Allen's testimony, Lincoln stressed that the mark on Metzker attributed to Armstrong's lethal blow could have been caused by the victim falling to the ground after being struck by Norris.

As the jury filed from the courtroom, Lincoln is reported to have turned to Mrs. Armstrong and said, "Aunt Hannah, your son will be free before sundown." The acquittal came quickly. When it did, Lincoln said thoughtfully, "I pray to God that this lesson may prove in the end a good lesson to him and to all."

### Target of body snatchers

After Abraham Lincoln was buried in 1865, authorities found it necessary to move his casket 17 times, mainly to prevent it from being stolen and held for ransom. That feat was almost achieved in 1876 by Big Jim Kenealy and his gang of counterfeiters. They concocted a weird plot to steal the body, rebury it elsewhere and then return it in exchange for money and the release of the outfit's master engraver, Ben Boyd, then doing 10 years in prison. Their plot was foiled when an informer working on counterfeiting matters infiltrated the gang and tipped off the Secret Service.

The would-be body snatchers were thwarted just as they were moving the casket, then kept in a mausoleum in a lonely section of forest two miles outside of Springfield, Ill. Nevertheless, the gang succeeded in eluding the Secret Service agents who swooped down on them. After 10 days all were rounded up, but Kenealy suddenly had a surprise for the authorities. He had previously determined that there was no law on the books making it illegal to steal a dead body, not even that of a martyred president. However, all the gang members were convicted and given the maximum sentence, one year in prison, for attempting to steal a coffin.

For the next two years the casket remained hidden under a pile of scrap lumber until it was moved again. Finally in 1901, it was locked in a steel cage and buried 10 feet below the floor of a national shrine in Springfield.

## Lindbergh kidnapping

No kidnapping in American history achieved more notoriety or produced more public clamor than the abduction of the Lindbergh baby in 1932. By its very nature, the crime inspired an incredible array of swindles, hoaxes and controversies. At the time, the depths of the Depression, Charles A. Lindbergh—Lucky Lindy—was a hero in an era of few heroes. He had enjoyed that stature since his epic flight from New York to Paris in May 1927. "Lindbergh," Frederick Lewis Allen was to write in his book *Only Yesterday,* "was a god"—and indeed he was. Consequently, the kidnapping of 20-month-old Charles A. Lindbergh, Jr., from the family's

home near Hopewell, N.J. was little short of sacrilege, a crime that outraged the public far more than even the Leopold-Loeb case of the previous decade.

The night of the crime, March 1, was particularly windy, and after Mrs. Lindbergh and the baby's nurse, Betty Gow, put the child to bed, the nurse remained with him until he was asleep. A short while later, Lindbergh heard a noise, but not hearing it again, he and his wife dismissed the sound as the wind. At about 10 p.m. the nurse, making her customary check, found the baby's bed empty. Searching around the house, Lindbergh discovered a homemade wooden ladder with a broken rung outside the nursery window, and he called the police.

Near the window sill he found a note written in broken English that indicated the writer might be German.

*Have fifty thousand dollars ready, 25,000 in twenty-dollar bills, 15,000 in ten-dollar bills, and 10,000 in five-dollar bills. In 4-5 days we will inform you where to deliver the money. We warn you for making anyding public or for notify the police. The child is in gut care. Indication for all letters are signature and three holes.*

But by that time the authorities had already been called in, and inevitably, the press and the nation soon learned of the crime. From then on, the case was nothing short of a three-ring circus. Everyone from the well-intended to a legion of crackpots and hoaxers got into the act. Police on various levels jockeyed for position in the investigative process. No one was clearly in charge, except possibly Lindbergh himself, who was impressed by certain investigators and unimpressed by others.

Symbols show location of the Lindbergh baby's room (A) and areas where kidnapper's ladder (B) and baby's bedding (C) were abandoned.

Initial theories about the crime revolved, quite naturally, around the possibility that the underworld was responsible for the kidnapping. Hearst columnist Arthur Brisbane championed the idea of releasing the notorious gangster Al Capone from prison to help find the child and return him to the Lindberghs. Since Brisbane had only a short time before he had to square a $250,000 tax claim, he quite possibly felt a sort of kinship with another man convicted on income tax charges. Within federal law enforcement circles, it was suggested that the aid of Lucky Luciano should be sought. Officially at least, nothing became of these proposals, although there is considerable reason to believe that

the Capone mob had set about framing an ex-convict, Robert Conroy, who had labored on the fringe of the outfit. He was found shot dead in August and there was later speculation that the mob had intended to pin the kidnapping on Conroy with manufactured evidence.

About a month after the abduction, a retired school principal, Dr. John F. "Jafsie" Condon, published a letter in the *Bronx Home News* in New York City offering to act as go-between in the return of the missing baby. Probably much to his surprise and that of the editor, the offer was accepted. A letter from a man who became known as Cemetery John provided facts that only the kidnapper could have known. A meeting was held in a cemetery between Jafsie and John, who raised the ransom demand to $70,000. John promised to send the baby's night clothes to prove he was the real kidnapper. Further negotiations dropped the ransom back down to $50,000.

At another meeting, with Lindbergh on hand, Jafsie handed over the money; all the bills had been marked, including $20,000 in gold certificates. The kidnapper said the baby could be found on a boat at Martha's Vineyard, Mass. A frantic Lindbergh rushed there but found no boat and no child. He had been duped.

On May 12, 1932 the body of a baby, identified by Lindbergh as his child, was found in a shallow grave just a few miles from the Lindbergh home. The ransom money eventually trapped the kidnapper, Bruno Richard Hauptmann, in September 1934, when an alert filling station attendant recognized a gold certificate given him by a customer as one of the marked bills and noted down the man's car license number. Hauptmann was traced through the license and over $11,000 of the ransom money was found in his garage. A U.S. Forestry Service "wood detective," Arthur Koehler, eventually identified the lumber yard that had cut the wood used to make the kidnap ladder and matched a rung of the ladder to a board in Hauptmann's attic.

Hauptmann's trial was held in January 1935 in Flemington, N.J., amidst a carnival atmosphere. Crowds stayed up all night to get seats in the courtroom, vendors sold Lindbergh baby dolls. During the trial Jafsie Condon identified Hauptmann as Cemetery John, and Lindbergh, who had been present at the second meeting with the kidnapper, identified the voice. A number of handwrit-

After he was taken into custody, Bruno Hauptmann consistently maintained he was innocent of the kidnapping.

ing experts linked the kidnap notes to the defendant, and wood expert Koehler's testimony proved unshakable.

Hauptmann was convicted despite his continued pleas of innocence. Yet there were many who felt Hauptmann had not been the only one involved in the plot. Among those dissatisfied with the verdict was New Jersey Gov. Harold Hoffman, whom others would accuse of using the case as a launching pad for a possible presidential bid. Gov. Hoffman clearly had need to move up higher in government so that he would have greater authority to conceal his current and past embezzlements of public funds. Gov. Hoffman stayed Hauptmann's execution to hear what was considered evidence of a new solution, but nothing developed. He also fired H. Norman Schwarzkopf as superintendent of the New Jersey State Police, calling the Lindbergh case "the

A crowd stayed up all night to get seats in the morning at the Hauptmann trial.

most bungled police job in history." That assessment was not shared by many others, including Lindbergh, who remained a firm friend of the lawman.

For a time, until Hauptmann's capture, Dr. Condon was suspected of being a confidence operator who had swindled Lindbergh out of the $50,000 ransom money. Gaston B. Means, a notorious political rogue who had for years operated in the shadowy fringes of law enforcement agencies in the federal government, swindled a scatterbrained socialite, Mrs. Evalyn Walsh McLean of Washington, D.C., out of $104,000 on the premise that he would use his underworld connections to retrieve the missing child. In another bizarre episode, one of the most-fabled detectives of the era, Ellis Parker, was convicted of kidnapping and torturing a disbarred lawyer, Paul H. Wendel, and of forcing him to confess that he and others and not Hauptmann were

involved in the kidnapping. Both Means and Parker died in prison on charges arising out of the Lindbergh case.

Perhaps the most bizarre aspect of the case was the long hours before Hauptmann's execution on April 3, 1936. A leading news commentator of the day, Gabriel Heatter, offered a play-by-play, minute-by-minute radio commentary to a public eager to hear about the final act in the drama and to learn whether Hauptmann would talk and implicate others during his final minutes. Hauptmann did not, denying his own guilt to the end.

Over the years many efforts have been made to shed more light on the case, including numerous attempts to portray Hauptmann as a mere scapegoat. The most formidable effort was a 1976 book by Anthony Scaduto, *Scapegoat, The Lonesome Death of Bruno Richard Hauptmann*, in which the author presents many contradictions in the evidence. According to the Scaduto thesis, police faked evidence against Hauptmann, and prosecution witnesses, state attorneys and even Hauptmann's own defense lawyers took part in distorting or suppressing evidence. However, despite the unearthing of considerable discrepancies, Scaduto failed to present solid proof that Hauptmann was the victim of a miscarriage of justice. Similarly, recent efforts to prove a New England man to be the "real" Lindbergh child—not at all an uncommon occurrence in celebrated cases of this type—have foundered.

See also: HAROLD GILES HOFFMAN.

## Lonergan, Wayne (1916– ) murderer
In one of New York City's most sensational murder cases, Patricia Burton Lonergan, a 22-year-old heiress to a $7 million brewery

fortune, was murdered in her bedroom on October 24, 1943. She had been strangled, bludgeoned by a pair of antique candlesticks and left naked on her bed.

Two months earlier, her husband had departed for his native Canada to join the Royal Canadian Air Force. However, it was discovered that he had been staying in a friend's apartment in New York City on the weekend of the murder. He was traced back to Toronto, arrested and returned to New York. At first, Lonergan, a bisexual, insisted he had spent the time in New York hunting for soldiers, but after 84 hours of interrogation he supposedly confessed that he had gone to Patricia's apartment and, after a quarrel, killed her, throwing his bloodstained uniform into the East River. His confession received a terrific play in the press, in part because of the concurrent admission that he had taken part in sex orgies and the fact that he had been the acknowledged lover of Patricia's father prior to their wedding. At one point Lonergan claimed to have killed his wife in self-defense during a fight.

The case against Lonergan was not the tightest on record. The police had neglected or failed to get Lonergan to sign his so-called confession. Moreover, there was no conclusive proof to show that he had visited the apartment or handled the candlesticks. Some legal observers felt he was convicted as much because of bisexuality as because of the evidence. The jury found him guilty of second-degree murder and he was sentenced to 35 years to life. After doing 21 years in Sing Sing, Lonergan was paroled in 1965 and deported to Canada.

## Long, Huey (1893–1935) assassination victim

The powerful Kingfish of Louisiana politics, first as governor and then as a U.S. senator,

flamboyant Huey P. Long was shot to death in 1935. At the time, he was among the most-beloved and most-hated men in the state and nation. His supporters called him "the one friend the poor has," while his foes considered him a "demagogue," a "madman" and the "destroyer of constitutional government." One group that was solidly in Huey's camp was the underworld, with whom he could always reach accommodation. When New York City Mayor Fiorello La Guardia started busting up the syndicate's slot machines, Long told Frank Costello, in effect, to bring his business down. The underworld shipped in one-armed bandits by the thousands, making New Orleans the illegal slot machine center of the country. The payoffs supposedly contributed the grease that kept the Long machine running.

On September 8, 1935, Long, although a U.S. senator at the time, was attending a special session of the Louisiana House of Representatives in Baton Rouge. As he walked down one of the capitol corridors with five bodyguards in attendance, a 29-year-old man, Carl Weiss, who was considered a brilliant medical doctor, stepped from behind a pillar and shot Long with a .32 caliber automatic. The Kingfish screamed and clutched his side as he ran down the hall. His bodyguards knocked Weiss to the floor, shooting him twice. As he struggled, a fusillade of 61 shots turned his white linen suit red with blood.

Weiss died on the spot. Long lived about 30 hours, as doctors vainly struggled to save his life. Weiss' exact motive for killing was never learned, other than that he and his family had long hated the Kingfish. However, there was another version of the assassination: Weiss had not killed Long at all.

There were two variations of this theory. According to one of them, a cut on Long's lip

**CROWD WHICH SURGED FROM HOUSE CHAMBER SCRAMBLED BACK WHEN FIRING COMMENCED.**

**LONG, FOLLOWED BY BODYGUARDS, LEFT THE HOUSE CHAMBER FOR THE GOVERNOR'S OFFICE DOWN THE HALL.**

**AS LONG TURNED, WEISS STEPPED FROM BEHIND POST, DRAWING GUN FROM SIDE TROUSER POCKET.**

**IN FRONT OF THE GOVERNOR'S DOOR LONG TURNED TO TALK WITH WHITE AND FOURNET.**

**BODYGUARD RODIN CLOSED WITH WEISS, THEN BACKED OFF FIRING FIRST SHOTS INTO HIS BODY.**

**FOURNET GRABS WEISS' ARM, DEFLECTING AIM.**

An artist's conception of the assassination of the Kingfish

had come from a punch in the mouth Weiss had given him. The enraged bodyguards, so the story goes, pulled their guns and started shooting wildly, and one of their shots fatally wounded the Kingfish. After killing Weiss, they took his gun and fired it. Since the bullet that killed Long passed right through his body, it was impossible to tell which of the many discharged bullets was the fatal one. In the other variation, Weiss had intended to kill Long but was gunned down before he could get off a shot. In either case the consensus was that Long's aides and bodyguards had put the blame on Weiss to protect themselves.

Long was buried on the landscaped grounds of the capitol he had built. A novel based on his career, *All the King's Men,* won the Pulitzer Prize, and the movie version won an Academy Award in 1939.

Further reading: *The Day Huey Long Was Shot* by David Zinman and *The Huey Long Murder Case* by Hermann B. Deutsch.

## Luetgert, Adolph Louis (1848–1911)
### murderer

Few murders have ever shocked the citizens of Chicago as much as the gruesome killing in 1897 of Louisa Luetgert by her husband, Adolph, the owner of a leading sausage-making business.

Luetgert had emigrated from his native Germany in the 1870s and, over the years, had acquired three distinctions: he made just about the best German sausages in the city; he was a man of enormous appetite and considerable girth, weighing about 250 pounds, and he had sexual appetites that equalled or exceeded his culinary one, having three regular mistresses at the time of his wife's demise and a bed installed at his plant for his many trysts.

Luetgert was relatively happy except for one thing: his hefty wife, Louisa. She annoyed him, so much so that he often felt, as he told one of his lovers, "I could take her and crush her." Actually, as the police were to surmise in 1897, he probably stabbed her to death with a huge knife. That much is conjecture because almost nothing of Louisa's body was ever found. After Adolph killed her, he did something that was to damage the sale of sausage meat in Chicago for a long time. He melted her body down in a vat at his meat plant and made her part of his sausages.

Louisa turned up missing on May 1, 1897. Adolph told her relatives that he had hired private detectives to find her and that he would not go to the police because, as a prominent businessman, he could not afford to have any scandal. Eventually, his wife's relatives went to the police, who in turn searched Adolph's sausage factory. After several searches the police emptied one of many steam vats and found some pieces of bone, some teeth and two gold rings, one a wedding band with the initials "L. L." engraved on it. Both rings belonged to Louisa Luetgert. Although Adolph insisted the bone fragments were animal, analysis identified them as human. The wedding ring was even more damning because the sausage maker's wife suffered from swollen joints in some of her fingers and had been unable to remove the ring for years. However, as the police theorized, she could have been melted out of it.

Luetgert's trial was sensational, although most unsavory. The evidence against him was formidable, especially when one mistress after another took the stand to testify against him. Convicted, Luetgert was sentenced to life at Joliet Prison, where he died in 1911.

## Malcolm X (1925–1965) murder victim

The murder of Malcolm X in New York City on February 21, 1965 remains steeped in controversy, although three men were convicted of the killing and sent to prison for life. Within the black community there remains a conviction that the police investigation was superficial, that one or more of the men charged were not the right men and that the crime itself may not have been the work of the Black Muslims or not of that group alone.

Malcolm X had risen to become the second most powerful figure in the Nation of Islam, at the time the official name for the Black Muslim separatist movement. He had been converted to the Black Muslims 15 years earlier while serving a prison term for burglary. A glib and powerful speaker, Malcolm X clearly represented a threat to the leader of the movement, Elijah Muhammad, and to his presumptive successor and son-in-law, Raymond Sharrief.

In 1964 Malcolm split away and formed his own group, the Organization of Afro-American Unity, after being suspended from his post by Elijah Muhammad. Tension built up between the two groups, and a week before his assassination Malcolm X's home was bombed. The next Sunday, February 21, he arrived at a mosque in Harlem to deliver a speech. As he stepped before the audience of 400, a disturbance broke out near the front rows. One man yelled to another, "Get your hands off my pockets—Don't be messin' with my pockets!"

As four of at least six bodyguards moved forward, Malcolm X said, "Now, brothers, be cool." At that moment another disturbance erupted further back in the audience. A smoke bomb was set off, and at that instant a black man with a sawed-off shotgun charged toward the stage and blasted Malcolm X in the chest. Two other blacks rushed forward with handguns and fired several bullets into the black leader's prone body.

For a moment the audience and most of Malcolm X's bodyguards froze and the killers raced off. One of the assailants, however, was shot in the thigh by a bodyguard. As he dropped at the front stairway exit to the ballroom, members of the audience surrounded him and started beating him until he was rescued by police officers.

Immediately after the assassination, the police, the media and Malcolm X's supporters believed the killing was the work of the Black Muslims, and a Muslim mosque was burned in retaliation. However, the assailant trapped at the scene, 22-year-old Talmadge Hayer, married and the father of two children, could not be identified as a Black Muslim. Two other men arrested later by the police and tried with Hayer were Black Muslims, but both denied any involvement. Hayer admitted his guilt and said he had three accomplices, whom he refused to name, but declared neither of the other two defendants, Norman 3X Butler, 27, and Thomas 15X Johnson, 30, were part of the plot.

After a while, most blacks agreed that Butler and Johnson were the wrong men, since both were well-known Black Muslims and, as such, would have had difficulty penetrating the security at the mosque. In addition, Norman 3X Butler had been treated at Jacobi Hospital in the Bronx on the morning of the assassination for thrombophlebitis; he had had his right leg bandaged and had been given medication. Some observers who claim no real investigation was made find the idea of a physically impaired assassin being used in the plot unbelievable. Oddly, several of those present, including three of Malcolm X's lieutenants and bodyguards, vanished.

## Manson, Charles (1934– ) murder cult leader

The highly publicized leader of a "family," or self-aggrandizing cult, Charles Manson burst on the California scene in shocking style, even in a state long thought inured to bizarre bloodletting. On August 9, 1969 Charles "Tex" Watson and three female accomplices, Patricia Krenwinkel, Susan Atkins and Leslie Van Houten, entered the Beverly Hills estate of film director Roman Polanski, who was away at the time, and murdered his pregnant wife, actress Sharon Tate, and four others— Abigail Folger, heiress to the Folger coffee fortune; Voyteck Frykowski, a Polish writer and producer, who was living with Folger; Jay Sebring, a hairstylist; and 18-year-old Steven Earl Parent. The five were shot, stabbed and clubbed to death, with Sharon Tate begging to be allowed to live for the sake of her unborn baby. The killers used the victims' blood to scrawl crazed slogans and words like "Pig" and "War" on the walls. During the slaughter Watson kept screaming, "I am the devil and I have come to do the devil's work!"

Two nights later, the shocking process was repeated at the home of Leno and Rosemary La Bianca; they were butchered and the same sort of bloody messages were scrawled all over their home.

The murderers were soon traced back to the Manson family. Manson, at 34, had done time in several prisons and reform schools for such charges as procuring and forgery. After his last release from prison, he had set up a sort of commune for a cult of shiftless hippies and drifters at the Spahn Ranch outside Los Angeles, once a filming location for Hollywood studios. At the ranch the cult practiced free love, experimented with drugs and conducted pseudo-religious ceremonies built around Manson as a Christlike figure. When Manson ordered guerrilla tactics, his followers practiced guerrilla tactics, and when he told them to kill, they killed.

After their capture none of the actual killers or Manson, who had directed them, showed any sign of remorse over the horrify-

Charles Manson (right) and two of his female cultists, Patricia Krenwinkel (left) and Leslie Van Houten, were in a jovial mood at a court appearance after their arrest. All were convicted of murder.

ing crimes. At their trial—during which a number of Manson's shaved-head female followers kept daily vigil outside the courthouse—the prosecutor called Manson "one of the most evil, satanic men who ever walked the face of the earth." For a time the three women defendants offered to admit their guilt if Manson was declared innocent. Manson waved off their offer, telling the court: "I have done my best to get along in your world, and now you want to kill me. I say to myself, 'Ha, I'm already dead, have been all my life . . . I don't care anything about any of you."

All were found guilty and sentenced to die, but they were spared the death penalty because of the Supreme Court ruling outlaw-

ing capital punishment and were given life instead. They have been eligible for parole since 1978. In 1980 Manson was turned down on his third annual application for parole. The parole board advised him to train for a trade as part of his rehabilitation, but Manson said: "I'll stay here forever. I'm too old. I can't do too much. I like to sit around, smoke grass, read the Bible now and then."

See also: HELTER SKELTER.

**Manton, Martin T.** (1880–1946) crooked judge
The only federal judge ever imprisoned for corruption, Martin T. Manton was something of a courtroom wunderkind. When Woodrow Wilson named him district court

judge, he was, at the age of 36, the youngest federal jurist in the country. Within a year and a half he had moved up to the appellate court; in 1922 it was said that he missed an appointment to the Supreme Court by an eyelash. Over a 10-year period Manton produced 650 opinions, an output very few judges have ever equaled. However, it developed that his opinions were for sale. Soliciting a bribe in one case, Manton was quoted as saying, "While I'm sitting on the bench, I have my right hand and my left hand."

In 1939 Manhattan District Attorney Thomas E. Dewey accused him of taking bribes with both hands and even employing an agent to negotiate the sale of verdicts. The charges against Manton were considered so incredible that he had no trouble convincing Judge Learned Hand and two former presidential candidates, Al Smith and John W. Davis, to appear as character witnesses at his trial. Nonetheless, he was found guilty. Pleading his own appeal before the Supreme Court, Manton came up with a novel argument: "From a broad viewpoint, it serves no public policy for a high judicial officer to be convicted of a judicial crime. It tends to destroy the confidence of the people in the courts." The High Court was unimpressed, however, and turned down his appeal. Manton served 19 months at the federal prison in Lewisburg, Pa. and died a broken man in 1946.

### Mather, Cotton (1663–1728) promoter of Salem witch trials

The American colonial clergyman Cotton Mather, it has been said, was simultaneously the most intelligent and the most stupid man this country has ever produced. He was the author of no less that 450 books on many erudite subjects, but he was also obsessed by witches. With his fiery sermons, Mather was probably the man most responsible for the Salem witchcraft mania of 1692. He encouraged the persecutions, which finally ended only because of public revulsion. Among the many contributions Dr. Mather made on the general subject of witchcraft was the theory that the devil spoke perfect Greek, Hebrew and Latin, but that his English was hampered by an odd accent.

### Maxwell, Robert (1923–1991) intercontinental superswindler

While the 1980s have been called the decade of the superswindler—producing such financial felons as Michael Milken, Ivan Boesky, Charles Keating, and the like—Robert Maxwell was in a class of his own.

Maxwell, a flamboyant Czech-born British publisher, was regarded by many as a brilliant ringmaster who fought his way up from poverty and personal tragedy to build a financial empire that made him one of the business world's most feared operators. In the 1980s Maxwell eagerly sought the mantle of savior of downtrodden newspapers, such as Britain's Mirror Group newspapers and New York's *Daily News*.

Then began what may be called Maxwell's "Operation Siphon." It will take years into the 21st century to unravel the full extent of Maxwell's depredations, but it became clear that he and perhaps a few others siphoned off at least $1.63 billion from pension funds and the two flagship companies of his publishing empire, Mirror Group and Maxwell Communications Corp. The total losses to the pension funds and other creditors will at some point escalate by many billions of dollars more.

Maxwell died at sea, having either fallen, been pushed or jumped from his luxury yacht, *Lady Ghislaine.* Was he murdered to be silenced? Had he died accidentally? Or had he finally decided the jig was up and taken his own life? Of the alternatives, the last seems the more likely since, according to investigators, he faced certain exposure in a matter of days.

Actually the most amazing aspect of his crimes was that Maxwell had gotten away with them for so many years, considering that 20 years earlier Great Britain's Board of Trade found that he was not "in our opinion a person who could be relied on to exercise proper stewardship of a publicly quoted company." Nevertheless, Maxwell continued to thrive, proving that nothing succeeds in fraud like excessive success. Even while picking up the nickname "The Bouncing Czech," Maxwell blithely went from one megadeal to the next, using looted assets to keep afloat the heavily indebted private companies at the heart of his empire.

In the firestorm after Maxwell's death, even the most austere elements of the British press descended to colorful and livid terms to denounce him as a "fraudster on a grand scale." Whittam Smith, editor of *The Independent,* declared, "He was a crook. Shareholders other than his family were lambs to be fleeced; pensions were fair game." Peter Jenkins wrote in the same publication: "Ask anyone with knowledge of financial matters the secret of his success, and they would explain how he could make money move from bank to bank, company to company, faster than the eye could see. Some called this wizardry business, but most knew in their hearts that Maxwell was simply not kosher, no friend of widows and orphans."

Superswindler Robert Maxwell was for a time hailed as the savior of the ailing *New York Daily News* when he took it over. Then he began what was later called "Operation Siphon," looting pension funds at the News and his other holdings and cheating creditors out of many billions.

Within a month of Maxwell's death, his financial empire had crumbled in bankruptcies. Perhaps Maxwell knew the house of cards was rushing headlong to collapse. In a television interview shortly before his death, Maxwell said in response to a question that in the hereafter he couldn't say if he would meet his "maker . . . or the banker."

Maxwell left a few somewhat laughing—but far many more stone-cold broke.

### Menendez Brothers    parent killers

In one of the most explosive California murder cases of the late 1900s—even coming close to rivaling the notorious O. J. Simpson trial—two brothers, Lyle Menendez, 21, and Erik Menendez, 18, shotgunned their wealthy parents to death in 1989. But was it a crime or self-defense?

The boys' shocking defense was that they had killed their parents, entertainment executive Jose Menendez and Kitty Menendez, because, they said, they feared their parents were going to kill them to prevent them from revealing years of sexual and emotional abuse by the couple. Both brothers said they had been sexually abused by their father between the ages of 6 and 8. So they slaughtered their parents with a pair of shotguns as they watched television in the Beverly Hills mansion. The prosecution charged that the brothers committed their crime to inherit an estate valued at $14 million and pointed to the brothers' wild spending spree after the slayings. Lyle got himself a Porsche and Erik a private tennis coach. The brothers at first claimed alibis, and it was not until Erik confessed to his therapist, who notified the law, that they were arrested.

The brothers' first trial was televised and became almost the obsession that the Simpson trial caused not long afterward. A feisty defense lawyer, Leslie Abramson, became a media star as she managed to pull out a hung jury after filling the record with tales of parental mistreatment and provoking nationwide outrage at the "abuse excuse."

It was charged in some legal circles that the televising of the trial made the sensationalism of the case so compelling that a conviction was impossible. In the second trial however the judge banned television and excluded much of the lurid abuse testimony, which was relegated to the possible punishment phase of the proceedings. The judge also rejected the defense's argument of "imperfect self-defense," which reasoned that even if there was no real threat of attack, the brothers' fears were genuine. The judge ruled the argument was invalid since it was the siblings who had set up the final confrontation with their parents. The brothers had indeed laid in wait for their parents.

On March 20, 1996, the Menendez brothers were convicted of first-degree murder. They were both sentenced to life imprisonment without the possibility of parole. What may have been even more crushing for the brothers was that they were not confined to the same institution. Erik was confined at the California State Prison in Sacramento County and Lyle at the California Correctional Institution at Tehachapi.

## Milken, Michael R. (1946– ) king of junk bonds

As a result of the scandals and prosecutions of the 1980s and early 1990s a debate left unsettled was who among the perpetrators did the most damage and walked away with the most loot. For a time Ivan Boesky was labeled by the press as the most "successful." However, Boesky could make the point that he was nowhere near being the biggest crook in American finance. He could point to Michael R. Milken, the junk bond king of Drexel Burnham Lambert, Inc., who was nailed after Boesky's cooperation.

Milken had risen to fame as the main force creating the huge market for junk bonds, the high-yield, high-risk debt securities that marked the corporate takeover boom of the 1980s. Milken did not go down easily, spending an estimated $1 million a month for several years fighting the federal government's case against him. He finally reversed his tactics and pleaded guilty in 1990 to six felony counts involving securities fraud and agreed to pay the lion's share of a cash settlement by himself and his cohorts, which was eventually fixed at $1.3 billion in fines and restitution costs to victims.

Still, there were those who objected to the deal, insisting that Milken had forced the government to drop the more serious charges of racketeering and insider trading. They also complained about his being able to keep about $125 million of his personal fortune. In addition, his immediate family maintained more than $300 million in assets, meaning that the settlement could leave the convicted junk bond dealer with close to a half billion dollars. Milken drew a 10-year prison term, with sentencing judge Kimba M. Wood declaring, "When a man of your power in the financial world, at the head of one of the most important banking houses in this country, repeatedly conspires to violate, and violates, securities and tax laws in order to achieve more power and wealth for himself and his wealthy clients, and commits financial crimes that are particularly hard to detect, a significant prison term is required in order to deter others."

The 10-year sentence was not permanent. Milken negotiated with the government and provided evidence against others (although critics said his offerings were less than adequate). For his cooperation Judge Wood reduced Milken's sentence to 33 months and 26 days so that he could be released on parole after 24 months. The judge said she also took into account Milken's good behavior in prison, where he had been tutoring other prisoners and had set up a prison library. Milken was also sentenced to 1,800 hours of community service. Barred from doing any more stock deals, Milken hardly maintained a low profile in business matters.

## Molineux, Roland B. (1868–1917) accused murderer

The least-remembered figure involved in the murder of Mrs. Katherine Adams, which proved to be one of New York's most sensational and most enduring mysteries, was the victim herself. All she did was drink some poison, die and get buried. Instead, the "Molineux Case" was named after the handsome and dashing young man who, depending upon which verdict one believes, either did or did not poison the elderly widow.

In 1898, at the age of 30, Roland Molineux moved with grace and ease in the city's high society. He was the son of Brigadier Gen. Edward Leslie Molineux, who had served with considerable honor in the Civil War and was a leading citizen of Brooklyn and a power broker within the Republican Party. With an excellent education behind him, Roland had a brilliant future as a chemist. He also possessed considerable charm—attested to by the fact that he had been named correspondent in a divorce case at the tender age of 15.

A fine physical specimen, Molineux was a member of the Knickerbocker Athletic Club and national amateur horizontal bar champion. Because of his social standing and athletic prowess, he exerted considerable influence on club affairs and usually got his way. One member he apparently didn't get his way with was Henry C. Barnet, who annoyed Molineux by courting a young lady named Blanche Cheeseborough even after she had become engaged to Molineux. However, in November 1898 Barnet died under mysterious circumstances. There was rumor that he had taken poison sent to him through the mail, but nothing came of the charge and Molineux and Blanche were married.

Meanwhile, Molineux developed a new feud, this time with Harry Cornish, the athletic director of the club. Actually, they had been at odds for a couple of years, mainly because Cornish did not seem to show the proper deference to the officious Molineux.

Then Cornish bested Molineux in a weight-lifting tournament, and the angry Molineux went to the club's board of directors and demanded Cornish be fired for various offenses. The board rejected Molineux' demands and the young athlete resigned in a huff.

On December 23, 1898 Cornish received a bottle of Bromo Seltzer in the mail from an anonymous donor. He considered it the work of a club wag, twitting him not to overdrink during the holidays. On December 28 Mrs. Adams, his landlady, complained of a splitting headache and the helpful Cornish fixed her a Bromo. She drank it and complained of its bitter taste. Cornish took a tiny sip and said he noticed nothing. Moments later, Mrs. Adams writhed in agony on the floor and died a half hour later. Cornish became deathly ill from his small sip.

Cornish had retained the wrapping the Bromo Seltzer had been mailed in, and suspicion soon centered on Molineux when a number of handwriting experts identified the writing on it as his. Other handwriting samples linked him to the poison that apparently had been sent to Barnet. Molineux was charged with the Adams killing, and press indignation and public hysteria ran high against him by the time he was brought to trial. The trial lasted three months and cost a staggering $200,000. Five hundred potential jurors were questioned before 12 could be selected. After eight hours of deliberation they found Molineux guilty and he was sentenced to die.

At this point Molineux' father financed a massive appeal effort. John G. Milburn, the Buffalo lawyer in whose home President William McKinley had died of an assassin's bullet, finally won a retrial on the ground that the judge had allowed the jury to hear evidence about the Barnet matter although it had no bearing on the case under consideration.

During his 18 months on death row Molineux had written a book of prison tales called *The Room with the Little Door,* which critics hailed as the work of a most sensitive and gifted writer. By the time the new trial began, the public atmosphere had changed. The previous hysteria had faded and Molineux was now viewed as a talented man of letters. The defense marshaled just as many handwriting "experts" on its side as the prosecution had in the previous proceedings, not a difficult accomplishment considering the state of that art at the time. Molineux' lawyer also produced a woman named Anna Stephenson, the wife of a policeman, who said she had been at the General Post Office when the poison was originally mailed. She assured the court she had seen a man mail a package addressed to Harry Cornish at the Knickerbocker Club and that man was not Molineux. In fact, the man had looked something like Cornish himself.

It turned out the woman could not see very well, but she insisted her vision had been perfect in 1898. Her husband was called to the stand and he advised the jurors to pay his wife no mind. The jury did not follow his advice and acquitted Molineux in four minutes.

Molineux was now a greater celebrity than ever. Newspapers hired him to write about other murder trials and he published a number of books. In the meantime, his wife, who had stood by him during his ordeal, divorced him. Later, she tried to appear in vaudeville as Blanche Cheeseborough Molineux, but her former husband took legal action to prevent it. In 1913 Molineux wrote a play, which David Belasco produced, called *The Man Inside,* about a reformed criminal. During its run Molineux, demonstrating his own ordeal had not left him unscathed, caused scenes at the theater and had to be ejected on a number of occasions.

Later that year he was committed to an asylum, where he died in 1917. Upon his death a police official declared the Adams murder had been considered closed since the time of Molineux's second trial.

## Moore, Nathaniel Ford (1883–1910)
### suspected murder victim

Few deaths aroused as much gossip and scandal in Chicago as that of playboy Nathaniel Ford Moore, the 26-year-old son of James Hobart Moore, president of the Rock Island Railroad and one of the nation's most influential capitalists. There were many back in 1910 who firmly believed Nathaniel Moore had been murdered and that belief persists to this day.

Young Moore supposedly found a check for $100,000 under his breakfast plate on his 21st birthday and became a playboy that night, visiting Chicago's and America's most-renowned and fabulous bordello, the Everleigh Club. For the next five years he was a regular there. His final visit was the night of January 8, 1910, when he showed up drunk. The strict rule of the Everleigh Club prohibiting the admittance of any customer in an inebriated condition was relaxed in Moore's case. However, one of the Everleigh sisters, Minna, refused to allow him to be served any more wine, which set off an argument between her and one of her girls, Moore's favorite, whom the playboy always tipped lavishly. The harlot marched out of the club, vowing vengeance on the Everleighs.

Moore himself left about 1 A.M. About 30 hours later, at dawn of January 10, Minna Everleigh received a telephone call from the harlot who had paraded out of the club in such a rage. Tearfully, the girl told Minna that Moore had died in a fashionable brothel run by Madam Vic Shaw. She also imparted the intelligence that Madam Shaw and some other madams along South Dearborn Street, members of the Friendly Friends, a society of brothel owners who constantly plotted against the Everleigh sisters because their club siphoned off so much of the "playboy money," had come up with a bizarre plot to plant Moore's body in the Everleigh Club furnace.

Minna Everleigh, accompanied by some supporters, marched on the Shaw brothel and forced her way in. She confronted Madam Shaw, who finally admitted to the presence of young Moore's corpse. Minna insisted the police be called and stood by while the young heir's body was removed to the family's Lake Shore Drive home, rather than her furnace. According to Minna Everleigh, Moore had died of a murderous overdose of morphine in his champagne, but the official investigation indicated death was due to heart disease. The investigation's finding, however, did not stop the whispering that there had indeed been a murder but that the family had used its power to limit the scandal to the proportions it had already achieved. The facts were never fully established to everyone's satisfaction.

The furnace plot became a part of Chicago folklore, adopted by the Capone gang for use when an unwanted stiff had to be removed from a mob resort called the Four Deuces. The boys would haul the corpse to the cellar of a competing establishment and put it in the furnace. Then the manager of the Four Deuces would complain to the police that the competition was running an illegal crematorium. In the ensuing investigation the rival resort would be so ripped up by police looking for additional "bodies" that it could never reopen.

See also: EVERLEIGH SISTERS.

**Nathan, Benjamin** (1813–1870) murder victim
The murder in 1870 of philanthropist Benjamin Nathan, described inaccurately as "the richest man in New York," remains to this day a tantalizing unsolved crime.

At 6 A.M. on July 28, 1870, Washington Nathan went downstairs in the family mansion at 12 West 23rd Street for a drink of water to soothe his regular hangover. He passed his father's bedroom, looked in and received, presumably, a shock. Benjamin Nathan lay dead on the floor, his features and clothing covered with blood and gore. He had been repeatedly struck on the head with an 18-inch carpenter's "dog." A safe in the room had been opened and there were signs of a struggle. There were also indications that the killer, rather than hurrying from the place after the crime, had leisurely washed up in a basin on the dresser. The murderer had not been very neat, leaving a bloody handprint on the wall.

While within 24 hours rewards totaling $47,000 were offered, the case was never solved. Police suspicion centered on dissolute Washington Nathan, who was known to have had terrific rows with his father over his lavish spending, but a case against him could never be proved. Washington was provided with an alibi for part of the time when the murder may have been committed by a "lass of the pavements," as the papers called her.

In 1879 Washington Nathan, still keeping up his dissolute ways, was paying court to an actress named Alice Harrison when a former inamorata named Fanny Barrett, who had followed him, whipped out a revolver and shot him in the neck. When it appeared that Washington would require an operation to remove the bullet, Chief of Police George W. Walling worked out a plan to have him questioned after the operation as he was coming out of the anaesthetic in the hope he would say something about his father's murder. But the bullet came out by itself, thwarting that strategy.

A much better technique became apparent too late, some three decades after the murder, when incredulous New York police were prevailed upon by Scotland Yard to take the thumb smudge of a man arrested for a New York hotel theft and send it to London.

There, it was matched up to a print found on a jewel case in a robbery. Some New York police historian then remembered the blood-stained prints of all five fingers on one hand of Nathan's murderer had been left on the wall, but the fingerprinting detection method had not yet been developed.

### Novarro, Ramon (1899–1968) Hollywood murder victim

During Hollywood's golden age, revelation of a male star's homosexuality could destroy his career. Two stars subjected to such sexual disclosure were the great "Latin lovers" Rudolph Valentino and Ramon Novarro. There is little doubt that the speculation was correct. The two were fast friends and in 1923 Valentino presented Novarro with what was described as "a black lead, Art Deco dildo inscribed with Valentino's silver signature." Newsmen capitalized on such intelligence to infer that the two great lovers were not "real men," and the more outspokenly homophobic referred to them as "faggots."

Upon Valentino's death in 1926, the dark, often brooding Novarro inherited the mantle as the world's greatest Latin lover. The Hollywood publicity mill linked him romantically with Greta Garbo and Myrna Loy, which Novarro outspokenly denied. So publicists switched to presenting him as a deep, pensive man. They apparently both started then quashed the rumor that Novarro was considering entering a monastery, brooding over Valentino's death. If he were indeed considering such a move, more likely it was by the mid-1930s when Novarro's popularity was on the wane. He left Hollywood and performed for some years abroad as a singer. When he returned to California to try to

Ramon Novarro, the great lover and the great lover of films, faced a hapless death in real life.

reinvigorate his screen career, he was disappointed by the public's lack of interest and took more to drinking in his lavish home in North Hollywood. He was seldom seen in the company of women and was well known to young male prostitutes, who he picked up cruising Los Angeles.

In October 1968 two runaway brothers from Chicago, Paul and Tom Ferguson, accompanied Novarro to his home. Their interests, however, were not the same as those of Novarro. After several hours of drinking, Paul Ferguson ended up naked in the Novarro home, where he became enraged at the aging actor. Paul was notorious for his contempt for "faggots." In a vicious attack he seized Novarro's trademark ivory-tipped cane and beat the filmstar into unconsciousness. Paul continued battering Novarro until finally Tom begged him to stop. By then Novarro was certainly mortally wounded.

The panicky brothers tried to make the situation look like a robbery, smashing furniture, emptying drawers and binding the bloody Novarro's wrists and ankles and jamming the cane between his thighs. They further sought to leave a false clue by scrawling "Larry" around the house. In another tact, they wrote on a mirror: "Us girls are better than fagits [sic]."

The pair dressed themselves in some of Novarro's elegant clothes and foolishly dumped their own bloody clothes in a neighbor's yard where the police readily found them. The clothes aided the police search that located the pair. Tried for murder, they were sentenced to life imprisonment. The Fergusons, however, were paroled after seven years, at the time a typical term, especially in light of the prevailing homophobia.

## Ohio Gang   Harding Administration grafters

Without doubt, the so-called Ohio Gang, a group of political cronies from Ohio who put Warren G. Harding in politics and eventually in the White House, took more from the public coffers in their two-year and five-month stay in Washington than any other corrupt group in American history. Including Teapot Dome, their total depredations have been estimated to total as much as $300 million, or five to 10 times what the Tweed Ring made off with.

The unofficial head of the Ohio Gang was President Harding's attorney general Harry M. Daugherty, who had guided Harding's political career from 1900 until his triumphant arrival in Washington in 1921. The Ohio Gang, as the group was soon labeled, let it be known that they had come to Washington for only one reason, to make money. A price tag was placed on everything they controlled. Judgeships, lucrative Prohibition-agent jobs, public lands and oil reserves were all up for sale. Bribes and payoffs were made at the House on 16th Street. The Little Green House on H Street featured poker games, bathtub gin and women to convince the dubious to join the graft game.

Daugherty and his Ohio henchman, Jess Smith, are believed to have a hand in every payment of graft, and there is little doubt that Harding knew much and suspected more. "My God," he told William Allen White, "this is a hell of a job. I have no trouble with my enemies. I can take care of them all right. But my damn friends, White, they're the ones that keep me walking the floor nights."

Harding didn't really spend much time walking the floors; he sat in on the poker games. Actually, the president didn't know how to control Daugherty and was a little afraid of him. Daugherty knew of Harding's illegitimate child and he had also advanced him $100,000, which he dropped in the stock market. As the stocks dipped, Daugherty's hold on Harding tightened.

The Ohio Gang's plundering was so massive that scandals started to break even before Harding died in 1923. There were rumors of frauds in the Veterans Bureau running as high as $200 million. Eventually,

Colonel Charles R. Forbes was sent to prison for taking kickbacks from contractors building veterans hospitals. Jess Smith, the Ohio Gang's bagman, killed himself and the newspapers speculated whether it was because of pangs of conscience or whether he had been murdered to ensure his silence. Albert B. Fall, Harding's secretary of the interior, served his time for his part in the Teapot Dome scandal along with oil man Harry Sinclair. Harry Daugherty narrowly escaped conviction in a bribery complicated case involving the alien property custodian. In the final analysis, the Ohio Gang could not have functioned if Harding had been a strong president, but Daugherty probably would not have promoted him if he had possessed that potential. As Sen. Frank Brandegee of Connecticut said at the time of his nomination, Harding was "no world-beater but he is the best of the second-raters."

See also: ALBERT BACON FALL, TEAPOT DOME SCANDAL.

## Olive, Isom Prentice "Print" (1840–1886)
murderer

The epitome of the arrogant big rancher, Texas-born Print Olive and his brother Bob owned one of Nebraska's greatest spreads. For many years he was a law unto himself, directing a brutal war against the homesteaders who, in his view, were crowding his range. Print Olive cut fences, destroyed crops and employed a cowboy army of over one hundred to terrorize the homesteaders, but the state of Nebraska kept siding with these settlers, a development that made the Olive brothers even more violent.

In November 1878 Bob Olive was killed in a shoot-out with two homesteaders, Luther Mitchell and Ami Ketchum. The two

men were arrested but, while being taken to a hearing, were handed over to Print Olive's men in exchange for cash. They were brought to the Olive ranch, where Print meted out his own version of frontier justice, shooting, hanging and—after dousing them with whiskey—burning them. For this outrage, which earned Print Olive the label "man burner," the cattle baron was brought to trial and, along with one of his chief aides, Fred Fisher, was sentenced to life imprisonment. When Olive's private army of cowboys threatened to break him free, President Rutherford B. Hayes, at the behest of the governor of Nebraska sent in several companies of mounted soldiers. Still, Print Olive bragged he would not remain in prison, and he proved right. Within two years, during which he spent $250,000 in legal fees, he was released and a new trial was ordered. It was never held, however, because the witnesses had "scattered."

Print Olive soon moved on to Colorado, where he gained a reasonable amount of acceptance over the next few years. However, his code remained as violent as ever. In 1886 in Trial City, Colo. Olive came across a former cowhand employee named Joe Sparrow, who owed him $10. Olive demanded the money in a saloon confrontation. When the smoke cleared, the cattle baron was dead.

## Oswald, Lee Harvey (1939–1963) assassin of John F. Kennedy

At 12:30 P.M. on November 22, 1963, President John F. Kennedy was shot to death in Dallas, Tex. with a mail-order rifle belonging to Lee Harvey Oswald. Oswald was an employee of the Texas School Book Depository and, as such, had access to a sixth-floor window that provided a perfect vantage for the sniping. As the motorcade passed, Oswald apparently fired three times, killing Kennedy and badly wounding Texas Gov. John B. Connally, who was sitting directly in front of the president in the executive limousine.

Ever since, there has been a dispute over whether or not Oswald was the only gunman and whether additional shots were fired by others. Critics of the Warren Commission, which investigated the assassination and concluded that Oswald had acted alone, have insisted, with varying degrees of plausibility, that the commission's reconstruction of the events was based on fallacies and physical improbabilities such as the commission's theory that a single bullet hit both Kennedy and Connally.

After the shooting Oswald concealed his rifle among some crates and casually walked from the building. He went home, secured a pistol and went out again. When stopped by Dallas policeman J. D. Tippit, Oswald shot the police officer four times, killing him. He took refuge in a movie house without purchasing a ticket and was apprehended there by police officers. When approached by the officers, he pointed his gun at them but it misfired.

Oswald consistently denied having killed either Kennedy or Tippit, although several witnesses identified him as Tippit's killer and his palm print was found on the weapon used to kill Kennedy. A check into Oswald's background produced a picture of a misfit and an apparent on-again, off-again believer in communism. He had received a hardship discharge from the marines in 1959 because of an injury his mother had suffered, but he did not stay home long to help her. Instead, he traveled to the USSR using funds the source of which has never been identified. He gave

up his American citizenship, went to work for the Soviets on radar installations and married the daughter of a KGB colonel. After two and a half years Oswald tired of life in the Soviet Union and decided to move back to America with his family. After obtaining a loan from the U.S. State Department, he returned and settled in New Orleans, where he seems to have divided his political affiliations between such diverse groups as the right-wing China Lobby and the left-wing Fair Play for Cuba Committee. He also had links with persons who were known conduits for arms and money provided by the CIA to counterinsurgency forces. Thus, Oswald may have been a Soviet agent, a CIA agent or plant or just a plain kook.

Oswald did not live long enough to provide an answer to that question or why he had killed the president. Two days after his apprehension he was shot to death by Jack Ruby, a Dallas nightclub operator, as police were transferring him to the county jail. The murder was shown live on television, as the media covered Oswald's movements. That such a valuable prisoner could be so easily assassinated was shocking and led to a bitter denunciation of Dallas law officials.

While the Warren Commission found that Oswald had acted alone in his assassination of the president and that Jack Ruby similarly had killed Oswald on his own, the controversy was not stilled. Dozens of books have been written attacking the conclusions of the commission, all pushing various conspiracy theories. New Orleans District Attorney James Garrison put forth the most fantastic claims of a vast plot to eliminate Kennedy from power.

In December 1978 the House Select Committee on Assassinations issued a report that challenged the Warren Commission's findings. Much of the committee's conclusions that Kennedy "was probably assassinated as a result of a conspiracy" was based on a study of the noises in Dallas' Dealey Plaza at the time of the murder. The acoustical study led the probers to conclude "the evidence established a high probability that two gunmen fired" at Kennedy that day. The panel said, however, that it was "unable to identify the other gunman or the extent of the conspiracy." Another conclusion, based on the evidence available, was that the Soviet Union, Cuba, organized crime or anti-Castro groups had not been involved. The committee flatly stated that none of the U.S. intelligence agencies—the CIA, the FBI or the Secret Service—were implicated. However, the agencies were criticized for their failings prior to and at the time of the assassination and during the ensuing probes.

At the time some members of the panel objected to the findings, protesting that they represented a rush to judgment precipitated by the acoustic evidence. After the panel's report, the matter was put in the hands of a new scientific panel that became known as the Committee of Ballistic Acoustics of the National Research Council and was funded by a grant from the National Science Foundation. Staffed by top-drawer experts from Harvard, MIT, the University of California, Columbia and Princeton as well as from research centers at Bell Telephone Laboratories, Xerox, IBM and Trisolar Corporation and an expert from the Firearms National Laboratory Center of the Department of the Treasury, the group concluded that there was no extra shot fired that would have suggested a conspiracy. The firm finding was, "The acoustic analyses impulses attributed to gunshots were recorded about one minute after the president had been shot and the motorcade had been instructed to go to the hospital."

It must be said, a number of conspiracy theorists conceded the point. However, others did not. A story made the rounds that they could not abandon their claims concerning the acoustics since they had written entire books on the premise. To concede the point meant their books would have to be moved from the nonfiction to the fiction shelves.

Similarly, conspiracy theorists who found Oswald innocent, or misused or framed, pointed to the staggering fate of so many material witnesses in the affair. In the three years following the Kennedy and Oswald murders, no fewer than 18 witnesses died. Six were shot to death, two committed suicide, three died in car accidents, one was killed by a karate blow to the neck, one bled to death from a throat slashing, three suffered fatal heart attacks and two expired from natural causes. The reserved London *Sunday Times* engaged an actuary to determine the mathematical probability of these occurrences. He concluded their odds were 100,000 trillion to one.

The newspaper killed the story after just one edition and amended its findings, most probably having gotten a storm of scientific protest. A spokesman for the *Times* later told the House Select Committee on Assassinations, that the claim was "a careless journalistic mistake and should not have been published. . . . There was no question our actuary having got his answer wrong."

He explained the actuary was asked about such a number of people out of the United States dying within a short period of time, to which he replied the odds were very high. However, if he had more correctly been asked about the odds of that happening from a pool based on the Warren Commission Index dying within a given period, the result would have been much lower. The newspaper's spokesman said, "Our mistake was to treat the reply to the former question as if it dealt with the latter—hence the fundamental error in our first edition report, for which we apologize."

Indeed, a chief researcher for the HSCA reported, "We had thus established the impossibility of attempting to establish, through the application of actuarial principles, any meaningful implications about the existence or absence of a conspiracy."

Despite the *Sunday Times* retraction and the Select Committee's findings, critics still cite the 100,000 trillion figure—typical is Robert J. Groden's 1993 book *The Killing of a President,* which sports a foreword by Oliver Stone, which used the *Sunday Times* figures with no reference to the newspaper's retraction—or at least claim the death rate is far above the norm. Of course, a supposedly abnormal death rate is a vital part of the thesis of Stone's movie, *JFK.*

It is rather easy to compile a collection of 100 theories that Oswald did not do it or most certainly, did not do it alone. The problem is that these theories are contradictory to one another, and that hardly makes the remaining one any more right than the 99 others.

Thus we are left with Oswald, a man frustrated with the idea that he was a failure and was sexually at odds with his wife. And we are left with the conclusion of Professor James W. Clarke in *American Assassins: The Darker Side of Politics,* which views Oswald as "a mercurial, anxiety-ridden young man who, the facts suggest, could have been turned away from his deadly assignment with a kind word and loving embrace."

See also: JACK RUBY.

## Pantages rape trials   Hollywood frame-up scandal

He was called Alexander the Great, perhaps a remarkable sobriquet for Alexander Pantages, who emigrated from Athens, Greece, and worked as a shoeshine and newspaper boy. Although he could hardly read or write English, through cunning, hard work and a moderate stroke of luck, Pantages made a small fortune in the Alaska gold rush around the turn of the 20th century. That gave him enough of a stake to become a leading force in the American entertainment industry.

He bought a run-down Seattle theater and staged vaudeville entertainments. He was so adept at this, he soon accumulated 60 very profitable theaters. Early on he grasped the enormous profits to be gained by use of Thomas Edison's motion picture projector, and he added movies to his theaters to complement his stage shows. In the 1920s, Pantages merged his theaters with those of Radio-Keith-Orpheum (RKO) into one of the richest theatrical operations in America. Pantages became a true financial power-house; when he talked many in Hollywood listened and even quaked.

Slight at 128 pounds, the 54-year-old Pantages knew how to run roughshod over other Hollywood giants and made scores of enemies. One primary example was Joseph Kennedy, the father of the future U.S. president. Joe Kennedy was eager to become an important Hollywood player. He had a relatively small-potatoes investment in a studio—FBO Pictures—and if he could buy the Pantages chain, he could realize his ambitions.

Kennedy approached Pantages with a buy-out offer. By that time—the late 1920s—Pantages had at least mastered broken English, had no interest in selling his theaters to Kennedy, but, he said, according to Hollywood scuttlebutt, "I sella you a ticket."

Pantages was well known as a womanizer and had a casting couch on which many would-be starlets secured performances in his stage shows and perhaps the movies. Following his affront to Kennedy, Pantages became mired in scandal.

A 17-year-old stagestruck high-school dropout, Eunice Pringle, claimed Pantages had raped her in his office, or more exactly in a janitor's broom and mop closet in the office. The Hearst and Chandler newspapers had a field day with the story, as well as the subsequent trial with its graphic details of how the alleged rape was carried out. At the trial the newspapers discovered "the sweetest 17 since Clara Bow" and "a full-blown beauty," "An Innocent Defiled." Descriptions of Pantages offered different characterizations. He was "The Great God Pan" . . . "His Foreign Goatedness Caught Out!". . . "Lechery Exposed" . . .

Pringle appeared at the trial as "Miss Innocent" from Central Casting. She had a long bowed pigtail, a blue dress with Dutch collar and cuffs, black stockings, black felt "Mary Jane" shoes, gloves and a wee purse. She could have passed, observers agreed, for 12 or 13. And she sobbed throughout her testimony.

The defense was handled by a young Jerry Giesler, who would become Hollywood's most flamboyant and effective defense lawyer. Giesler ridiculed Pringle's story of the rape—that the frail Pantages held her mouth with his right hand, knocked her to the floor, managed to undress himself and rip away her clothing with his left hand alone without the healthy girl being able to get away. Pervading this line was the fact that Pantages could easily have had sex with any number of willing females any day of his choice.

To break down Pringle's Mary Jane pose, Giesler insisted she wear the outfit she had on when the alleged attack took place. Pringle appeared before the jury in a provocative red dress, clinging and low cut, fully made up and looking very much the sexy female rather than the virginal little girl.

Then Giesler sought to introduce evidence that Pringle was a sexual sophisticate who lived "in sin" with her agent, dancer Nick Dunaev, a man reputed to skate on the line between right and wrong, and that she had sexual affairs with many other men. However, the judge ruled such matters irrelevant.

After being deadlocked for some time, the jury voted to convict, and the judge sentenced Pantages to 50 years in San Quentin. Giesler appealed the conviction on the basis that the judge had prevented him from presenting vital evidence and that three women jurors claimed they had been pressured into voting to convict. The California Supreme Court ordered a new trial.

This time around the jury found Pantages not guilty. One juror described how the panel had gone through the process of "eliminating the witnesses we believed had not told the truth until we got to the testimony we felt was acceptable." None of the jurors believed Pringle's testimony.

Pantages left San Quentin a free man, his reputation restored. In Hollywood there was much speculation whether Pringle and Dunaev were capable of concocting the fake story on their own. There was strong belief that someone else was behind the plot, and that person was named in private but not in print.

Some years later when Pringle was on her deathbed, she confessed that Joe Kennedy was behind the frame-up and that besides paying her and Dunaev he had promised that after he had absorbed Pantages' empire, he would take care of Pringle by making her a star performer on the Pantages circuit.

## Patterson, Nan (1882–?) accused murderer

The 1904 case, one the New York newspapers dubbed The Girl in the Hansom Cab, had everything the readers of the new yellow journalism could want: a Floradora Girl, at the time the most dazzling of Broadway figures; a big-spending gambler and race horse owner; a jealous wife, and a murder mystery.

Gorgeous Nan Patterson was a Floradora Girl, not a member of the original sextette but a replacement for one who had married a millionaire. All Floradora Girls, the public believed, were destined to marry millionaires. Nan, a doll-faced, stagestruck young thing, had made it to the Great White Way after eloping in her teens. She later fell for, instead of a millionaire, a married gambler, Francis Thomas Young, known to his friends as Caesar. Young, who was what might be called a cad, and Nan were constantly seen together at the races, at gambling spas and at all the top hotels and restaurants. However, Young also had a wife, whom he wouldn't or couldn't give up. He kept his wife in one New York hotel and Nan in another on the same block. It made the gambler's life a hectic one. He paid for Nan's divorce, and in 1904 he finally decided to divorce his wife and run off with Nan. But his wife talked him out of that plan and the couple reconciled. Feeling she could win back her husband from Nan by separating them, she convinced Young to sail to Europe with her on June 4.

The day before his departure, Young spent his time with Nan Patterson. The pair drank heavily and quarreled, Nan still trying to get him to change his mind. Early the following morning, they had a make-up breakfast and entered a hansom cab for a ride down Broadway. Suddenly, there was the sound of an explosion inside the cab. Nan was heard to cry out: "Look at me, Frank. Why did you do it?"

What Nan Patterson claimed Young had done was shoot himself in the chest, out of anguish over having to leave her. It was a peculiar story in that, as newspaper sketches would explain to their eager readers, Young would have had to have been a contortionist to have inflicted the wound that had killed him. In addition, somehow the dying man had managed to put the gun back in his pocket.

Nan was arrested for murder. The state's version was that she had pulled out a gun, and when Young grabbed it, she had pulled the trigger. During two sensational trials Nan took the stand and stuck to her story despite vigorous cross-examination. In neither case could the prosecution get better than a hung jury, and speculation arose that the state simply would never be able to get a jury of 12 men to visualize a smoking pistol in such a lovely woman's hand. The district attorney's office tried a third time, with the same predictable result. In her prison cell Nan was deluged with messages of sympathy and not a few offers of marriage. It was all too much for the authorities. Ten days after the third trial, the judge granted a motion that she be discharged, and a crowd of 2,000 persons cheered her as she was released. Children sang in the streets:

*Nan is free, Nan is free,*
*She escaped the electric chair,*
*Now that she's out in the open air.*

That night Nan Patterson got gloriously drunk at one plush Broadway spot after another. She soon was offered starring roles in top musicals, but her career collapsed when theatergoers discovered she had no acting or other talent. Nan then reconciled with her ex-husband and they remarried. However, the union again soon ended in divorce, and The Girl in the Hansom Cab just faded away.

## Peacock, Dr. Silber C. (1896–1936) murder victim

Few murdered persons have ever been more unjustly maligned than was Dr. Silber C. Peacock, a successful and wealthy Chicago pediatrician who was killed on the night of January 2, 1936.

Dr. Peacock had left his home at 10:05 P.M. to answer what was to prove to be a fake emergency call about a sick child. Hours later, he was found dead in his Cadillac, shot, slashed and viciously clubbed. Dr. Peacock did not appear to have been robbed of his money or valuables (it was subsequently discovered that $20 had been taken), and the public and the newspapers soon began a series of speculations about him. Among other things, he was said to have been the victim of a narcotics robbery, a leading narcotics dealer, the keeper of a secret love nest, a habitue of underworld dives and a society abortionist. All these allegations eventually proved groundless. For example, the charge of keeping a "swank love nest," as one newspaper put it, started because his wife could not identify an apartment key that was found in his possession at the time of his death. Eventually, the police discovered it was the key to the apartment of the parents-in-law of a Chicago deputy coroner, who, during his investigation, had somehow inadvertently dropped it among the effects found on the dead man.

Finally, 10 weeks after the slaying, four young men were arrested and confessed to the murder. They had plotted to rob a physician, selected Peacock's name out of hundreds of doctors listed in the classified telephone directory and lured him to his death with a telephone call. When he had resisted, they killed him and fled. Three of the culprits—Emil Reck, Robert Goethe and Durland Nash—went to prison for 199 years plus four consecutive terms of one year to life. The fourth, 17-year-old Mickey Livingston, drew a 30-year sentence.

## Percy, Valerie (1945–1966) murder victim

Senatorial candidate Charles H. Percy's 21-year-old twin daughter Valerie was killed in the family's mansion in Kenilworth, Ill. on September 18, 1966. At about 5 A.M. Percy was awakened by his wife's screams. He immediately turned on a switch that set off a piercing burglar alarm atop the 17-room suburban home and rushed to Valerie's bedroom, where he found the girl still alive but mutilated by numerous stab wounds. She died shortly thereafter. Hearing a noise, Valerie's stepmother had investigated and come upon a shadowy intruder standing over the girl's bed. He had shined a flashlight in the woman's face and, while she was temporarily blinded, successfully made his escape.

The case shocked the country and for a time its political impact in the Senate race between Percy and 74-year-old Senate Democrat Paul Douglas was hard to gauge. Some political observers concluded the tragedy produced a significant sympathy vote for Percy that helped him win the election although Douglas later admitted that Percy had already pulled ahead of him in the summer.

From the beginning, there appeared to have been a sexual motive behind the Percy murder, indicating the act of a person harboring a strong sexual animosity toward the girl. Over the next several years the case remained unsolved despite Sen. Percy's offer of a $50,000 reward and an intensive police investigation, in which 14,000 persons were questioned and 1,317 leads followed up. A total of 19 confessions were made—all false.

A youth in Tucson, Ariz. confessed to the murder in October 1966 but later denied it. In 1971 police in South Yarmouth, Mass. reported that a 24-year-old man had admitted committing the Percy killing and 17 other murders as well. Confession number 18, another phony, was made by a 26-year-old suspect in a Las Vegas murder case. The final one came from a 27-year-old man in Miami, who not only claimed he had killed Valerie but John F. Kennedy, Robert F. Kennedy and Martin Luther King as well.

By 1973, the authorities considered the murder solved, although they agreed there would probably never be a prosecution. Reporter Art Petacque of the *Chicago Sun-Times* broke the case by obtaining a statement from a Mafia operative, 58-year-old Leo Rugendorf, who oversaw the activities of a gang of cat burglars that had robbed the homes of wealthy people all over the country. Rugendorf, near death from heart disease, fingered burglars Francis Hohimer and Frederick Malchow, who had plunged to his death from a railroad trestle in 1967 after escaping from a Pennsylvania prison. Hohimer at the time was doing 30 years in the Iowa State Penitentiary for armed robbery.

Rugendorf said Hohimer told him shortly after the murder: "They'll get me for the Valerie Percy murder. The girl woke up, and I hit her on the top of the head with a pistol." In addition, the reporter was able to get corroboration of Rugendorf's claim from Hohimer's younger brother, Harold, who reported Frank was "real nervous and uptight" the day after the murder. Harold said his brother had told him he "had to 'off' a girl."

Harold Hohimer further stated: "I asked him why he had to do someone in, and he said it was because the girl made a lot of noise and they got in a fight. I asked him, 'What score are you talking about?' and he said, 'It's all in the newspapers and on the radio today.' He was talking about the Valerie Percy thing."

Yet another acquaintance of Frank Hohimer claimed Frank had told him two weeks before the murder that he had cased the Percy mansion and intended to rob it. After maintaining his silence for a while, Frank Hohimer consented to answer questions put to him by Petacque and investigators. He denied killing Valerie and denied being in the Percy mansion. Instead, he accused Malchow of the murder, stating that on the morning of the crime Malchow had come to his flat in blood-soaked clothes.

In 1975 Frank Hohimer wrote a book about his criminal past, *The Home Invaders*, admitting a number of burglaries, including a robbery of Elvis Presley's mansion in Memphis, but holding to his version of the Percy murder.

Without physical evidence linking Malchow or Hohimer to the murder, officials admit, there is no chance anyone will ever be prosecuted for the murder of Valerie Percy. The offer of $50,000 reward has been withdrawn. Reporter Petacque won a Pulitzer Prize for his work on the story.

## Phillips, David Graham (1868–1911) murder victim

David Phillips, one of the most popular novelists of the first decade of the 20th century, achieved posthumous fame as the only writer ever to be murdered because of a character he created.

One day late in 1910 a neurotic 21-year-old member of Philadelphia society, Fitzhugh

Goldsborough, picked up one of Phillips' novels, *The Fashionable Adventures of Joshua Craig,* which was plotted largely around a scatterbrained, selfish young socialite. Goldsborough had an elder sister, a frivolous member of Philadelphia society who seemed to match Phillips' character in one unflattering detail after another. He also had an explosive temper and had often come to blows with persons who had said anything he took to be un-kind about his sister. Goldsborough whipped himself into a murderous frenzy over Phillips' apparent insult.

On January 23, 1911 Phillips left his Gramercy Park apartment in New York City; as he walked through the park, he was confronted by a disheveled, haggard-looking young man. Fitzhugh Goldsborough pulled out a pistol and screamed, "Here you go!" and then shot the author several times. As Phillips fell to the ground mortally wounded, Goldsborough glanced at horrified passersby and said, "Here I go!" He put the gun to his temple and pulled the trigger, killing himself. Police soon uncovered the motive for Goldsborough's act, but never found any indication that the victim had ever known or even heard of the murderer's sister.

### Puente, Dorothea (1929– ) mass murderess with a "heart of gold"

Dorothea Gray, or, to use her third of four married names, Dorothea Puente, was in the 1980s much celebrated in Mexican-American circles as a rich woman who did much to help the down and out in Sacramento. She made large contributions to the Mexican-American Youth Association and was much respected at social events connected with the Mexican-American community and called "La Doctera" for her solicitude of the needy, especially men and women facing a lonely old age. The fact that she danced at charity balls with Governor Jerry Brown increased her status in the eyes of the Mexican community.

In reality Dorothea, in her fifties, was a killer, in many respects similar to the infamous Belle Gunness, who at the turn of the 20th century killed would-be suitors for their money and buried them in her farmyard in La Porte, Indiana. Dorothea buried her victims in the yard of her mansion. Her victims weren't suitors but down-and-outers she made so much a show of giving care and comfort in their declining years.

Dorothea had been an outlaw in many ways for many years, but no one knew that, as she had gone through several marriages with new identities. She came from a family of cotton pickers and was raised off and on by a drunken mother. She was sent to an orphanage when she was nine and later lived with a variety of relatives, including some of her older brothers and sisters.

In her teens she worked as a waitress and later moved on to prostitution. She engaged in various confidence games and more prostitution so that by the 1960s she owned a half-dozen brothels. In fact, her mansion previously had been a rather imposing bordello. She ran through four husbands but in her supposed good works for the lonely aged, she had hit upon a good thing.

She lived lavishly on the top floor of her white Victorian mansion while all her "boarders"—as she liked to call them—lived below. Her lodgers seemed to have few complaints. They received good care, good food and their own color TV sets. To them Dorothea was an angel, the soul of compassion. Dorothea lived well herself and was also an ardent gardener. The source of her seemingly endless wealth was that garden. It was where she buried her victims.

Dorothea saw to it that her lodgers filed their Social Security payments when they were due, but she would show up at the Social Security office to arrange that she be named payee on the checks, explaining that her lodgers were not competent to handle their own money and that, as a relative, she was taking care of them. A typical instance was that of Alvaro (Burt) Montoya, who was, Puente informed the government, her cousin and somewhat retarded. So Montoya's $637 stipend went directly to Dorothea and would keep on coming until Montoya died.

That was a problem for Dorothea; she had to ensure that Montoya and her other lodgers went on living, or better still, that they died without the government knowing. This created the best circumstance for Dorothea, since it left her with vacancies to fill in her mansion—and additional payments from more retirees. The only hitch would be if a pensioner died outside of the mansion, on the street or in a hospital, and a death certificate was made out. That would end Puente's control of the money. Therefore, Dorothea killed her boarders and while everyone else in the mansion was asleep, she would plant the bodies in holes other lodgers dug in her ever-expanding garden to accommodate more new "plants."

For a time various social workers were quite happy to send their clients to Dorothea, but in time they found the elderly persons were disappearing. Sometimes, Dorothea explained this away by saying they had gone to stay with relatives in Mexico—or in fact with some of Dorothea's in-laws who seemed to have the same desire to help the unfortunate of the world.

The juggling of so many disappearing oldsters had to make some social workers suspicious, and eventually the police were notified. At first the authorities were thrown off by the very fine surroundings Puente offered the lonely oldsters, but finally her criminal past emerged, and while she insisted she had turned her life around years earlier, authorities asked for permission to do some digging in her yard.

Puente had to comply, and soon searchers turned up a deposit of lime 18 inches from the surface in a corner of the yard. Digging further, they found bits of clothing and a leg bone with bits of skin. That, however, was not sufficient evidence to prove Puente had committed murder. She explained that a shallow hole had been dug where the bone was recovered and that she had poured lime in it merely to soften the earth.

Before any charges could be filed, the law would have to find more evidence of foul play. Crime scene technicians, heavy-equipment operators, forensic anthropologists and other diggers scoured the yard. In the meantime, Puente left the mansion with one of her lodgers, allegedly to meet a cousin. She didn't return. Just after she left, a second body was uncovered, then another and another. In a few days a total of seven bodies were found, and there was every indication that more were to come, one lodger ending up in a box on the side of the Sacramento River.

Puente had escaped the city by taxi, first to Stockton and then, by Greyhound bus, to Los Angeles. Even with the hunt for her on, Dorothea could not resist trying a scam on a retired handyman named Charles Willgues. Her intended victim grew suspicious and called the Los Angeles CBS news bureau, which sent out a film crew together with local police. Puente was captured and brought to trial, and on August 26, 1993, a jury—after almost six weeks deliberation—found her guilty of killing three of the victims, making use of the drug flurazepam.

The jury's real hangup was agreeing on a sentence. The judge then sentenced Puente to life imprisonment without parole.

## Ramsey, JonBenet (1990–1996) young beauty pageant queen murder victim

Few murders during the late 1900s drew more attention—and public outrage—than that of JonBenet Ramsey, the six-year-old beauty pageant queen. Her body was found the day after Christmas 1996 in her family's opulent home in Boulder, Colorado. John Ramsey, the girl's father, told authorities he found a ransom note but then discovered the little girl's lifeless body in a windowless basement room. The child had been beaten and strangled, but had not, as later often stated, showed signs of sexual assault.

Mr. and Mrs. Ramsey informed investigators that they frequently left their doors unlocked at night, a common behavior in the area. The house did have an alarm system but it generally was not set since JonBenet and her older brother had accidentally set it off on a number of occasions.

JonBenet's murder achieved international notoriety, because she had been brought up as an adult-style beauty pageant queen and to many as a sex symbol. Rumors fed on rumors that she had been sexually abused for some time. Indeed for many the exhibiting of the beautiful young child in such pageants was in itself a form of child abuse.

However, the criminal investigation foundered over the next years. There were reports of deep friction between police investigators and the prosecuting attorney's office. It was claimed that the initial police investigation was so flawed and the crime scene so compromised the gathering of credible forensic evidence was impossible. After working on a number of avenues, investigators kept returning to the parents since there seemed to be no one else to investigate. There were charges made in the media that the Ramseys had failed to cooperate with the authorities in their investigation. More than a year after the murder, John and Patsy Ramsey turned over the clothing they had been wearing the night before their daughter's body was found. The long continuing inquiry got no further in a grand jury investigation which failed to come up with any finding.

Finally the Boulder County D.A. Alex Hunter concluded the grand jury proceedings, although the word was the investigation was "not over by any means."

The seeming stalling of the case did not please public opinion which by vast majorities wanted a criminal trial to proceed. In the ensuing furor, Colorado Governor Owens announced he was considering appointing a special prosecutor to continue the case. However, in the end it appeared there was at the moment no credible evidence with which to proceed, and the governor later dropped this plan. He did however point the finger at the Ramseys, which proved popular with the public if not with considerable segments of the legal community.

By the turn of the century the murder remained unsolved. If a helpless child was not accorded justice, she did suffer yet another indignity. On October 21, 1999 it was reported that vandals had defaced Jon-Benet's tombstone.

## Ray, James Earl (1928– ) assassin of Martin Luther King, Jr.

On April 4, 1968 the Rev. Dr. Martin Luther King, Jr., the acknowledged leader of the black civil rights movement and an advocate of Gandhian principles of nonviolent resistance, was in Memphis, Tenn. to lend support to a controversial strike by the city's sanitation workers. That evening King stepped out onto the balcony of his room at the Lorraine Motel and was shot and mortally wounded by an assassin firing from a bathroom window of a nearby rooming house. A 30.06-caliber rifle bullet struck King in the right side of the jaw, penetrated his neck and severed his spinal cord. The force of the bullet was so powerful it ripped his necktie completely off his shirt.

Items left by the assassin were traced to cities as far away as Los Angeles and Atlanta.

Through fingerprints the murderer was identified as a white man named James Earl Ray, a minor criminal who had no apparent reason for killing King. After the murder Ray fled to Canada and in May he went to London on a Canadian passport, showing a remarkable sophistication at eluding capture. He took a mysterious side trip to Lisbon, came back to London and was about to fly to Brussels when he was apprehended on June 8. He was returned to the United States in July.

Over the years Ray has continued to be a controversial figure. Certainly, a number of details appear to indicate the existence of a broad plot to kill King. Some have even claimed that the FBI was involved in his death and that Ray was merely a scapegoat. Nothing of the sort has ever been proved, although there is no doubt that the agency did much to besmirch King's character both before and after his death.

A retired FBI man who had worked in the agency's Atlanta office at the time of the King assassination told of deep anti-King feelings prevalent there and how one agent literally had leaped for joy when he learned King had been killed. The FBI was forced to admit it had wiretapped King's home and sent Mrs. Coretta King letters that implied her husband was involved sexually with several other women. When King was scheduled to receive the Nobel Peace Prize in 1964, the FBI had even sent a letter to him intimating he should commit suicide before the award was given. It read in part: "King—there is only one thing left for you to do. You know what it is. You have just 34 days in which to do it. It has definite practical significance. You are done. There is but one way out. . . ."

J. Edgar Hoover had been incensed by the thought of King getting the Nobel Peace Prize and had called him "the most notorious liar in the country." Hoover had authorized the investigation of King's sex life and ordered many of the illegal harassments used against him. The director had even inspired a news story that caused King to switch from his initial choice of a white-owned hotel to the Lorraine Motel, where he was shot.

James Earl Ray seemed too much of a misfit to be involved in so monumental a case as the King assassination. A 10th-grade dropout, he held nothing but menial jobs until 1946, when he joined the army. He was discharged in December 1948 for "ineptness and lack of adaptability to military service." After that, he had a string of arrests for some bush-league armed robberies, small-time smuggling and burglaries. He also served three years for forgery. He broke out of the Missouri State Prison in April 1967 but was considered such an unimportant criminal that the reward for his capture amounted to only $50. While Ray was being hunted for the King murder, his father insisted that if he had done the job, "he couldn't have planned it alone; he wasn't smart enough for that."

After he was apprehended and brought back to the United States, Ray pleaded guilty to murdering King and drew 99 years. Within 24 hours he attempted to reverse his plea and insisted on dropping his original attorney, Percy Foreman, and getting a new lawyer. He maintained he was innocent and that "Raoul," a shadowy figure known only to Ray, had sent him to Memphis to take part in a gun-smuggling operation and had passed him money and orders. He said he did not know who had killed King.

During hearings on the King murder held by the House Select Committee on Assassinations in 1978, a St. Louis man, Russell G. Byers, told the panel he had been offered $50,000 in late 1966 or early 1967 to arrange King's death. He said the offer had come from two men, John Kauffmann and John Sutherland, acting on behalf of a group of businessmen. Both Kauffmann and Sutherland were now dead and their widows said they did not believe they could have taken part in such a plot. It developed that the FBI had been aware of Byers' allegations in 1973, but the information had not been passed on to agents investigating the King assassination. A spokesman for the FBI said that the handling of the information was in "violation of established rules and procedures," but that the bureau was satisfied a simple misfiling had occurred through "administrative error," rather than a deliberate attempt to block the investigation. Since the agent responsible for handling the information had retired, there was, the spokesman said, no need for a formal inquiry into the matter.

In any event, Byers said he suspected that Sutherland and Kauffmann had planned to recruit him as a dupe who would take the blame for the murder but not actually carry it out. Byers' story prompted House investigators to look for links between Byers or Kauffmann and Sutherland and Ray's escape from the penitentiary in April 1967. The committee heard testimony that Ray had committed the murder in the hope of collecting a $50,000 bounty, and in December 1978 it concluded there was a "likelihood" of a conspiracy. The panel found that "no federal, state or local government agency was involved in the assassination of Dr. King," although it did say the Domestic Intelligence Division of the FBI was guilty of "gross" abuse of its legal authority in its surveillance of King and that the Justice Department had "failed to supervise adequately" that division.

James Earl Ray remains the only person ever convicted in the King murder case and has been behind bars since 1969 save for a three-day period when he escaped from prison. On that occasion his escape lacked the financing and planning which had marked his flight prior to the murder of King and he was quickly retaken.

## Ribicoff, Sarai (1957–1980)  murder victim

The murder of Sarai Ribicoff, a 23-year-old member of the socially prominent Connecticut Ribicoffs and the niece of Senator Abe Ribicoff, was to have an immense effect on the attitudes of Californians toward crime and indeed led to a surge in the purchase of guns for personal use in the state which was to last for years.

Graduated from Yale the previous year, Sarai had become a staff reporter for the Los Angeles *Herald Examiner* and was recognized as a talented member of the staff. On November 12, Sarai had dinner with John Shoven, 33, a Stanford economics professor, at Chez Hélène, a fashionable French restaurant on a busy thoroughfare in Venice. They left the restaurant about 10 P.M. and were but a few steps outside when a horrific incident ensued. They were confronted by two African-American youths, one of whom was waving almost nonchalantly a 9-mm automatic. It was obvious that the gunman was under the influence of some sort of drug.

In an effort to avoid a confrontation, Shoven led his date into the street, in the hope there would be oncoming traffic. The two youths followed menacingly. The couple then moved, ill-advisedly, in the shadow of an unfenced lawn. Thinking better of the situation, they made a beeline back toward the restaurant but were overtaken as they reached the sidewalk. The gunman had clearly been studying Shoven's gold watch and Sarai's gold chain with a small gold pendant with a diamond chip. It had been a gift from her mother.

Cut off from the restaurant, the couple was menaced by the gunman, who kept saying repeatedly: "This is for real. This is for real." As the gunman's companion grabbed Shoven's wallet containing about $200 in cash, the latter asked that his assailants leave his credit cards and I.D.

Meanwhile the gunman shoved Sarai to the sidewalk and demanded her purse, which she did not have. She struggled as her attacker seized the pendant. Shoven stared in horror, as perhaps did his assailant who was yanking his gold watch free, when the gunman cocked the pistol poised in Sarai's back. He pulled the trigger and the shot echoed off the pavement. Sarai gasped what were to be her dying breaths. The gunman fired two more shots into his helpless victim and took off with his booty, as did his companion.

Next door in a crêpe restaurant kitchen, 22-year-old Oscar Benitez, an illegal immigrant from Salvador, heard the shots and took off after the fleeing pair. He saw them run into a nearby vacant building on Fifth Avenue. Police, informed by Benitez when they arrived, followed a trail of blood to the second floor but found no one. They did recover Shoven's empty wallet.

Back at the crime scene a clue turned up. There was a bloodstain just below Sarai's knee, where she had not been hit. It turned out to be Type O blood; the victim's blood type was A. The bullet that had killed Sarai had bounced off the concrete and nicked the killer's arm.

Checking at nearby emergency rooms, the police found one where Frederick Jerome

Thomas, having Type O blood, had been treated. Thomas was well known to police. A high school graduate, although functionally illiterate, he was baron of the Venice angel dust pushers and a leader of the Crips, the city's most dangerous street gang. He was taken into custody at midnight. His accomplice, Anthony LaQuin McAdoo, surrendered the following day. McAdoo, 19, had never been in serious trouble and had never been known to use drugs, unlike Thomas, who was popularly held to have consumed almost as much PCP as he sold. McAdoo had been in Thomas' company because he desperately needed cash to repair his car.

The murder of Sarai Ribicoff sent shock waves through Los Angeles' citizenry, including the liberal community that counted Sarai as one of their own. The *Herald Examiner*, noted as a liberal voice, became outspoken in favor of vigorous prosecution of criminals. It fueled more outrage when it dug up the fact that Thomas had been arrested six months earlier for possession of four ounces of PCP and that the district attorney's office had not prosecuted him.

The prosecution made a deal with McAdoo to testify against Thomas in exchange for a sentence of 25 years with the chance of parole in 17. Thomas seemed to be a certain candidate for the gas chamber, but he escaped the death penalty. McAdoo's testimony proved to be an aid to Thomas when he explained to the jury that just before Thomas shot Sarai she tried to resist as he attempted to pull the gold pendant free of her neck. Apparently, that was regarded by the jury as a somewhat extenuating circumstance for Thomas. The jurors, including seven women, voted narrowly to decline the death penalty, opting to sentence Thomas to life imprisonment with no chance for parole.

Now once again shockwaves swept the city, the outrage perhaps equaling that felt by whites years later when O. J. Simpson was acquitted on criminal murder charges. Belle Ribicoff, Sarai's mother, expressed her horror: "Have we reached the point as a society where someone who struggles with an attacker becomes responsible for his own murder?"

Even Los Angeles' large liberal community, long in favor of gun control, now focused increasingly on the city's crime rate, which was exceeding that of New York City. Actor Sylvester Stallone became one of the cofounders of the Beverly Hills Gun Club, which showed patrons how to pick calibers for maximum stopping power as well as the secrets of fast and accurate shooting. And in the half-year following Sarai's murder, the number of women in California applying for tear gas permits soared from 26,000 to 341,000.

Eventually, support for gun control soared as the memory of the Ribicoff murder faded against the spate of more recent violent shootings. By 1999 however, California was easily in the forefront for gun control and in that year the state enacted the nation's toughest and most comprehensive ban on assault-style weapons.

## Rice, William Marsh (1816–1900) murder victim

One of Texas' more famous millionaires, William Marsh Rice had but one ambition in his later years: to give his adopted state, which had made him rich, an institution of higher learning as a memorial to himself. His life was ended by a bizarre murder plot to rob his estate, most of which was intended for the founding of that institution.

Rice had garnered a fortune in oil, land and hotels. At the age of 80, he had buried two wives, had no children and was living alone in New York. He hired 23-year-old Charles F. Jones as a combination nurse and secretary and by 1900 he so trusted Jones that he allowed him to handle all his banking affairs.

At the time, Rice was involved in a legal dispute over part of his fortune. Before his second wife died, she made up a will disposing of half of Rice's money, to which she was entitled under the community property law in Texas, where the couple had been living. Rice countered that he was actually a resident of New York and only visited Texas and that therefore all the money rightfully was his. Nonetheless, he made out a will leaving almost all of his estate to establish "The Rice Institute." One of Rice's adversaries was a brash Texas lawyer with a shady past, a man named Albert T. Patrick, who went to New York to gather proof that Rice's claim of residency in that state was a fraud. In fact, Patrick had something else in mind. He was out to get the Rice millions for himself. After promising secretary Jones a fortune, he drew him into the plot.

Although Rice had made a will in 1896 for the establishment of the school, Patrick set about producing a new will that would name him the chief beneficiary. In this new will Rice's relatives would receive much more money, making them far more likely to support it than the original. He also left $5,000 to each of the prospective trustees of the new school, whom Rice had named in the authentic will. "They'll be glad to forget about the school," Patrick told Jones. "Every man has his price. You know, any man in Houston can be bought for five thousand dollars."

On September 24, 1900 Patrick sent an office boy to Rice's bank with a check for $65,000. It was made out to Abert T. Patrick but endorsed by Albert T. Patrick. Because of the faulty endorsement, it was rejected. When the boy returned with the correct endorsement, the bank became suspicious and called Rice to verify his signature. Jones answered the phone call and said the check was authentic, but he was nevertheless asked to put Mr. Rice on the phone. The secretary replied that Rice was not available. Later that same day the bank called again; this time Jones said his employer had died.

As a matter of fact, Rice had been dead when the check was first presented for payment. Jones had tiptoed into Rice's room while he was asleep and covered his face for 30 minutes with a sponge soaked in chloroform. Then he called Patrick, who in turn arranged for a Dr. Walter Curry to examine the body. Dr. Curry signed a death certificate that declared Rice had succumbed to "old age, weak heart and collocratal diarrhea with mental worry."

Meanwhile, Patrick informed Rice's bank that he held another check for $65,000 as well as an assignment of all his bonds and securities. The bank wondered why Rice had left everything to Patrick. Patrick said: "Frankly, the old gentleman admired me. He was just stuck on me. He thought I was the most wonderful man in the world. Said he never met anyone he liked better."

Nevertheless, the bank and a number of Rice's relatives and proposed trustees of the school insisted on a post-mortem, which revealed traces of mercury in the dead man's organs and congestion of the lungs caused by "some gas or vapor." On October 4 Patrick and Jones were arrested on charges of forgery and confined in the Tombs Prison.

Patrick, who until then had exercised considerable authority over Jones, ordered his accomplice to confess to the murder and assume the entire guilt. Jones slit his throat with a pen knife and spent two weeks recuperating in Bellevue Hospital.

When he was returned to the Tombs, Jones first stated that Patrick had administered the fatal chloroform to the old millionaire. Then he admitted he had done it after Patrick had showed him a picture of his two smiling daughters and said he could not kill anyone.

Patrick was brought to trial for murder in January 1902. The proceedings lasted 10 weeks and the testimony filled 3,000 pages. Jones turned state's evidence and, in exchange, was not charged with anything. He spent five days on the witness stand. Patrick was convicted and sentenced to death in the electric chair.

Patrick's long fight for freedom has been described as one of the blackest chapters in New York's legal history. A wealthy brother-in-law reportedly poured thousands into the battle. Patrick spent four years and seven months in the death house, during which time he saw 17 others go to the chair. Finally, in December 1906 Gov. F. W. Higgins commuted his sentence to life imprisonment. Patrick, the star boarder on death row, announced: "I refuse to accept the governor's commutation. I propose to continue my fight for freedom."

He shuttled back and forth to various courts with all sorts of arguments. In one court he argued that he was legally dead and, as such, could not be kept in Sing Sing. It could be that everyone wearied of the entire matter, but in any event, on November 28, 1912 Gov. John A. Dix gave Patrick a complete pardon, noting in a brief comment that "an air of mystery has always surrounded the case." The governor's act was, to say the least, controversial, but so was the fact that Jones, the actual killer, had not even been tried for the murder.

In a certain sense, all the parties in the case came out fairly well off. Rice Institute was endowed and grew to be the nation's wealthiest school on a student per capita basis. Patrick eventually became a man of property before he died in 1940 at the age of 74. Ironically, even Jones ended up with a fair sum of money, which he inherited from his family. When he committed suicide in 1954 at the age of 80, his neighbors in Baytown, Tex. had no idea he was *the* Jones who had been involved in the Rice murder. However, it was not a guilty conscience that prompted him to take his life but fear of becoming an invalid and dependent on strangers.

## Rich Men's Coachmen's Club criminal organization

One of the strangest criminal organizations in history was the Rich Men's Coachmen's Club, which appeared in Chicago in the 1880s. Among the city's coaching set the true sign of social importance was to have English grooms and coachmen, since English fashion still represented the ultimate authority in the Gem of the Prairie. The social order became somewhat scrambled as many of these English grooms and coachmen who flooded Chicago attempted to exploit and bully their employers, getting away with such behavior, because the crowning disaster in the city's society was to lose one's English servant.

The field became so lush that a number of Yankee imposters posed as Englishmen to get coachmen's jobs. A leading faker of this ilk was one John Tilbury, who won a position with Victor Fremont Lawson, the owner of the *Chicago Daily News.* Tilbury's real name was James McGraw and he really hailed from New York City, but he affected a perfect accent and had provided himself with impressive forged credentials. Tilbury saw there were enormous opportunities for dishonest coachmen if their activities could be properly organized.

He formed the Rich Men's Coachmen's Club, headquartered in Lawson's barn, where both business and social meetings were held. The latter activities included drinking and carousing and betting on dog and cockfights. Business meetings consisted of reports on mansions that could be burglarized; valuable dogs that could be stolen and sold, trained as fighters or returned to their owners for ransom; and family secrets that could be used for blackmail. Honest servants of rich families were appalled by the actions of Tilbury's gang. They informed their employers and wrote anonymous letters to the police accusing various coachmen of being former inmates of British jails or deserters from the British army. However, most employers refused to believe such charges against their coachmen, restrained by their own pride in having British servants or the threat of blackmail. Nonetheless, Lawson may have breathed a sigh of relief when Tilbury left his employ to join the staff of Mrs. Hollis M. Thurston, a leading figure in Chicago society. No doubt Mrs. Thurston was proud of her catch of a coachman who claimed to be a former guards officer and the disinherited member of a titled family.

Some three months later, Tilbury had gathered enough dirt on the Thurston family to approach his mistress and inform her he wanted $12,500 to remain silent about certain family scandals. Mrs. Thurston was made of stern stuff and informed private detectives, who seized Tilbury at the mansion as the blackmail money was paid to him. The detectives then turned him over to the police. When the story broke in the newspapers the next day, the *Chicago Times* reported: "Chicago society has turned white with dread."

At Tilbury's trial, Mrs. Thurston was subjected to a withering cross-examination, which attacked her conduct and character. In the end, Tilbury was freed on the ground that the private detectives hired by the woman had violated his rights. However, the police thereafter hounded Tilbury and some other crooked coachmen until they finally left town and the Coachmen's Club was dissolved.

### Roosevelt, Theodore (1858–1919) would-be assassination victim

On October 14, 1912 Theodore Roosevelt, then running for the presidency as the Bull Moose candidate, left a dinner at Milwaukee's Hotel Gilpatrick to deliver a campaign speech at the Milwaukee Auditorium. As he entered an open car, a plump, short little man with receding light brown hair stepped to within six feet of him and fired a .38 Police Positive. The bullet hit Roosevelt in the chest, and he lurched into the backseat of the car. When the assailant leveled his gun for a second shot, an associate of Roosevelt, Elbert E. Martin, downed him with a flying tackle. Several policemen pounced on the would-be assassin and dragged him off.

Fortunately for Roosevelt, the bullet had penetrated a metal spectacles case in his breast pocket and gone through a 50-page speech manuscript that had been folded twice. It had then smashed into a rib but most of its lethal force had already been spent.

Roosevelt's assailant was a 36-year-old ex-saloon owner named John Nepomuk Schrank, who was suffering from a severe mental illness. On September 15, 1901, the day after William McKinley had died of an assassin's bullet and Roosevelt succeeded to the presidency, Schrank dreamed that McKinley's ghost came to him and accused Roosevelt of the murder. From that day on, Schrank hated Roosevelt, and when Roosevelt dared to run for what Schrank considered to be a third term, he loathed him even more. Then one night in 1912 McKinley's ghost reappeared in Schrank's dreams and begged him not to let a "murderer" become president. Schrank determined to kill Roosevelt, and he left his home in New York and followed the candidate around the country. He got close enough in Chicago and Chattanooga to get in a shot, but he lost his nerve. In Milwaukee his nerve did not fail him.

The bullet had entered Roosevelt's chest so deeply that doctors decided against removing it and the ex-president carried it in his body until his death from natural causes in 1919. He said the bullet bothered him no more than if he were carrying it in his vest pocket. Schrank was declared insane and spent the rest of his life in mental institutions in Wisconsin. When Theodore Roosevelt died, Schrank said he was sorry because "he was a great American." However, when Franklin Delano Roosevelt ran for a third term in 1940, Schrank was enraged. He told doctors that if he were free he would shoot this Roosevelt also. Schrank died of a heart ailment on September 15, 1943, exactly 42 years after he first dreamed of McKinley's ghost.

### New York police commissioner
Theodore Roosevelt's reputation as a reformer originated during his three years as a police commissioner in New York City,

from 1895 to 1897. He was instrumental in rooting out departmental corruption in the entrenched, politically protected regimes of Chief Inspector Alexander S. Williams and Big Bill Devery, who for a time even held the post of chief of police. Roosevelt won acclaim for starting the process of promotion based on merit rather than politics, a revolutionary idea in 19th century New York. He also pioneered a bicycle squad, a telephonic communications system and special training for new recruits, another unheard-of procedure. Later, Roosevelt lent powerful support to the Pennsylvania State Constabulary, which was to become the model for modern state police organizations. In 1908, as president, he set up the Bureau of Investigation, the forerunner of the FBI.

An admirer of men of action, Roosevelt made some lamentable mistakes, for example, naming Pat Garrett, the killer of Billy the Kid, to the post of customs collector. Garrett was murdered in 1908. In 1905 he had tried to appoint the aging Bat Masterson to the post of U.S. marshal for the Oklahoma Territory. Masterson, who realized the president did not understand that an era had ended, declined the offer as diplomatically as possible. "I am not the man for the job," he wrote Roosevelt, ". . . and if I were marshal some youngster would try to put me out because of my reputation. I would be bait for grown-up kids who had fed on dime novels. I would have to kill or be killed. No sense to that. I have taken my guns off, and I don't ever want to put them on again."

### Ross, Charles Brewster (1870–?)
**kidnapping victim**
When four-year-old Charley Ross was taken from his Philadelphia home on July 1, 1874

and held for ransom, it was the first case of this type to achieve nationwide notoriety; "poor little Charley Ross" soon became a household phrase.

The boy's wealthy father, Christian K. Ross, received a note demanding $20,000 and immediately contacted the police, although he had been cautioned not to. Ross then entered into tortuous negotiations with the kidnappers, who set up three separate meetings over the next few months to collect the ransom. The criminals did not keep any of these appointments, apparently because they correctly suspected the police had set traps.

Meanwhile, New York City police identified a known criminal, William Mosher, as one of the kidnappers by matching his handwriting with that on the ransom notes. On the night of December 13, 1874, Mosher and another notorious burglar, Joey Douglass, were both fatally wounded while attempting a burglary in Brooklyn. Before dying, Mosher admitted the kidnapping and named Douglass as an accomplice. He would not reveal the whereabouts of the

"What happened to poor Charley Ross?" became one of the most haunting and persistent questions of the late 19th century.

William Mosher and Joey Douglas were both shot in a burglary attempt in Brooklyn. Before dying, Mosher admitted the pair had been involved in the Ross kidnapping, but he would not reveal the whereabouts of the child.

child, however. Suspicion now centered on William Westervelt, an ex-New York policeman with an unsavory reputation. Westervelt was soon identified as the man seen near the Ross home before the crime who had asked numerous questions about the financial worth of Christian K. Ross. Despite this evidence, Westervelt would admit nothing about the kidnapping, even after being found guilty of charges related to the abduction and sentenced to seven years.

Upon his release Westervelt faded into obscurity, but the Ross case would not, despite underworld rumors that Westervelt had definitely been in charge of holding the child and, as the hunt had intensified, had panicked and drowned the boy in the East

River. The Ross family spent the next 20 years tracking down leads, spending a fortune on some 500 separate journeys. But the era's most haunting question, "What happened to poor little Charley Ross?" remained unanswered.

## Rubinstein, Serge (1909–1955) financier and murder victim

In 1955 financial wizard and convicted draft dodger Serge Rubinstein was not considered a very likable person. In fact, the government was trying to deport him as an undesirable. Someone considered him even less desirable and on January 27 bound and strangled him to death in his luxurious five-story home on New York's Fifth Avenue.

A White Russian émigré, he burst upon the American scene a few years before World War II as the enfant terrible of the financial world and fattened an already swollen personal fortune by destroying, through devious means, a succession of companies and their stockholders. He was forced to take time from that unsavory activity to do 2 1/2 years in prison for failure to serve in the army during World War II, having falsely claimed Portuguese citizenship.

Upon his release Rubinstein went right back to his financial double-dealing. In 1949 he was indicted for stock fraud, mail fraud and violation of the Securities Acts. It was charged that he had made $3 million profit by buying Panhandle Producing and Refining stock at less than an average of $2 a share, driving the price up with false rumors and having the company pay dividends it hadn't earned and then, after he had liquidated his holdings, selling short when the public found out the truth and the stock started to fall. After a vigorous two-year battle, Rubinstein

was acquitted of stock fraud and was ready for more capers.

He also led the life of a man-about-Manhattan, recruiting a large selection of lady friends, most of whom had keys to his home and whom he would often summon in the middle of the night to make a quick visit.

Early on the morning of January 27, 1955, Rubinstein returned home with a blonde he had taken to dinner. After a short time the blonde left. Apparently, Rubinstein read for a while and then telephoned another blonde acquaintance and asked her to come over. The woman, roused from her sleep, said she was too tired.

Excluding his murderer or murderers, the second blonde was the last person Rubinstein spoke to in his life. A little after 8 A.M. Rubinstein's butler brought a breakfast tray to his bedroom and found him dead. Clad in black silk mandarin pajamas, he lay sprawled on his back, his hands and feet bound with Venetian-blind cord. Strips of wide adhesive tape were plastered across his mouth and wound around his throat. It was obvious he had been strangled and the early theory was that the adhesive tape had done the job, perhaps inadvertently. At first, it was thought Rubinstein had been the victim of a kidnap attempt and had been killed in error. However, the autopsy showed he had died by manual strangulation. He had been throttled by someone with powerful hands.

Police developed many theories. One postulated that business enemies had been responsible; another claimed it had been "a mob job—a syndicate job"; yet another attributed the murder to a robbery attempt gone awry. The previous August, Rubinstein had filed charges against three men for attempting to extort $535,000 from him. In all, the police questioned literally thousands of persons whose names Rubinstein had written in several loose-leaf notebooks. It appeared he was in the habit of writing down the name of every person he met who might ever be useful to him, either for business or pleasure. Business contacts, friends, enemies, associates, prison mates and girlfriends, both past and present, were hauled in and interrogated, all to be caught in the limelight of intensive newspaper coverage.

The more sensational newspapers had a field day with several of the murdered man's lady friends because of his written comments about them or because of the fact that he seemed to have kept a number of them under surveillance. In one case Rubinstein had even hidden a small battery-operated transmitter under a woman's bed to record her bedside conversations. Later, he had confronted her with the recording of her amorous conversation with a date. When the story of the recorder broke in the newspapers, the girl said, with a certain ingenuousness, "Now everyone in New York knows my bed squeaks."

Despite a flurry of investigative activity, the murder remained unsolved.

## Ruby, Jack (1911–1967) killer of Lee Harvey Oswald

Even as the nation was still in shock over the assassination of President John F. Kennedy, millions watched on television as the president's accused killer, Lee Harvey Oswald, was shot to death in the Dallas, Tex. city jail on November 24, 1963. The murderer was 52-year-old Jacob Rubenstein, better known as Jack Ruby, a local nightclub operator.

Oswald, flanked by lawmen, was being escorted through the basement of the municipal building to a waiting armored truck that was to take him to the county jail when Ruby stepped out from a cluster of newsmen, thrust a snub-nosed .38-caliber revolver at Oswald's left side and fired a single shot. Clutching his side, Oswald slumped to the concrete floor, writhing in pain. He lost consciousness without saying a word and 86 minutes later, at 1:07 P.M., he died while undergoing emergency surgery.

Ruby was described as an ardent admirer of President Kennedy and his family who had become distraught about his murder. In the ensuing controversy over the assassination and whether or not Oswald had acted alone, as the Warren Commission later found, Ruby was pictured as a player involved in an intricate plot to kill Kennedy and, later, to silence Oswald, who may have been the actual killer or merely a scapegoat. Despite several scenarios arriving at these various conclusions, no positive link between Oswald and Ruby has ever been established.

Ruby was convicted of Oswald's murder. While awaiting a retrial on appeal, he was transferred in December 1966 to a hospital where he was found to be suffering from cancer. He died the following January 3 of a blood clot in his lung.

That same day a three-minute conversation between Ruby and his brother Earl tape-recorded in the hospital in December was made public. In it Ruby said he had known that Oswald was going to be transferred to the county jail the morning of November 24 but added that his presence at the jail was due to his having made an "illegal turn" behind a bus that put him in the jail parking lot. He said he had no recollection of the moment he shot Oswald. "It happened in such a blur . . . before I knew it . . . the officers had me on the ground."

Ruby angrily denied a rumor that he had met Oswald at his nightclub before the assassination, saying, "It's fabrication." He told his brother he always carried a gun because of various altercations he had had in his club and because he carried fairly large amounts of cash at times.

Ruby's demand that he be given a lie detector test to prove he had acted alone in the murder of Oswald was denied because, it was said, his physical condition would make such a test valueless.

See also: LEE HARVEY OSWALD.

## Sage, Russell (1816–1906) would-be murder victim

On December 4, 1894 a bearded stranger entered the offices of Russell Sage, the financial tycoon. He carried a carpetbag containing, he informed a secretary, bonds from John D. Rockefeller for personal delivery to Mr. Sage. There was a small meeting going on in Sage's office, but Mr. Rockefeller's bonds were always welcome and the messenger was ushered in. Silently, the bearded man handed Sage a typewritten note that read: "I hold in my hands ten pounds of dynamite. If I drop it on the floor it will tear the building to pieces and everyone with it. For $1,250,000 it shall not drop. Yes or no?"

Sage reacted with the ruthlessness for which he was infamous. He grabbed one of his low-paid clerks, shoved him toward the bearded man and, at the same time, broke for the door. There was a deafening explosion. A secretary and the bearded stranger were killed. Five others, including the clerk Sage used as a human shield, were badly injured. The clerk later sued Sage and was awarded $40,000.

The only clue the police had was the head of the bearded stranger, but they could not identify him. Investigators theorized that there was a gang of mad anarchists on the loose aiming "to rid the country of millionaires." Meanwhile, Ike White, a legendary reporter for the *New York World* sifted through the wreckage and found a button. He washed if off and determined it bore the identification of a Boston tailor. In time, White was able to identify the bomber as Henry L. Norcross, a frustrated inventor. The *World* broke the story with a huge picture of the bearded head and a one-word headline: "IDENTIFIED!" It was one of the most sensational scoops in American newspaper history.

## Shakur, Tupac (1971–1996) unsolved murder victim

It has been observed by many that in some cases at least rap music and crime are soul mates. Certainly the point could be made concerning rap star Tupac Shakur. Shakur had frequently romped on the very edge of deadly violence.

Within the parameters of the violent elements in the rap world, Shakur had more than one scrap with violence. In 1994 he was the victim of a shooting at Quad Records in New York. Shakur made no bones about a rap group being involved in setting him up for that near fatal attack.

When Shakur was 10 years old he told a minister of his ambition to be a revolutionary when he was older. His mother, Afreni Shakur, was a founding force of the New York branch of the Black Panther Party, and his father was once suspected in a plot to blow up police stations and department stores. His stepfather was convicted in planning the robbery of a Brink's armored truck in which two guards were killed. If nothing else, Shakur's history helped explain why he was considered to have done a brilliant acting job as a gangster in a 1992 movie, *Juice*.

By 1996 Shakur was at the top of the heap in the rap music world, but had built up a full line-up of Shakur haters. Some of those haters were obviously in Las Vegas on September 7, 1996 when Shakur arrived to attend the heavyweight battle between Mike Tyson and Bruce Seldon at the MGM Grand Hotel. Shakur and Tyson were to appear later at Club 662. The match ended quickly, Tyson being declared the winner after only 109 seconds. Shortly after the fight Shakur and his bodyguards engaged in a scuffle with a man near the hotel's Grand Garden. Around 11 P.M. Shakur was riding in a new black BMW sedan belonging to and being driven by Suge Knight of Death Row Records to the club where the Shakur-Tyson party was soon to get under way.

About a mile from the Strip a light-colored Cadillac occupied by three or four men pulled up beside the BMW and a man in the backseat of the Cadillac aimed a semiautomatic pistol from the window and let loose a barrage of an estimated 13 shots. One shot grazed Knight's head. Five other slugs ripped into Shakur. Three other cars were in the entourage with the BMW occupied by Shakur's bodyguards and friends, and these vehicles and a couple of others took off in pursuit of the killer Cadillac but that car made it away through heavy Las Vegas traffic.

Shakur and Knight were taken to University Medical Center where Shakur underwent a total of three operations. During the first just after the shooting, Shakur's right lung was removed to halt internal bleeding. In the next days Shakur would have two more operations but on September 14 he died.

Police had no dearth of possible motives, including street gang revenge for the quarrel Shakur had after the match. It turned out that person was allied with the Crips while Knight was a friend of the Bloods. Police also theorized about the group Shakur had accused of the New York City attack on him. There was also speculation that the motive might have been money since Knight had not long ago taken out a $1 million dollar policy on Shakur's life. Other observers felt there probably was yet another motive hidden in Shakur's violent life. In any event the murder of the rap star went unsolved.

## Sheppard, Samuel H. (1924–1970) accused wife murderer

A leading osteopath in the Cleveland area, Dr. Samuel Sheppard was convicted of murdering his wife, Marilyn, on July 3, 1954

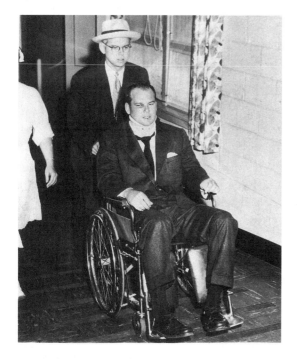

Sam Sheppard had to be wheeled to his wife's funeral with his neck in a brace, allegedly the work of a "bushy-haired stranger" who had murdered his wife. Sheppard was convicted of her murder but cleared 12 years later.

after a sensational trial that attracted national and international attention.

Marilyn Sheppard had been slain with more than 25 blows to the head in the upstairs bedroom of the couple's suburban home, which fronted on Lake Erie. She was 31 at the time and four months pregnant. Dr. Sam, as the newspapers labeled him, said he had been awakened by his wife's screams and the sounds of a terrible fight. When he came to his wife's aid, he said, he had been knocked unconscious by a "bushy-haired stranger."

The murder took on a sex scandal tone when Sheppard admitted he had been having an affair with Susan Hayes, a young, attrac-

tive medical technician at Bay View Hospital, where the doctor worked. Both Dr. Sam and Miss Hayes admitted their relationship on the witness stand. Probably this fact as much as any of the evidence resulted in a guilty verdict and a life sentence for Sheppard. Meanwhile, many voices were raised proclaiming Dr. Sam's innocence. Newspapers and magazines took up the crusade, as did the noted mystery writer Erle Stanley Gardner. With the aid of a new lawyer, F. Lee Bailey, Dr. Sam was released from the Ohio State Penitentiary in 1964 pending a new trial. The Supreme Court upheld his release, sighting "prejudicial publicity" and a "carnival atmosphere" at the first trial.

Bailey kept his client off the stand at the second trial, which was held in 1966, and attacked the prosecution's case as "ten pounds of hogwash in a five pound bag." The jury agreed, finding Dr. Sam innocent 12 years after his first conviction.

Following his acquittal, Sheppard married a woman who had befriended him by mail during his time in prison, and regained his medical license. However, in 1968 Sheppard's second wife sued for divorce, saying she feared for her safety living with him. Subsequently, Dr. Sam turned professional wrestler, but his health began to fail and he died in 1970.

In 1995 Sam Reese Sheppard filed suit seeking monetary damages for his father's 10 years of wrongful imprisonment. In 1998 Sheppard's body was exhumed and, according to the son's attorney, new DNA evidence excluded Dr. Sheppard as a suspect. However, the State of Ohio, which had apparently exhibited little interest in doing DNA checks earlier decided to exhume Marilyn Sheppard's body to check her DNA, an official saying, "Right now, there is no positive pro-

After the murders of Nicole Simpson and Ron Goldman, the most famous picture of O.J. Simpson was not of any of his football exploits, but the LAPD mug shot of his arrest.

file of Mrs. Sheppard's DNA, and we need that so we can start answering some of the questions being raised by the plaintiffs."

Under Ohio law, the state could be required to pay $25,000 for each year of imprisonment, plus lost income and other expenses. In 2000 a court ruled in favor of the state, but the ruling was subject to appeal.

### Simpson case   "Trial of the Century"

The trial for murder of former football star O. J. Simpson was not without reason called the "Trial of the Century." In the "starring role" was O. J. Simpson, who gained well-deserved fame in college and professional football and later remained in the public eye as a television sportscaster and pitchman and as a supporting actor in a number of films, especially the comic *Naked Gun*

movies. Clearly he had hurdled the color barriers and was a huge and popular success in the world at large. He had a beautiful wife, Nicole Brown Simpson, and seemed to live an ideal life among the rich and famous in the Los Angeles–Hollywood scene.

That clearly changed when Simpson's wife was murdered and he was charged with the crime. There were other unusual aspects to the case, such as the preponderance of DNA evidence introduced and discussed. Above all, the Simpson trial became a media event; millions of people from coast to coast listened to every word of the trial broadcast in what was undoubtedly television overkill.

The violence in the case was gruesome enough. Nicole, 35, and her friend Ron Goldman, 25, were killed on June 12, 1994, outside the doorway of Nicole's condominium at 875 South Bundy Drive in Brentwood. The evidence appeared to be that

Goldman had been savagely stabbed first, and then Nicole. After the crime Los Angeles police followed Simpson's car in what became known as the "slow speed chase." There was speculation that Simpson, a passenger in the car driven by an old football buddy, was near to killing himself—the pro-Simpson people insisting that was because he was suffering from the loss of his wife while the anti-Simpson group attributed his despair to guilt resulting from what he'd done. The chase became a long spectacle, with viewers along the freeway cheering Simpson and yelling "Juice!" an old accolade from his football days. Finally Simpson in effect gave himself up, and the whole spectacle shifted to the legal system. While Simpson did remain the center of attention, other players from Judge Lance Ito to colorful prosecution figures as well as defense attorneys hired by Simpson and dubbed by the media as the "dream team," became very recognizable and in some cases idolized or reviled.

The prosecution insisted Simpson had the time and inclination to commit the murders in a jealous rage, while the defense made the investigators into sort of defendants themselves. The defense claimed the police used shoddy investigative techniques and fabricated evidence. They sought to dismiss the DNA evidence submitted by the prosecution as not credible and compromised by controversial handling of evidence, such as by one detective carrying around with him for more than a day a vial of Simpson's blood. The defense mocked Detective Mark Fuhrman's claim that he found a glove containing blood carrying the DNA of Simpson and the victims. (In one trial highpoint, Simpson was asked to put on the glove, but he could not, because it was too small, giving birth to a famous quote to the jury by lead defense attorney Johnnie Cochran Jr.: "If it doesn't fit, you must acquit."

The defense lawyers claimed Fuhrman was a racist and that the white officer harbored a grudge against Simpson stemming from a 1985 incident in which he smashed the windows of his wife's car with a baseball bat. The defense inferred to the jury that Fuhrman had sprinkled blood found on the crime scene from a blood sample Simpson had given when the bodies were discovered.

The jury acquitted Simpson quickly, which brought charges that since 10 members of the panel were African-American, the jury was itself prejudiced. The reaction to the verdict followed racial lines, with 64 percent of whites and only 12 percent of blacks believing Simpson was probably guilty, while 59 percent of blacks and 11 percent of whites thought he was probably innocent.

As time passed, public opinion against Simpson solidified and when Simpson was sued in civil court by relatives of Nicole Brown Simpson and Ron Goldman, he was convicted, a result that involved no criminal consequences. However, a judgment for $33.5 million for wrongful death was imposed on Simpson, and virtually all his wealth was taken from him by law, and he was stymied in various efforts to resume any kind of career.

It could not be said that the racial divide widened by the case narrowed subsequently.

### Sirhan, Sirhan Bishara (1944– ) assassin of Robert F. Kennedy

The early morning of June 5, 1968 was a moment of triumph for Senator Robert F. Kennedy, brother of President John F. Kennedy, who had been assassinated in

1963. He had just won the California presidential primary, defeating Senator Eugene McCarthy, and emerged for the first time as the likely winner of the Democratic nomination. That evening he delivered a victory speech in Los Angeles' Ambassador Hotel. After the speech the senator was walking toward a rear exit when a 24-year-old Palestinian, Sirhan Bishara Sirhan, approached carrying a Kennedy campaign poster, behind which he had concealed a .22-caliber eight-shot Iver Johnson pistol. He fired several shots at Kennedy, three of which hit home. Two struck Kennedy in his armpit and would not have been fatal. The third entered the side of his head behind the right ear. Kennedy fell, mortally wounded, while his assailant was wrestled into submission by the senator's bodyguards, including former sports stars Rafer Johnson and Rosey Grier. As they did so, Sirhan wildly emptied his weapon into the crowd, wounding five persons.

Kennedy died at 1:44 the following morning.

Sirhan was proud of his act. He joked with police officers, made them taste his coffee to make sure it was not poisoned and even spoke sorrowfully about how violent the society had become. He was particularly upset about the terrible things the Boston Strangler had done.

Meanwhile, some witnesses claimed 10 shots had been fired, leading to speculation that Sirhan might not have acted alone. A possible explanation was that some of Kennedy's bodyguards' guns had been accidentally discharged in the melee.

During Kennedy's speech, a campaign worker, Sandy Serrano, stepped out onto a hotel balcony to escape the smoke and heat. While she was there, two men and a young woman in a white polka-dot dress went by her into the building. Later, after the shooting, the trio rushed out and Serrano was "nearly run over." The woman wearing the polka-dot dress shouted, "We shot him!" When Serrano asked whom they had shot, the woman replied, "We shot Kennedy!"

The police eventually turned up a woman named Cathy Fulmer, but Serrano was unable to identify her as the one in the polka-dot dress. Fulmer was found dead in a motel room some days after Sirhan was convicted of the assassination.

Sirhan freely confessed his act and was convicted and sentenced to death, a fate he escaped when the Supreme Court abolished capital punishment in 1972. In the streets of Arab capitals throughout the Middle East, posters appeared hailing "Sirhan Bishara Sirhan, a commando not an assassin." "Commando sources" were quoted as saying the posters were designed to convey the idea that in shooting Kennedy, Sirhan was acting on behalf of all dispossessed Palestinians by striking at a supporter of Israel—Kennedy.

Currently, Sirhan remains in prison, actively pursuing a parole.

**Spooner, Bathsheba** (1746–1778) murderess
Bathsheba Spooner, the Tory Murderess, was convicted and sentenced to death in 1778 in the first capital case tried in American jurisdiction in Massachusetts, and quite possibly, her subsequent ill fate was the result of her lowly political repute. Not that Bathsheba was innocent of the charges against her. She admitted conspiring with and assisting her lover and two escaped British soldiers in the murder of her husband, the elderly Joshua Spooner, but she most likely would have earned herself a lesser punishment had she possessed more revolutionary fervor.

Bathsheba was the daughter of Timothy Ruggles, chief justice of the Massachusetts Court on Common Pleas under crown rule. With the onset of the Revolution, Ruggles had been forced to flee to Canada. Bathsheba remained behind in that fateful year of 1776 and married 63-year-old Joshua Spooner, a retired merchant. Although old Spooner was rather apolitical, he was soon branded as a Tory sympathizer because of his marriage to the daughter of a leading Tory. It was not a situation to his liking and probably explained why he was so happy when he came home one day in the winter of 1778 to find his 31-year-old wife had taken in Ezra Ross, a handsome 20-year-old soldier in the Revolutionary Army who had been wounded in the chest during a recent campaign. Ross had literally collapsed outside the Spooners' door in the hamlet of Brookfield, near Worcester. With his wife, a suspected Tory, now nursing a Revolutionary hero, Spooner knew that the wagging rebel tongues would still.

Of course, his wife's care for the soldier had little to do with political sentiments; within a few months she would inform her recuperating patient that she was "with child." Bathsheba also told young Ross they would have to kill her husband before he learned of their affair and cast them both out of his lavish keep. Ross agreed to her suggestion in the abstract, but in practice he proved unavailing. She suggested poisoning her husband, but Ross, who said he could face any man musket to musket, backed off from such a low deed. Then Spooner had to journey to Boston to look after his investments and Ross went with him. Bathsheba's lover was supposed to kill her husband on the return trip and blame the murder on the British, but the pair returned together.

By this time Bathsheba Spooner had decided her young lover just wasn't going to do her bidding; so she recruited two passing British soldiers to carry out the plot. Whether James Buchanan and William Brooks were deserters or escapees from Revolutionary custody was of small consequence to Mrs. Spooner. The important thing was that they were willing to perform any deed which would earn them some gold. With Buchanan and Brooks backing him, Ross waylaid Spooner as he came staggering home one midnight from Ephraim Cooley's tavern. The three clubbed the old man to death and dumped his body into a well at the side of the house.

A maid fetching water the next morning discovered the bucket covered with a film of blood and sounded the alarm. Old Spooner's body was raised and it was found to be devoid of purse, snuff box, silver shoe buckles and watch. Obviously, he had been murdered and robbed. Perhaps if they had kept a low profile, Ross, Brooks and Buchanan might have escaped detection, but with foolish abandon, they took to wearing their loot, and within days the trio was arrested. Servants in the Spooner household then came forth with tales of having heard the three in conspiratorial conversations with Mrs. Spooner. One servant, coachman Alexander Cumings, said he had come into the parlor and observed the men burning their clothing, which appeared to be bloodstained in the fireplace. The victim's money box lay open on the table and its contents divided up in neat piles.

It was, to say the least, a rather open-and-shut case, especially when Bathsheba confessed she had masterminded the murder of her husband to keep him from learning of her affair with young Ross. The case was tried by William Cushing, chief justice of the Massachusetts Supreme Court and later a member of the U.S. Supreme Court, and prosecuted by Robert Treat Paine, a signer of the Declaration of Independence. Defense attorney Levi Lincoln, who was to become attorney general under Thomas Jefferson, came up with the rather novel defense that since the plot had been so openly planned and botched, Bathsheba must have been "insane." He added that because only one of the three men had struck the fatal blow, the jury could not convict more than one of them and, lacking absolute proof against any of the three, it would have to release them all. Unmoved by the defense attorney's arguments, the jury found the four guilty. They were all sentenced to be hanged.

The sentences were scheduled to be carried out on June 4, 1778 but were postponed through the intercession of the Rev. Thaddeus MacCarty, a Worcester minister, who visited the condemned woman in her cell to discuss her spiritual future. Mrs. Spooner once more admitted her part in the crime but for the first time confessed the full story, including the fact that she was pregnant. If that were so, and the Rev. MacCarty was certain it was, both English law and custom forbade her execution. Urged on by MacCarty, the Massachusetts Council granted a stay until July 2 and ordered that "two men midwives and twelve discreet lawful matrons" conduct an examination "by the breast and by the belly" to determine the accuracy of the claim.

Their unanimous finding was that Bathsheba Spooner was not pregnant, which led MacCarty to charge that their opinion had been colored by their political sympathies. He empaneled his own jury of three men midwives and three lawful matrons.

After they conducted an examination, all the men and one of the women declared Bathsheba was pregnant, but the two other women said she was not. In any event, the MacCarty panel had no legal standing, and even Bathsheba gave up the fight.

She made a final request in a letter to the council

*that my body be examined after I am executed by a committee of competent physicians, who will, perforce, belatedly substantiate my claims. I am a woman, familiar with my bodily functions, and am surely able to perceive when my womb is animated. The midwives who have examined me have taken into greater account my father's Royalist leanings than they have the stirrings in my body which should have stirred their consciences. The truth is that they want my father's daughter dead and with her my father's grandchild.*

Thousands attended the four hangings in Worcester on July 2, the dispute over Bathsheba's condition still raging. The crowd did not disperse until later that afternoon when a committee of surgeons completed an autopsy and rather reluctantly made their report public. In the executed woman's womb they had found "a perfectly developed male foetus, aged between five and six months."

Some latter-day historians have insisted that the Spooner case was so etched on the conscience of the citizens of Massachusetts that never again was a female condemned to death in the state, with or without a plea for mercy because of pregnancy. That theory is certainly open to debate, but one definite result of the affair was that certain male midwives and discreet lawful matrons needed a lengthy period of remorse before they could once more walk the streets of Worcester without downcast eyes.

## Stewart, Alexander Turney (1803–1876)
### grave-robbing victim

The nation's most sensational grave robbery was the removal of the bones of A. T. Stewart, two years after he died in 1876, from the churchyard of the venerable St. Mark's-in-the-Bouwerie in New York City. Since Stewart was the greatest of the merchant princes of his era and a multimillionaire, the grave ghouls demanded a ransom of $200,000 for the return of the body. Negotiations over the ransom continued for two years through newspaper personal columns until finally the ghouls agreed to accept $20,000.

The transaction was made at midnight on a lonely country road. The chief ghoul, using the assumed name of Henry Romaine, and two others took the money in exchange for a bag of bones, which were later definitely established as Stewart's. The identities of the grave robbers were never learned, although various police authorities claimed the crime was the work of either the notorious bank robber George Leonidas Leslie or the fence Travelling Mike Grady.

The Stewart family reburied A. T. Stewart's bones in the mausoleum of the Cathedral of the Incarnation in Garden City, Long Island, protected thereafter by an intricate burglar alarm system.

## Stompanato, Johnny (1926–1958) "justifiable homicide" victim

The death of Johnny Stompanato, a 32-year-old ex-bodyguard for gambler Mickey Cohen, in April 1958 was labeled a case of

Body snatchers turn over a bag containing the bones of the late merchant prince A. T. Stewart for $20,000 ransom.

"justifiable homicide," harkening back to Hollywood's real life murder and scandal days in the 1920s and 1930s. For a year prior to Stompanato's death, he had been the romantic interest of Lana Turner, at 38 still one of Hollywood's most glamorous actresses. Then, as the saying went, Turner "didn't pick up his option."

On the night of April 4 Cheryl Crane, the 14-year-old daughter of Lana Turner and Stephen Crane, the second of Turner's four husbands, was present when an argument broke out between her mother and the gangster. As the girl later related to police:

*I was in my room talking to mother when he came in and began yelling at her. She told him "I don't want to argue in front of the baby."*

*Then mother and he went into mother's room and I went to the door to listen. He kept saying that he was going to have her cut and disfigured. I thought he was going to get her.*

*I ran downstairs to the kitchen and grabbed the first big knife I could find and raced back upstairs.*

*I stood outside the bedroom door, right around the corner.*

*Then I heard him say, "I'll get you if it takes a day, a week or a year. I'll cut your face up. I'll stomp you. And if I can't do it myself I'll find somebody who will—that's my business."*

*I went into the room and I said, "You don't have to take that, mother." Then I pushed the knife into his stomach with all my might.*

The husky gangster crumpled without a word, according to both mother and daughter.

At a coroner's inquest, a week later, Lana Turner was the star performer, describing the killing as well as her relationship with Stompanato. The gangster had been advised to get out of England in 1957 after he had threatened Turner with a razor. Despite this difference, the pair reconciled, and shortly before Stompanato's death they had returned from a two-month stay in Acapulco, Mexico.

The actress said:

*. . . I swear, it was so fast. I truthfully say I thought she had hit him in the stomach.*

*As best I remember, they came together. But I still never saw the blade. Mr. Stompanato grabbed himself here [indicating the abdomen].*

*And he started to move forward, and he made almost a half-turn and he dropped on his back and when he dropped, his arm went out, so that I still didn't see that there was blood or a wound until I ran over to him and I saw his sweater was cut.*

*And I lifted the sweater up and I saw this wound. I remember only barely hearing my daughter sobbing. And I ran into my*

*bathroom which was very close. And I grabbed a towel. I didn't know what to do. Then I put a towel on Mr. Stompanato.*

A medical report indicated the knife had severed the aorta and that the victim had died within minutes.

After hearing the evidence, the coroner's jury returned a verdict of justifiable homicide.

Cheryl Crane was a heroine, Lana Turner was a heroine and Johnny Stompanato was memoralized by Hollywood screenwriters who found ways to incorporate the drama into movie scripts.

## Sumner, Charles (1811–1874) U.S. Senator and assault victim

The halls of Congress have been the scene of numerous acts of violence, most perpetrated by outsiders, of course. Perhaps the most criminal attack by one congressman upon another occurred in 1856 in what was, in a personal sense, a preview of the coming Civil War. On May 19 Sen. Charles Sumner of Massachusetts delivered a fiery attack on the proslavery forces, charging that Sen. Andrew P. Butler of South Carolina had embraced "the harlot, Slavery" as his "mistress." Three days later, Rep. Preston S. Brooks, Butler's nephew and also a native of South Carolina, strode onto the Senate floor to avenge the insult to his uncle. As Sumner sat at his desk writing, Brooks charged at him and proceeded to beat him over the head with the heavy cane he was carrying. Sumner toppled to the floor under the savage barrage, tearing the desk from its moorings as he struggled to move away. Brooks pounded on Sumner's head until his cane broke. Two Georgia senators watching nearby were reported to have chuckled at the attempted murder. Sumner survived the assault, although he was nearly blinded in one eye and was disabled for a number of years. As for Rep. Brooks, he was showered with gifts of canes and whips from southern admirers. From that date until secession, many congressmen appeared on the legislative floor armed with pistols or bowie knives or both.

### Switzer, Carl "Alfalfa" (1927–1959) shooting victim

From the age of eight, Carl "Alfalfa" Switzer was perhaps the most recognizable kid star in Hollywood with his freckled face, bobbing Adam's apple, and everpresent cowlick. Featured in the irrepressible *Our Gang* comedies along with the likes of Spanky, Buckwheat, Darla and Porky, Switzer performed in 60 of these Hal Roach pictures with an endearing off-key singing voice and banjo eyes that earned him the admiration of millions of American kids. But as it must to all kid stars, adolescence overtook him, and in 1942 he could not continue in his role.

Switzer took the end of his juvenile stardom more crushingly that did most young stars, and he became embittered while still trying to string together some sort of screen career—with very little success. A few "mature" roles came his way, but the feeling was that he could not escape his persona as Alfalfa. He had held a few nonacting jobs and drank a good deal by the 1950s. Then the old *Our Gang* comedies came to television as the *Little Rascals*. Everyone connected with that operation made money but not the *Our Gang* kids, who had no TV residuals in their contracts since at the time no one thought television would ever amount to much.

The situation made Switzer even more bitter. If it were not for friends like Henry Fonda and Roy Rogers, Switzer would probably have gotten no more acting work. Rogers booked him for a couple of minor appearances on his television show and Fonda got him a few minor movie roles. Switzer married a Kansas heiress, but that union collapsed after four months.

Switzer had to take bartending jobs and tried to build a career as a hunting guide, being quite a proficient hunter. Through Fonda, he lined up the backing for a good hunting expedition and in need of a good hunting dog, he borrowed one belonging to a friend, a welder named Bud Stiltz. Unfortunately, the dog ran off, which upset his owner, Stiltz. Switzer felt bad himself and posted a $35 reward for the dog.

The dog was found by a man who brought it to the tavern where Switzer tended bar to claim his reward. Elated, Switzer laid out drinks for the man in addition to giving him the reward money. Later, Switzer was upset

As an *Our Gang*er, Carl "Alfalfa" Switzer was at times a gentle bully. In real life he proved later to be more violent, which led to his death.

211

when the tavern insisted he make good on the drinks.

As days passed, Switzer got it in his head that Stiltz owed him $50. Stiltz objected, pointing out that Switzer had lost the dog and was on his own when he entertained the day's finder with drinks.

Switzer felt he needed all the money he could get. He'd finally landed a small supporting job in *The Defiant Ones* and felt if he could hang on in Hollywood, he still might have an acting career. But he kept brooding about Stiltz and finally, after a long drinking bout with a studio buddy, the pair headed to Stiltz' home. His studio pal flashed a movie police badge at the door and demanded to be let in. When the door opened a crack, the pair pushed their way in.

Switzer demanded the $50, and he and Stiltz engaged in a heated shouting match. Finally Switzer seized a heavy clock from a table, and yelled, "I going to take $50 out of your face!" He swung at Stiltz, smashing him in the forehead just above his right eye, causing a gush of blood. Clutching his forehead, Stiltz retreated into his bedroom with Switzer in pursuit. The dog owner opened a closet and produced a .38-caliber revolver. A struggle ensued, with a wild bullet smashing into the wall.

Switzer forced his foe back into the closet and slammed the door. Fearful that Stiltz would emerge firing from the closet, Switzer drew a switchblade knife from his pocket. Switzer brandished the knife as Stiltz came forward, gun in hand. "He's trying to kill me," Switzer cried and swung his knife, hitting only air. Stiltz fired, hitting Switzer in the stomach.

Switzer died in an ambulance on the way to a hospital. It had been a silly dispute, one having about as much logic as the *Our Gang* kids' pranks.

As Alfalfa Switzer had been known to millions, but even his tragic death garnered him little public recognition, as he had the misfortune to die on the same day as fabled director Cecil B. DeMille. The media splashed DeMille's obituary over all the newspapers and television. Most accounts of Switzer's death ran only a paragraph or two. A friend was quoted as saying later, "I think he would have been happy to have gone out with a splash of front-page publicity, but once again he was reduced to a bit player role."

Stiltz was cleared by a coroner's inquest, which found Switzer's death a case of justifiable homicide.

## Swope, Colonel Thomas B. (1825–1909)
### murder victim

An elderly multimillionaire, Colonel Thomas B. Swope was the central figure in a bizarre 1909 murder plot that shocked Kansas City, Mo.

Swope, a bachelor, lived in a mansion with his brother's widow, a nephew and four nieces. A fifth niece had just moved into her own home nearby, having married a Dr. B. C. Hyde. Dr. Hyde had obviously thought he was marrying into money, so one can understand his sudden dismay when he learned that Swope was preparing to change his will, leaving most of his money to charity. A man of quick action, Hyde gave both Swope and his lawyer such a fast-acting poison that the two men immediately "died of heart failure." Hyde, escaping suspicion for this strange double death, was not satisfied with just his wife's share of the Swope fortune, however, and calmly prepared to murder the other young heirs so that his wife would also inherit their shares of the estate. Before the authorities stopped him, he had fatally poisoned one and almost killed the other four with typhoid germs.

Although the evidence against Hyde was staggering, he was able to avoid conviction in three sensational trials. Found guilty the first time, Hyde won a reversal on technical grounds. The second trial ended in a mistrial and the third in a hung jury. Finally in 1917, the indictment against Hyde was dismissed and he quickly departed, never having spent a single day in prison for one of the most diabolical schemes of the era.

### Taylor, William Desmond (?–1922) victim of unsolved murder

With Hollywood reeling from the Fatty Arbuckle case, movie executives needed anything but another scandal for which the film industry could be excoriated. But that is what they faced when someone pumped two .38-caliber bullets into the heart of film director William Desmond Taylor the night of February 1, 1922. The case would never be solved, for many, many reasons. Not the least of which was that someone, upon finding the body, thought it was more advisable to notify studio executives than the police. After all, who really ran Hollywood?

Studio brass dispatched their people to the scene to launch an immediate cover-up operation. As a result, much of the potential evidence was in all likelihood tampered with. Taylor, somewhere around 45 years old—his past was hazy—was a notorious ladies' man, and many who heard about his murder turned up at his house to get rid of any evidence that might involve them in scandal.

Among those who sped to the murder scene was 28-year-old Mabel Normand, a leading comedienne of the day and the chief

One of the many speculations about the Taylor murder was this one favored by the *New York Daily News*, which had the killer dressed in male attire but walking like a woman.

rival to Mary Pickford, "America's Sweetheart," in box office appeal. Mabel was searching for letters revealing she had a $2,000-a-week cocaine habit and that Taylor had helped her out, it was said, by beating up a drug dealer supplying her with the stuff. And there were love letters.

Why hadn't the police been summoned? It seemed a studio doctor examined Taylor's body and surmised death had been the result of natural causes, perhaps a chronic stomach ailment. Only later when the body was turned over to authorities was blood discovered, as was a bullet hole. From the doctor's assessment, Paramount studio brass felt they were right in assuming Taylor's death had not been a matter for the police.

Normand had been the last person known to have seen Taylor alive. She had dropped in to the director's bungalow about 7:05 P.M. She said Taylor had seen her off to her chauffeur-driven limousine around 9 o'clock, after lending her a book by Sigmund Freud when he noticed some trashy magazines in the car.

It soon developed Taylor had a string of lady friends. A picture of Mary Pickford occupied a favored spot in his bachelor quarters. She said that not only did she know nothing about the murder but that she was America's Sweetheart. There were two damsels, one young, one older, who had got to the murder scene too late, their way blocked by police. They were Mary Miles Minter and her ever-watchful mother. They were very much enraged when the police refused them entry. Miss Minter, allegedly 17 years old, had been a rage in a number of Charlie Chaplin films.

One reason the Minters had tried to crash the murder scene soon became apparent. During the police search a scented note on Mary's stationery fluttered out of a book. The note was short, sweet and very, very passionate. It read:

Dearest:
I love you—I love you—I love you.
XXXXXXXXXXXXXXXXXX!
Yours always,
Mary.

The eighteenth *X* was two inches high so "Dearest" would know how devoted she was.

Mary made it clear that she truly meant what she wrote in the note. She later said, "I loved him deeply, and tenderly, with all the admiration a young girl gives to a man with the poise and position of Mr. Taylor." She insisted that despite all her devotion, she and Taylor, an ex-British army officer (a matter of some dispute), had merely been good friends.

And Mary insisted she knew nothing about all those bits of lingerie found in the Taylor home. None, she said, was hers. There was, for instance, a mysterious pink silk nightie with a butterfly on the back that was quickly discovered. Then there was a collection of silky, lacy lingerie, nightgowns and underwear, each item meticulously tagged with a date. There were love letters from other actresses and secret photographs of many of them. Taylor seemed to have been a multifaceted collector and connoisseur.

Mary, however, had a way of dominating the Taylor gossip. There was her remarkable performance at the director's garish funeral, which Taylor would no doubt have liked to use in one of his films. Mary kissed the corpse on the lips and then arose to declare that her dreamboat had whispered something to her even in death. She said it sounded like "I shall love you always, Mary."

Now the police investigation was in full swing, with the cops off on one wild goose chase after another. In the first two months, some 300 people, some even in South America and Europe, confessed to the murder. The public loved all this but really wanted more specific identification of the owners of all those uncovered unmentionables.

If the authorities identified any or all of those persons, they did not reveal one. Each

Taylor cataloged the unmentionables of his conquests. Denying they were sexually involved with Taylor were *(clockwise from upper left)* actresses Mary Miles Minter, Mabel Normand and Mary Pickford. Pickford especially insisted she and Taylor were just friends, and besides, she was "America's Sweetheart."

lead petered out after the other. Studio brass launched a campaign to save Mary. When the public found it upsetting that a 17-year-old girl could get involved with an older man, the studio insisted she was really 21, no, make that 22. The idea of a girl pretending to be younger than she was didn't wash with the public. Nor did Mabel Normand's pretending to be older than she was.

Both women ended up almost as tragically as did Taylor himself. American moviegoers exhibited a prudery that has since largely vanished. But at the time they wanted no more to do with Mary Miles Minter, and she was forced to retire. But at least she managed a comfortable retirement from an investment trust her mother had established.

Mabel Normand did try to do some movies, including one in 1923 called *Suzanna* that was described as her funniest ever. Hardly anyone went to see it. Still there was some belief Normand could weather the storm in time, but in 1924 she happened to be around when her chauffeur put a bullet into another gentleman, apparently in a dispute over her favors. Then she was named corespondent in another man's divorce suit. Mabel took refuge in more and different drugs. Her health ruined, she died of tuberculosis in 1930.

Perhaps the real legacy of the Taylor murder was that it led to Hollywood "going moral" by launching the Hays Office under the leadership of Will Hays, the Presbyterian postmaster-general of the Harding Cabinet. In due course that experiment would run out of gas.

## Teapot Dome scandal

The term "Teapot Dome" has become a catch phrase for governmental corruption and graft taking. Early in the ill-fated Harding Administration, Secretary of the Interior Albert B. Fall declared that the oil reserves at Teapot Dome, Wyo. and Elk Hills, Calif., which had been set aside for use by the U.S. Navy, were being drained by adjacent commercial operations and that consequently they should be leased out to private interests. It so happened that Fall had a number of close friends who would benefit from this decision, and in 1922, without allowing competitive bidding on the property, he secretly signed lease contracts with Edward L. Doheny and Harry F. Sinclair, two oil millionaires known for their freewheeling tactics. The two oil men, who figured to clear as much as $100 million from their leases, found ways to show their gratitude. Doheny slipped Fall $100,000 in a black bag, while Sinclair used a roundabout method to see that the secretary got a $260,000 "loan" in Liberty Bonds.

After the press and a senatorial inquiry headed by Thomas J. Walsh of Montana dug out the facts, the government canceled the leases, a decision eventually upheld by the Supreme Court. Oil man Doheny shocked the nation by dismissing his $100,000 payment as "a mere bagatelle." Criminal cases involving Doheny and Fall and Sinclair and Fall were tried but resulted in acquittals, although Sinclair was given nine months for contempt of court and Fall, tried separately, was found guilty of bribery charges and drew a one-year prison term. It can be argued that Fall was made the "fall guy" for all the scandals of the Harding Administration, in which even larger sums were siphoned out of the Treasury.

See also: ALBERT B. FALL.

## television quiz show scandal

In 1959 the television broadcast industry was rocked by a quiz show scandal when it was

On-the-air photos of Charles Van Doren (top) and Herbert Stempel (below) show them going through the prearranged quiz show charade that made Van Doren for a time the most celebrated "egghead" in the nation.

established that many big-money winners had been provided with the answers to questions. Several recent highly acclaimed winners were exposed as frauds, perhaps the most shocking being Charles Van Doren, a 33-year-old Ph.D. who came from one of the nation's top intellectual families.

Van Doren, a $5,500-a-year instructor at Columbia University, had won $129,000 on NBC's "Twenty-One" after having been sup-

plied with a trumped-up script in advance. Later, Van Doren said he had been convinced to take part in the quiz show because it would be a boon "to the intellectual life, to teachers, and to education in general." He added, "In fact, I think I have done a disservice to all of them."

On the basis of his new fame as a quiz winner, Van Doren got a $50,000-a-year post with NBC, but in the aftermath of the exposures he lost that position as well as his teaching job at Columbia.

In the ensuing investigation New York District Attorney Frank Hogan found that of 150 persons who had testified before a grand jury about the quiz fixes, about 100 had lied. From 1959 to 1962, 18 contestants who had "won" from $500 to $220,500 on now-defunct quiz shows pleaded guilty to perjury and were given suspended sentences, although they could have been fined and imprisoned for three years. The punishment seemed sufficient, considering the fact that nothing was done to the corporate sponsors, some of whom, according to confessions by the shows' producers, had decided whether a contestant would be bumped or allowed to survive as a contestant.

Abroad the scandal generally was viewed as demonstrating a failing in American life. France's *France-Soir* saw a parallel between Van Doren's confession and Vice President Nixon's campaign-fund confession and observed: "In America, more than anywhere, contrition is a form of redemption. A sinner who confesses is a sinner pardoned." Nixon would survive to be pardoned again, but Van Doren never returned to public life.

## Thaw, Harry Kendall (1872–1947) murderer

At first, quite a few people felt that railroad heir Harry Kendall Thaw did what was right and proper when he shot Stanford White, the distinguished architect, on the roof garden of New York's Madison Square Garden in 1906. Revelations showed that millionaire White had a hobby of seducing young girls. One of his amusements, it would be alleged, was having them put on little girls' dresses and cavort, legs flying, on a red velvet swing in a heavily curtained, lavishly decorated miniature Taj Mahal he maintained on the West Side.

One girl White so despoiled was the beautiful Evelyn Nesbit, who became his mistress at the age of 16, by which time she had already posed for Charles Dana Gibson's painting *The Eternal Question* and had adorned the chorus of many hit shows, including "Floradora." Then in 1905, at the age of 19, Evelyn left White to become engaged to Thaw, whom she married the following year. Thaw was the wastrel heir of a Pittsburgh railroad tycoon who had reduced his allowance to a paltry $2,000 a year. However, he had a doting mother who gave him another $80,000 so that he could pursue the wild life. Among other bad habits that would soon become public knowledge, Thaw maintained an apartment in a New York brothel where he would entice young girls under the promise of winning them a show business career. Once he had them in the apartment, Thaw often would whip the girls, a treatment he soon inflicted on his new bride. Thus, there emerged a bizarre triangle: a lascivious architect with 50 elegant New York City buildings to his credit and a lascivious wastrel with $40 million in his future contending over gorgeous Evelyn, destined to become the fantasy idol of millions of American men and boys. Irvin S. Cobb was to describe her to enthralled newspaper readers as having "the slim, quick grace of a fawn, a head that sat on her flawless throat as a lily on its stem, eyes that were the color of blue-brown pansies and the size of half dollars, a mouth made of rumpled rose petals." Was it any wonder that the assassination of Stanford White enjoyed as much publicity as had that of President William McKinley a few years earlier?

At age 34 Thaw was no doubt going slowly mad. On a European cruise he finally cracked up and beat Evelyn until she "confessed" all her past sins with White. To stop the whippings, Evelyn was later to admit she told Thaw even more than had happened.

Thaw was now totally insane with jealousy. He forbade his wife to mention White by name but instead refer to him as "the Bastard" or "the Beast." Being rather on the genteel side, Evelyn more often simply called him "the B." Then on the evening of June 25, 1906, Thaw and his wife were attending a musical at the dinner theater on the roof of Madison Square Garden. Also in the audience was Stanford White. Suddenly, Thaw arose from his seat and strolled through the audience to within four feet of White. He drew a revolver and fired two times at the architect's head, killing him instantly. As the victim slumped to the floor, Thaw fired a final shot into his shoulder. Then he announced with evident satisfaction: "You deserve this. You ruined my wife."

Thaw unloaded his weapon, scattering the cartridges onto the floor, and held the gun aloft, indicating he meant no harm to others. He was quickly arrested and hustled off to jail.

While awaiting trial, Thaw had all his meals catered from Delmonico's, and his mother announced she was prepared to spend a million dollars to save her son. She hired the famous California trial lawyer Delphin Delmas to defend him. Even before the opening of the trial, Delmas began spreading stories that transformed bounder Thaw into a defender of American womanhood. Various of White's escapades with teenage girls were leaked to the press and the Rev. Charles A. Eaton, who numbered John D. Rockefeller among his parishioners, delivered a sermon in Thaw's defense. "It would be a good thing," Rev. Eaton said, "if there were a little more shooting in cases like this."

District Attorney William Travers Jerome, the uncle of Winston Churchill, saw what the defense was trying to do and reacted with an angry declaration that he would personally try the case. "With all his millions," Jerome roared, "Thaw is a fiend. In the conduct of his trial, I shall prove that no matter how rich a man is, he can't get away with murder in New York County!"

Tickets to the sensational trial were scalped at $100, and 80-odd world famous artists and writers, including Cobb, Samuel Hopkins Adams and James Montgomery Flagg, covered the proceedings. The prosecution's case was brief and simple: Thaw had shot and killed White. The high point for the defense came when Evelyn took the stand and, as the saying went, told all. Dressed in a plain blue frock with a white collar, big schoolboy tie and black velvet hat, she told, in dewy innocence, of the bizarre love games she played with White, often wearing a little girl dress with her hair hung back. It was a tale that would have enraged a statue. She sobbingly told of her ultimate deflowering, which White had accomplished by giving her drugged champagne that rendered her helpless. In rebuttal, the prosecutor elicited damaging testimony from a leading toxicologist, Dr. Rudolph Witthaus, who pointed out that Evelyn's story of the drugged champagne was dubious. No drug known to science would have worked as rapidly as she described without also killing the victim.

But what was such evidence worth against the word of Evelyn Nesbit—"a wounded bluebird, a soiled Broadway sparrow," as the press referred to her.

A group of alienists examined Thaw and pronounced him legally sane, but throughout the trial he alternately scribbled incoherent notes to his lawyers, cried like a baby and flew into rages until his eyes bugged out and "his face would turn purple."

In a flowery summation, defense attorney Delmas told the jury that his client had been temporarily seized by "*dementia Americana* . . . that species of insanity which makes every home sacred . . . makes a man believe that his wife is sacred. . . . Whoever stains the virtue of his wife has forfeited the protection of human laws and must look to the eternal justice and mercy of God. . . ."

The gentlemen of the jury could not agree on a verdict. A year later, a new trial was held. Prosecutor Jerome decided his previous tactic of attacking Evelyn's rape story had boomeranged, so this time he stipulated she spoke the truth. Evelyn looked more lovely and Thaw acted more mad. The jury returned a verdict of "not guilty, on the ground of his insanity at the time of the commission of the act."

Thaw, however, did not go free. He was declared criminally insane and imprisoned for life in a mental institution at Matteawan, N.Y. His mother spent tens of thousands of dollars on legal hearings trying to win his freedom. Then in 1913 Thaw escaped from the asylum, fled to Canada and was finally retaken. While he was on the loose, Evelyn Nesbit announced: "Harry Thaw has turned out to be a degenerate scoundrel. He hid behind my skirts through two dirty trials and I won't stand for it again. I won't let lawyers throw any more mud at me." She then signed a contract to appear in vaudeville at $3,500 a week.

A battery of lawyers kept Thaw from going back to Matteawan and in 1915 a court declared him sane. The following year he celebrated his new freedom by horsewhipping a teenage boy. Before going off to the asylum once more, Thaw divorced Evelyn. He emerged from Matteawan in 1922 and embarked on a new career of wild living. Evelyn Nesbit continued to appear in vaudeville for many years and, sporadically, in some less austere nightclubs and gin mills. She eventually retired to a career in ceramics in California. Harry Thaw continued to roam the world, spending his millions, until his death in 1947.

### Todd, Thelma (1906–1935) Hollywood actress and alleged murder victim

She was dubbed the "Vamping Vixen," the "Hot Toddy," and the "Ice Cream Blonde," but she easily outdistanced this sort of Hollywood hype. Beautiful Thelma Todd was recognized as a sparkling comedienne who easily made the transition from silents to talking movies because of her genuine talents. Most remembered for her roles with the Marx Brothers in successful box office hits as *Monkey Business* and *Horse Feathers,* she also appeared with Buster Keaton, Laurel and Hardy, Bing Crosby, Cary Cooper, Joe E. Brown, and ZaSu Pitts, her closest female friend. In most of these appearances Thelma was regarded as the real draw. From 1926 to 1935 she appeared in an amazing 109 films, virtually all very successful. The saying was that many actors and directors were ready to kill to get her in their films.

Thelma had a most adoring legion of fans, a situation that made her rich beyond the hope of a young girl with limited acting training. Her road to Hollywood had been amazingly easy. She won a beauty contest as Miss Massachusetts, and a family friend

When Thelma Todd, the striking heartthrob of the 1920s and '30s, died in her car under mysterious circumstances, the rumor mills never stopped, and murder theories about the case continued into the next century.

showed pictures of her to Paramount producer Jesse Lasky, who sight unseen, offered her a contract. Thelma was sent to a studio acting school in Astoria, New York, and progressed so rapidly she was ready to move to the top in Hollywood. Her delightfully throaty voice in the talkies soon made her the darling of movie audiences.

Extremely bright, Thelma often told friends she had to realize her fame would have to fade with age and that she had to set herself up for the future. One course she set out on was a half-interest, along with director and producer Roland West, in a swank Palisades roadhouse called "Thelma Todd's Sidewalk Cafe," which became a mecca for the rich and famous of the sun-and-beach-loving film colony. Some would later insist that the cafe was the reason for Thelma's tragic fate, but that was just one theory among many.

On the evening of December 16, 1935, Thelma Todd's body was found by her maid in her garage, set well atop the cliff above Thelma's apartment, which was situated above the cafe.

The actress was slumped on the steering wheel of her Packard convertible with its top down. The car's ignition was turned on. Like other sudden deaths that had upset the big studios in recent years, there was a vested interest by certain forces to see to it that there be no suggestion of foul play. But there were problems in advancing the theory that Thelma had committed suicide—especially since she was very much at the peak of her career. Her face was bloody and there was blood on the evening gown and mink coat she had worn to a late Saturday night party given in her honor at the Trocadero, one of Hollywood's top nightspots. The blood seemed to raise the possibility that she had been batted about after being driven home by her limousine driver. That in turn raised the possibility that she had been beaten and placed in her car and the ignition turned on.

And there were other whispers. Thelma seemed to be having a secret affair with a very rich and powerful man from San Francisco. She told actress Ida Lupino, who was at the party, about him and said she expected to see him shortly, perhaps right after the party. Thelma inferred it was very, very important that she not reveal his identify, presumably as that would result in a very messy situation.

Then again there was the fact that Thelma did seem quite fearful recently, for a time hiring bodyguards and on some occasions she instructed her driver to pick up speed, fearing they were being followed. Thelma did mutter things about "eastern gangsters." That element was not unknown in Hollywood. Lucky Luciano operating out of New York had set about targeting spots where the mob could establish secret gambling operations on an upper floor. The mob was very interested in Thelma's cafe, but Thelma had refused them. Could she have been ordered killed by Luciano as an object lesson to owners of other choice spots so they would be less inclined to refuse similar offers?

A lot of criticism was placed on director West, who although he had his own apartment in the complex had moved in with Thelma. He had not attended the Trocadero affair and said later that he had jokingly warned if she wasn't home by 2 A.M. he would lock her out. As a point of fact he did lock her out, and he claimed he never heard her come home. And even though he did not see her all day and night Sunday, he had not looked for her.

There were other loose ends. Thelma had had a terrible argument at the party with her ex-husband, talent agent Pat DeCicco, who had shown up with two starlets.

While all these factors were tossed into the mix, an inquest ruled that Thelma Todd had committed suicide, a finding with which Hollywood's brass was most comfortable. The film colony was at the time in its do-good phase, with all scandals deemed detrimental to the industry.

However, because of public opinion a second inquest was held before a grand jury. This time the verdict was that Thelma died "by carbon monoxide poisoning," leaving open that chance that she had not killed herself but had died accidentally because she was curled up in the convertible with the motor on to stay warm through the night. There did seem to be a hole in that theory since she could have curled up not in her open convertible but instead in the car right next to it, a new Lincoln sedan, which obviously would have provided much more warmth.

Then true Hollywood mania raged. In which car had Todd really died, and was her body transferred?

Again criticism centered on her housemate, director West, who insisted he never heard Thelma trying to get in—although neighbors insisted the actress had created a loud ruckus. Also, West failed to locate Thelma Sunday day or evening. West was the only one ever to pay a price in the tragedy. He could not shake off public suspicion and was never able to direct another movie.

In succeeding years the Thelma Todd story never died. Decades later theories are still being advanced, which say powerful forces protected the killer, utilizing perjured testimony and official corruption. Despite claims and counterclaims, it is now firmly established that the verdict on the Todd case still must reside in the "unsolved" files.

## Truman, Harry S (1884–1972) intended assassination victim

On November 1, 1950 a uniformed White House guard, Donald Birdzell, was at his post in front of Blair House, across the street from the Executive Mansion, where President Harry S Truman was staying while repairs were being made at the White House. Suddenly, Birdzell heard a faint, metallic click and turned his head. Ten feet away, a neat, dark man in a pin-striped blue-green suit was silently and carefully aiming a German F-38 automatic pistol at him. It went off just as Birdzell jumped for the street—a prescribed Secret Service action to draw fire away from the house where the president was staying so that he would not catch a stray bullet. The first assault on a president of the United States in his Washington residence was underway.

Birdzell landed on the streetcar tracks on Pennsylvania Avenue, turned and began firing back. The gunman put a bullet in his leg, dropping him to one knee. Another slug ripped into Birdzell's good leg and he pitched forward. As other guards and Secret Servicemen went into action, a second attacker darted up to the guard at the west sentry booth, pulled out a Luger and began shooting at point-blank range. A uniformed sentry, Leslie Coffelt, went down with bullets in the chest, stomach and legs. He died a short while later. Plainclothesman Joseph Downs toppled over, shot in the stomach.

There was one last burst of gunfire. The wounded Birdzell, stretched out flat with his pistol held braced at arm's length on the pavement before him, shot the first gunman in the chest as he frantically tried to reload. The would-be assassin sprawled out, his hat awry, his heels kicking. The second gunman

Would-be presidential assassin Oscar Collazo lies wounded at the foot of the steps to Blair House.

lurched backward over a low boxwood hedge, dead with a bullet through his ears.

In the heavy silence that followed, Secret Serviceman Floyd Boring saw President Truman in his undershirt peering out the window of an upstairs room, where he had been napping.

"Get back, Mr. President!" Agent Boring shouted. "Get back!"

Truman stepped back while a few Secret Service agents converged on the scene. Most remained at their posts, on guard against further attacks.

The wounded gunman was identified as Oscar Collazo and his dead partner as Griselio Torresola. In Torresola's pocket were found two letters from a fiery Puerto Rican nationalist, Pedro Albizu Campos.

While newspaper front pages were filled with details of the assassination attempt, a key factor failed to get the prominence it deserved. Although Torresola and Collazo started with the assassin's greatest asset—the element of surprise—they failed to penetrate even the outer rim of presidential protectors. Backing up the uniformed White House police was an agent sitting in a nearby office building with a clear view of Blair House. His duty was to drop any attacker who made it to the doorway of Blair House. However, even if the attackers had gotten through the door, they would have faced an agent stationed inside the entrance with a submachine gun in his lap.

There was another agent on the stairway, one in front of Truman's door and others in surrounding rooms. It was estimated that the assassins would have had to kill at least 20 Secret Servicemen before getting within sight of the president.

How much faith President Truman placed in the Secret Service was pointed up by the fact that a few hours after the attack he delivered a speech and unveiled a statue before a large crowd in Arlington—all as though nothing had happened.

Collazo recovered from his wounds and was convicted and sentenced to death for the murder of Coffelt. President Truman commuted his death sentence to life imprisonment. On September 6, 1979 President Jimmy Carter, "for humane reasons," commuted his life sentence to time served and on September 10 he was released from prison.

## von Bülow, Claus (1926– ) cleared of attempted murder charges

For some 19 years until late 1999, and presumably much longer, Martha "Sunny" von Bülow had been in a coma in a vegetative state with no medical expectation of ever regaining consciousness. That situation led to two of the most sensational trials of the 1980s, during which her husband, Danish-born socialite Claus von Bülow, was accused of seeking to either kill her or cause her death by denying her required medication to alter her hypoglycemic (low blood sugar) condition.

The prosecution presented the evidence offered by Maria Schrallhammer, Sunny's longtime private maid, that she had seen a little black bag with a vial of "insulin" and a hypodermic syringe. The maid also testified that von Bülow seemed uncaring when his wife suffered attacks, once waiting until Sunny was "barely breathing" before summoning a doctor. That coma was due to an apparent drug overdose.

Then on December 21, 1980, Sunny was found unconscious on the floor of her bath-room in the couple's fashionable Newport, Rhode Island, mansion. She was rushed to a hospital, later transferred to a Boston hospital and then to Columbia Presbyterian Medical Center in New York City, where she thereafter remained in a coma, vegetative and in a fetal position.

The prosecution felt it had a powerful case against von Bülow. Von Bülow was well-to-do but not in the same league financially with his wife. Educated in England at Cambridge University, he had worked for a time for J. Paul Getty, advising the oil billionaire on legal and diplomatic matters. When the von Bülows were married they soon became much sought after by the social elite, and were distinguished for their elegant dinner parties. They were both patrons of the arts, and Claus became a profitable investor in *Deathtrap*, a highly acclaimed Broadway comedy thriller, ironically about a husband who plans to kill his wife for her fortune. That was what the prosecution alleged was von Bülow's intent in real life. It said von Bülow wanted to inherit his share of his wife's fortune, amounting to about $14 mil-

Socialite Claus von Bülow was portrayed in the press as weeping as he entered the mansion he once shared with his comatose wife, Sunny. Actually he apparently was reacting to a greeting given him by the family's two pet dogs (not shown).

lion, and then marry his mistress, Alexandra Isles, a beautiful socialite and former television soap-opera actress.

The prosecution won the first trial on two counts of assault with intent to murder and von Bülow was sentenced to 30 years imprisonment but was freed under $1 million bail. Von Bülow appealed the verdict, a process he assigned to Harvard professor Alan Dershowitz. In the Rhode Island Supreme Court Dershowitz argued that von Bülow's "little black bag" and its supposedly incriminating contents had been illegally seized and used against the defendant. Von Bülow's 1982 conviction was thrown out. However, Sunny's two children by a previous marriage,

Prince Alexander von Auersperg and his sister, Princess Annie Laurie von Auersperg Kneissl, again filed charges that their stepfather tried to kill their mother.

The second trial was held in 1985. A brilliant defense attorney, Thomas Puccio, advised by Dershowitz, brought in experts who testified that drugs and alcohol, rather than insulin, had caused Sunny's comas. It was claimed that Sunny had injected herself with mixtures of Demerol and amphetamines and that von Bülow's extramarital affairs had greatly depressed her. Von Bülow was quoted as saying Sunny had lost interest in sex after their daughter, Cosima, was born in 1967, and that was why he had sought the attentions of another woman. Medical experts for the prosecution testified that only insulin injections could have caused the comas. Thus the jurors were left to debate the testimony of experts on both sides. Even Isles, von Bülow's mistress, testified against him.

In his summation after nine weeks of sensational testimony, which was a delight to the tabloid press, Puccio implored the jury to consider only the real facts in the case. He admitted it was "not a pretty picture. Mr. von Bülow was cheating on his wife and he was stringing Alexandra Isles along. No matter what you think of Mr. von Bülow's conduct of his marriage, please don't hold that fact against him in this case." The jury on June 10, 1985 acquitted the 58-year-old defendant.

Sunny's two children by her previous marriage then filed a $56-million lawsuit against von Bülow. They sought to bar von Bülow from collecting $120,000 a year from a trust fund Sunny had established for him, claiming he had falsely influenced her while planning to do her in. Meanwhile Cosima was disinherited by her maternal grandmother because she had stood by her father and could have provided him with money. In 1986 von Bülow tried to settle the matter by divorcing Sunny and giving up all claims to any of her fortune, estimated in total to be somewhere between $25 and $40 million, if the children dropped the suit against him and gave their half-sister, Cosima, her fair share of the estate left by Sunny's mother. The offer was rejected, but the following year the parties came to an agreement. Von Bülow renounced all claims to Sunny's fortune and agreed not to write any books about the case. Cosima gained one-third share of her grandmother's estate.

## Waite, Dr. Arthur Warren (1887–1917)
murderer

In 1916 Dr. Arthur Warren Waite, a leading New York dental surgeon and a brilliant germ culture researcher at Cornell Medical School, committed two of this country's most-celebrated poison murders. He is remembered, however, not so much for his deeds as for his style, which, if nothing else, proved that a knowledge of medical science doesn't necessarily make a person an efficient killer.

Dr. Waite was an exceptionally handsome man in his late twenties. Tall, athletic and debonair, he had made a considerable impact on New York's Upper West Side society. An expert tennis player, he won several tournaments; Franklin P. Adams and other well-known tennis addicts considered him to be the best player on the local courts. Waite was also devoting a good deal of attention to making himself a millionaire. That he figured to do by wiping out his wife's parents, millionaire drug manufacturer John E. Peck and his wife of Grand Rapids, Mich. When the Pecks, in their seventies, passed away, Waite's wife stood to inherit approximately $1 million.

Mrs. Peck came to visit the Waites for Christmas in 1915. Waite took his mother-in-law out driving with the windshield open in a pouring rain so as to bring on pneumonia. He put ground glass in her marmalade. He sprayed her throat with bacteria and viruses known to cause influenza, anthrax, diphtheria and streptococcus. Some of Mrs. Peck's friends commented on how well she looked, and she did have a nice rosy-cheeked face. Finally, however, the old woman died on January 30, 1916, with doctors attributing her death to kidney disease. Waite wasn't at all sure whether she had died because of or in spite of what he had given her, but he was determined that no one else would know either. He had his mother-in-law cremated, which he said was her last request.

Mr. Peck, saddened by his wife's death, came to visit the following month. While consoling him, Waite filled his galoshes with water, dampened his bedsheets while he slept, opened a container of chlorine gas in his bedroom while he slept and even fed him a mixture of burned flypaper and veronal. When Peck developed a sniffle, Waite gave him a nasal spray laced with tuberculosis bacteria. Nothing happened.

Becoming desperate, he gave the old man 18 grains of arsenic, presumably enough to kill a team of horses. Peck took to bed but did not die. Finally, Waite took a pillow and smothered him to death. That, of course, worked, and Waite went out celebrating with his mistress. He was seen by a woman friend of the family, who thought it was callous of him to be carrying on in such fashion with his father-in-law's body not even cold. In an anonymous letter to the authorities, she accused the dentist of poisoning Mr. and Mrs. Peck. Large amounts of arsenic were found in Mr. Peck, and police investigators traced the poison to Waite, who finally confessed his entire plot.

Waite died in the electric chair at Sing Sing on May 24, 1917. He was annoyed when guards came to escort him to the death chamber because they interrupted his reading of a volume of Robert Browning's poetry. Waite marked with a pencil the last lines he had read:

*"Life's a little thing!*
*Such as it is, then,*
*pass life pleasantly. . . ."*

### Webster, John White (1791–1850) murderer

A crime that might have been spawned by the imagination of an Edgar Allen Poe and has been called "America's classic murder" occurred in Boston on the afternoon of November 23, 1849. Dr. George Parkman, for whom the Parkman Chair of Anatomy had been established at the Massachusetts Medical College, called on Dr. John White Webster at the school to demand repayment of a loan. Dr. Webster (MA, MD, Harvard) who led a rather notorious wild life, said he could not make payment, whereupon Parkman shouted, "I got you your professorship and I'll get you out of it." In a rage Webster grabbed a heavy piece of kindling wood and smashed Parkman in the head. Parkman fell to the floor. When Webster examined him, he found Parkman was dead. The confrontation took place in a laboratory in the basement of the medical college building.

Webster dragged the body into an adjoining room and placed it in a huge sink. He then climbed in the sink and calmly began dissecting the corpse. When he finished, he incinerated the pieces in his assay oven. Some larger pieces he put in a vault used for storing the bones of dissected bodies.

Quite naturally, the disappearance of Dr. Parkman caused a considerable stir and the college posted a reward of $3,000 for the apprehension of his apparent abductors. One of the few leads in the case came from Dr. Webster, who told of Dr. Parkman coming to visit him and accepting a $483 payment on his loan. The authorities theorized that the money provided a possible motive for robbery and continued their search. They did not suspect Dr. Webster. However, a college janitor named Ephraim Littlefield did. He had noticed that on the afternoon of the disappearance the wall behind Dr. Webster's assay oven had been very hot. When he later mentioned the fact to Dr. Webster, the latter seemed nervous and said he had been doing some experiments. The next day, in an uncharacteristic gesture of generosity, Webster gave the janitor a Thanksgiving turkey, but the gift only heightened Littlefield's suspicions. A week after the disappearance, he used a crowbar to take some bricks out of Webster's vault and found a fleshy pelvis and parts of a leg. When the

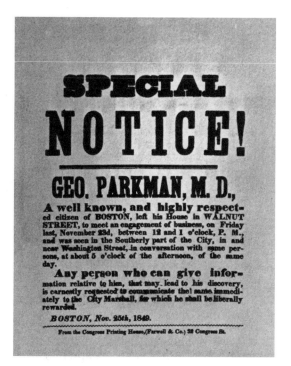

A city marshall poster asking for information concerning the whereabouts of Dr. George Parkman before his grisly fate was determined.

police were summoned, they made other grisly finds, including the most incriminating, that of Parkman's teeth in Webster's oven.

The trial of Dr. Webster in 1850 was a sensation. Among those testifying were Oliver Wendell Holmes, who by then occupied the Parkman Chair, Drs. W. T. G. Morton and C. T. Jackson, the discoverers of ether, and Jared Sparks, president of Harvard. Newspapers as far away as New Orleans sent special correspondents, and instant booklets relating the testimony appeared. Since an estimated 60,000 persons showed up to view the trial, the judge ordered that spectators could sit in the balcony for only 10 minutes at a time.

Webster pleaded not guilty and insisted the cut-up parts belonged to a routine cadaver, but the clinching evidence against him was the positive identification of Parkman's teeth by dentists. After an 11-day trial Webster was found guilty. Prior to his hanging on August 30, 1850, he made a full confession.

### Weger, Chester (1939– ) murderer

The savage robbery and murder of three well-to-do Chicago matrons in Starved Rock State Park, Ill. in March 1960 attracted nationwide attention. In investigative circles it is remembered as one of the most embarrassing cases in the annals of scientific detection. Police laboratory tests that should have pointed to the killer did not, and the murderer, 21-year-old Chester Weger, managed to do what many experts had claimed was the impossible, beat the lie detector, not once but twice.

The bodies of the women, Mrs. Lillian Oetting, Mrs. Mildred Lindquist and Mrs. Frances Murphy, wives of prominent businessmen, were found bound with twine and hidden in a cave. Nearby was a bloodied tree limb, some four inches thick, with which their killer had battered them to death. During the long investigation hundreds of persons were questioned. For a time the most promising suspect was Chester Weger, a dishwasher employed at the park's lodge. He was reported to have had a scratched face on the day the women had been murdered.

When police interrogated him, they discovered he had a bloodstained leather jacket, which they immediately sent to the police laboratory. While tests were being made on the jacket, Weger agreed to submit to a lie detector examination. The conclusion was that he was telling the truth when he denied any connection with the brutal crime. Then the laboratory analysis of the jacket found the stains were animal blood, as Weger had claimed. Authorities, reluctant to give up on the youth as a suspect, gave him another lie detector test. Once more, he passed with flying colors.

Weger was dropped as a suspect, as were all other local persons, and the police concluded that the women had been the victims of a transient thief. Two local deputies, Wayne Hess and William Dummett, were not convinced, however. They went back to the twine used on the women, which was originally thought to be of too common a type to be traced. The officers found the twine was a 20-strand variety and compared it with the twine used at the Starved Rock Lodge; it too had 20 strands. The lodge had bought the twine from a Kentucky manufacturer, who informed the officers that very few of his customers purchased that kind of twine. The lodge, in fact, was the only one in Illinois.

The deputies again centered their investigation at the lodge. Since the original investigators had casually dismissed the twine as a clue, the two deputies wondered if perhaps the rest of the inquiry had been just as poorly handled. Among other clues, the officers secured Weger's jacket again but this time sent it to the FBI Laboratory in Washington. Technicians there identified the stains as being human blood and most likely from the same group as that of one of the victims.

Weger was once more a suspect, but there was the troublesome matter of the lie detector tests. A top expert, John Reid of Chicago, was called in to perform a new test. This time the machine clearly indicated Weger was lying when he denied committing the murders. Meanwhile, Hess and Dummett had searched the records of previous crimes in the area and found a case in which a girl had been raped not long before the triple murders. The victim had been tied up with twine exactly like the cord used in the murders. Given a number of photographs of various men, she readily picked out one of Weger as her attacker.

Confronted with this new evidence plus the revised blood analysis and the incriminating polygraph findings Weger confessed. On March 4, 1961, Weger's 22nd birthday, he was convicted of the three murders and was later sentenced to life imprisonment.

Reid was asked how he could account for two previous failures by the lie detector before he, unlike the previous examiner, was able to get the incriminating results. "Simple enough," he said. "It's all a matter of technique—in knowing how to conduct such an experiment effectively." Weger himself had an entirely different rationale. "Before the tests," he said, "I just swallowed a lot of aspirin and washed it down with a bottle of Coke. That calms a guy down, you know. Why I didn't do that before this other guy tested me I'll never know."

## Welch, Bernard Charles, Jr. (1940– )
### master thief and murderer

Described by police as a one-man crime wave, Bernard C. Welch, Jr., was a remarkable master thief whose career ended in December 1980, when he was apprehended for the Washington, D.C., murder of Dr. Michael J. Halberstam, a noted cardiologist and author. Through the years since 1965, when he was 25, Welch was arrested a total of 25 times but avoided confinement on a number of occasions by jumping bail or escaping detention. His main activity was burglary, and often when free on bond, he went about committing additional thefts. He specialized in stealing furs, art objects, rare coins and silverware. Wherever he went, Welch lived in style, paying cash for luxurious houses, in one case almost $250,000 up front.

It can only be guessed how much money Welch made from 1965 to 1980 despite several years in prison during that time; it may have been anywhere from $10 to $20 million. Francis M. Mullen, assistant director of the Federal Bureau of Investigation, said of him after his capture in 1980:

> Welch has operated as a one-man crime cell; that's why he has been so hard to catch. . . . He has been so smart, melting much of the stuff to prevent it from being traced. He was a loner, so that it reduced the chance of someone close turning him in. He specialized in burglary, the type of crime hardest to solve. He was lucky, he never walked into one of our sting operations. And he was talented and well-trained.

From 1974—when he escaped from New York's Dannemora Prison by hiding on the grounds following a softball game and scaling a 25-foot fence after dark—to 1980, Welch was perhaps the FBI's most-sought criminal, with 15,000 circulars describing him and his method of operation distributed to police.

During those six years Welch continued his big-money capers and lived high on the hog, finally winding up in Great Falls, one of the more affluent suburbs of Falls Church, Va. He lived with his common law wife and three children in a $245,000 house, into which he poured an estimated $750,000 worth of improvements, including a huge indoor swimming pool and an environmental room that allowed for alteration of temperature and humidity to simulate both Arctic and Saharan conditions as well as everything in between. He surrounded his home with a security system, which, one newspaper noted, "the Central Intelligence Agency, 10 miles down the road, might envy." Spotted under the eaves of the home were a host of remote-controlled closed-circuit television cameras that swept the tree-decorated lawn in all directions. Weight sensors could detect footsteps on the grass and microphones in the outside walls would signal any attempt to enter.

Welch simply informed his neighbors, to whom he proudly exhibited his personal art collection, that he was a stockbroker (so successful that he had no need to take on any new clients). He also maintained a summer home in Duluth, Minn. and told a different story there about his profession. He was a fur dealer to the nation's wealthiest.

On the night of December 5, 1980, Welch burglarized four affluent homes in the Washington, D.C. area before invading the house of Dr. Halberstam. When Halberstam unexpectedly confronted him, Welch violated his cardinal rule against violent crime and shot the doctor. Halberstam managed to get in his car and was driving to a nearby hospital when he saw his assailant and swerved his car to hit him. Halberstam died on the operating table a short time later.

After Welch's apprehension, his Virginia home was located and searched. It took some 20,000 pages to catalog the stolen loot found in his basement, more than 50 boxes and crates. About 2,000 burglary victims from the D.C. area were invited to try to claim over $4 million in stolen goods recovered by the police.

In May 1981 Welch was sentenced to nine consecutive terms of life in prison. He would be eligible for parole in 143 years.

## Whitney, Richard F. (1888–1974) financial manipulator

Richard Whitney, former president of the New York Stock Exchange, earned himself two quite different nicknames during his checkered career. The epitome of conservative respectability, he was charged by the Bankers' Pool with handling the purchase of millions of dollars in stock on Black Thursday in 1929 in an effort to reinforce public confidence in the market; for his efforts he became known as the Strongman of Wall Street. In 1938 it was discovered that Whitney had misappropriated the securities of the clients of his bond company to cover his own losses. Renamed the Wolf of Wall Street, Whitney was sent to Sing Sing. He served three years and never returned to the Street, disappearing from sight for a time and then turning up as the manager of a fiber mill in Florida. He died in obscurity in 1974 at the age of 86.

## Wilder, Christopher (1945–1984) rich serial killer

Australian-born Christopher Wilder early on showed tendencies of sexual and violent behavior that were not at all mitigated by his family's wealth which may indeed have placed him in an independent position that allowed him to develop into a frightening serial killer in the United States.

With his Australian mother and American naval officer father, Wilder lived in a number of U.S. cities, as his father's duties required. The family eventually returned to Australia.

At the age of 17, Wilder was accused of taking part in a gang rape on a Sydney beach, for which he was sentenced to one year's probation with required counseling that involved group therapy and electroshock treatments. These seemed to have had no positive effects. Wilder married at 23, but the marriage soon collapsed, his wife charging sexual abuse. By this time Wilder was into nude photography, which he used in attempts to extort sex from his subjects. Charges stemming from this account were dropped when none of the women thus abused would testify in court.

Wilder felt it was prudent to leave Australia, and in time he relocated to Florida. He had the financial ability to prosper in construction and electrical contracting, and he lived a lavish lifestyle. He then got on to doing the important things in his life, setting up a photo studio in his apartment as a more convenient way to lure women to his photo shoots, which frequently degenerated into sexual attacks. In time Wilder had run-ins with the law as well as his parents, who stayed with him for a time. Not knowing what to do with him, they returned to Australia, after settling a considerable sum of money on their son. On his own, Wilder raped a teenager, lacing her pizza with knockout drops. For this he was sentenced to five years on probation, with the requirement that he undergo psychological counseling and treatment from a sex therapist.

With a net worth estimated at $2 million, Wilder became involved in car racing, competing in the Miami Grand Prix and Sebring races. He also started getting blackouts and would vanish for two or three days, later telling friends he had no idea what he had been doing.

Presumably a number of sexual crimes forced Wilder back to Australia in 1982. He promptly got in trouble in an incident involving two 15-year-old girls and was brought up on charges. His parents put up $350,000 bail, and Wilder took off for the United States once more, where he pretended nothing was wrong.

But now his killer instincts took over. In February 1984 Wilder took part in the Miami Grand Prix and was outraged when he finished 17th. Rosario Gonzalez had a worse fate. She worked at the event distributing samples and was approached by Wilder. By that evening she had disappeared, her body never found. Then Wilder started dating lovely Beth Kenyon, who had been a finalist in the Miss Florida contest. Beth told her parents Wilder, who was known to have a wild reputation, was a perfect gentleman with her. But in March she informed her parents she was breaking off with Wilder. That same month Beth disappeared, and a coast-to-coast manhunt produced no results. Not long after that, Wilder kidnapped Terry Ferguson from a Florida shopping mall. Her body, stabbed numerous times with an instrument resembling a filet knife, was found in a snake-infested creek. Witnesses identified Wilder as the abductor of 21-year-old Terry.

Then Wilder abducted a college co-ed from a shopping mall in Tallahassee, took her to a Bainbridge, Georgia, motel where he sealed her eyes shut with super glue. He continually raped her and subjected her to electrical shocks. Wilder was hitting her with a hair dryer in the bathroom, but the co-ed managed to scream even though her hands and mouth were taped. Panicked, Wilder fled the room, muttering "excuse me" to other motel guests in what they described as a light Australian accent.

The murder spree continued as Wilder kidnapped 21-year-old Susanne Logan in Oklahoma City. Her body was found in the town reservoir in Milford, Kansas. She had been stabbed and raped and had bite marks on her breasts.

A 16-year-old girl kidnapped and stabbed repeatedly near Gary, Indiana, survived Wilder's predation by pretending to be dead. There were other cases, such as a co-ed in Beaumont, Texas, who was stabbed to death and dumped in a canal.

By now the FBI had tied Wilder to many of these slayings and had him at the head of its Ten Most Wanted List. New victims turned up in Colorado and Las Vegas, where Michelle Korfman, a casino executive's daughter, was approached by a man about competing in *Seventeen* magazine's cover contest. She finally turned up in the Los Angeles County morgue.

Investigators expected Wilder to head for the Australian outback, but he did not. He turned east and in Victor, New York, abducted Beth Dodge, a 33-year-old Sunday school teacher. Her body turned up in Rochester.

Now the manhunt for Wilder concentrated on watching for him to try to slip into Canada. Instead he turned up in Colebrook, New Hampshire. He undoubtedly was looking for another female victim, but he was now being hunted as well. Two state troopers passed a service station where Wilder had stopped for gas. Wilder, who had been sporting a bushy beard, had shaved it off, leaving his tanned face pale where the beard had been. The troopers closed in on Wilder and called out to him to stop. Instead, Wilder ran swiftly to his car and seized a .357 Magnum revolver. One of the officers hurled his body at Wilder and two shots followed as they wrestled for the gun. A bullet passed through Wilder and pierced the officer's chest, coming within an inch of killing him. The second shot killed Wilder.

## Williams, Edward Bennett (1920–1988)
defense lawyer

F. Lee Bailey, one of the most famous lawyers in the country once said, "If I ever got in trouble, he's the one I'd want representing me." Bailey was referring to a burly Washington lawyer with the face of a middle-aged cherub, Edward Bennett Williams. Even men who despised Williams, and that included many prosecutors, rival lawyers and even former attorneys general such as Robert F. Kennedy, have admitted he may be the best lawyer in the tradition of Clarence Darrow in recent decades.

Williams was not a "scorecard"-type lawyer, with X number of defendants of whom only a minute percentage go to prison. His success record was once estimated to be about 70 percent, an amazing figure for a lawyer whose clients have included Sen. Joseph McCarthy, Jimmy Hoffa, Adam Clayton Powell, Bobby Baker, Frank Costello, Aldo Icardi, *Confidential* magazine, and assorted admitted gamblers and accused Russian spies. Costello probably best summed up the attitude of Williams' clients toward the lawyer when he said: "What I like about Ed Williams is that he'll go up against any of 'em—J. Edgar Hoover, Bobby Kennedy, even President Johnson. He doesn't pull back. He's not afraid."

Opponents naturally saw him in a different light; he was called everything from "ruthless" and a "hypocritical trickster" to "the biggest egotist in the law since William Jennings Bryan" and "a man who would have defended Eichmann if there was enough money in it."

Some years ago Williams had a favorite riposte for his critics: "I'm called the Burglar's Lobby in Washington because I defend people like Frank Costello. The Sixth Amendment of the Constitution guarantees the right of legal counsel to *everyone*. It does not say to everyone *except* people like Frank Costello."

Once when Williams was defending Jimmy Hoffa during Robert Kennedy's tenure as attorney general, Kennedy said he'd "jump off the Capitol dome" if he lost the case. When Hoffa was acquitted, Williams offered to provide Kennedy with a parachute, thus ending a long friendship between the two.

Some of his opponents charged Williams with perverting the Constitution; he saw what he did as defending it. He probably had done more to restrain overzealous congressional committees than any other lawyer. One example was the case of Aldo Icardi, accused of committing one of the most vicious murders in World War II. On a 1944 Office of Strategic Services (OSS) mission, Icardi and OSS Maj. William V. Holohan parachuted behind enemy lines in northern Italy. Holohan, who had taken along a large number of gold coins for use on the mission, disappeared. Six years later, his corpse was fished out of an Italian lake.

Williams told an interviewer:

*Shortly thereafter, a Pentagon press release charged Icardi with Holohan's murder. Five years after that, a Congressional committee called Icardi to testify, and he denied committing the crime. He was promptly indicted on eight counts of perjury, which, if conviction resulted, could potentially have forced him to spend forty years in prison. So I went to court and proved, to the satisfaction of the judge, that two members of the*

*Congressional committee had called Icardi not for any valid legislative purpose, but because they were deliberately looking for a perjury indictment against him. In effect, here were two Congressmen assuming the triple roles of prosecutor, judge, and jury—yet every schoolboy knows that our freedom as a nation is protected by a delicate separation of powers between the legislative, judicial and executive branches of government. In acquitting Icardi, the court clearly defined the line between Congress as a lawmaker and Congress as a grand jury.*

In his continuing battle against government prosecutors Williams once made shambles of a Treasury agent who had meticulously prepared an income tax case against Adam Clayton Powell. The agent withered under Williams' fire, admitted errors in the government's calculations and acted more like a defendant than like the prosecution's leading witness. In the end, the judge threw out two counts against Powell and the third and final count ended in a hung jury—a remarkable conclusion considering Powell had paid only about $900 in taxes on a gross income of $70,000.

Williams was long a thorn in the side of police investigators engaged in illegal eavesdropping, winning a Supreme Court landmark decision against the practice in the early 1960s. The case involved three gamblers who ran a $40,000-a-day sports betting parlor in a row house on 21st Street, N.W., Washington, D.C. The police moved into the house next door and drove a spike into the common wall between the two buildings. The spike, part of an electronic listening device, was inserted into a duct, converting the entire heating system into a sort of microphone, which allowed police to record scores of conversations involving gambling transac-

tions. Based on that evidence, the three gamblers were convicted and given long prison terms. Williams took over the case and argued before the Supreme Court that the police eavesdropping was "more subtle and more scientifically advanced than wiretapping" and was the grossest sort of violation of the rights of the defendants to be secure from unreasonable searches and seizures. It was no different from the police smashing into a house in the middle of the night without a search warrant. The Supreme Court threw out the convictions.

Williams never saw the contradiction in defending—at approximately the same time—Sen. McCarthy and several of the Hollywood writers accused of communism during McCarthy's heyday in the 1950s. Certainly, McCarthy wanted Williams because he wanted the best possible defense in his fight to escape Senate censure, but the case against him was ironclad and Williams lost.

Williams undoubtedly took the McCarthy case because he had an abiding hatred for the encroaching power of the congressional investigative committees and what he has called "the legislative lynch." He later told a reporter: "When Estes Kefauver first ran roughshod over the rights of the hoodlums in 1950, the country was amused. Then the leftist intellectuals, who didn't spring to the defense of the hoodlums, found that their turn was next. While this was going on labor thought it was funny but they soon discovered that they were being clobbered." In 1961 Williams was further amused to hear spokesmen for the business community deploring the abuse of business by congressional committees. He commented: "Nobody cares until it hurts him. That's why I'm interested in stopping such chain reactions—back where they hit the weak and the degraded—before they get started."

In later years Williams often visited law schools to try to convince young lawyers and students to take up criminal law, to concern themselves with human rights instead of property rights. "You look at the curricula of the top law schools," he once noted, "and you find that they are stepped in such courses as Real Property, Taxes, Estates, and Torts, all of which are required subjects. You generally find that Criminal Law and Constitutional Law are elective courses, which very few students take."

He died in 1988.

## Winchell, Walter (1897–1972) gossip columnist

A controversial gossip columnist and influential radio commentator, Walter Winchell played an important role in a number of crime stories. He was on speaking terms with several leading gangsters and, at the same time, a close friend of FBI Director J. Edgar Hoover. Even his detractors had to admit Winchell scored numerous crime scoops. He was the first to link Albert Anastasia to the murder of a private citizen, Arnold Schuster, after Schuster had spotted bank robber Willie Sutton and tipped off the police. He came up with a number of scoops in the Murder, Inc. case, and because he was trusted by the underworld, he was chosen to arrange the details of the surrender of Louis "Lepke" Buchalter to Hoover in 1939. Lepke was driven to Fifth Avenue and 28th Street, where he got out of a car and walked over to one in which Winchell was sitting behind the wheel. Winchell stared at Lepke intently for a moment, turned to his stocky companion in the back and said, "Mr. Hoover, this is Lepke."

Hoover nodded, opened the rear door and motioned for Lepke to get in. Lepke later said he had wanted Winchell to act as intermediary to guarantee he would not be shot down while surrendering.

In his later years Winchell ranted in his column over the level of street crime in New York City and told friends he would not venture out after dark without carrying a gun. Winchell, the King of Broadway, felt hostage on the streets that had been his beat for so many years.

## Wood, Isaac (?–1858) mass poisoner

The largest all-in-the-family poisoning plot in American history was perpetrated by Isaac Wood at Dansville, N.Y. in the 1850s.

The first to die was Isaac's brother David, who owned a huge estate in the area. David Wood was struck down unexpectedly by a strange malady in May 1855. Before the year was out, his wife Rhoda and his three children had died of the same strange sickness. Isaac Wood had slowly poisoned all five so that he could gain control of the estate; he accomplished that goal by acting as administrator. Isaac then took his wife and child to live in New Jersey, where he murdered them as well. Now a rich man, he moved on to a new life in Illinois.

Before leaving for Illinois allegedly to bear his grief alone, Wood had leased his brother's home to a tenant named Welch. Shortly after the murderer departed, Welch found three packs of arsenic in the barn. The arsenic had been wrapped in legal papers that assigned Isaac Wood full authority over the estate after the death of his brother and his family. That link and the fact that all of Isaac Wood's relatives had died under similar circumstances were sufficient evidence to doom him. Wood was brought back to New York, tried and hanged on July 9, 1858 at Geneseo.

## Wylie, Janice (1942–1963) murder victim

The gruesome murders of Janice Wylie, the 21-year-old daughter of author Max Wylie and niece of writer Philip Wylie, and her roommate, 23-year-old Emily Hoffert, on August 28, 1963 shocked New York City, and caused a legal controversy for years thereafter.

The bodies of the two women were found bound together in their Manhattan apartment. Both had numerous stab wounds and Janice Wylie had been eviscerated. The newspapers depicted the murders as a ritualistic sort of sexual crime. Eight months after the murders the police charged a semiliterate 19-year-old black named George Whitmore, Jr., with the crime. He had been arrested in the Brownsville section of Brooklyn on a charge of attempted rape, which, said the police, he admitted along with the murder of a woman in Brooklyn and the Wylie-Hoffert homicides. A few weeks later, Whitmore repudiated the three confessions, insisting he had been beaten and otherwise coerced into making them. In all, he was brought to trial four times on various charges.

In his own version of how he was made to confess, Whitmore, whose IQ was at various times estimated to be between 60 and 90, wrote: "I am the kind of boy that like to have fun. . . . I don't like to be hurt nor me hurt anyone witch I'd never did. But when I first came to New York I was aquised of doing things I know nothing about."

Whitmore said that when he denied the attempted rape in the Brooklyn precinct house, he was "hit many times." He went on:

*Then I was so squared that I was shakeing all over. And before I know it, I was saying yes. I was so squared if they would have told me name was tom, dick or harry I would have said yes . . .*

*Then I was asked about the killing in the city on 88 St. But I was squared in to saying yes. They would say George Didn't you do so and so here and so and so there. I wouldn't say anything.*

*They would would say shour you did. Then they would write it down. And go over it with me. Then call in some more men, and ask me the same quition again. I would just repeat what I just learned. . . .*

*I got enemies witch I never had. But I hope some time he or she will soon find out that I was the wrong boy. God will see to it. . . . God knows that I didn't do these things, and if I keep praying he will help me. . . .*

*Just bying here it can chang your life it can make you want to make something of your life when you get out it can also make you relazice many other things to. You learn to to fell sorry for other people as well as your self. So take it from me and witch what you are doing. I am a boy who never been in trouble before and went to jail for non-thing. . . .*

In 1965 Whitmore was cleared in the Wylie-Hoffert homicides following a confession made by Richard Robles, a 22-year-old drug addict who was subsequently convicted and sentenced to life imprisonment. Whitmore's experiences, especially the discredited confessions, were cited by the Supreme Court in the landmark Miranda decision, which led to curbs on police powers to question suspects, and by the New York legislature in a 1965 statute that largely abolished capital punishment.

Whitmore was also cleared of the third murder accusation after newspapers turned up evidence that the white detectives had been biased against him and the Manhattan and Brooklyn district attorneys' offices found proof that he was innocent. However, he was still convicted three times of the attempted rape charge. In 1973, after Whitmore had served a total of four years in prison, it was found that the prosecution had withheld from the defense evidence which would have cleared him in the rape case as well.

Whitmore filed suit against the city in 1973 charging false arrest and wrongful imprisonment, but in 1979 a judge ruled that the statute of limitations in the Wylie-Hoffert case had run out by 1973 and that in the rape case there was no proof of "actual malice" on the part of the Brooklyn district attorney's office. The judge said he felt an "emotional strain" in ruling against Whitmore and suggested that the wrong-man victim seek redress from the legislature, which had the power to grant him a financial settlement.

## Zangara, Joseph (1900–1933) assassin

Virtually every presidential assassination or attempt has produced speculation of a deeper and more insidious plot. Joseph Zangara's attempt to kill Franklin D. Roosevelt on February 15, 1933 in Miami is unique in that the conspiracy theory posits the president-elect was not even the target and that Zangara, in fact, killed the man he was supposed to, Mayor Anton J. Cermak of Chicago. According to the majority of experts, the idea that Zangara was a Capone hit man is nonsense. Nevertheless the theory has long been held by many crime historians and Chicago journalists. A leading expert, Judge John H. Lyle, probably as knowledgeable as any non-Mafia man on the subject of Chicago crime, emphasizes "Zangara was a Mafia killer, sent from Sicily to do a job and sworn to silence."

Before the shooting, Cermak had been trying to get rid of the Capone mob so that gangsters under his control could take over crime in Chicago, and a current journalistic theory held that he had fled to Miami because he feared the Capones were going to assassinate him. The fact that Zangara had won several pistol-shooting awards when he was in the Italian army and that he fatally wounded Cermak without even hitting Roosevelt provided additional weight to the theory that the intended victim of the assassination was Cermak. However, when Zangara opened fire on the car carrying Roosevelt and Cermak, he hit four bystanders, casting doubt on his ability as a marksman.

If Zangara kept his silence in a monumental criminal plot, he had not maintained his peace on political matters since his arrival in the country in 1923. Employed off and on as a mill hand in New Jersey, he had railed about "capitalist presidents and kings." According to his later confession, he would have been just as likely to have tried to kill Calvin Coolidge or Herbert Hoover as Roosevelt; he happened to select FDR only because he was in Miami when Roosevelt was there. "I see Mr. Hoover first I kill him first," he said at his trial. "Make no difference. Presidents just the same bunch—all same." Zangara clung to that line to the day of his execution. Of Cermak, he said, "I wasn't shooting at him, but I'm not sorry I hit

Joseph Zangara was almost stripped of all his clothing by those who seized him after his unsuccessful attempt to assassinate President-elect Franklin D. Roosevelt.

him." Zangara claimed he might have tried to kill King Victor Emmanuel III had he remained in the Italian army.

In the death chamber Zangara said: "There is no God. It's all below. . . . See, I no scared of electric chair." Sitting down in the chair, he glared at the witnesses with contempt. "Lousy capitalists." His last words were: "Goodby. *Addio* to all the world. Go ahead. Push the button."

See also: ANTON J. CERMAK.

# PHOTO CREDITS

# BIBLIOGRAPHY

Following is a bibliography of selected resources for further reading on crimes and the rich and famous as well as the history of crimes in America in general.

Adams, Ramon F. *Burs Under the Saddle*. Norman: University of Oklahoma Press, 1964.

Adler, Polly. *A House Is Not a Home*. New York: Popular Library, 1954.

Allen, Frederick Lewis. *Only Yesterday, An Informal History of the Nineteen Twenties*. New York: Harper & Bros., 1931.

———. *Since Yesterday*. New York: Harper & Bros., 1940.

Asbury, Herbert. *The Gangs of New York*. New York: Alfred A. Knopf, Inc., 1927.

———. *The Barbary Coast, An Informal History of the San Francisco Underworld*. Garden City, N.Y.: Garden City Publishing Company, Inc., 1933.

———. *Sucker's Progress*. New York: Dodd, Mead and Company, Inc., 1938.

———. *Gem of the Prairie*. New York: Alfred A. Knopf, Inc., 1940.

———. *The French Quarter, An Informal History of the New Orleans Underworld*. New York: Alfred A. Knopf, Inc., 1940.

———. *The Great Illusion: An Informal History of Prohibition*. New York: Doubleday & Co., 1950.

Berger, Meyer. *The Eighty Million*. New York: Simon & Schuster, 1942.

Block, Eugene B. *The Wizard of Berkeley*. New York: Coward-McCann, 1958.

———. *Great Train Robberies of the West*. New York: Coward-McCann, 1959.

———. *Great Stagecoach Robbers in the West*. New York: Doubleday & Co., Inc. 1962.

———. *Fifteen Clues*. Garden City, N.Y.: Doubleday & Co., Inc., 1968.

Bolitho, William. *Murder for Profit*. New York: Harper & Bros., 1926.

Bonanno, Joseph. *A Man of Honor, The Autobiography of Joseph Bonanno*. New York: Simon & Schuster, 1983.

Boswell, Charles, and Lewis Thompson. *The Girls in Nightmare House*. New York: Gold Medal, 1955.

———. *Practitioners of Murder*. New York: Collier, 1962.

Brynes, Thomas. *Professional Criminals in America*. New York: Chelsea House, 1969.

Burns, Walter Noble. *The One-Way Ride*. Garden City, N.Y.: Doubleday, Doran & Company, 1931.

Caesar, Gene. *Incredible Detective: The Biography of William J. Burns*. Englewood Clifs, N.J.: Prentice-Hall, 1968.

Chandler, David. *Brothers in Blood: The Rise of the Criminal Brotherhoods*. New York: Dutton, 1975.

Churchill, Allen. *A Pictorial History of American*

*Crime.* New York: Holt, Rinehart & Winston, 1964.

Coates, Robert M. *The Outlaw Years: The History of the Land Pirates of the Natchez Trace.* New York: The Literary Guild of America, 1930.

Collins, Ted, ed. *New York Murders.* New York: Sloan & Pearce, 1944.

Crouse, Russell. *Murder Won't Out.* New York: Pennant Books, 1953.

Croy, Homer. *He Hanged Them High.* Duell, Sloan & Pearce, 1952.

DeFord, Miriam Allen. *Murders Sane & Mad.* New York: Abelard-Schuman, Ltd., 1965.

Demaris, Ovid. *Captive City.* New York: Lyle Stuart, Inc., 1969.

DeVol, George. *Forty Years a Gambler on the Mississippi.* New York: H. Holt & Company, 1926.

Drago, Harry Sinclair. *Outlaws on Horseback.* New York: Dodd, Mead & Company, 1964.

Eisenberg, Dennis; Uri Dan; and Eli Landau. *Meyer Lansky, Mogul of the Mob.* New York & London: Paddington Press Ltd., 1979.

Elman, Robert. *Fired in Anger.* Garden City, N.Y.: Doubleday & Company, Inc., 1968.

Emrich, Duncan. *It's an Old Wild West Custom.* New York: The Vanguard Press, Inc., 1949.

Emery, Edward Van. *Sins of New York.* New York: Frederick A. Stokes, 1930.

———. *Sins of America as "Exposed" by the Police Gazette.* New York, Fredrick A. Stokes Co., 1931.

Frank, Judge Jerome, and Barbara Frank. *Not Guilty.* Garden City, N.Y., Doubleday & Company, Inc., 1957.

Godwin, John. *Alcatraz 1868–1963.* New York: Doubleday & Co., 1963.

———. *Murder USA.* New York: Ballantine Books 1978.

Gosch, Martin A., and Richard Hammer. *The Last Testament of Lucky Luciano.* Boston: Little, Brown, 1975.

Hammer, Richard. *Playboy's Illustrated History of Organized Crime.* Chicago: Playboy Press, 1975.

Hecht, Ben. *A Child of the Century.* New York: Simon & Schuster, 1954.

———. *Charlie, The Improbable Life and Times of Charles MacArthur.* New York: Harper & Bros., 1957.

Horan, James D. *Desperate Men.* New York: G. P. Putnam Sons, 1949.

———. *Pictorial History of the Wild West.* New York: Crown Publishers, Inc. 1954.

———. *The Desperate Years.* New York: Crown Publishers, Inc., 1962.

———. *The Pinkertons, The Detective Dynasty That Made History.* New York: Crown Publishers, Inc. 1967.

Hynd, Alan. *Murder, Mayhem and Mystery.* New York: A. S. Barnes & Co., 1958.

Jackson, Joseph Henry. *San Francisco Murders.* New York: Duell, Sloan and Pearce, 1947.

Johnston, James A. *Alcatraz Island Prison.* New York: Charles Scribner's Sons, 1949.

Karpis, Alvin, with Bill Trent. *The Alvin Karpis Story.* New York: Coward McCann & Geoghegan, Inc., 1971.

Katcher, Leo. *The Big Bankroll, The Life and Times of Arnold Rothstein.* New York: Harper & Bros., 1959.

Katz, Leonard. *Uncle Frank: The Biography of Frank Costello.* New York: Drake, 1973.

Kefauver, Estes. *Crime in America.* New York: Doubleday & Co., 1951.

Kilgallen, Dorothy. *Murder One.* New York: Random House, 1967.

Klein, Alexander, ed. *Grand Deception.* New York: J. B. Lippincott & Company, 1955.

———. *The Double Dealers.* Philadelphia and New York: J. B. Lippincott & Company, 1958.

Kobler, John. *Capone.* New York: G. P. Putnam's Sons, 1971.

Kohn, George C. *Encyclopedia of American Scandal.* New York: Facts On File, 1989.

Lawes, Warden Lewis Edward. *Twenty Thousand Years in Sing Sing.* New York: R. Long & R. R. Smith, Inc., 1932.

Lewis, Alfred Henry. *The Apaches of New York.* New York: G. W. Dillingham Company, 1912.

———. *Nation-Famous New York Murders.* G. W. Dillingham Company, 1914.

McLoughlin, Denis. *Wild and Wooly.* Garden City, N.Y.: Doubleday & Company, Inc., 1975.

Maas, Peter. *The Valachi Papers.* New York: G. P. Putnam's Sons, 1968.

Messick, Hank. *Lansky.* New York: G. P. Putnam's Sons, 1971.

Morrel, Ed. *The Twenty-fifth Man.* Montclair, N.J.: New Era Publishing Co., 1924.

Murray, George. *The Legacy of Al Capone.* New York: G. P. Putnam's Sons, 1975.

Ness, Eliot, with Oscar Fraley. *The Untouchables.* New York: Julian Messner, 1957.

Newton, Michael. *Hunting Humans.* New York: Avon Books, 1992.

Pearson, Edmund L. *Studies in Murder.* New York: MacMillan Company, 1926.

———. *More Studies in Murder.* New York: Harrison Smith & Robert Haas, Pub., 1936.

Peterson, Virgil. *Barbarians in Our Midst.* Little, Brown & Co., 1936.

———. *The Mob.* Ottawa, Illinois: Green Hill Publishers, Inc., 1983.

Radin, Edward D. *12 Against the Law.* New York: Bantam Books, 1952.

———. *12 Against Crime.* New York: Collier Books, 1961.

Reid, Ed. *Mafia.* New York: Random House, 1952.

———. *The Grim Reapers.* Chicago: Henry Regnery Co., 1969.

Reid, Ed, and Ovid Demaris. *The Green Felt Jungle.* New York: Trident Press, 1963.

Rodell, Marie F. *New York Murders.* New York: Duell, Sloan and Pearce, 1944.

Salerno, Ralph, and John Tompkins. *The Crime Confederation.* New York: Doubleday & Co., 1969.

Sann, Paul. *The Lawless Decade.* New York: Crown Publishers, Inc., 1957.

Scott, Gini Graham. *Homicide: 100 Years of Murder in America.* Lincolnwood, Illinois: Roxbury Park, 1998.

Smith, Alton. *Syndicate City.* Chicago: Henry Regnery Co., 1954.

Sondern, Frederic, Jr. *Brotherhood of Evil: The Mafia.* New York: Farrar, Straus & Cudahy, 1959.

Stone, Irving. *Clarence Darrow for the Defense.* New York: Doubleday & Co., 1941.

Tallant, Robert. *Ready to Hang.* New York: Harper & Bros., 1952.

Teresa, Vincent, with Thomas C. Renner. *My Life in the Mafia.* Garden City, New York, Doubleday & Company, 1973.

Teresa, Vincent. *Teresa's Mafia.* Garden City, New York: Doubleday & Company, Inc., 1975.

Toland, John. *The Dillinger Days.* New York: Random House, 1963.

Touhy, Roger, with Ray Brennan. *The Stolen Years.* Cleveland: Pennington Press, Inc., 1959.

Turkus, Burton B., and Sid Feder. *Murder, Inc.: The Story of the Syndicate.* Farrar, Straus & Young Co., 1951.

Turner, Wallace. *Gambler's Money.* Boston: Houghton Mifflin Co., 1965.

Wendt, Lloyd, and Herman Kogen. *Lords of the Levee.* New York: Bobbs-Merrill, 1943.

Wilson, Frank J., and Beth Day. *Special Agent.* New York: Holt, Rinehart & Winston, 1965.

Whitehead, Don. *The F.B.I. Story.* New York: Random House, 1956.

Wolf, Marvin J., and Katherine Mader. *L.A. Crime.* New York: Facts On File Publications, 1986.

Wooldridge, Clifton R. *Hands Up! In the World of Crime or Twelve Years a Detective.* Chicago: Police Publishing Co., 1901.

# Index

Boldface page numbers indicate main headings.

## A

Abramson, Leslie 164
Acosta, Carlos 133, 134
Adams, Albert J. **1–2**
Adams, Franklin P. 231
Adams, Katherine 165
Adams, Samuel 60
Adams, Samuel Hopkins 221
Ade, George 97
Adler, Polly **2–3**, 23
Adonis, Joe 64
Ah Hoon **3–4**
Alaska gold rush 179
Alcatraz prison **4–6**, 53
Alger, Horatio 127
Allen, Charles 150
Allen, Frederick Lewis 151
Allen, John **6–7**
Allen, Lizzie **7–8**, 10
Allison, Dorothy **8–9**
Altgeld, John Peter **9–10**, 73
Alton, Josie. *See* Arlington, Josie
*American Assassins: The Darker Side
    of Politics* (Clarke) 177
American Continental Corp. 134,
    135
American Telephone and Telegraph
    12
*American Tragedy, An* (Dreiser) 105
America's Sweetheart 215, 216, *217*
Amsler, Joseph C. 136
anarchists
    Altgeld, John P. and 9–10
    Berkman, Alexander 28–30
    Czolgosz, Leon 71–72
    Goldman, Emma 28, 30
Anastasia, Albert 64, 79, 240
Andersonville Prison 149
Andrews, Shang **10–11**
Animal Rescue League 40
Annenberg, Moses L. "Moe" **11–12**

Annenberg, Walter 12
Anselmi, Albert 53
Antar, Eddie 68
Antar, Sam 68
Anton, Rev. Henry 61
Apache Kid 87
Arbuckle, Roscoe "Fatty" **12–13**, 215
Arlington, Josie **13–15**
Arlington, The **13–15**
Armstrong, Hannah 150
Armstrong, Jack 150
Armstrong, William "Duff" 149–150
Arnold, Keith 65
arson 91–93, 101, 139, 149, 174
Ashley, Bob 16
Ashley, John **15–17**
Ashley, William 25
asphyxiation 75–77, 88, 231. *See also*
    strangulation victims
assassination attempt victims
    Dewey, Thomas E. 79–80
    Ford, Gerald R. 19, 104, 122
    Gaynor, William J. 17–18
    Jackson, Andrew 17, 122, 131
    Reagan, Ronald viii, 19, 33, 34, 59,
        122–123
    Roosevelt, Franklin D. 18, 56,
        243–244
    Roosevelt, Theodore 18, 66, 72,
        194–195
    Seward, William 61, 148
    Truman, Harry S 18, 122,
        225–226
    Wallace, George 19, 42–43
*Assassination in America* (McKinley)
    17
assassination victims **17–19**. *See also*
    murder victims
    Garfield, James A. 17, 110–112
    Kennedy, John F. 18, 174–177, 183,
        198, 205–206

Kennedy, Robert F. 19, 183,
    205–206, 238
King, Martin Luther, Jr. 18, 183,
    188–190
Lincoln, Abraham 17, 146–151
Long, Huey P. 18, 155–156
Malcolm X 18, 159–160
McKinley, William 17, 71–72, 166,
    195
assassins
    Booth, John Wilkes 17
    Butler, Norman "3X" 18
    Czolgosz, Leon 17, 71–72
    Guiteau, Charles Julius 17,
        110–112
    Hayer, Talmadge 18, 160
    Johnson, Thomas "15X" 18
    Oswald, Lee Harvey 18, 174–177,
        198–199
    Ray, James Earl 18, 188–190
    Sirhan, Sirhan Bishara 19, 205–206
assassins, would-be 183
    Berkman, Alexander 28–29
    Bremer, Arthur Herman 19, 42–43
    Collazo, Oscar 18, 225, 226
    Fromme, Lynette Alice "Squeaky"
        19
    Gallagher, James J. 18
    Genovese, Vito 64
    Hinckley, John W., Jr. 19
    Lawrence, Richard 17
    Moore, Sara Jane 19
    Schrank, John Nepomuk 18,
        194–195
    Secret Service, U.S. and 103–104
    Torresola, Griselio 18, 225
    Zangara, Joseph 18, 243–244
assault 63, 133, 210–211, 228. *See
    also* wounded victims
Astor Place Opera House 19–20
Astor Place Riots 19–20

Atkins, Susan  160
Atlanta Boys Convoy  4
Atlanta Penitentiary  6, 64
Attell, Abe  33
Atzerodt, George  17, *147*
Auburn Prison  72, 106
Auersperg, Prince Alexander von  228, 229
Aurelio, Thomas  62

**B**

Bailey, F. Lee  **21–22**, 119, 203, 238
Baker, Bobby  238
Baker, Lt.  148
Baker, Rosetta  **22**
Bakker, Rev. Jim  **22–23**
"Ballad of Bonnie and Clyde, The" (Parker)  38–39
Bankers' Pool  236
bank robbers
  Ashley gang  15–17
  Dillinger gang  80–88, 118
  Hearst, Patty  118, 119
  Sutton, Willie  240
Barker, Doc  6
Barnaby, Josephine  109
Barnet, Henry C.  165, 166
Barnum, P. T.  46, 49
Barrett, Fanny  169
Barrow, Blanche  37, 38
Barrow, Buck  37, 38
Barrow, Clyde  **36–39**
Barrows, Sydney Biddle  viii, **23–25**
Barrymore, John  97
Baum, W. Carter  85
Beatles  59, 120
Becker, Charles  65
Beckwith, Charles T.  57
Beckwith, Sir Jennings  25
Beckwourth, Jim  **25**
Bedford Hills Correctional Facility  115
Belasco, David  167
Bell Telephone Laboratories  176
Benchley, Robert  3
Benhayon, Henry  41
Benitez, Oscar  190
Benjamin N. Cardozo School of Law  88
Benson, Margaret  **25–26**
Benson, Scott  **26**
Benson, Steven  **26**

Bergdoll, Grover Cleveland  **26–27**
Berger, Meyer "Mike"  **27–28**
Berkman, Alexander  **28–30**
Beverly Hills Gun Club  191
Bickford, Maria  **30–32**
Bigley, Elizabeth. *See* Chadwick, Cassie
Billy the Kid  195
Biograph Theater  86
Birdzell, Donald  225
Bixby, A. L.  41
Black Hand threats  54–55
Black Muslims  18, 159–160
Black Panther Party  42, 202
Black Sox Scandal  **32–33**
*Blood and Money* (Thompson)  vii, 122
Bloods  202
Bloomingdale, Alfred  viii, **33–36**
Bloomingdale, Betsy  34, 35
Board of Trade (Great Britain)  163
Boesky, Ivan  36, 49, 146, 162, 164
bombings
  Benson family  26
  Berkman, Alexander  28
  Chapman family  138
  Fugmann, Michael  139
  Haymarket  9–10
  *Los Angeles Times*  73
  Malcolm X  159
  Sage, Russell  201
  World Trade Center  134
Booth, John Wilkes  17, 147–148
bordellos. *See* brothel(s)
Borden, Abby  39
Borden, Andrew  39–40
Borden, Emma  39, 40
Borden, Lizzie  **39–41**, 109
Boring, Floyd  225
Boston Female Anti-Slavery Society  **105**
Boston Strangler  21, 206
Botkins, David  89
Bowers, Cecelia  41–42
Bowers, J. Milton  **41–42**
Bowery Gang  90
Boyd, Ben  150

Boyd, Percy  38
Brady, James S.  19, 122
Brandegee, Frank  174
Bremer, Arthur Herman  19, **42–43**
Breslyn, Joseph  110
Brewster, William  24
Brisbane, Arthur  152
"broadcloth mob"  **105**
Bromo Seltzer  166
Brooks, Preston S.  210–211
Brooks, William  207
brothel(s)  86. *See also* madams; prostitutes
  Arlington  13–15
  Capone, Al and  51–52
  Everleigh Club  96–98, 167
  Friendly Friends and  167
  House of Mirrors  8
  John Allen's Dance House  6–7
  Mother Herrick's Prairie Queen  7
  Puente, Dorothea and  184
  Senate  7
  Sutherland, Annie and  43, 44
  Thaw, Harry Kendall in  220
Brown, Billie  105–106
Brown, Jerry  184
Brown, Joe E.  222
Browning, Robert  232
Bryan, William Jennings  75, 238
Buchalter, Louis "Lepke"  240
Buchanan, James  207
Buchanan, Dr. Robert  **43–44**
Bulette, Julia  **45–46**
Buntline, Ned  19
Burdell, Dr. Harvey  **46–49**
Burdell, Theo  46
Bureau of Alcohol, Tobacco and Firearms  104
Bureau of Investigation  195. *See also* FBI (Federal Bureau of Investigation)
burglars. *See also* thieves
  Douglass, Joey  196
  Gallory, Richard G.  116
  Graham, Barbara and  107–108

Harsh, George S.  116
Hearst, Patty  118
Hohimer, Francis "Frank"  183
Lawson, Victor Fremont  194
Malchow, Frederick  183
Mosher, William  196
Ray, James Earl  189
Rugendorf, Leo  183
Tilbury, John  194
Burke, Honest John  47
Burns, William "Sleepy Bill"  33
Burr, Aaron  **49**
Butcher, Jacob "Jake" Franklin  **49**
Butler, Andrew P.  210
Butler, Norman "3X"  18, 160
Byers, Russell G.  189

**C**

California Correctional Institution  164
California State Prison  164
Campos, Pedro Albizu  225
capital punishment  88–90
  Harsh, George S. on  116
  Manson, Charles and  161
  New York State on  241
  Supreme Court, U.S. on  21, 89, 161, 206
Capone, Alphonse "Scarface Al"  **51–53**
  at Alcatraz  6
  Berger, Meyer on  27–28
  Cermak, Anton J. and  18, 56
  furnace plot and  167
  Leibowitz, Samuel S. and  143
  Lindbergh kidnapping and  152
  *Scarface* and  120
  tax evasion by  11
  Zangara, Joseph and  243
Capote, Truman  60
Carillo, Jose Antonio  25
Carnegie, Andrew  28, 57–58
Carnegie Steel Co.  28
Carroll, Earl  **53–54**
Carroll, Tommy  85, 86
Carson, Ann  54

Carson, John 54
Carter, Jimmy 18, 123, 226
Caruso, Enrico 54–55
Case of the Ragged
    Stranger 119–120
Casey, James P. 56–57
Cassidy, Butch 87
Cassini, Dennis 42
Castiglia, Franceso. See
    Costello, Frank
Catcher in the Rye
    (Salinger) 59
Cathcart, Countess Vera
    53
Caverly, John R. 74, 144
Cayuga Democratic Club
    66, 67
CBS 146, 185
Cejnar, Jack 85
Cemetery John 152–153
Cermak, Anton J. "Ten Per-
    cent Tony" 18, 56–57,
    243–244
Chadwick, Cassie 57–58
Champion, Nathan D.
    "Nate" 58
Chaplin, Charles 18
Chaplin, Charlie 12, 216
Chapman, Mark David 59
Chapman, Mrs. James A.
    138
Cheeseborough, Blanche
    165, 166
Chicago Edison 127
Chicago White Sox 32–33
China Lobby 175
Chivington, John M. 25
Choate, Rufus B. 31, 32
Chrysler Corporation 77
CIA (Central Intelligence
    Agency) 175, 176
Cicotte, Eddie 33
Cincinnati Redlegs 32–33
Circus Saints and Sinners
    124, 125
Citizens National Bank of
    Oberlin 57
Civilian Conservation
    Corps (CCC) 85
Civil War 45, 93, 113,
    165, 210
Clark, Dora 65
Clark, Lewis 60, 61
Clark, Russell 82, 83, 84,
    85
Clarke, Donald Henderson
    100
Clarke, James W. 177

Clinton, Henry L. 48
Clutter family 60
Coast Guard, U.S. 5, 15
Cobb, Irvin S. 220, 221
Cochran, Johnnie, Jr. 205
Cody, John Patrick 102
Coffelt, Leslie 18, 225,
    226
Cohen, Mickey 209
Cole, Teddy 5
Coll, Vincent "Mad Dog"
    142–143
Collazo, Oscar 18, 225,
    226
Collins, George 43
Colner, Andrew 108
Colosimo, Big Jim 52, 120
Colson, Charles W. 42
Colt, Caroline. See Hen-
    shaw, Caroline
Colt, John C. 60–62
Colt, Samuel 60–62
Columbia Presbyterian
    Medical Center 227
Comiskey, Charles A.
    32–33
Committee of Ballistic
    Acoustics 176
Commonwealth Edison
    127
Complete Scarsdale Med-
    ical Diet, The (Tarnower)
    114
Condon, Dr. John F. "Jaf-
    sie" 152, 153, 154
Congress, U.S. 27, 99,
    124, 210–211, 238–240
Connally, John B. 175
Conroy, Robert 152
conspiracy. See also
    swindlers
    Atzerodt, George 147,
        149
    Bakker, Jim 23
    Booth, John Wilkes
        147–149
    Cook, Dr. Frederick A.
        62
    Herold, David 147, 148,
        149
    Jackson, Andrew and 17
    Johnson, Andrew and
        148
    Kennedy, John F. and
        175–177
    King, Martin Luther, Jr.,
        and 188, 189
    Mudd, Dr. Samuel 149

O'Laughlin, Michael 149
Paine, Lewis 147, 149
Roosevelt, Franklin D.
    and 243–244
Spangler, Edward 149
Surratt, John H. 149
Surratt, Mary 147, 149
Constitution, U.S. 238
Continental Press Service
    12
Cook, Dr. Frederick A. 62
Cook County Jail 120
Coolidge, Calvin 243
Cooper, Gary 222
Cooper, James Fenimore
    60
Coppolino, Carl 21
Cora, Charles 55
Corbett, Boston 149
Corbett, James J. "Gentle-
    man Jim" 97
Cornell Medical School
    231
Cornish, Harry 165–166
Costello, Frank 2, 62–65,
    155, 238
counterfeiters 54, 150–151
Court of Appeals, U.S. 90
Cowley, Sam 86
Coy, Bernie 5
Coy, Wayne 82
Crabb, Christopher Colum-
    bus 8
Craft, Gerald 65
Crane, Cheryl 209–210
Crane, Stephen 65–66, 209
Cranston, Alan 134–135
Crater, Joseph Force 66–68
Crazy Eddie 68
Crick, Francis 88
Crips 191, 202
Crosby, Bing 222
Crouse, Russel 96, 137
Crowe, Pat 136
Crow Indians 25
Crown Point Jail 84, 85
Cudahy, Edward A., Jr.
    136
Cumings, Alexander 207
Cumpanis, Ana 86
Cunanan, Andrew viii,
    69–71
Cunningham, Emma 47,
    48
Cuomo, Mario 115
Curry, Dr. Walter 192
Cushing, William 208
Czolgosz, Leon 17, 71–72

D
Dakota, the 59
Dana, Charles 60
Dannemora Prison 235
Darby, Helen 95
d'Arlington, Lobrano. See
    Arlington, Josie
Darrow, Clarence Seward
    10, 73–75, 144, 238
Daugherty, Harry M. 99,
    173, 174
Davis, Angela 42
Davis, Jefferson 149
Davis, John W. 162
Davis, T. Cullen vii, viii
Davis, Warren Ransom
    131
Day Huey Long Was Shot,
    The (Zinman) 156
Death Row Records 202
Debs, Eugene V. 73
DeCicco, Pat 224
Declaration of Indepen-
    dence 208
DeConcini, Dennis 135
DeFreeze, Donald 118, 119
Dekker, Albert 75–77
Dekker, Jan 76
Delahanty, Thomas K. 19,
    122
Delmas, Delphin 221, 222
DeLorean, John 77–79
DeMille, Cecil B. 212
Democratic Party
    during Astor Place riots
        19
    Costello, Frank and 62
    Dekker, Albert in 76
    Dillinger, John and 83
    during draft riots 90, 93
    Kennedy, Robert F. in
        206
    Leibowitz, Samuel S. in
        143
    Savings and Loan scandal
        and 135
    Wallace, George in
        42–43
Department of Justice, U.S.
    4
Depression
    Costello, Frank during
        64
    Crater, Joseph Force dur-
        ing 66–67
    Dillinger, John during
        80–88

Hoffman, Harold Giles
 during 124
Insull, Samuel during
 127–128
kidnappings during
 135–136, 151
Whitney, Richard F. dur-
 ing 236
Dershowitz, Alan 228
DeSalvo, Albert 21
DeSapio, Carmine 62
Deubler, Mary. *See* Arling-
 ton, Josie
Deubler, Peter 14
Deutsch, Hermann B. 156
Devery, Big Bill 195
Devil's Island, America's.
 *See* Alcatraz prison
Dewey, Thomas E. 2,
 **79–80**, 162
Dickinson, Charles **131**
Dietrich, Walter 82
*Dillinger: Dead or Alive?*
 (Nash and Offen) 87
Dillinger, John Herbert 37,
 **80–88**
Dimmig, John 41
Diners Club 34
Dirty Dozen 81
District of Columbia Jail
 112
Dix, John A. 193
DNA evidence **88–90**,
 203–205
Dodge, Beth 237
Dodson, Richard Lee 9
Doheny, Edward L. 99,
 100, 218
Donahue, Phil 25
Douglas, Paul 182
Douglass, Joey 135, 196
Downs, Joseph 225
draft dodgers 26–27, 90,
 93, 197
draft riots **90–93**
Dreiser, Theodore 105
Drexel Burnham Lambert,
 Inc. 36, 146, 164
drug traffickers 64, 77–79
duels 49, 113, 131
Dummett, William 234
Dunaev, Nick 180
Dyer, Oliver 6

**E**

Earley, Mark 89
Eaton, Charles A. 221
Eckel, John J. 47, 48

Edison, Thomas A. 127,
 179
Eisemann-Schier, Ruth 136
Elwell, Joseph Bowne
 **95–96**
embezzlers 123–125,
 127–128, 153
Emig, William 117
Empire Club 20
*Encyclopedia of American*
 *Crime* vii
Everett, Samuel 61–62
Everleigh, Ada **96–98**
Everleigh, Minna **96–98**,
 167
Everleigh Club 96–98, 167
extortion 54–55, 197–198

**F**

Fair Play for Cuba Com-
 mittee 175
Fall, Albert Bacon **99–100**,
 174
Fallon, William J. **100–102**
Farley, James J. 56
*Fashionable Adventures of*
 *Joshua Craig, The*
 (Phillips) 184
Fashion Institute of Tech-
 nology 24
Fawcett, Farrah 122
Faye, Tammy 23
FBI (Federal Bureau of
 Investigation)
 Bremer, Arthur Herman
  and 42, 78
 Dillinger, John and 85,
  86, 87
 DNA testing and 88
 Green, Eddie and 87
 Harris, Emily and 115,
  119
 Harris, William and 115,
  119
 Hearst, Patty and 115,
  119
 on Hinckley, John 123
 Kennedy, John F. and
  176
 kidnapping gangs and
  136
 King, Martin Luther, Jr.,
  and 188, 189
 Moore, Sara Jane and
  104
 Nelson, Baby Face and
  87
 on Padgett, Randall 89

Sage, Anna and 87
St. Louis police and 110
Van Meter, Homer and
 87
 on Weger, Chester 234
 Welch, Bernard Charles,
  Jr. and 235
 on Wilder, Christopher
  237
 Winchell, Walter and
  240
 Yoshimura, Wendy and
  115
FBO Pictures 179
Federal Avaiation Adminis-
 tration (FAA) 59
Federal Deposit Insurance
 Corporation (FDIC) 49
Federal Home Loan Bank
 134
Felsch, Oscar 33
Ferber, Nat 102
Ferguson, Miriam "Ma"
 38
Ferguson, Paul 170
Ferguson, Terry 236
Ferguson, Tom 170
Ferrare, Cristina 77
Fielden, Samuel 10
Finch, Barbara **102–103**
Finch, Dr. Raymond
 Bernard 102–103
fingerprinting 169–170,
 188
Firearms National Labora-
 tory Center 176
Fisher, Fred 174
Five Points Gang 51, 90,
 93
Flagg, James Montgomery
 221
Flegenheimer, Arthur
 "Dutch Schultz." *See*
 Schultz, Dutch
Floradora Girls 181
Floyd, Pretty Boy 37
Flynt, Larry 35
Folger, Abigail 160
Folsom Prison 118
Fonda, Henry 211
Forbes, Charles R. 174
Ford, Bob 87
Ford, Gerald R. 19, 104,
 122
Ford's Theatre 147
Foreman, Percy 21, 189
Forest Products Laboratory
 138

Forestry Service, U.S. 138,
 153
forgers
 Chadwick, Cassie 57
 Irving, Clifford 128–129
 Jones, Charles F. 192
 Manson, Charles 160
 Patrick, Albert T. 192
 Ray, James Earl 189
Forrest, Edwin 19
Fort, Dr. Joel 119
Foster, Jodie 123
Four Deuces 167, 168
"Four hundred" assassina-
 tion list **103–104**
Fowler, Gene 100
Frank, Jerome 89
Franklin, Rufus "Whitey"
 6
Franks, Bobby 143–144
Franks, Jacob 143, 144
fraudsters. *See also* embez-
 zlers; swindlers
 Bakker, Jim 23
 Cook, Dr. Frederick A.
  62
 Cunningham, Emma 48
 DeLorean, John 78–79
 Ohio Gang and 173
 Van Doren, Charles
  219–220
Frechette, Evelyn "Billie"
 83, 84, 85
Freud, Sigmund 216
Frick, Henry Clay 28–30
Friendly Friends 167
Fromme, Lynette Alice
 "Squeaky" 19
Frykowski, Voyteck 160
Fugmann, Michael 139
Fuhrman, Mark 205
Fulmer, Cathy 206

**G**

Gaiteau, Charles Julius 17
Gallagher, James J. 18
Gallory, Richard G. 116
Galluccio, Frank 51, 52
Gambino, Carlo 64
gamblers, gambling
 Adams, Albert J. 1–2
 Annenberg, Moses L.
  11–12
 Black Sox scandal 32–33
 Burke, Honest John 47
 Capone, Al 52–53
 Cohen, Mickey 209
 Costello, Frank 64, 155

Elwell, Joseph Bowne 96
Hargraves, Dick 113
Lansky, Meyer 64
Luciano, Lucky 64, 224
Ragen, James M. 12
Rich Men's Coachmen's Club 194
Rosenthal, Herman 65
Williams, Edward Bennett and 238, 239
Young, Francis Thomas 181
Gandil, Charles Arnold "Chick" 33
Garbo, Greta 170
Gardner, Erle Stanley 203
Garfield, James A. 17, 110–112
Garrett, Pat 195
Garrison, James 175
Garrison, William Lloyd 105
Gary, Joseph E. 10
Gates, Bet-A-Million 97
Gauvreau, Emile 12
Gaynor, William J. 17–18
General Motors Company 77
Genovese, Vito 64–65
Gentlemen's Riot 105
Getty, J. Paul 227
Gibson, Charles Dana 220
Giesler, Jerry 180
Gillette, Chester 105–106
Gillis, Lester 85
Gilmore, Geary 65
Girl in the Hansom Cab, The 180, 181
Giunta, Hop Toad 53
Glenn, John 134, 135
Goethe, Robert 182
Goldman, Emma 28, 30
Goldman, Ron vii, 204–205
Goldsborough, Fitzhugh 183–184
Goldstein, Buggsy 143
Gonzales, Dr. Thomas A. 106–107
Gonzalez, Rosario 236
Goodrich, William 13
Gordon, Roger 42
Gordon, Waxey 79
Gosch, Martin A. 80
Gourlay, Jennie 148
Gow, Betty 151
Grady, Mike 209

grafters, political 99–100, 173–174, 218
Graham, Barbara 107–109
Graham, Henry 107
Grant, Frederick 65–66
Grant, Julia Dent 147
Grant, Ulysses S. 17, 109, 147
Graves, Dr. Thomas T. 109–110
Gray, Dorothea. See Puente, Dorothea
Gray, L. Patrick 42
Great Chicago Fire of 1871 7, 92
Great Mouthpiece, The (Fowler) 100
Greeley, Horace 92
Green, Eddie 85, 86–87
Greenlease, Robert C. "Bobby," Jr. 110, 136
Grier, Rosey 206
Groden, Robert J. 177
Guimares, Alberto Santos 137
Guiteau, Charles Julius 110–112
gun control 191
Gunness, Belle 184

**H**

Hahn, Jessica 22–23
Halberstam, Dr. Michael J. 234, 235
Hall, A. Oakley 48
Hall, Camilla 118
Hall, Carl Austin 110
Hamer, Frank 39
Hamilton, Alexander 49
Hamilton, John 82, 85, 86
Hamilton, Polly 86
Hamilton, Ray 37, 38, 39
Hamm, William A., Jr. 136
Hammer, Richard 80
Hammond, Percy 97
Hand, Learned 162
Hankins, Effie 8, 96
Hansen, Edmund 108
Harding, Warren G. 99, 100, 173, 174, 218
Hargraves, Dick 113
Hargrave Secret Service 84
Harris, Carlyle 43, 44
Harris, Emily 115–116, 119, 136
Harris, Ira 147

Harris, Jean S. viii, 113–115
Harris, William 115–116, 119, 136
Harrison, Alice 169
Harsh, George S. 116
Hart, Alex 117, 118
Hart, Brooke 116–118
Hart, Monmouth 61
Harvard School for Boys 143
Hauptmann, Bruno Richard 124, 136, 138, 139, 153–154
Hawkins, Eva 10
Hayer, Talmadge 18, 160
Hayes, Robert 88
Hayes, Rutherford B. 174
Hayes, Susan 203
Haymarket affair 6, 9
Haynes, Richard "Racehorse" vii, 21, 22
Hays, Will 218
Hayward, Susan 109
Haywood, Big Bill 73
Head, Sam 31, 32
Heady, Bonnie Brown 110, 136
Hearst, Patricia "Patty" 9, 21, 22, 115–116, 118–119, 136
Hearst, William Randolph 9, 11, 101, 102, 118, 152, 180
Heatter, Gabriel 154
Hecht, Ben 27, 119–120
Henninger, Ronald 9
Henry, prince of Prussia 97
Henshaw, Caroline 61, 62
Hermitage USA 23
Herold, David 17, 148
Hershfield, Harry 124
Hess, Wayne 234
Hickman, Edward 136
Hickock, Richard E. 60
Higgins, F. W. 193
Hill, Ann 121
Hill, Joan Robinson 121–122
Hill, Dr. John vii, 121–122
Hinckley, John W., Jr. 19, 59, 122–123
Hip Sings 3–4
Hoffa, Jimmy 238
Hoffert, Emily 241
Hoffman, Harold Giles 123–125, 153

Hogan, Frank 220
Hohimer, Francis "Frank" 183
Hohimer, Harold 183
Holley, Lillian 84
Holloway, Jerome 65
Holmes, John Maurice 116–117
Holmes, Oliver Wendell 233
Holohan, William V. 238
Home Invaders, The (Hohimer) 183
Homicide: 100 Years of Murder in America (Scott) 70
Hoover, Herbert 52, 243
Hoover, J. Edgar 86, 188, 238, 240
House of Mirrors 8
House of Representatives, U.S. 43
House on 16th Street 173
House Select Committee on Assassinations (HSCA) 175–176, 189
Huey Long Murder Case, The (Deutsch) 156
Hughes, Archbishop 91
Hughes, Howard 120, 128–129
Humphrey, Hubert 42
Hunt, E. Howard 42
Hunter, Alex 187–188
Huntley, Ada 10
Hyde, Dr. B. C. 212–213

**I**

IBM 176
Icardi, Aldo 238–239
Immigration Bureau 86
In Cold Blood (Capote) 60
Indiana, Gary 69
Indiana State Reformatory 82
Innocence Project 88–89
Insull, Samuel 127–128
International News Service 85
Iowa State Penitentiary 183
Irving, Clifford 128–129
Irving, Washington 19, 60
Irwin, John W. 136
Islam, Nation of 159–160
Isles, Alexandra 228, 229
Ito, Lance 205

## J

Jackson, Andrew 17, 122, **131**
Jackson, Dr. C. T. 233
Jackson, Rachel 131
Jackson, Shoeless Joe 33
Jacobson, Susan 8
James, Jesse 15, 80, 87
James Street gang 51
Jefferson, Thomas 49, 208
Jeffreys, Dr. Alec 88
Jenkins, Peter 163
Jerome, William Travers 221, 222
Jewish Defense League 133, 134
John Allen's Dance House 6–7
Johnson, Andrew 17, 148, 149
Johnson, Lyndon B. 238
Johnson, Rafer 206
Johnson, Thomas "15X" 18, 160
Johnson County War 58
Johnston, James A. 4
Joliet Prison 145, 157
Jones, Charles F. 192–193
Jones, William Daniel 37–38
Judson, Edward Z. C. 19, 20
junk bonds 164–165
Justice Department, U.S. 189

## K

Kach Party 133
Kahane, Rabbi Meir **133–134**
Kansas State Penitentiary 60
Karpis, Alvin "Creepy" 6, 136
Kauffmann, John 189
Keating, Charles H., Jr. 49, **134–135**, 162–163
Keating Five 134–135
Keaton, Buster 222
Keenan, Anna Marie. *See* King, Dot
Keenan, Barry W. 136
Kefauver, Estes 239
Kefauver Committee 63, 64
Kelly, George "Machine Gun" 6, 136

Kelly, Kathryn 136
Kendall, Carol Lynn Benson 26
Kenealy, Big Jim 150–151
Kennedy, John F. 18, 174–177, 183, 198, 205–206
Kennedy, Joseph "Joe" 179
Kennedy, Mike 62
Kennedy, Robert F. "Bobby" 19, 183, 205–206, 238
Kenyon, Beth 236
Ketchum, Ami 174
kidnappers **135–137**
Amsler, Joseph C. 136
Bonnie and Clyde 38
Crowe, Pat 136
Douglass, Joey 135, 196
Eisemann-Schier, Ruth 136
Gilmore, Geary 65
Hall, Carl Austin 110, 136
Harris, Emily 115–116, 136
Harris, William 115–116, 136
Hauptmann, Bruno Richard 136, 138
Heady, Bonnie Brown 110, 136
Hickman, Edward 136
Holloway, Jerome 65
Irwin, John W. 136
Karpis, Alvin "Creepy" 136
Keenan, Barry W. 136
Kelly, George "Machine Gun" 136
Kelly, Kathryn 136
Krist, Gary Steven 136
LaMarca, Angelo John 136
Leopold, Nathan "Babe" 143–144
Loeb, Richard "Dickie" 143–144
Mosher, William 135, 196
Robinson, Michael 137
Schoenfeld, James 137
Schoenfeld, Richard Allen 137
Seadlund, John Henry 136
Seale, Arthur 137
Seale, Irene 137

Smith, Byron 65
Taylor, Thomas 137
Westervelt, William 135, 196
Wilder, Christopher 236–238
Williams, William A. H. 137
Woods, Frederick Newhall, IV 137
kidnap victims **135–137**
Arnold, Keith 65
Brooke, Hart 116–118
Craft, Gerald 65
Cudahy, Edward A., Jr. 136
Dodge, Beth 237
Ferguson, Terry 236
Franks, Bobby 143–144
Greenlease, Robert C. "Bobby," Jr. 110, 136
Hamm, William A., Jr. 136
Hearst, Patty 115–116, 118–119, 136
Lindbergh, Charles A., Jr. 135, 136, 151–154
Logan, Susanne 237
Mackle, Barbara Jane 136
Mattson, Charles 136
Murphy, Reginald 137
Parker, Marion 136
Reso, Sidney J. 137
Reville, E. B. 136
Reville, Jean 136
Ross, Charles Brewster "Charley" 135, 195–197
Ross, Charles S. 136
Shorter, Baxter 108
Sinatra, Frank, Jr. 136
Urschel, Charles F. 136
Wais, Marshall J. 137
Weinberger, Peter 136
Wendel, Paul H. 154
killers. *See* murderers
*Killing of a President, The* (Groden) 177
Kinder, Mary 83, 84
King, Coretta 188
King, Dot **137–138**
King, James 55
King, Martin Luther, Jr. 18, 183, 188–190
Kinsey, Alfred 3
Kline, Deborah Sue "Debbie" 8–9

Kline, Jane 9
Kneissl, Princess Annie Laurie von Auersperg 228, 229
Knickerbocker Athletic Club 165, 166
Knight, Suge 202
Koehler, Arthur **138–139**, 153
Korfman, Michelle 237
Kozol, Dr. Harry 119
Krenwinkel, Patricia 160, 161
Krist, Gary Steven 136

## L

La Bianca, Leno 120, 160
La Bianca, Rosemary 120, 160
La Guardia, Fiorello 80, 155
Lait, Jack 97
Landis, Kenesaw Mountain 33
Langer, William 6
Lansky, Meyer 63–64, 79, 80
Lardner, Ring 97
Larsen, Marie 95
Lasky, Jesse 223
*Last Testament of Lucky Luciano, The* (Gosch and Hammer) 80
Lawrence, Jimmy 87
Lawrence, Joel 31
Lawrence, Richard 17, 131
Lawson, Louise 138
Lawson, Victor Fremont 193–194
Leach, Matt 83, 85
Leavenworth prison 62
LeBlanc, Antoine **141**
Lee, Lulu 11
Lee, Robert E. 148
*Legal Medicine and Toxicology* (Gonzales) 107
Leibowitz, Samuel S. **141–143**
Leishman, John 28, 29
Lennon, John 59
Leopold, Nathan "Babe" 74, **143–145**
Lepke, Louis 79, 143
Leslie, George Leonidas 209
Leslie, Harry 83, 86
Levine, Dennis 36, **146**

Lewisburg Penitentiary 146, 162
Lexow Committee 66
*Life Plus 99 Years* (Leopold) 145
Lima Jail 83
Lincoln, Abraham 17, 90, **146–151**
Lincoln, Levi 208
Lincoln, Mary Todd 147
Lincoln Savings and Loan 134, 135
Lindbergh, Anne Morrow 151
Lindbergh, Charles A., Jr. 124, 135, 136, 138, 139, **151–154**
Lindbergh, Charles A. "Lucky Lindy" 151, 153–154
Lindquist, Mildred 233–234
Lindsay, Vachel 10
Littlefield, Ephraim 232
Little Green House on H Street 173
Liu Fook 22
Livingston, Mickey 182
Lobrano, Philip 14
Loeb, Richard "Dickie" 74, **143–145**
Logan, Susanne 237
Lonergan, Patricia Burton 154–155
Lonergan, Wayne **154–155**
*Lonesome Road, A* (Harsh) 116
Long, Huey P. 18, **155–156**
looting 90, 91, 92, 93. *See also* embezzlers; robbery victims; swindlers; thieves
Loy, Myrna 170
Luciano, Lucky 2, 51, 63–64, 79–80, 152, 224
Luetgert, Adolph Louis **156–157**
Luetgert, Louisa 156–157
Lupino, Ida 224
Lutz, Philip, Jr. 84
Lyle, John H. 56, 243
Lynn, Ray 17

### M

MacArthur, Charles 27, 119–120
MacCarty, Rev. Thaddeus 208
Mackle, Barbara Jane 136
Macomber's 43, 44
Macready, William Charles 19, 20
madams
  Barrows, Sydney Biddle viii, 23–25
  Bulette, Julia 45–46
  Everleigh sisters 96–98, 167
  Fallon, William J. and 100–102
  Paulus, Lilla 122
  Puente, Dorothea 184
  Sage, Anna 86
  Shaw, Vic 167
  Stanford, Sally 107
Madeira School for Girls 114
Madison Square Garden 220, 221
Madsen, David 70
Magnuson, John 138
Maitland, Cleo 97
Makiki Mental Health Clinic 59
Makley, Fat Charley 82, 83, 84, 85, 87
Malchow, Frederick 183
Malcolm X 18, **159–160**
Mammoth Oil Co. 99
*Man Inside, The* (Molineux) 167
Manson, Charles 19, 35, 120, **160–161**
Manton, Martin T. **161–162**
Marshall, Mr. 137–138
Martin, Elbert E. 194
Marx Brothers 222
Maryland State Penitentiary 43
Massaro, Jim 146
Masterson, Bat 195
Mather, Cotton **162**
Matson, Charles 136
Maxwell, Robert **162–163**
Maxwell Communications Corp. 162
"Mayflower Madam" viii, **23–25**
Maynard, Lottie 10
McAdoo, Anthony LaQuin 191
McCarthy, Eugene 206
McCarthy, Joseph 76, 238, 239
McCarthy, Mary 11
McCarthy, Timothy J. 19, 122
McErlane, Frank 11
McGovern, George 43
McGraw, James 194
McGraw-Hill Book Co. 128–129
McGuirk's Suicide Hall 6
McKinley, James 17
McKinley, William 17, 57, 71–72, 166, 195, 220
McLean, Edward B. 100
McLean, Evalyn Walsh 154
McMullin, Fred 33
McNamara, James 73
McNamara, John J. 73
McNutt, Paul V. 82, 83, 84, 86
Means, Gaston B. 154
Medina, Ernest L. 21
Mencken, H. L. 30
Menendez, Erik **163–164**
Menendez, Lyle **163–164**
Methvin, Henry 39
Metropolitan Opera 54
Metzker, James "Pres" 149–150
Mexican-American Youth Association 184
Meyner, Robert B. 124, 125
Miami Grand Prix 236, 237
Middleton, Clarence 17
Middle West Utilities 127
Miglin, Lee 70
Milburn, John G. 166
Milken, Michael R. 49, 162–163, **164–165**
Millain, John 46
Miller, Robert Lee, Jr. 88
Millie, Bad 11
Mineo, Sal viii
Minter, Mary Miles 216, *217*, 218
Miranda decision 241
Mirror Group 162–163
Missouri State Prison 189
Mitchell, J. Kearsley 138
Mitchell, Luther 174
Mobley, Hanford 17
Molineux, Edward Leslie 165
Molineux, Roland B. **165–167**
Monkey Trial 75
Montoya, Alvaro "Burt" 185
Moody, Priscilla 31
Moore, James Hobart 167
Moore, Nathaniel Ford **167–168**
Moore, Sara Jane 19, 104
Moran, Bugs 53
Morgan, B. F. 82
Morgan, Vicki viii, 33–36
Morton, Dr. W. T. G. 233
Mosher, William 135, 196
Moss, Lizzie 11
Mother Herrick's Prairie Queen 7
Mudd, Dr. Samuel 148, 149
Muhammad, Elijah 159
Mullen, Francis M. 235
Mulrooney, Edward P. 68
Muni, Paul 120
Murder, Inc. 28, 64, 80, 143, 240
murderers. *See also* assassins; poisoners
  Allen, John 6
  Altgeld, John P. and 9–10
  Anastasia, Albert 240
  Anselmi, Albert 53
  Arbuckle, Roscoe "Fatty" 12–13
  Ashley, Bob 16
  Becker, Charles 65
  Beckwourth, Jim 25
  Benson, Steven 25–26
  Bonnie and Clyde 36, 37, 38, 39
  Borden, Lizzie 39–41
  Bowers, J. Milton 41–42
  Brooks, William 207
  Buchanan, James 207
  Buchanan, Robert 43–44
  Capone, Al 52–53
  Casey, James P. 56–57
  Chapman, Mark David 59
  Clark, Russell 83
  Coll, Vincent "Mad Dog" 142–143
  Collazo, Oscar 225, 226
  Colt, John C. 60–62
  Coppolino, Carl 21
  Cora, Charles 55
  Costello, Frank 62–65
  Cunanan, Andrew 69–71
  Dillinger, John 80–88
  Fallon, William J. and 100–102

Ferguson, Paul 170–171
Ferguson, Tom 170–171
Fugmann, Michael 139
Gallory, Richard G. 116
Garrett, Pat 195
Genovese, Vito 64–65
Gillette, Chester **105–106**
Gilmore, Geary 65
Goethe, Robert 182
Goldsborough, Fitzhugh 184
Graham, Barbara 107–109
Graves, Dr. Thomas T. **109–110**
Hall, Carl Austin 110, 136
Hargraves, Dick 113
Harris, Jean S. 113–115
Harsh, George S. 116
Hauptmann, Bruno Richard 136, 138, 139
Heady, Bonnie Brown 110, 136
Hickman, Edward 136
Hickock, Richard E. 60
Holloway, Jerome 65
Jones, Charles F. 192–193
Ketchum, Ami 174
LaMarca, Angelo John 136
LeBlanc, Antoine 141
Leibowitz, Samuel S. and 141–143
Leopold, Nathan "Babe" 74, 143–145
Livingston, Mickey 182
Loeb, Richard "Dickie" 74, 143–145
Lonergan, Wayne 154–155
Luetgert, Adolph Louis 156–157
Magnuson, John 138
Makley, Far Charley 83
Manson, Charles 160–161
McErlane, Frank 11
Medina, Ernest L. 21
Menendez, Erik 163–164
Menendez, Lyle 163–164
Mitchell, Luther 174
Nash, Durland 182
Nelson, Baby Face 85

Nosair, Sayyid A. 133–134
Olive, Isom Prentice "Print" 174
Patrick, Albert T. 192–193
Paulus, Lilla 122
Pierpont, Harry 83
Prendergast, Robert 73
Puente, Dorothea 184–186
Reck, Emil 182
Robles, Richard 241
Ross, Ezra 207
Ruby, Jack 18, 175, 198–199
Ryan, Joseph Hugh 103
Scalise, John 53
Seadlund, John Henry 136
Seale, Arthur 137
Sheppard, Sam 21
Smith, Byron 65
Smith, Perry E. 60
Smith, Richard 54
Spooner, Bathsheba 206–209
Thaw, Harry Kendall 220–222
Thomas, Frederick Jerome 190–191
Vandiver, Bobby 121–122
Waite, Dr. Arthur Warren 231–232
Wanderer, Carl 119–120
Webster, John White 232–233
Weger, Chester 233–234
Weiss, Dr. Carl 18, 155
Welch, Bernard Charles, Jr. 234–236
Wilder, Christopher 236–238
Yale, Frankie 52
Zangara, Joseph 56, 57, 243–244
murderers, accused
    Hayes, Robert 88
    Miller, Robert Lee, Jr. 88
    Molineux, Roland B. 165–167
    Padgett, Randall 89
    Patterson, Nan 180–181
    Sheppard, Sam 202–204
    von Bülow, Claus 227–229
    Wilhoit, Gregory 90

murder victims. *See also* assassination victims
Adams, Samuel 60
Ah Hoon 3–4
Allison, Dorothy on 8–9
Anastasia, Albert 64
Arnold, Keith 65
Baker, Rosetta 22
Bickford, Maria 30–32
Billy the Kid 195
Bulette, Julia 45
Burdell, Dr. Harvey 46–49
Capone, Al 51–52
Carroll, Tommy 86
Carson, John 54
Cermak, Anton J. 18, 56–57, 243–244
Champion, Nathan D. 58
Chapman, Mrs. James A. 138
Clutter family 60
Coffelt, Leslie 225, 226
Colosimo, Big Jim 52
Craft, Gerald 65
Deubler, Peter 14
Dickinson, Charles 131
Dillinger, John 86
Douglass, Joey 196
during draft riots 91
Elwell, Joseph Bowne 95–96
FBI agents 87
Ferguson, Terry 237
Finch, Barbara 102–103
Folger, Abigail 160
Franks, Bobby 143–144
Frykowski, Voyteck 160
Garrett, Pat 195
Gianni Versace 69, 70–71
Goldman, Ron 205
Gonzales, Dr. Thomas A. and 107
Green, Eddie 86–87
Greenlease, Robert C. "Bobby," Jr. 110
Halberstam, Dr. Michael J. 234, 235
Hamilton, Alexander 49
Hamilton, John 86
Hansen, Edmund 108
Hart, Brooke 116–118
Hill, Joan Robinson 121–122
Hill, Dr. John 121–122
Hoffert, Emily 241

Kahane, Rabbi Meir 133–134
Kennedy assassination witnesses 176
Ketchum, Ami 174
King, Dot 137–138
King, James 55
Kline, Deborah Sue "Debbie" 9
La Bianca, Leno 120, 160
La Bianca, Rosemary 120, 160
Lawson, Louise 138
Lennon, John 59
Lindbergh, Charles A., Jr. 136, 139
Lindquist, Mildred 233–234
Loeb, Nathan "Babe" 145
Logan, Susanne 237
Lonergan, Patricia Burton 154–155
Luetgert, Louisa 156–157
Madsen, David 70
Makley, Far Charley 87
Mattson, Charles 136
Menendez, Jose 164
Menendez, Kitty 164
Metzker, James "Pres" 149–150
Miglin, Lee 70
Mitchell, Luther 174
Monahan, Mabel 108
Morgan, Vicki 35
Mosher, William 196
Murphy, Frances 233–234
Nathan, Benjamin 169–170
Nelson, Baby Face 87
Nitti, Frank 56
Novarro, Ramon 170–171
O'Banion, Dion 52
O'Brien, H. J. 92–93
Oetting, Lillian 233–234
Olive, Bob 174
Oswald, Lee Harvey 175, 198–199
Parent, Steven Earl 160
Parker, Marion 136
Parkman, Dr. George 232–233
Peacock, Dr. Silber C. 182

Peck, John E. 231–232
Peck, Mrs. John E. 231–232
Percy, Valerie 182–183
Phillips, David Graham 183–184
Pierpont, Harry 87
prison guards 5
Ragged Stranger 119–120
Ramsey, JonBenet 187–188
Ray, Nick 58
Reese, William 70
Reville, Jean 136
Ribicoff, Sarai 190–191
Rice, William Marsh 191–193
Ross, Charles S. 136
Rubinstein, Serge 197–198
Ryan, Joseph Hugh 103
Sarber, Jess 83
Sayre, Mr. and Mrs. 141
Schuster, Arnold 240
Sebring, Jay 160
Secret Service agent 103
Seminole sub-chief 16
Shakur, Tupac 201–202
Sheppard, Marilyn 202–204
Simpson, Nicole Brown 205
Spooner, Joshua 207
Stica, Ronald 8
Stompanato, Johnny 209–210
Swope, Thomas B. 212–213
Tarnower, Dr. Herman 114–115
Tate, Sharon 160
Taylor, William Desmond 215–218
Thurmond, Thomas H. 118
Tippit, J. D. 175
Todd, Thelma 222–224
Trail, Jeffrey 70
Vandiver, Bobby 122
Van Meter, Homer 87
Versace, Gianni 69–70, 71
Wanderer, Ruth 119–120
Weinberger, Peter 136
Weiss, Dr. Carl 18, 155
White, Stanford 220–221
Wylie, Janice 241–242

Young, Guard 108
Youngblood, Herbert 85
murder victims, alleged
Dekker, Jan 75–77
Moore, Nathaniel Ford 167–168
Murphy, Frances 233–234
Murphy, Reginald 137
Murray, George 11
My Last Million Readers (Gauvreau) 12

N

Nabisco 146
Nash, Durland 182
Nash, Jay Robert 87
Nathan, Benjamin **169–170**
Nathan, Washington 169
National Association of Fraud Examiners 68
National Research Council 176
National Science Foundation 176
National Socialist (Nazi) Party of America 123
Nation-Wide News Service 11, 12
Navy, U.S. 218
NBC 219–220
Neebe, Oscar 10
Negro Orphanage 92, 93
Nelson, Baby Face 37, 85, 87
Nesbit, Evelyn 220–222
Neufeld, Peter 88
Newberry, Teddy 56
New Mexico State Penitentiary 100
New Testament 7
New York Stock Exchange 236
New York Times
on Annenberg, Moses L. 12
on Bergdoll, Grover Cleveland 27
Berger, Meyer at 27–28
on Borden, Lizzie 41
on capital punishment 89, 90
Nitti, Frank 56
Nixon, Richard M. 12, 43, 220
Norcross, Henry L. 201
Normand, Mabel 215, 216, 217, 218

Norris, Dr. Charles 107
Norris, James 149–150
North Side Gang 52, 53
Nosair, Sayyid A. 133–134
Not Guilty (Frank) 89
Novarro, Ramon **170–171**

O

O'Banion, Dion 52, 120
O'Banion Gang 53
O'Brien, H. J. 92
Oetting, Lillian 233–234
Offen, Ron 87
Office of Strategic Services (OSS) 238
Ohio Gang 99, **173–174.** See also Teapot Dome Scandal
Ohio State Penitentiary 87, 203
O'laughlin, Michael 149
Old Testament 21
Olive, Bob 174
Olive, Isom Prentice "Print" **174**
On Leongs 3–4
Only Yesterday (Allen) 151
Ono, Yoko 59
Organization of Afro-American Unity 18, 159
Oswald, Lee Harvey 18, **174–177**, 198
Otis, Harrison Gray 73
Owens (Colorado governor) 188

P

Packard Corporation 77
Padgett, Randall 89
Paine, Lewis 17, 147
Paine, Robert Treat 208
Pan-American Co. 99
Pancoast, Marvin 34
Panhandle Producing and Refining 197–198
Pantages, Alexander **179–180**
Paramount Studios 223
Parent, Steven Earl 160
Paresis Hall 6
Parker, Bonnie **36–39**
Parker, Ellis 154
Parker, John F. 149
Parker, Marion 136
Parkman, Dr. George 232–233
Patrick, Albert T. 192–193

Patterson, Haywood 142
Patterson, Nan **180–181**
Paulus, Lilla 122
Payne, John Howard 60
Peacock, Dr. Silber C. **182**
Pearson, Edmund 40
Peary, Robert E. 62
Peck, John E. 231
Peck, Mrs. John E. 231
Pennsylvania Railroad 81, 144
Pennsylvania State Constabulary 195
Percy, Charles H. 182–183
Percy, Valerie **182–183**
Perez, Juan 25
perjury 54, 146, 220, 238–239
Perkins, Emmett 108
Perry, Nancy Ling 118
Petacque, Art 183
Pfeiffer, Ken 9
Philadelphia Prison 54
Phillips, David Graham **183–184**
Pickford, Mary 215, 216, 217
Pierpont, Harry 82, 83, 84, 85, 87
Piquett, Louis 84
Pitchfork, Colin 88
Pitts, ZaSu 222
Poe, Edgar Allan 60, 61, 232
poisoners 25
Hyde, Dr. B. C. 213
Waite, Dr. Arthur Warren and 231–232
Wood, Isaac 240–241
poison victims
Adams, Katherine 165
Adams, Mrs. 166
Barnaby, Josephine 109
Barnet, Henry C. 165, 166
Beckwourth, Jim 25
Cornish, Harry 166
Potts, Helen 43
Sutherland, Annie 44
Swope, Thomas B. 212
Wood, David 240
Wood, Rhoda 240
Polanski, Roman 160
Porter, Robert 23
Postal Service, U.S. 133, 166
Potts, Helen 43

Powell, Adam Clayton 238, 239
Prendergast, Robert 73
Presley, Elvis 183
Pringle, Eunice 180
Prohibition 3, 16, 51–54, 63, 173
prostitutes. *See also* brothel(s); madams
Adler, Polly 2–3
Allen, John and 6–7
Allen, Lizzie 7–8
Andrews, Shang and 10–11
Arlington, Josie 13–15
child 123
Clark, Dora 65
during draft riots 91–92
Fallon, William J. and 100–102
on freight train 141
Graham, Barbara 107–109
Luciano, Lucky and 80
Novarro, Ramon 170
Paulus, Lilla 122
Puente, Dorothea 184
Vandiver, Bobby and 122
Puccio, Thomas 228, 229
Puente, Dorothea **184–186**
Purvis, Melvin 86
Putnam, George Palmer 60

**Q**

Quad Records 202

**R**

Ragen, James M. 12
Rallings, George 92
Ramsey, John 187–188
Ramsey, JonBenet **187–188**
Ramsey, Patsy 187–188
rape victims
Cutler, Zelma 88
Fowler, Anne Laura 88
Kline, Debora Sue "Debbie" 9
Logan, Susanne 237
Pringle, Eunice 180
Rappe, Virginia 12
rapists 88
Dodson, Richard Lee 9
Patterson, Haywood 142
Pitchfork, Colin 88
Scottsboro Boys 141–142

Weger, Chester 234
Wilder, Christopher 236–238
Rappe, Virginia 12
Rathbone, Henry 147
Ray, James Earl 18, **188–190**
Ray, Nick 58
RCA 12
Reagan, Nancy 34
Reagan, Ronald viii, 19, 33, 34, 59, 122–123
Reck, Emil 182
*Red Badge of Courage, The* (Crane) 65
Red Cross 45
Red Sash Gang 58
Red Scare roundups 30
Reese, William 70
Reid, John 234
Reilly, Edward J. 138
Reles, Abe 28, 143
Republican Party
Annenberg, Moses L. in 11–12
Dillinger, John and 83
during draft riots 93
Guiteau, Charles Julius in 111
Hoffman, Harold Giles in 123–124
Molineux, Edward Leslie in 165
Savings and Loan scandal and 135
Reso, Sidney J. 137
Reville, E. B. 136
Reville, Jean 136
Revolutionary War 207–208
Ribicoff, Abe 190
Ribicoff, Belle 190, 191
Ribicoff, Sarai **190–191**
Rice, William Marsh **191–193**
Rice Institute 191, 192, 193
Rich Men's Coachmen's Club **193–194**
Riegle, Donald W. 135
Ripley, Beulah 14
Risbergand, Charles "Swede" 33
RKO (Radio-Keith-Orpheum) 179
Roach, Hal 211
Roaring Twenties 100–102

robbery victims
Brink's 202
Clutter family 60
Percy, Charles H. 183
Ribicoff, Sarai 190
Rice, William Marsh 191–193
Shoven, John 190
Spooner, Joshua 207
Robinson, Ash 121, 122
Robinson, Michael 137
Robles, Richard 241
Rockefeller, John D. 201, 221
Rock Island Railroad 167
Rockwell, Norman 59
Roe, Ralph 5
Rogers, Hugo 62
Rogers, Roy 211
Rogers, Will 85
Rolfe, James "Sunny Jim" 117–118
Romaine, Henry 209
*Room with the Little Door, The* (Molineux) 166
Roosevelt, Franklin D.
assassination attempt on 18, 56, 243–244
Cermak, Anton J. and 56, 57
Cook, Dr. Frederick A. and 62
on draft evaders 27
as New York State Governor 66
Schrank, John Nepomuk on 195
Zangara, Joseph and 56, 57
Roosevelt, Theodore 18, 66, 72, **194–195**
Rosenthal, Herman 65
Rosetti, Frank 62
Ross, Charles Brewster 135, **195–197**
Ross, Charles S. 136
Ross, Christian K. 196
Ross, Ezra 207
Rothstein, Arnold "the Brain" 33
Royal Canadian Air Force 116, 155
Rubenstein, Jacob. *See* Ruby, Jack
Rubinstein, Serge **197–198**
Ruby, Earl 198, 199
Ruby, Jack 18, 175, **198–199**

Rugendorf, Leo 183
Ruggles, Timothy 207
rumrunners, rumrunning 15, 16–17
Ryan, Joseph Hugh 103
Rynders, Isaiah 19, 20

**S**

Sage, Anna 86, 87–88
Sage, Russell **201**
St. Valentine's Day Massacre 53
Salem witch trials 162
Salinger, J. D. 59
Salvation Army 105
Sandburg, Carl 145
Sand Creek Massacre 25
San Francisco Committee of Vigilance 56
San Gabriel Mission 25
San Quentin prison 109, 118, 180
Santos, Jack 108
Sarber, Jess 83, 84, 85
Saunders, Geraldine 76
Savings and Loan (S&L) scandal **134–135**
Sayre, Mr. and Mrs. 141
Scaduto, Anthony 154
Scalise, John 53
*Scapegoat, The Lonesome Death of Bruno Richard Hauptmann* (Scaduto) 154
"Scarsdale Diet" doctor viii, 114–115
Scheck, Barry 88–89
Schoenfeld, James 137
Schoenfeld, Richard Allen 137
Schrallhammer, Maria 227
Schrank, John Nepomuk 18, 194–195
Schultz, Dutch 2, 27, 79–80
Schuster, Arnold 240
Schwab, Michael 10
Schwarzkopf, H. Norman 153–154
Scopes, John 75
Scotland Yard 169
Scott, Gini Graham, Ph.D. 70
Scottsboro Boys 141–142
Seabury probe 67
Seadlund, John Henry 136
Seale, Arthur 137

Seale, Irene 137
Sebring, Jay 160
Sebring Races 236
Secret Army Organization (SAO) 42
Secret Service, U.S.
  Fromme, Lynette Alice "Squeaky" and 19
  Kennedy, John F. and 176
  Lincoln, Abraham and 151
  Reagan, Ronald and 19, 122
  Roosevelt, Theodore and 72
  Truman, Harry S and 225–226
Securities Acts 197–198
Securities and Exchange Commission 146
securities fraud. See swindlers
Seldon, Bruce 202
Seminole Indians 15, 16
Senate, The 7
Senate, U.S. 10, 134–135, 155–156
Serrano, Sandy 206
Seward, William 61, 148
Shakespeare, William 19
Shakur, Afreni 202
Shakur, Tupac 201–202
Shapiro, Gurrah 79
Sharrief, Raymond 159
Shaw, Vic 167
Sheppard, Dr. Samuel H. "Sam" 21, 202–204
Sheppard, Marilyn 202–204
Sheppard, Sam Reese 203
Shorter, Baxter 108
Shoven, John 190
Siegel, Bugsy 143
Simmons, Zachariah 1
Simpson, Nicole Brown vii, 204–205
Simpson, O. J. vii–viii, 89, 163, 164, 191, 204–205
Sinatra, Frank, Jr. 136
Sinclair, Harry F. 99, 100, 174, 218
Singleton, Ed 82
Sing Sing prison 55, 155, 193, 232, 236
Sirhan, Sirhan Bishara 19, 205–206
sleepwalking 30, 31–32

Smith, Al 162
Smith, Byron 65
Smith, Jess 173, 174
Smith, Pegleg 25
Smith, Perry E. 60
Smith, Richard 54
Smith, Whittam 163
Snodgrass, George 47
Snyder, Simon 54
Soltysik, Patricia 118
Spahn Ranch 160
Spangler, Edward 149
Sparks, Jared 233
Sparrow, Joe 174
Spawl, Lucy 47
Spawl, Mr. 47
Spooner, Bathsheba 206–209
Spooner, Joshua 206, 207–208
Stallone, Sylvester 191
Stand, Bert 62
State Department, U.S. 175
Stephenson, Anna 166
Sterling, Ross 37
Stewart, Alexander Turney 209
Stica, Ronald 8
Stiltz, Bud 211, 212
stock fraud. See swindlers
Stompanato, Johnny 209–210
Stone, Oliver 177
Storyville 14
Stotesbury, E. T. 138
strangulation victims. See also asphyxiation
  Bulette, Julia 45
  Burdell, Dr. Harvey 47
  Greenlease, Robert C. "Bobby," Jr. 110
  Lonergan, Patricia Burton 155
  Ramsey, JonBenet 187–188
  Rubinstein, Serge 197–198
Strauss, Pittsburgh Phil 143
Strauss, Richard 70
Strongman of Wall Street. See Whitney, Richard F.
Stroud, Robert 6
suicide
  Adams, Albert J. 2
  at Alcatraz prison 6
anarchists 10

Berkman, Alexander 30
Colt, John C. 61, 62
Cunaan, Andrew 69–71
Gonzales, Dr. Thomas A. and 107
Graves, Dr. Thomas T. 110
Hargraves, Dick and 113
Jones, Charles F. 193
Kennedy assassination witnesses 176
Smith, Jess 174
Sullivan, Bridget 39
Sullivan, Christy 62
Sullivan, John J. 67
Sullivan, Joseph "Sport" 33
Sumner, Charles 210–211
Supreme Court, U.S.
  on capital punishment 21, 89, 161, 206
  Cushing, William on 208
  on illegal eavesdropping 239
  Leibowitz, Samuel S. and 142
  Manton, Martin T. and 162
  Miranda decision 241
  on Sheppard, Sam 203
  Teapot Dome scandal and 218
Surratt, John H. 149
Surratt, Mary 17, 147
Suskind, Richard 128
Sutherland, Annie 43
Sutherland, John 189
Sutton, Willie 240
swindlers
  Boesky, Ivan 36, 49, 146, 162, 164
  Butcher, Jake 49
  Chadwick, Cassie 57–58
  Crazy Eddie 68
  Fallon, William J. and 100–102
  Guimares, Alberto Santos 137
  Insull, Samuel 127–128
  Irving, Clifford 128–129
  Keating, Charles, Jr. 134–135, 162
  Levine, Dennis 36, 146
  Maxwell, Robert 162–163
  Means, Gaston B. 154
  Milken, Michael 49, 162–163, 164–165

Rubinstein, Serge 197–198
Whitney, Richard F. 236
Switzer, Carl "Alfalfa" 211–212
Swope, Thomas B. 212–213
Symbionese Liberation Army (SLA) 115–116, 118–119
syndicate, national crime 62–65, 79–80, 155

T

Tammany Hall 62, 66
Tarnower, Dr. Herman viii, 114–115
Tate, Sharon 35, 160
tax evaders
  Annenberg, Moses L. 11, 12
  Brisbane, Arthur 152
  Capone, Al 6, 11, 53
  Costello, Frank 64
  Crazy Eddie 68
  DeLorean, John 78–79
  Farley, James J. 56
  Levine, Dennis 36, 146
  Powell, Adam Clayton and 239
  Schultz, Dutch 2
  Taylor, Thomas 137
  Taylor, William Desmond 215–218
Teapot Dome scandal 99–100, 173, 174, 218
television quiz show scandal 218–220
terrorists 9–10, 115–116, 133. See also anarchists; Symbionese Liberation Army (SLA)
Texas School Book Depository 174–175
Thaw, Harry Kendall 220–222
"Thelma Todd's Sidewalk Cafe" 223, 224
They Always Call Us Ladies (Harris) 115
thieves. See also bank robbers; burglars; embezzlers; swindlers
  Barrow, Clyde 36–39
  Beckwourth, Jim 25
  Burdell, Dr. Harvey 47
  Casey, James P. 55

Costello, Frank 63
Dekker, Albert and 76
Dillinger, John 80–88
Graham, Barbara 108
Graves, Thomas T. 109
Hickock, Richard E. 60
Parker, Bonnie 36–39
Red Sash Gang 58
Smith, Perry E. 60
Weger, Chester 233–234
Welch, Bernard Charles, Jr. 234–236
Thomas, Frederick Jerome 190–191
Thompson, George **105**
Thompson, Kit 10
Thompson, Thomas 122
Thornton, Roy 37
*Three Month Fever: The Andrew Cunanan Story* (Indiana) 69
Thurmond, Thomas H. 116–117, 118
Thurston, Mrs. Hollis M. 194
Tilbury, John 193–194
Tippit, J. D. 175
Tirrell, Albert 30–32
Tirrell, Cynthia 32
Todd, Thelma **222–224**
Tombs Prison 60–61, 62, 192–193
tong wars 3–4
Torresola, Griselio 18, 225
Torrio, Johnny 51, 52
Tortora, Anthony 8
Tory Murderess 206–209
Trail, Jeffrey 70
Treasury Department, U.S. 104, 176, 239
Tregoff, Carole 102–103
Trisolar Corporation 176
True, John L. 108
Truman, Harry S 18, 122, **225–226**
Tryforos, Lynne 114
Turkus, Burton 80
Turner, Lana 209
Twain, Mark 45
Tweed Ring 2, 173
Tyson, Mike 202

**U**

Ulasewicz, Anthony 42
Union Theological Seminary 6
Unruh, Howard 28
Urschel, Charles F. 136

**V**

Valentino, Rudolph 170
Vandiver, Bobby 121–122
Van Doren, Charles 219–220
Van Houten, Leslie 160, *161*
Van Meter, Homer 81, 82, 85, 87
Versace, Gianni viii, **69**, **70–71**
Veterans Bureau 173
Victor Emmanuel II, king of Italy 244
Virginia and Truckee Railroad 45
Virginia City Fire Co. 45
Volstead Act 53
von Bülow, Claus **227–229**
von Bülow, Cosima 228, 229
von Bülow, Martha "Sunny" 227–229

**W**

Wais, Marshall J. 137
Waite, Dr. Arthur Warren **231–232**
Wallace, George 19, 42–43
Walling, George W. 61, 169
Walsh, Thomas J. 218
Walters, Barbara 42
Wanderer, Carl 119–120
Wanderer, Ruth 119–120
War Department, U.S. 4, 147, 148
Warner, Frankie 11
Warner Brothers 13
Warren, Joseph A. 64
Warren Commission 175, 177, 198
Washington, Earl, Jr. 89
Watkins, Stewart 103

Watson, Carrie 7
Watson, Charles "Tex" 160
Watson, John 88
Weaver, George "Buck" 33
Webster, Dr. John White **232–233**
Weger, Chester **233–234**
Weinberger, Peter 136
Weiss, Dr. Carl Austin 18, 155
Weiss, Ed 97–98
Weiss, Hymie 120
Welch, Bernard Charles, Jr. **234–236**
Wells, Floyd 60
Wells Fargo 45
Wendel, Paul H. 154
West, Roland 223, 224
West, William H. 109
Westervelt, William 135, 196
Whalen, Grover A. 64
Whig Party 17
White, Ike 27, 44, 201
White, Stanford 220–221
White, William Allen 173
Whitmore, George, Jr. 241
Whitney, Richard F. **236**
Wilder, Christopher **236–238**
Wilhoit, Gregory 90
Wilkins, M. H. F. 88
Willard, May 11
Willgues, Charles 185
Williams, Alexander S. 195
Williams, Claude 33
Williams, Edward Bennett **238–240**
Williams, Old Bill 25
Williams, William A. H. 137
Wilson, Woodrow 161
Winchell, Walter **240**
witchcraft 162
Witthaus, Dr. Rudolph 221
Wolfe, William 119
Wolf of Wall Street. *See* Whitney, Richard F.
Wood, David 240
Wood, Isaac **240–241**
Wood, Rhoda 240

Woods, Frederick Newhall, IV 137
World War I 119, 124
World War II 116, 197, 238–239
Worrell, Mrs. 109
wounded victims
Acosta, Carlos 133, 134
Birdzell, Donald 225
Brady, James S. 19, 122
Clark, Dora 65
Delahanty, Thomas K. 19, 122
Downs, Joseph 225
Frick, Henry Clay 29–30
Gaynor, William J. 17–18
Hargraves, Dick 113
McCarthy, Timothy J. 19, 122
Nathan, Washington 169
Rathbone, Henry 148
Reagan, Ronald viii, 19, 33, 34, 59, 122–123
Sumner, Charles 210–211
Wallace, George 19, 42–43
Wylie, Janice **241–242**
Wylie, Max 241
Wylie, Philip 241
Wyoming Stock Growers' Association 58

**X**

Xerox Corporation 176

**Y**

Yale, Frankie 52
Yoshimura, Wendy 115, 118
Young, Francis Thomas "Caesar" 181
Young, Guard 108
Youngblood, Herbert 84, 85

**Z**

Zangara, Joseph 18, 56, 57, **243–244**
Zinman, David 156